40 architects under 40

Jessica Cargill Thompson

40 architects under 40

40 Architekten unter 40

40 architectes de moins de 40 ans

TASCHEN
KÖLN LONDON MADRID NEW YORK PARIS TOKYO

CONTENTS

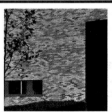

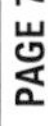

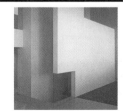

INTRODUCTION

Who are the Richard Rogers, Norman Fosters, Tadao Andos and Richard Meiers of tomorrow? Who will be designing the landmark buildings of the 21st century? Who will be responsible for shaping the 21st-century city? And who will be defining the architectural styles of the next decade?
Gathering 40 young practices from 21 countries, this book is an attempt to spotlight some of those people. All under or just over 40 - "young" in a profession where it takes at least seven years to qualify and where more than a decade can elapse between initial sketches and a building reaching completion - they represent a cross-section of the best in their field. As yet their body of built work is limited, but their vision and potential can be seen in imaginative projects that range from furniture, private residences and small urban interventions to major public buildings.
Though a range of styles can be seen, Modernism is still a dominant force, given new twists by technological developments in materials and construction, while the philosophy of deconstructionism has had a profound impact on architectural thinking, allowing architects to escape the tyranny of "four walls and a roof". Strides in glazing technology, for example, mean that glass can be used uninterrupted on wide expanses, and architects can create different effects such as etching, printing and sandwiching things between panes.
But the most profound influence on today's architects has been digital technology. This affects not only the way business is done, allowing drawings and photographs to be sent around the world in an instant, but the very nature of space itself. Computer games create whole virtual worlds, and with the aid of a mouse we can walk round buildings long before they are built. These ideas have been explored most fully by the

Wer sind die Richard Rogers, Norman Fosters, Tadao Andos und Richard Meiers von morgen? Wer wird die prägenden Bauten des 21. Jahrhunderts entwerfen? Wer wird das Aussehen der Städte des 21. Jahrhunderts und die architektonische Formensprache des nächsten Jahrzehnts bestimmen?
Dieses Buch unternimmt den Versuch, auf 40 junge Architekturbüros aus 21 Ländern aufmerksam zu machen. Alle unter oder knapp über 40 Jahre alt – und damit »jung« in einem Beruf, für den man eine mindestens siebenjährige Ausbildungszeit braucht und in dem zwischen ersten Skizzen und fertigem Bau mehr als zehn Jahre vergehen können –, repräsentieren sie einen Querschnitt der besten ihres Fachs. Noch ist die Zahl ihrer realisierten Bauten begrenzt, aber ihre visionäre Kraft und ihr Potential schlagen sich in einfallsreichen Projekten nieder.
Trotz einer großen stilistischen Vielfalt ist die Moderne, abgewandelt durch die technische Weiterentwicklung von Materialien und Bauweisen, noch immer eine bestimmende Größe. Dem weit reichenden Einfluss der dekonstruktivistischen Philosophie ist es indes zu verdanken, dass die Architekten der Tyrannei der »vier Wände mit Dach« entkommen konnten.
Den stärksten Einfluss auf die heutige Architektenschaft hat jedoch die Computertechnik. Sie verändert nicht nur geschäftliche Abläufe dadurch, dass Zeichnungen und Fotografien in Sekunden um die ganze Welt geschickt werden können, sondern auch das Wesen des Raums. Mit Hilfe der Maus können wir in Bauten umhergehen, lange bevor sie errichtet sind.
Diese Möglichkeiten werden von dem New Yorker Büro Asymptote voll ausgeschöpft, das ebenso viele virtuelle wie »reale« Bauten schafft. Dabei stellen die Architekten alte Vorstellungen vom Wesen des Raums in Frage

Qui sont les Richard Rogers, Norman Foster, Tadao Ando et Richard Meier de demain ? Qui dessinera les édifices marquants du XXIe siècle ? Qui façonnera les villes du nouveau millénaire ? Quels sont les hommes et femmes qui définiront les styles architecturaux de la décennie à venir ?
En présentant 40 jeunes studios de 21 pays différents, ce livre a pour ambition de mettre en lumière certains de ces créateurs des formes de demain. Tous ont à peine 40 ans, ou un tout petit peu plus – ce qui est jeune dans une profession où il faut au moins sept ans pour être qualifié, et où plus de dix ans peuvent s'écouler entre les premières esquisses et l'achèvement d'un bâtiment –, et représentent une sélection des meilleurs représentants de leur discipline. Leurs réalisations concrètes sont encore limitées, mais leur vision et leur potentiel sont déjà manifestes dans des projets inventifs.
En dépit de la diversité des styles, le modernisme reste une force dominante, tout en prenant des aspects nouveaux suite à l'évolution des matériaux et des méthodes de construction. Parallèlement, la philosophie de la déconstruction a profondément marqué la pensée architecturale, libérant celle-ci de la tyrannie des « quatre murs et un toit ».
Le facteur qui a le plus profondément marqué l'architecture contemporaine est toutefois la technologie informatique. Cela affecte non seulement la façon de traiter les dossiers (un plan ou des photographies peuvent être envoyés à l'autre bout du monde en un instant), mais la conception même de l'espace architectural. En créant des mondes virtuels, l'informatique permet de « parcourir » un bâtiment bien avant qu'il ne soit construit.
Les possibilités offertes par ces constructions virtuelles ont été explorées à fond par le bureau new-yorkais Asymptote, qui crée autant de structures numériques

New York practice Asymptote, who create as many virtual electronic structures as they build real ones, constantly challenging old concepts about the nature of space and focusing on experience rather than tangible details. Their building projects bombard users with electronic information and effects, building walls out of video images and controlling environments with computers.

The tremendous advances in computer technology also mean that complex three-dimensional structures can be modelled relatively easily. Frank O. Gehry's Guggenheim Bilbao is perhaps the most spectacular testament to the abilities of computer modelling, but its possibilities have also inspired younger architects: Shuhei Endo's spirals and arches of corrugated steel, MVRDV's Villa VPRO that folds in the middle, Ben van Berkel's house based on the mathematics of the Möbius band, Sancho-Madridejos's folding planes, Shigeru Ban's undulating roofs of cardboard tubing.

While competitions have provided practices such as Studio Granda, Gigon/Guyer and Berger + Parkkinen with a chance to shine on landmark buildings such as art galleries and town halls, other architects have made valuable contributions to the urban fabric on a smaller scale. Shuhei Endo's Transtation O in Japan, Andreas Hild's bus shelter and recycling station in Germany, and Manuelle Gautrand's colourful glass toll stations on the A16 motorway in France lift the spirit where ill-designed standard issue pieces leave one cold.

Where opportunities for young architects tend to be on a smaller scale and include a high proportion of interiors work, many broaden their remit to include furniture design. This has long been a popular sideline for architects, resulting in some classic pieces, and younger architects such as Claesson Koivisto Rune,

und konzentrieren sich auf die Raumerfahrung statt auf greifbare Details. Ihre Projekte bombardieren die Nutzer mit elektronischen Informationen und Effekten, Wänden aus Videobildern und computergesteuerten Umgebungen.

Die ungeheuren Fortschritte in der Computertechnologie ermöglichen es zudem, dreidimensionale Objekte relativ einfach zu modellieren. Frank O. Gehrys Guggenheim Bilbao ist das vielleicht spektakulärste Zeugnis der Möglichkeiten computergestützten Entwerfens. Junge Architekten ließen sich davon anregen: Shuhei Endos Spiralen und Bögen aus gewelltem Stahlblech, MVRDVs in der Mitte geknickte Villa VPRO, Ben van Berkels von den mathematischen Prinzipien des Möbius'schen Bands angeregtes Haus, Sancho-Madridejos' gefaltete Ebenen, Shigeru Bans wellenförmig bewegte Dächer aus Papprohren.

Während Wettbewerbe Büros wie Studio Granda, Gigon/Guyer und Berger + Parkkinen die Möglichkeit eröffneten, sich mit markanten Bauten wie Kunstmuseen und Rathäusern zu etablieren, steuerten andere Architekten kleiner dimensionierte, gleichwohl wertvolle Beiträge zum urbanen Gefüge bei. Shuhei Endos Transtation O in Japan, Andreas Hilds Bushaltestelle und Recyclinganlage in Deutschland sowie Manuelle Gautrands farbenfrohe, gläserne Mauthäuschen an der A16 in Frankreich begeistern durch ihre überraschenden und ungewöhnlichen Lösungen.

Viele jüngere Architekten erweitern ihr Repertoire um Möbelentwürfe. Dieser beliebten Nebentätigkeit sind einige klassische Stücke zu verdanken. Kollektionen jüngerer Architekten wie Claesson Koivisto Rune, Thomas Sandell und UT wurden von bedeutenden Möbelherstellern übernommen und könnten eines Tages ebenso zu Sammlerstücken werden wie eine Vase von Alvar Aalto oder der Hill House-Stuhl von Charles Rennie Mackintosh.

qu'il n'en construit de réelles, sans cesser d'interroger les anciens concepts concernant la nature de l'espace, et en privilégiant la perception et le vécu plutôt que les détails tangibles. Leurs constructions et projets bombardent les utilisateurs d'informations et d'effets électroniques tels que des murs d'images vidéo ou des environnements contrôlés par ordinateur.

Grâce aux progrès fulgurants de l'informatique, il est également devenu relativement facile de simuler de complexes structures tridimensionnelles. Le Guggenheim Bilbao construit par Frank O. Gehry constitue sans doute le témoignage le plus spectaculaire du potentiel de la modélisation informatique, laquelle a inspiré plus d'un architecte de la jeune génération. Mentionnons les spirales et arcades en tôle ondulée de Shuhei Endo ; la Villa VPRO due à MVRDV, repliée au centre ; la maison de Ben van Berkel basée sur le modèle mathématique du ruban de Möbius ; les plans plissés de Sancho-Madridejos ; les toitures ondoyantes en tubes de carton de Shigeru Ban ...

Tandis que des concours internationaux ont permis à des bureaux d'architectes comme Studio Granda, Gigon/Guyer ou Berger + Parkkinen de briller en réalisant des musées d'art, hôtels de ville et autres édifices prestigieux, d'autres architectes ont apporté une précieuse contribution au tissu urbain à une échelle plus modeste. Le Transtation O de Shuhei Endo au Japon, l'abribus et la déchetterie d'Andreas Hild en Allemagne, les expressives barrières de péage en verre de Manuelle Gautrand sur l'autoroute A16 en France, élèvent l'esprit là où des constructions banales ne susciteraient qu'ennui.

Les jeunes architectes se tournent souvent vers le design de meubles. Cette activité secondaire pratiquée de longue date par les architectes a produit des pièces dont certaines sont devenues classiques. Des modèles conçus

Thomas Sandell and UT have had collections commissioned by major furniture manufacturers that could one day become as collectible as an Aalto vase or Mackintosh ladder back chair.
Though telecommunications, travel and the media continue to play their part in breaking down national stereotypes, differing economic, political, topographical and climatic conditions create regional trends.
In Europe, it has been hard to ignore the Netherlands, where a generation of architects just turning 40 have been creating fantastical buildings full of humour and imagination that totally destroy convention. Much of this controlled eccentricity can be attributed to the influence of Rem Koolhaas, through his teaching at the Technical University of Delft in the 80s and his Rotterdam-based practice OMA through which have passed Winy Maas of MVRDV and Willem Jan Neutelings, as well as American-born Swiss architect Mike Guyer. Represented here are the bizarre but strangely functional buildings of MVRDV, the wonderfully tactile work of Neutelings Riedijk, and the defiantly cerebral work of UN Studio, led by Ben van Berkel and Caroline Bos. Others not featured in this book that stand out include NOX' and oosterhuisassociates' abstract metallic water pavilion at the Oosterschelde and NL Architects' rubber-clad heat transfer station in Utrecht.
Switzerland and Austria have also been a talking point, with practices such as Herzog + de Meuron and Peter Zumthor garnering international respect and commissions for their sensuous minimal Modernism. Following close behind them are Zurich-based Gigon/Guyer, who have already enjoyed numerous successes in competitions for museums and art galleries; featured here are the Museum Liner in Appenzell and an extension for the Oskar Reinhart Collection am Römerholz in

Wenngleich Telekommunikation, Reisen und die Medien auch weiterhin ihren Teil dazu beitragen, nationale Stereotypen zu unterlaufen, bringen unterschiedliche ökonomische, politische, topographische und klimatische Bedingungen regionale Trends hervor.
In Europa sind vor allem die Niederlande zu nennen, wo eine Generation knapp 40-jähriger Architekten großartige Bauten voller Witz und Phantasie plant, die sich über alle Konventionen hinweg setzen. Ein großer Teil dieser gebändigten Exzentrik ist dem Einfluss von Rem Koolhaas und seiner Lehrtätigkeit an der Technischen Hochschule Delft in den 80er-Jahren zu verdanken. In seinem Rotterdamer Büro OMA waren Winy Maas von MVRDV und Willem Jan Neutelings ebenso beschäftigt wie der in Amerika geborene Schweizer Architekt Mike Guyer. Hier sind die bizarren, gleichwohl seltsam funktionalen Bauten von MVRDV vertreten, die wunderbar haptischen Projekte von Neutelings Riedijk sowie die provokant-intellektuellen Arbeiten von UN Studio, geleitet von Ben van Berkel und Caroline Bos.
Auch die Schweiz und Österreich können bedeutende Architekten vorweisen; Büros wie Herzog + de Meuron und Peter Zumthor erringen mit ihrem sinnlichen minimalistischen Modernismus internationale Anerkennung und Aufträge. Auch die Zürcher Bürogemeinschaft Gigon/Guyer konnte bereits zahlreiche Erfolge in Wettbewerben für Museen und Kunstgalerien verbuchen. Hier werden ihr Museum Liner in Appenzell und ein Erweiterungsbau der Sammlung Oskar Reinhart am Römerholz in Winterthur vorgestellt. Gerade erst 40, findet man sie regelmäßig neben bekannten Namen auf den prestigeträchtigen Listen internationaler Wettbewerbe. In Wien traten Berger + Parkkinen durch ihren Masterplan für die Botschaften der Nordischen Länder in Berlin ins Rampenlicht, die zu den gelungensten Botschaftsgebäuden in der neuen

par des architectes de la jeune génération, notamment Claesson Koivisto Rune, Thomas Sandell et UT, ont été repris par de grands fabriquants de meubles ; un jour, ils deviendront peut-être aussi recherchés par les collectionneurs qu'un vase d'Alvar Aalto ou la chaise « Hill House » de Charles Rennie Mackintosh.
A une époque où les télécommunications, les voyages faciles et les médias contribuent plus que jamais à faire tomber les stéréotypes nationaux, les différences de conditions économiques, politiques, topographiques et climatiques créent des tendances régionales.
En Europe, il serait difficile d'ignorer les Pays-Bas, où une génération d'architectes atteignant tout juste la quarantaine a réalisé des constructions fantastiques pleines d'humour et d'imagination, défiant toutes les conventions. Cette excentricité contrôlée peut être attribuée en grande partie à l'influence de Rem Koolhaas, grâce à son enseignement à l'université technique de Delft pendant les années 80, et à son bureau de Rotterdam, par lequel sont passés Winy Maas de MVRDV et Willem Jan Neutelings, ainsi que l'architecte suisse (né aux Etats-Unis) Mike Guyer. Mentionnons les bâtiments bizarres mais étonnamment fonctionnels de MVRDV, les réalisations merveilleusement tactiles de Neutelings Riedijk, ou le travail aussi audacieux que cérébral d'UN Studio, dirigé par Ben van Berkel et Caroline Bos.
La Suisse et l'Autriche ont également attiré l'attention grâce à des bureaux comme Herzog + de Meuron et Peter Zumthor, dont le modernisme minimaliste et sensuel a suscité de grands éloges ainsi que des commandes au plan international. Ils sont suivis de près par le bureau zurichois Gigon/Guyer, qui a d'ores et déjà remporté plusieurs concours concernant des musées et galeries d'art – en particulier le Musée Liner d'Appenzell et l'extension de la Collection Oskar Reinhart am Römerholz à Winter-

Winterthur. Though only just turned 40, they already have a reputation that now sees them regularly featured on prestigious international competition lists alongside established names. In Vienna, Berger + Parkkinen have been thrust into the limelight through their masterplan for the Nordic embassies complex in Berlin, among the most exciting of the new embassies to be built in the new German capital. Showing promise but yet to build up enough work to be included in the shortlist of 40 architects here are: young Austrian deconstructivists Geistlweg Architektur; Andreas Kleboth, Julia Fügenschuh and Christof Hrdlovics from the growing pool of talent in Innsbruck; Wolfgang Prix's protegés Vienna-based Poor Boy's Enterprise; and fresh young Zurich partnership Vehovar & Jauslin, who are currently designing the Artplage exposition to be held in Yverdon-les-Bains in 2002.

Spain spent most of the 90s recovering from the post-Franco exuberance of the Barcelona Olympics and Seville Expo of 1992. As it climbed back out of recession towards the end of the 90s it focused not on grand gestures (Guggenheim Bilbao aside) but on community facilities, civic centres, sports facilities, educational buildings and public housing, providing valuable opportunities for the next generation of architects. They have responded with purer, more restrained forms, concentrating on expressive volumes and planes rather than showmanship. The upbeat "Barcelona Style" of the early 90s as epitomised by Alfredo Arribas and Javier Mariscal has been supplanted by a much more sober style associated with European minimalism/ modernism, espoused by Madrid-based architect and lecturer Alberto Campo Baeza, who taught many of the new architects at the Escuela Técnica Superior de Arquitectura de Madrid (ETSAM).

deutschen Hauptstadt zählen. Viel versprechend, aber noch ohne ausreichend realisierte Entwürfe, um in die vorliegende Auswahl aufgenommen zu werden, sind die jungen österreichischen Dekonstruktivisten von Geistlweg Architektur; Andreas Kleboth, Julia Fügenschuh und Christof Hrdlovics aus dem wachsenden Kreis junger Talente in Innsbruck; das von Wolfgang Prix geförderte, in Wien ansässige Poor Boy's Enterprise sowie die unlängst gegründete Zürcher Gemeinschaft Vehovar & Jauslin, die die für das Jahr 2002 in Yverdon-les-Bains geplanten Artplage-Ausstellung gestaltet.

In Spanien waren die 90er-Jahre überwiegend von der Erholung vom post-Franco'schen Überschwang der Olympiade in Barcelona und der Expo '92 in Sevilla geprägt. Mit Überwindung der Rezession am Ende der 90er-Jahre standen – abgesehen vom Guggenheim Bilbao – weniger Großprojekte als städtische Einrichtungen, Bürgerzentren, Sportanlagen, Schulbauten und der öffentliche Wohnungsbau im Vordergrund, was einer jungen Architektengeneration entscheidende Chancen bot. Sie reagierte mit klareren, gemäßigteren Formen und beschränkte sich auf expressive Volumina und Flächen statt auf Effekthascherei. An die Stelle des von Alfredo Arribas und Javier Mariscal verkörperten optimistischen »Barcelona-Stils« der frühen 90er-Jahre trat eine eher rationale, mit dem europäischen Minimalismus/Modernismus assoziierte Richtung, für die sich der Madrider Architekt und Hochschullehrer Alberto Campo Baeza einsetzt; viele der jungen Architekten zählten an der Escuela Técnica Superior de Arquitectura de Madrid (ETSAM) zu seinen Schülern.

In England konzentriert sich das Architekturgeschehen nach wie vor auf London. Eine Vielzahl erstklassiger Architekturschulen, darunter die Architectural Association, das Royal College of Art und die Bartlett School, zieht eine interessierte Studentenschaft an, die nach dem

thur. Bien qu'ils aient tout juste 40 ans, leur réputation leur vaut déjà de figurer aux côtés de bureaux confirmés sur les listes de prestigieux concours internationaux. A Vienne, Berger + Parkkinen viennent de connaître la célébrité grâce à leur plan directeur pour le complexe réunissant les ambassades des pays scandinaves à Berlin – une des réalisations « diplomatiques » les plus fascinantes de la nouvelle capitale allemande. Mentionnons également de jeunes architectes prometteurs, mais qui n'ont pas encore suffisamment construit pour être inclus dans notre sélection : les déconstructivistes autrichiens du bureau Geistlweg Architektur ; Andreas Kleboth, Julia Fügenschuh et Christof Hrdlovics, issus de l'important réservoir de talents d'Innsbruck ; à Vienne, Poor Boy's Enterprise, dont le mentor est Wolfgang Prix ; et les nouveaux associés zurichois Vehovar & Jauslin, qui préparent actuellement la mise en espace de l'exposition Artplage, prévue pour 2002 à Yverdon-les-Bains, en Suisse.

L'Espagne a passé une bonne partie des années 90 à se remettre des excès post-franquistes illustrés par les Jeux Olympiques de Barcelone et l'Expo '92 de Séville. En émergeant de la récession à la fin de la décennie, elle a fait porter ses efforts moins sur des gestes de prestige (à l'exception du Guggenheim Bilbao) que sur des équipements municipaux, centres civiques, installations sportives, écoles et logements sociaux, autant d'occasions précieuses pour les architectes de la nouvelle génération. Ils ont réagi en créant des formes plus pures et plus maîtrisées, des volumes et plans expressifs plutôt que des effets trop voyants. Le flamboyant « style de Barcelone » du début des années 90, incarné par Alfredo Arribas et Javier Mariscal, a été supplanté par un langage nettement plus sobre associé au modernisme minimaliste européen, prôné par l'architecte et conférencier Alberto Campo Baeza, basé à Madrid, où il eut pour élèves de

In the UK, architectural activity is still centred on London, where a wealth of top architectural schools (including the Architectural Association, Royal College of Art and Bartlett school) draw an exciting mix of students, who often stay in the capital after they have graduated, taking advantage of a rich cultural scene, access to large practices and the recent millennial building frenzy. After a particularly harsh recession in the early 90s that hit construction especially hard, a vibrant scene has built up in the late 90s with a great deal of cross-fertilisation of ideas between architecture and other creative disciplines such as fine art and theatre. Multidisciplinary practices such as FAT, Softroom, Urban Salon, Muf, and Wells Mackereth venture into areas such as multimedia, exhibition design, street furniture, community consultation, art, set design and urban regeneration. Most subsist on a diet of teaching, bar design, exhibitions and loft conversions, waiting for a big breakthrough such as a competition win for a public building.

Adjaye and Russell have found success with a string of commissions for young British artists such as Jake and Dinos Chapman and Chris Ofili, as well as exploring traditional building techniques in Ghana. David Adjaye is now trying to break into the American market with an inspiring media, performing arts and athletic centre planned for downtown Boston, Massachusetts. Niall McLaughlin, a Geneva-born Irishman living in London, has won several awards and much respect for his Carmelite monastery chapel and sacristy and a photographer's hide, which show a lightness of touch unencumbered by any overt stylising.

Scandinavia has rediscovered its roots and accepted that it is possible to enjoy simplicity and tradition without descending into the tweeness of Carl Larsson.

Abschluss häufig in der Hauptstadt bleibt und von der vielfältigen Kulturszene, vom Zugang zu großen Büros und dem jüngsten Millennium-Bauboom profitiert. Nach einer einschneidenden Rezession in den frühen 90er-Jahren, von der besonders die Bauwirtschaft betroffen war, entstand in den späten 90ern eine lebendige Szene, geprägt vom regen Ideenaustausch zwischen Architektur und anderen kreativen Disziplinen wie bildender Kunst und Theater. Multidisziplinäre Büros wie FAT, Softroom, Urban Salon, Muf und Wells Mackereth unternehmen Vorstöße in Bereiche wie Multimedia, Ausstellungsdesign, Straßenmöblierung, Kunst, Bühnenbild und Stadterneuerung. Die meisten halten sich mit Lehraufträgen, dem Design von Bars, Ausstellungen und Loftausbauten über Wasser und warten auf den großen Durchbruch, wie die erfolgreiche Teilnahme an einem Wettbewerb für ein öffentliches Gebäude.

Adjaye and Russell haben Erfolg mit einer Reihe von Aufträgen junger britischer Künstler wie Jake und Dinos Chapman und Chris Ofili, beschäftigen sich aber auch mit traditionellen Bautechniken in Ghana. David Adjaye versucht gegenwärtig mit einem interessanten Bürgerzentrum für die Innenstadt von Boston auf den amerikanischen Markt vorzudringen. Der in Genf geborene und in London lebende Ire Niall McLaughlin wurde mit mehreren Preisen ausgezeichnet und konnte mit seiner Kapelle und Sakristei für den Londoner Karmel ebenso überzeugen wie mit einem Fotografenunterstand. Seine Arbeiten sind frei von stilistischen Zwängen und zeugen von einer Leichtigkeit, die sich nicht um oberflächliches Styling kümmert.

Skandinavien hat seine Wurzeln wieder entdeckt und gelernt, dass es möglich ist, sich an Schlichtheit und Tradition zu erfreuen, ohne in die Idyllik eines Carl Larsson abzurutschen. Helle Hölzer, weiß verputzte Wände, klare

nombreux jeunes architectes à la Escuela Técnica Superior de Arquitectura (ETSAM).

En Grande-Bretagne, l'activité architecturale reste concentrée à Londres, où de nombreuses écoles d'architecture de haut niveau (notamment l'Architectural Association, le Royal College of Arts et Barlett School) attirent une foule bigarrée d'étudiants, qui restent souvent dans la capitale après avoir fini leurs études. Ils y trouvent une riche scène culturelle et la possibilité de travailler pour des bureaux réputés, sans oublier le récent boom de la construction dû au changement de millénaire. Après une période de forte récession au début des années 90, qui avait durement touché le bâtiment, une scène très dynamique a vu le jour à la fin de la décennie, avec un fertile échange d'idées entre l'architecture et d'autres disciplines créatrices telles que les beaux-arts et le théâtre. Des bureaux pluridisciplinaires comme FAT, Softroom, Urban Salon, Muf ou Wells Mackereth font des incursions dans le multimédia, la conception d'expositions, le mobilier urbain, la vie associative, l'art, le décor de théâtre et/ou de cinéma, et la réhabilitation urbaine. La plupart subsistent grâce à l'enseignement, la décoration de bars, les expositions et l'aménagement de lofts, en attendant une percée décisive telle qu'une victoire à un concours public.

Adjaye and Russell ont connu le succès grâce à une série de commandes de jeunes artistes britanniques, notamment Jake et Dinos Chapman et Chris Ofili, tout en explorant les techniques de construction traditionnelles au Ghana. David Adjaye essaie maintenant de s'introduire sur le marché américain avec une exaltante maison de quartier projetée pour Boston. Niall McLaughlin, Irlandais natif de Genève, a gagné plusieurs prix – et un grand respect – pour son couvent de carmélites et pour un refuge campagnard destiné à une photographe, qui témoignent

Blond woods, white walls, clean lines, simplicity and functionality have all become bywords for Scandinavian design. Working in an urban context one has Thomas Sandell, who has led Stockholm's charge towards modern Scandinavian design through his fashionable interiors and furniture. Claesson Koivisto Rune, also based in Stockholm, use architectural trickery such as screens and cutaways to create complex spaces that are inescapably fresh, modern and predominantly white.
In more isolated settings, architects are responding to dramatic landscapes with dramatic architecture. Jarmund/Vigsnæs's headquarters for the governor of Svalbard on Spitsbergen, Norway's most northerly outcrop, digs itself into the snow leaving a severe angular silhouette like a crashed stealth bomber. Søren Robert Lund's ARKEN Museum of Modern Art in Ishøj responds to its coastal setting with a deconstructed building representing a pile of flotsam and jetsam.
The German tendency towards function over form too often manifests itself in buildings that are overly functional but worthy. However, some more imaginative practitioners are able to inject a little more life into their art and even begin to have fun. Schneider + Schumacher's bright-red Info-Box really brightened up Berlin's Potsdamer Platz during surrounding construction work and has become much more loved than the corporate structures that now encircle it. Munich-based Andreas Hild enjoys being provocative, upsetting the sensibilities of the establishment critics by juxtaposing kitsch motifs with urban situations such as a 19th-century wallpaper design on a bus shelter, faux mahogany on social housing, or the ghostly shadow of ornate stonework on the facade of a Berlin apartment block.
In New York, there has been little opportunity for new building of any kind, and recent architectural projects

Linien, Schlichtheit und Funktionalität sind zum Inbegriff skandinavischen Designs geworden. Thomas Sandell, meist in urbanem Kontext tätig, ebnete mit seinen trendgerechten Interieurs und Möbeln Stockholm den Weg an die Spitze des modernen skandinavischen Designs. Das ebenfalls in Stockholm ansässige Büro Claesson Koivisto Rune schuf durch architektonische Kunstgriffe wie Wandschirme und Ausschnitte komplexe Räume, die, überwiegend weiß gehalten, frisch und modern wirken.
In abgelegeneren Gegenden reagieren die Architekten auf dramatische Landschaften mit angemessener Architektur. Jarmund/Vigsnæs' Präsidium des Gouverneurs von Svalbard auf Spitzbergen, Norwegens nördlichstem Vorposten, duckt sich mit einer scharfkantigen Silhouette, die an einen abgestürzten Stealthbomber denken lässt, in den Schnee. Søren Robert Lund nimmt bei seinem ARKEN Museum of Modern Art in Ishøj die Lage an der Küste zum Anlass für ein dekonstruiertes Gebäude, das einem Treibholzstapel gleicht.
Die deutsche Tendenz, der Funktion Vorrang vor der Form zu geben, schlägt sich zu oft in zwar achtbaren, doch übermäßig funktionalen Bauten nieder. Einigen phantasievolleren Architekten gelingt es jedoch, lebendigere und unterhaltsamere Bauwerke zu schaffen. Schneider + Schumachers knallrote Info-Box belebte den Potsdamer Platz in Berlin während der Bauarbeiten erfolgreich und erfreut sich nun weit größerer Beliebtheit als die mittlerweile fertiggestellten Konzernzentralen. Der Münchener Andreas Hild schmückt eher konventionelle Bauaufgaben mit Kitschmotiven, wie im Falle des altmodischen Tapetenmusters an einer Bushaltestelle, dem Mahagoni-Imitat am sozialen Wohnungsbau oder dem gespenstischen Schatten reicher Steinmetzarbeit auf der Fassade eines Berliner Wohnhauses.

d'une grande légèreté de dessin, sans s'encombrer d'une stylisation trop affichée.
La Scandinavie a redécouvert ses racines, et réalisé qu'il est possible d'épouser la simplicité et la tradition sans pour autant tomber dans le style minimisant de Carl Larsson. Bois clairs, murs blancs, lignes rigoureuses, simplicité et fonctionnalité sont devenus synonymes du design scandinave. Dans le contexte urbain, signalons notamment Thomas Sandell, qui a dirigé en Suède l'offensive du design scandinave contemporain avec ses élégants intérieurs et meubles. Claesson Koivisto Rune, également basé à Stockholm, utilise des procédés tels que des écrans ou des découpes pour créer des espaces complexes, dont la fraîcheur égale la modernité.
Dans des cadres plus isolés, les architectes ont réagi à des paysages sauvages par une architecture non moins frappante. Le quartier général du gouverneur de Svalbard construit par Jarmund/Vigsnæs au Spitzberg, pointe la plus septentrionale de Norvège, s'enfouit dans la neige, laissant émerger une austère silhouette angulaire qui évoque un bombardier écrasé. Le Musée d'art moderne ARKEN à Ishøj, dessiné par Søren Robert Lund, reflète le site côtier par un édifice déconstruit semblable à un amas d'épaves rejetées par la mer.
En Allemagne, la tendance privilégiant la fonction au détriment de la forme se manifeste trop souvent par des bâtiments hyper-fonctionnels mais d'une pesante gravité. Quelques architectes inventifs réussissent cependant à injecter un peu plus de vie dans leur art, et commencent même à s'amuser. L'Info-Box rouge de Schneider + Schumacher a mis un peu de gaieté dans la Potsdamer Platz de Berlin alors qu'elle était cernée par d'énormes chantiers, et a fini par être bien plus appréciée du public que les immeubles commerciaux qui l'entourent. Le munichois Andreas Hild introduit des motifs kitsch dans un

tend to be limited to interiors. However, the city's rich art scene makes it a natural home for architects such as Simon Ungers and Asymptote, who divide their time between art and architecture, creating installation pieces for major galleries and buildings that exist as pieces of outdoor sculpture.

Elsewhere in America, where there is more space, architects are keen to respond to the natural environment. Thompson and Rose's Atlantic Center for the Arts is woven into the Florida jungle, while Wendell Burnette's studio and house in Phoenix, Arizona, creates what he describes as "a giant Band-Aid" for a crevasse in the rocky desert landscape.

The Japanese continue to rework International Modernism into their own uncompromising forms. Like Tadao Ando, Kisho Kurokawa and Fumihiko Maki before them, newer arrivals on the Japanese architectural scene continue to push building forms and technologies to their limits. Shigeru Ban's Wall-less House - essentially a continuous plan folded over to enclose an open-plan space - and Shuhei Endo's wrap-around skins and swirls of corrugated steel rewrite the rule book. In building technology, Ban has developed his hallmark paper tube as an environmentally efficient building component, and Ushida Findlay have worked with wire mesh and sprayed concrete shells to create amorphous sculptural shapes that are easy to build and provide good insulation.

In south-east Asian countries, where the economic boom has fed a vast construction programme, particularly in Hong Kong, China and Malaysia, young architects have had the chance to design big commercial projects. However, more often than not this has resulted in soulless commercialism and the subsuming of architectural creativity by corporate ostentation. Within this, a few

In New York entstanden in jüngster Zeit wenig Neubauten, architektonische Projekte beschränken sich in der Regel auf Interieurs. Dennoch fühlen sich Architekten wie Simon Ungers und Asymptote, die sich ebenso intensiv mit Kunst wie mit Architektur befassen, von dieser Stadt mit ihrer reichen Kunstszene angezogen. Sie entwerfen Installationen für bekannte Galerien und konzipieren Bauten, die wie Landschaftsskulpturen wirken.

In anderen Teilen der Vereinigten Staaten, wo es mehr Raum gibt, sind die Architekten bestrebt, auf den natürlichen Kontext zu reagieren. Thompson und Rose flechten ihr Atlantic Center for the Arts in die subtropischen Wälder Floridas, während Wendell Burnettes Atelier- und Wohnhaus in Phoenix, Arizona, nach seinen Worten einem tiefen Spalt im felsigen Wüstengelände als »riesiges Pflaster« dient.

Die Japaner verbinden die internationale Moderne mit ihren eigenen kompromisslosen Formen. Wie bereits Tadao Ando, Kisho Kurokawa und Fumihiko Maki treiben auch neuere Vertreter der japanischen Architekturszene Bauformen und -verfahren bis an ihre Grenzen. Shigeru Bans Wall-less House, das »Haus ohne Wände« – eigentlich eine fortlaufende, gebogene Fläche, die einen freien Raum umgibt – und Shuhei Endos umlaufende Verkleidungen und Wirbel aus gewelltem Stahlblech verabschieden sich von tradierten Regeln. Shigeru Ban entwickelt mit den für ihn charakteristischen Pappröhren ein umweltfreundliches Baumaterial.

Der Bauboom in den aufstrebenden Ländern Südostasiens, insbesondere aber in Hongkong, China und Malaysia, eröffnete jungen Architekten zahlreiche Gelegenheiten, große kommerzielle Projekte auszuführen. In den meisten Fällen entstanden jedoch seelenlose kommerzielle Bauten, bei denen die Kreativität des Architekten

contexte urbain : motif de papier peint du XIXe siècle. ornant un abribus, logements sociaux revêtus de faux acajou, ou reflet fantomatique d'anciens ornements en stuc sur la façade d'un immeuble d'appartements berlinois.

A New York, où l'on ne construit guère ces temps-ci, l'activité est en majeure partie limitée à l'architecture d'intérieur. La foisonnante scène artistique de la ville n'en convient pas moins à des architectes tels que Simon Ungers ou Asymptote, qui partagent leur temps entre l'architecture et l'art, réalisant des installations pour d'importantes galeries, et des bâtiments qui sont en fait des sculptures de plein air. Dans d'autres régions des Etats-Unis les architectes tirent parti de l'environnement naturel. Thompson and Rose ont conçu l'Atlantic Center for the Arts, qui s'intègre dans la jungle de Floride ; à Phoenix, Arizona, l'ensemble maison-atelier de Wendell Burnette recouvre d'« un pansement adhésif géant » une crevasse du paysage désertique et rocailleux.

Au Japon, les architectes continuent de réinterpréter le modernisme du style international selon leurs rigoureuses exigences formelles. Comme Tadao Ando, Kisho Kurokawa et Fumihiko Maki avant eux, les nouveaux acteurs de la scène architecturale japonaise continuent à repousser les limites des formes et des techniques de construction. La Wall-less House (« maison sans murs ») de Shigeru Ban, ou les peaux enveloppantes et les volutes de tôle ondulée de Shuhei Endo réinventent les règles du jeu. Dans le domaine de la technologie du bâtiment, Shigeru Ban a fait du tube en carton, matériau de construction respectueux de l'environnement, sa signature.

Dans les pays d'Asie du Sud-Est, où le boom économique a nourri un énorme programme de constructions, en particulier à Hong-Kong, en Chine et en Malaisie, de jeunes architectes ont eu la possibilité de dessiner de grands

lone voices have managed to follow their own agenda, though often working on a much smaller scale. Gary Chang's EDGE (HK) LTD and his previous company with Michael Chan, Edge, persevered in following their own vision, creating inspiring public spaces within the dense urban environment of Hong Kong. Mike Tonkin, now back in the United Kingdom after seven years on the island, employs lateral thinking to find his highly original solutions for conventional building types: curly fringes for a hair salon, a photographer's studio that itself is a giant pinhole camera, and a karaoke bar decorated with an abstract jungle motif because "we used to sing in the trees".
Countries dealing with past oppression of minorities and indigenous peoples are particularly sensitive to traditional building forms, and younger architects are rejecting Euro-centric styles that previously dominated the architecture of their countries. Henri Comrie + 'Ora Joubert explore the architectural demands of post-apartheid South Africa by acknowledging the constraints of a low-tech building industry. Simple construction methods and everyday materials are enriched through light, texture, and well-planned spaces - for example Comrie's Gordon Institute of Business Science, which responds to climatic conditions with open shady courtyards and thick ochre-coloured walls and Joubert's Huis Laubscher in Pretoria, a thatched roof supported on rough-hewn wooden posts.
In Australia and New Zealand, crinkly tin is ubiquitous as a building material, even in urban settings, where it serves as an homage to makeshift houses. Its most famous champions have been Roy Grounds, Glenn Murcutt, and Lindsay and Kerry Clare. Now it is becoming more mainstream. Images of Patrick Clifford's own house give the impression of a forest tree house

sich der Prachtentfaltung von Konzernen unterzuordnen hatte. In diesem Umfeld gelang es einigen wenigen, ihren eigenen Weg zu gehen, häufig jedoch in weit kleinerem Maßstab. Gary Changs Büro EDGE (HK) LTD und seine frühere Partnerschaft mit Michael Chan, Edge, verfolgten konsequent eigene Vorstellungen und schufen reizvolle öffentliche Räume im dicht bebauten Hongkong. Der nach siebenjähriger Tätigkeit in Hongkong nach England zurückgekehrte Brite Mike Tonkin bedient sich unorthodoxer Einfälle für konventionelle Gebäudetypen: »gelockte« Dekoration für einen Friseursalon, ein Fotoatelier, das einer riesigen Lochkamera gleicht und eine Karaoke-Bar, die mit einem abstrakten Dschungelmotiv dekoriert ist, weil »wir früher in den Bäumen sangen«.
Ein einfühlsamer Umgang mit traditionellen Bauformen ist in Ländern zu beobachten, die sich mit der einstigen Unterdrückung von Minderheiten und eingeborenen Völkern auseinandersetzen müssen. Junge Architekten lehnen die eurozentrischen Stile ab, von denen die Architektur ihrer Länder früher beherrscht wurde. Nach der Überwindung der Apartheid tragen Henri Comrie + 'Ora Joubert der kaum technisierten Bauwirtschaft Südafrikas Rechnung. Einfache Bauverfahren und profane Materialien werden durch Licht, Struktur und gut geplante Räume veredelt; Comrie reagiert bei seinem Gordon Institute of Business Science mit offenen, schattigen Innenhöfen und dicken, ockerfarbenen Wänden auf die klimatischen Bedingungen. Joubert reduziert ihr Huis Laubscher in Pretoria auf ein Reetdach, das von roh behauenen Holzpfosten getragen wird.
In Australien und Neuseeland ist Wellblech als Baumaterial allgegenwärtig, selbst in urbanen Kontexten, wo es als Zitat von Behelfsunterkünften verwendet wird. Seine bekanntesten Verfechter sind Roy Grounds, Glenn Murcutt und Lindsay und Kerry Clare. Inzwischen hat sich

édifices commerciaux. Il en résulte trop souvent un mercantilisme sans âme, la créativité architecturale étant subordonnée à l'ostentation des grandes entreprises. Quelques voix isolées ont néanmoins réussi à rester fidèles à leurs principes, bien qu'en travaillant souvent à une échelle nettement plus modeste. Le bureau de Gary Chang EDGE (HK) LTD et son prédécesseur Edge (en association avec Michael Chan), ont obstinément suivi leur vision personnelle en créant des espaces publics saisissants dans le dense tissu urbain de Hong-Kong. Il y a aussi Mike Tonkin, revenu en Grande-Bretagne après avoir travaillé plusieurs années dans l'île, dont la pensée latérale lui permet de trouver des solutions extrêmement originales à des projets fort conventionnels : décoration ondulée pour un salon de coiffure, atelier de photographe constituant une gigantesque chambre noire, bar karaoké décoré d'un motif abstrait évoquant la jungle parce que « jadis nous chantions dans les arbres ».
Les pays qui ont connu l'oppression des minorités et des populations indigènes sont particulièrement sensibles aux formes de l'architecture traditionnelle. Leurs jeunes architectes rejettent les styles « eurocentriques » qui ont longtemps dominé l'architecture de leurs pays. Henri Comrie + 'Ora Joubert explorent les besoins architecturaux de l'Afrique du Sud d'après l'apartheid en tenant compte des limites d'une industrie du bâtiment restée rudimentaire. Des méthodes de construction simples et des matériaux courants sont enrichis grâce à des espaces bien conçus et au traitement de la lumière et des textures. En témoignent notamment l'Institute of Business Science de Comrie, qui répond aux conditions climatiques par d'épais murs de couleur ocre et des cours ombragées, et la Huis Laubscher de Joubert à Pretoria, qui est pour l'essentiel un toit en chaume soutenu par des poteaux en bois grossièrement taillés.

rather than a family home in downtown Auckland, and the Wilson House by Crosson Clarke has the informality of a beach shack but still wins awards from New Zealand domestic lifestyle magazines.
Many of the names in this book are already in the ascendant with a small but growing body of work behind them. More in their late 20s and early 30s are beginning to show signs of promise and are about to tackle their first mega projects. London-based Foreign Office Architects Alejandro Zaero Polo and Farshid Moussavi are constructing the £150 million Yokohama International Ferry Terminal in Japan, which seems to defy mathematics. London-based Cécile Brisac and Edgar González in 1999 won the competition for the Museum of World Culture in Gothenburg, Sweden. Brad Cloepfil's Allied Works, based in Portland, Oregon, beat strong competition from Gigon/Guyer, Peter Zumthor, Herzog + de Meuron and others to design the new Forum for Contemporary Art museum in St Louis, Missouri, which is scheduled to open in 2002.
The architects included here have been selected to show the diversity, originality, beauty, quality and integrity at large at the younger end of the architectural spectrum. Together they present a snapshot of a particular generation; "40 architects under 40" is intended to be a reference book, a source of inspiration, and a glimpse of the future.

das Material weitgehend durchgesetzt. Ansichten von Patrick Cliffords Haus lassen eher an ein Baumhaus im Wald denken als an ein Einfamilienhaus im Zentrum von Auckland, und das Haus Wilson von Crosson Clarke Architects erinnert mit seiner provisorischen Erscheinung an eine Strandhütte, wird aber dennoch von Lifestylemagazinen in Neuseeland mit Preisen ausgezeichnet.
Der Aufstieg vieler in diesem Buch vorgestellten Architekten, die alle ein kleines, aber stetig wachsendes Œuvre vorweisen können, ist bereits abzusehen. Darüber hinaus gibt es viele Architekten im Alter von Ende 20 oder Anfang 30, die viel versprechende Ansätze zeigen und vor der Umsetzung ihrer ersten Großprojekte stehen: Die Londoner Architekten Alejandro Zaero Polo und Farshid Moussavi, die den Neubau des britischen Außenministeriums verantworten, errichten mit einem Budget von £ 150 Millionen das Yokohama International Ferry Terminal in Japan, das mathematische Regeln außer Kraft zu setzen scheint; Cécile Brisac und Edgar González, ebenfalls in London tätig, konnten 1999 den Wettbewerb für das Museum of World Culture in Göteborg für sich entscheiden; das von Brad Cloepfil geleitete Büro Allied Works mit Sitz in Portland, Oregon, setzte sich gegen die starke Konkurrenz von Gigon/Guyer, Peter Zumthor, Herzog + de Meuron und anderen im Wettbewerb um das neue Forum for Contemporary Art in St. Louis, Missouri, durch, das 2002 eröffnet werden soll.
Die vorliegende Auswahl von 40 Architekten soll die Vielfalt, Originalität, Schönheit, Qualität und Integrität der jüngeren Architekten zeigen – gemeinsam ergeben sie die Momentaufnahme einer Generation.

En Australie et en Nouvelle-Zélande, la tôle froissée, matériau omniprésent même dans un contexte urbain, est un hommage aux habitations de fortune. Ses champions les plus célèbres furent Roy Grounds, Lindsay and Kerry Clare et Glenn Murcutt. Maintenant, son utilisation est devenue courante. Les photos de la propre maison de Patrick Clifford donnent l'impression d'une maison dans la forêt, et non d'une résidence familiale en plein centre d'Auckland. La maison Wilson dessinée par Crosson Clarke a le naturel d'un cabanon de plage, ce qui ne l'empêche pas d'être distinguée par les magazines de décoration néo-zélandais.
Beaucoup des architectes présentés dans ce livre ont déjà réalisé une œuvre limitée mais qui ne cesse de s'accroître ; pour eux, l'avenir s'annonce bien. D'autres, plus jeunes d'une dizaine d'années, ont fait des débuts prometteurs et s'apprêtent à aborder leurs premiers « méga-projets ». Les architectes du ministère des Affaires étrangères britannique Alejandro Zaero Polo et Farshid Moussavi, basés à Londres, construisent à Yokohama, Japon, un terminal de ferry de £ 150 millions. En 1999, Cécile Brisac et Edgar Gonzáles, eux aussi établis à Londres, ont remporté le concours concernant le Musée de la Culture mondiale, qui sera construit à Göteborg, Suède. Allied Works, bureau dirigé par Brad Cloepfil à Portland, Oregon, a remporté face à une forte concurrence (Gigon/Guyer, Peter Zumthor, Herzog + de Meuron, etc.) le concours pour la construction du nouveau musée Forum for Contemporary Art à Saint Louis, Missouri, dont l'ouverture est prévue pour 2002.
Les 40 architectes présentés dans ces pages ont été choisis de sorte à refléter la diversité, l'originalité, la beauté, la qualité et l'intégrité dont témoignent dans leur ensemble les jeunes bâtisseurs. Ensemble, ils constituent une coupe transversale, ou un instantané, d'une génération.

THESOCIAL

Adjaye and Russell

24 Sunbury Workshops, Swanfield Street,
London E2 7LF, UK

tel + 44 20 7739 4969 fax +44 20 7739 3484 e-mail dadjaye@compuserve.com

David Adjaye

born	1966 Dar-es-Salam, Tanzania
studied	1986 Middlesex University; 1990 South Bank University; 1993 Royal College of Art, London; 1997 South Bank University
previous practices	Chassay Architects, London; David Chipperfield Architects, London; Eduardo Souto de Moura Architects, Oporto, Portugal
	1994 founded Adjaye and Russell

William Russell

born	1965 Marlborough, UK
studied	1986 University of Newcastle upon Tyne; 1993 Royal College of Art, London
previous practice	RMJM, London and Hong Kong; Pierre Yves Rochon, Paris
	1994 Partner, Adjaye and Russell

Selected projects

Soba Noodle Bar	1996	London, UK
Lunch @ Exmouth Market, Cafe	1997	Clerkenwell, London, UK
House extension	1998	St John's Wood, London, UK
The Social	1999	London, UK
Studio and home for Chris Ofili	1999	Shoreditch, London, UK
House for Eve and Ewan McGregor	1999	St John's Wood, London, UK
Gallery and house for Jake Chapman	2000	Shoreditch, London, UK
Dorchester Media Performing Arts and Athletic Center		Boston, Massachusetts, USA (feasibility study)
Church and school	2005	Accra, Ghana (awaiting funding)

After designing a string of central London eateries in the mid-90s, Adjaye and Russell have lately built up a clientele of celebrities drawn from London's cultural movers and shakers: a residence for Eve and Ewan McGregor, studio/houses for both Jake Chapman and Chris Ofili. At the same time the practice is extending its international interests in Ghana and the United States.
The practice approaches architecture as a craft, and likes to see itself as an atelier experimenting with unusual materials and techniques rather than as a

Nachdem sie in der Mitte der 90er-Jahre eine Reihe von Esslokalen im Londoner Zentrum entworfen hatten, rekrutiert sich die Klientel von Adjaye und Russel in jüngster Zeit aus der Szene der Stadt: ein Haus für Eve und Ewan McGregor, Ateliers und Wohnhäuser für Jake Chapman und Chris Ofili. Zugleich erweitert das Büro seine Tätigkeit nach Ghana und in die Vereinigten Staaten.
Adjaye and Russell betreiben Architektur als Handwerk und verstehen sich eher als Atelier, das mit ungewöhnlichen Materialien und Techniken experimentiert denn als herkömmliches Architekturbüro: grobe Industriemate-

Après avoir réalisé vers le milieu des années 90 une série de restaurants dans le centre de Londres, Adjaye and Russel se sont constitué une clientèle de célébrités dans le milieu culturel londonien : une résidence pour Eve et Ewan McGregor, des maisons-ateliers pour Jake Chapman ainsi que pour Chris Ofili. Parallèlement, ils étendent leur activité au niveau international, notamment au Ghana et aux Etats-Unis.
Le bureau aborde l'architecture comme un artisanat ; il aime se considérer comme un atelier expérimentant de nouveaux matériaux et techniques plutôt que comme un

standard architectural practice. This is evident in their unconventional use of harsh industrial materials for The Social bar, the glass wall that disappears into the ground on a North London house extension, cheap garden centre fencing used as a textural cladding at Lunch cafe, playful use of translucent and transparent materials altering light, depth and boundaries between spaces or underground natural ventilation for a church and school in Ghana. David Adjaye is also developing furniture and lighting ranges.

rialien für die Bar The Social, die verschiebbare Glaswand einer Hauserweiterung in North London, billige Zäunen aus dem Gartencenter zur strukturierenden Verkleidung im Café Lunch. Opake und transparente Materialien, die Licht, Tiefe und Raumgrenzen modifizieren, setzen sie spielerisch ein; für eine Kirche und Schule in Ghana verlegen sie die Frischluftzufuhr unter die Erde.
Neben seiner architektonischen Arbeit entwickelt David Adjaye auch Möbel- und Leuchtenkollektionen.

bureau d'architectes traditionnel – à témoin l'utilisation peu conventionnelle de matériaux industriels bruts pour le bar The Social, le mur de verre s'enfonçant dans le sol d'une extension de maison particulière de Londres Nord, des clôtures de jardin bon marché utilisées pour texturer des surfaces à Lunch, l'usage ludique de matériaux translucides et transparents modifiant la qualité de la lumière et brouillant les limites entre les espaces, ou encore la ventilation souterraine naturelle d'un ensemble église-école au Ghana. David Adjaye crée aussi des collections de meubles et de luminaires.

1999 **London, UK**

The Social

A former strip joint in London's Soho district, The Social bar has transformed the back-street dive into a fashionable drinking den. The challenging palette of materials is intentionally industrial: cast concrete seating, honeycomb panelling usually used on aeroplane fuselages, sheets of glass-reinforced plastic back-lit with fluorescent and tungsten lights, grey Eternite cladding as wall panels, Luxcrete floors, a steel staircase and bare light bulbs on steel poles. Spatially, ground and basement have been reversed, with the main bar downstairs and an oak-lined more private space above. Cutting back the front of the ground floor brings light down into the basement, and adds a sense of occasion through the double-height space.

Die Bar The Social, ein ehemaliges Striplokal im Londoner Viertel Soho, hat sich von der Hinterhofspelunke zum angesagten Szenetreff gemausert. Die mutige Materialpalette wirkt bewusst industriell: Sitzmöbel aus Fertigbeton, Wabenverkleidung, die gewöhnlich für Flugzeugrümpfe verwendet wird, Scheiben aus mit Glasfaser verstärktem Kunststoff, die von hinten mit Neon- und Tungstenlicht beleuchtet werden, graue Eternitplatten als Wandverschalung, Luxcreteböden, eine Stahltreppe und nackte Glühbirnen auf stählernen Pfosten. Erdgeschoss und Souterrain haben die Plätze getauscht: Die Hauptbar liegt im Tiefgeschoss, und ein mit Eichenholz getäfelter, intimerer Raum ebenerdig darüber. Die Verschiebung der Erdgeschossfront nach hinten lässt Tageslicht ins Souterrain dringen, und der Raum gewinnt durch seine doppelte Höhe eine besondere Atmosphäre.

Les propriétaires de The Social bar ont transformé une ancienne boîte de strip-tease mal famée en un bar très « tendance ». La gamme de matériaux est délibérément de nature industrielle : sièges en béton moulé, revêtements en nid d'abeille du type utilisé pour les fuselages d'avions, plaques de plastique armé de fibre de verre diffusant la lumière de lampes fluorescentes ou à incandescence, panneaux muraux en Eternit gris, planchers en Luxcrete, escalier en acier, pieds en acier portant des ampoules électriques nues. Spatialement, le rez-de-chaussée et le sous-sol ont été inversés, le bar à proprement parler étant au sous-sol, et un lieu plus intime, lambrissé de chêne, au niveau supérieur. Le rez-de-chaussée, partiellement en retrait, permet à la lumière du jour de pénétrer au niveau inférieur, et donne un caractère imprévu à cet espace à double hauteur.

The stark entrance, right, and the downstairs bar, left, which uses industrial materials such as glass-reinforced plastic wall panels and cast concrete tables

Rechts der nüchterne Eingang; links die Souterrain-Bar mit Industriematerialien wie Wa[illegible]elen aus glasverstärktem Kunststoff und Tis[illegible]s Fertigbeton

L'entrée est très austère (à dro[illegible]). A gauche, le bar du sous-sol ; les architectes ont utilisé des matériaux industriels : cloisons en plastique renforcé de fibre de verre, tables en plaques de béton.

SOCIAL THE SOCIAL THE SOCIAL THE SO
THE SOCIAL THE SOCIAL TH
SOCIAL THE SOCIAL THE SOCIAL

The street facade, above, and cosier wood-panelled upper bar, right

Oben die Straßenfassade, rechts die heimeligere obere Bar mit Holzvertäfelung

Ci-dessus, la façade. A droite, le bar du rez-de-chaussée ; ici, les murs lambrissés de bois créent une ambiance plus intime.

The 6 m sheet of glass separating kitchen from garden can be lifted up on hydraulic rams.

Die 6 m breite Glasscheibe zwischen Küche und Garten lässt sich mittels hydraulischer Drucksäulen anheben.

Des vérins hydrauliques permettent de lever la plaque de verre de 6 m de large séparant la cuisine du jardin.

1998 **St John's Wood, London, UK**

House extension

The steel, glass and concrete box extends from the back of the existing Victorian house at semi-basement level providing an open-plan family room and kitchen, with a generous roof terrace above. The most impressive feature is a single-sheet 6 m-wide glass wall separating the new space from the garden. With the kitchen work surface set at exactly the same level as the garden and the seamless glass wall able to rise up on hydraulic rams, interior and exterior are effectively treated as one continuous space.

Der kastenförmige Anbau aus Stahl, Glas und Beton schließt sich auf Souterrain-Niveau an das viktorianische Haus an und erweitert es um einen offenen Mehrzweckraum mit Küche; darüber befindet sich eine großzügige Dachterrasse. Besonders eindrucksvoll ist die 6 m breite Verglasung, die den neuen Raum vom Garten trennt. Da die Arbeitsfläche der Küche und der Garten exakt auf dem selben Niveau liegen und sich die nahtlose Glaswand mittels hydraulischer Drucksäulen anheben lässt, erscheinen Innen- und Außenraum tatsächlich als zusammenhängendes Ganzes.

La boîte en acier, verre et béton s'étendant à l'arrière d'une maison victorienne existant entre le niveau du rez-de-chaussée et celui du sous-sol, abrite une salle de séjour et cuisine à plan ouvert, surmontée d'un vaste toit-terrasse. Le trait le plus marquant est un pan de verre de 6 m séparant le nouvel espace du jardin. Le plan de travail de la cuisine étant situé exactement au niveau du jardin, et le mur de verre pouvant se lever grâce à un système hydraulique, l'intérieur et l'extérieur sont vraiment traités comme un espace continu.

Above, the kitchen work surface is flush with the patio, creating a seamless flow from indoors to outdoors. Left, the terrace on top of the kitchen.

Oben: Die Arbeitsfläche der Küche liegt auf einer Höhe mit dem Garten; so verschmelzen Innen- und Außenraum. Links die Terrasse über der Küche.

Ci-dessus : le plan de travail de la cuisine étant situé au niveau du patio, intérieur et extérieur se confondent. A gauche : la terrasse sur la cuisine.

2005 **Accra, Ghana**

Church and school

This Baptist complex includes a church, church hall, school and two pastoral residences set on a very steep site in the equatorial climes of Accra. David Adjaye has combined modern aesthetics with traditional Ghanaian building principles. The walls of the buildings will be made of an adobe and concrete mix, the roofs of metal sheeting, and rather than glazing, the architects will use wooden lattice-screens, which allow occupants to look out but no one to look inside. The buildings rest on a series of plenums (ventilation shafts) running beneath the site and up the back of the hill, providing a natural ventilation system.

Dieser baptistische Komplex umfasst Kirche, Gemeindesaal, Schule und zwei Wohnhäuser für Seelsorger auf einem sehr steilen Gelände in der Äquatorialzone von Accra. David Adjaye verbindet moderne Ästhetik mit traditionellen ghanaischen Bautechniken: Die Wände werden aus einer Mischung von Lehm und Beton, die Dächer aus Blechplatten bestehen, und anstelle von Verglasungen werden die Architekten Holzgitter verwenden, die die Bewohner hinaus, aber niemanden hinein sehen lassen. Die Bauten stehen auf einer Reihe von Belüftungsschächten, die unterhalb des Geländes zur Rückseite des Hügels verlaufen und so ein natürliches Belüftungssystem bilden.

Ce complexe baptiste comprend une église, un hall, une école et deux maisons pour les pasteurs, répartis sur un site en forte pente à Accra, ville au climat équatorial. David Adjaye a allié une esthétique moderne aux techniques de construction traditionnelles du Ghana. Les murs sont en brique crue et béton et les toits en tôle, tandis que les vitrages sont remplacés par des claustras permettant aux occupants de voir sans être vus. Les bâtiments reposent sur une série de puits de ventilation creusés sous le site et s'ouvrant sur le versant opposé de la colline, l'ensemble constituant un système de climatisation naturel.

A series of terraces lead down from the schoolhouse and church to the two pastoral residences.

Abgetreppte Terrassen führen vom Schulgebäude und der Kirche hinunter zu den beiden Wohnhäusern der Seelsorger.

Une série de terrasses descend de l'école et de l'église vers les deux résidences pastorales.

Cross-section across site/ Schnitt der Anlage/ Vue en coupe du site

1 **gardens/** Gärten/ jardins
2 **pastors' residences/** Wohnhäuser der Seelsorger/ résidences des pasteurs
3 **school's gardens/** Schulgärten/ jardins de l'école
4 **school/terraces with church above/** Schule und Terrassen mit darüberliegender Kirche/ école et terrasses donnant sur l'église
5 **bell tower/** Glockenturm/ clocher

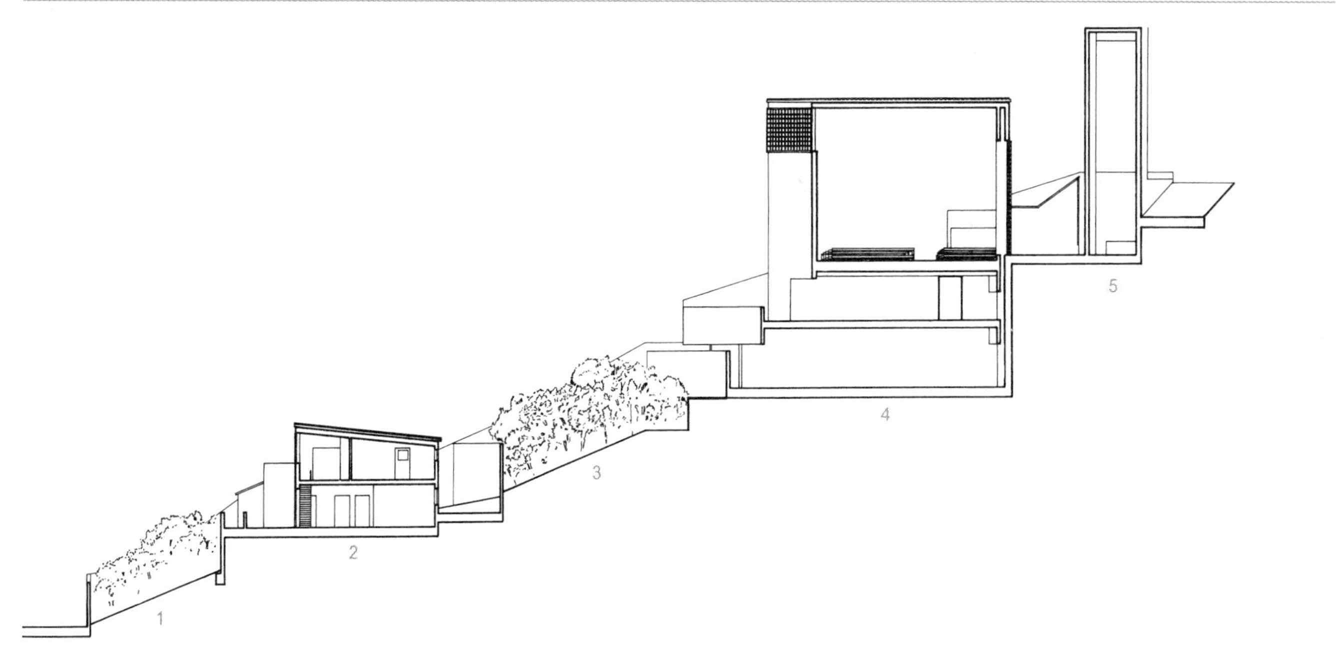

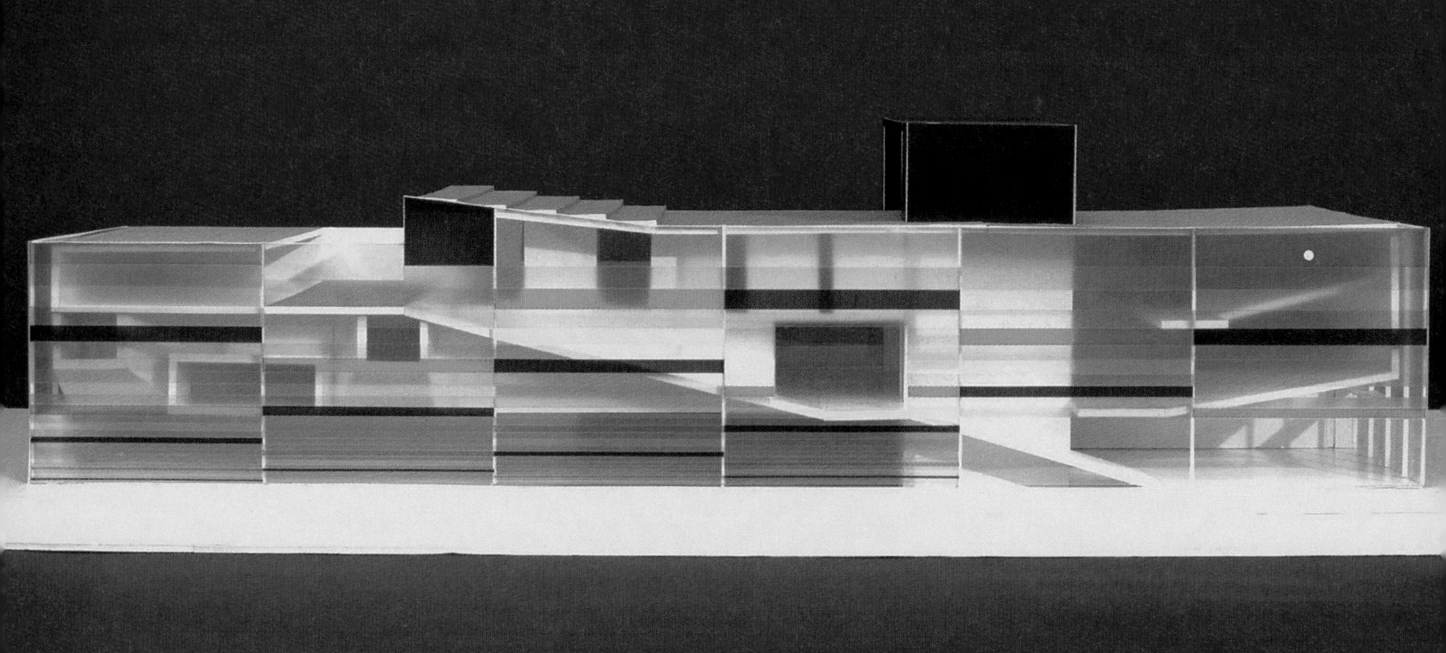

The new arts and athletic centre for Boston, Massachusetts, is conceived as "a window to the city".

Das geplante Kunst- und Sportzentrum für Boston, Massachusetts soll als »Fenster zur Stadt« fungieren.

Divers aspects du centre culturel et sportif prévu pour Boston, Massachusetts, telle une « fenêtre ouverte sur la ville ».

Dorchester Media Performing Arts and Athletic Center

Designed to house teaching facilities for sports, the performing arts and the media, and to provide a community centre in one of Boston's tenser neighbourhoods, the building will be divided vertically/horizontally into three sections, while maintaining flexibility and communication between them. Where the theatre's fly tower protrudes from the top of the block, David Adjaye envisions it to be used as an open air cinema screen. The street facade will be a colourful glazed wall designed in collaboration with an artist, "a window to the city", offering passers-by vignettes of the activities within. Work will start on site in 2002.

Das Zentrum soll Lehreinrichtungen für Sport, Bühnenkunst und Medien beherbergen und als Bürgerzentrum für eins der problematischeren Viertel von Boston dienen. Es wird vertikal und horizontal in drei Abschnitte unterteilt, die jedoch flexibel verbunden bleiben. Das aus dem Dach herausragende Bühnenhaus des Theaters kann nach Vorstellung Adjayes als Open-Air-Leinwand genutzt werden. Die Straßenfassade wird in Zusammenarbeit mit einem Künstler als farbig verglaste Wand gestaltet, als »Fenster zur Stadt«, das Passanten Detailansichten des Innenraums bietet. Die Bauarbeiten werden 2002 beginnen.

Destiné à accueillir des espaces d'enseignement du sport, des arts scéniques et des techniques médiatiques, et à doter d'un centre culturel l'un des quartiers les plus problématiques de Boston, l'édifice sera divisé verticalement/horizontalement en trois sections, entre lesquelles la flexibilité et les communications seront assurées. Adjaye envisage de faire de la tour abritant les cintres du théâtre, qui se dresse au-dessus du bloc, un écran de cinéma de plein air. La façade sur rue sera un mur vitré multicolore conçu en collaboration avec un artiste, une « fenêtre sur la ville » donnant aux passants des aperçus de l'activité du centre. Les travaux devraient commencer en 2002.

Jesús Aparicio Guisado

Conde de Peñalver 15 - 3° Izda, 28006 Madrid, Spain   tel +34 91 577 9446   fax +34 91 576 0796   e-mail raizdesiete@nagasys.es

Jesús Aparicio Guisado

born	1960	Madrid, Spain
studied	1984	Escuela Técnica Superior de Arquitectura de Madrid (ETSAM); 1989 Columbia University, New York (Fulbright Scholar)

Selected projects

Annex to the Parliament	1986	Madrid, Spain (project)
Chapel for the Incorrupt Heart and Arm of Santa Teresa	1987	Alba de Tormes, Salamanca, Spain
Sports complex	1991	Valdemoro, Madrid, Spain
Tourist centre	1995	Cadalso de los Vidrios, Madrid, Spain
Pavilion for the Giuseppe Terragni exhibition	1997	Madrid, Spain
Apartment building	1998	Santa Marta de Tormes, Salamanca, Spain

A student of Madrid-based architect Alberto Campo Baeza, who with architectural critic Kenneth Frampton supervised his doctoral thesis at the Escuela Técnica Superior de Arquitectura de Madrid (ETSAM), Aparicio's architecture is typical of the best work being produced by the substantial group of good young architects based in Madrid. Unlike the more flamboyant work that came out of Barcelona in the early 90s, the new Madrid crowd works in a style that is much purer and tectonic, concerned with space, planes, and objects rather than with superficial embellishments.

Jesús Aparicio Guisado has a particularly poetic approach to architecture based on a quest for beauty and spiritual experience. "My architecture is born of walls that define spatial volumes and trap beauty within, in the sense of place, function, construction, thereby creating dwellings of beauty. The idea of architecture consists in finding beauty in the elements of a project and making them, and with them, something inhabited and sublime. The union of beauty and dwelling takes place in the walls, the corporeal elements that define architecture."

A professor of building design at ETSAM, Aparicio has a strong academic approach with more theoretical than

Aparicio ist Schüler des Madrider Architekten Alberto Campo Baeza, der zusammen mit dem Architekturhistoriker Kenneth Frampton auch seine Doktorarbeit an der Escuela Técnica Superior de Arquitectura de Madrid (ETSAM) betreute. Sein Stil ist charakteristisch für die besten Arbeiten der großen Gruppe junger Architekten in der spanischen Hauptstadt. Anders als die eher extravaganten Arbeiten, die Anfang der 90er-Jahre in Barcelona entstanden, pflegt die neue Mannschaft in Madrid einen klareren, tektonischeren Stil, bei dem es mehr um Raum, Flächen und Objekte geht als um die Verschönerung von Oberflächen.

Jesús Aparicio Guisados Architekturauffassung ist besonders poetisch und wurzelt in der Suche nach Schönheit und geistiger Erfahrung. »Meine Architektur entsteht aus Mauern, die räumliche Volumina umgrenzen und Schönheit einfangen, im Sinne von Ort, Funktion und Konstruktion, wobei Orte der Schönheit geschaffen werden. Die Idee von Architektur besteht darin, Schönheit in den Elementen eines Projekts zu finden und daraus und mit ihnen etwas Bewohntes, Erhabenes zu machen. Schönheit und Wohnung vereinen sich in den Mauern, den greifbaren Elementen, die die Architektur bestimmen.«

Disciple de l'architecte madrilène Alberto Campo Baeza, qui dirigea sa thèse de doctorat à l'Escuela Técnica Superior de Arquitectura de Madrid (ETSAM) avec l'historien d'architecture Kenneth Frampton, Aparicio pratique une architecture typique des meilleures réalisations de l'important groupe de jeunes architectes de qualité actifs à Madrid. Contrairement au design exubérant venu de Barcelone au début des années 90, cette communauté madrilène travaille dans un style nettement plus pur et structurel, accordant plus d'importance aux espaces, aux plans et aux objets qu'aux enjolivements de surface.

Jesús Aparicio Guisado a une approche particulièrement poétique de l'architecture, fondée sur une quête de la beauté et de l'expérience spirituelle. « Mon architecture naît de murs qui définissent des volumes et y prennent la beauté au piège, de sorte que le lieu, la fonction et la construction créent des havres de beauté. L'idée de l'architecture consiste à découvrir la beauté dans les éléments d'un projet et d'en faire quelque chose d'habité, de sublime. L'union de la beauté et de l'habitat s'opère entre les murs, éléments concrets qui définissent l'architecture. »

Professeur de dessin d'architecture à l'ETSAM, Aparicio a une approche très universitaire, et a conçu davantage de

built projects. He is also a visiting professor at numerous top European schools of architecture, and has published widely his writings on architecture. Using architecture to mirror the universe and keep man within nature rather than cocooning him inside building, he ensures that one is always aware of the sky and the infinite space from within his buildings. His concept - as he is fond of repeating - is "architecture is the dwelling of beauty".

Der Professor für Entwurfslehre an der ETSAM hat ein stark akademisch geprägtes Architekturverständnis, und sein Œuvre umfasst mehr geplante als realisierte Projekte. Zudem lehrt Aparicio als Gastprofessor an zahlreichen führenden Architekturfakultäten Europas; seine Schriften zur Architektur sind weithin publiziert. Er nutzt Architektur, um das Universum zu spiegeln und bindet den Menschen an die Natur, statt ihn in Innenräume zu hüllen. So ist er stets darauf bedacht, dass man sich in seinen Bauten des Himmels und des unendlichen Raums bewusst bleibt. Sein Grundgedanke, den er gern wiederholt, lautet: »Architektur ist der Ort der Schönheit«.

projets théoriques que de réalisations concrètes. Il est également professeur associé de plusieurs écoles d'architecture européennes de haut niveau, et a beaucoup publié. Utilisant l'architecture pour refléter l'univers et relier l'homme à la nature plutôt que pour le protéger contre celle-ci, il veille à ce que l'occupant de ses bâtiments soit toujours conscient du ciel et des espaces infinis. Son concept, comme il aime à le répéter, est « L'architecture est le lieu où réside la beauté ».

Apartment building

Aparicio Guisado has created a rooftop paradise where shallow pools on the roof-terrace continue metaphorically into the apartments through the surface of table tops set at exactly the same height as the surface of the water.
Two huge holes are cut through the building so that the apartments within burst out of the confines of the walls. More subtly, perforated brick walls in the bedroom are seen as a means for the exterior to penetrate the interior. The architect describes them as "apartments of air and sky".
On this project Aparicio collaborated with Luis Ignacio Aguirre and Daniel Huertas Nadal.

Aparicio schuf mit seinem Apartmenthaus in Santa Marta de Tormes ein Dachparadies – die flachen Wasserbecken der Dachterrasse setzen sich metaphorisch in den Tischplatten in den Wohnungen fort, die exakt auf Höhe der Wasseroberfläche liegen.
In das Gebäude wurden zwei große Öffnungen geschnitten, so dass die Wohnungen die Begrenzungen ihrer Wände durchbrechen. Auf noch subtilere Weise lassen durchbrochene Backsteinwände im Schlafzimmer den Außenraum ins Innere dringen.
Bei diesem Projekt arbeitete Aparicio mit Luis Ignacio Aguirre und Daniel Huertas Nadal zusammen.

Jesús Aparicio Guisado a créé un paradis sur le toit-terrasse de cet immeuble d'appartements, ponctué de bassins qui se poursuivent métaphoriquement dans les appartements, où les plateaux des tables sont exactement à la même hauteur que la surface de l'eau.
L'immeuble est percé de deux énormes puits, de sorte que les appartements échappent à la limite des murs. Plus subtilement, les murs en brique perforés des chambres permettent à l'extérieur de faire irruption dans les espaces intérieurs. L'architecte les décrit comme des « appartements d'air et de ciel ».
Ce projet a été réalisé en collaboration avec Luis Ignacio Aguirre et Daniel Huertas Nadal.

Far left, roof terrace. Left, glass lift shaft open to the sky.

Ganz links die Dachterrasse; links der nach oben offene, verglaste Liftschacht

Page de gauche, une partie du toit-terrasse. Ci-contre, la cage d'ascenseur vitrée s'ouvre sur le ciel.

Above, the table surface is flush with the terrace pool. Right, Aparicio cuts into the block on the upper level.

Oben: Die Tischplatte liegt exakt auf Höhe des Wasserbeckens auf der Terrasse. Rechts: Aparicio kerbt den Bau im Obergeschoss ein.

Ci-dessus : la table est au niveau du plan d'eau de la terrasse. A droite : Aparicio a découpé le niveau supérieur du bloc.

Exterior space is framed between white space, grass and sky. Trees grow straight up through the slabs.

Der Außenraum wird von dem weißem Pavillon, Rasen und Himmel gerahmt. Bäume wachsen ungehindert durch die Platten.

A l'extérieur, les volumes sont délimités par des plans blancs, par le ciel et la végétation. Des arbres poussent à travers les dalles de béton.

1997 **Madrid, Spain**

Pavilion for the Giuseppe Terragni exhibition

The exhibition is located between a garden and the Paseo de la Castellana, Madrid. The point of departure for Aparicio was existing "walls" - "the green of the garden, the indigo ceiling of the sky, the trees as vertical elements and the grey facade of the Nuevos Ministerios building". Into these Aparicio inserted a floor and ceiling slab as an outdoor pavilion, and a vertical wall to enclose part of the garden. Trees grow straight through floor and ceiling regardless. Superimposed elements set up veiled views through the pavilion and new relationships between spaces as one moves around it. Pure white, it is a sanctuary of contemplation and silence. On this project Aparicio collaborated with Héctor Fernández Elorza.

Der Pavillon für die Giuseppe Terragni-Ausstellung liegt zwischen einem Garten und dem Paseo de la Castellana in Madrid. Ausgangspunkt waren vorhandene »Wände« – »das Grün des Gartens, die tiefblaue Decke des Himmels, die Bäume als vertikale Elemente und die graue Fassade des Nuevos Ministerios-Gebäudes.« Hier fügte Aparicio eine Bodenplatte und eine Decke ein und schuf so einen Freiluftpavillon. Eine Mauer, die einen Teil des Gartens umschließt, ergänzt das Ensemble. Bäume wachsen ungehindert durch Fußboden und Decke; einander überschneidende Elemente modifizieren den Blick des Besuchers und lassen stets neue Beziehungen zwischen den Räumen entstehen. Aparicio realisierte dieses Projekt zusammen mit Héctor Fernández Elorza.

Le site de l'exposition Giuseppe Terragni étant pris entre un jardin et le Paseo de la Castellana à Madrid, le point de départ du projet était les « murs » existants : le vert du jardin, le plafond indigo du ciel, les arbres constituant des éléments verticaux et la façade grise des nouveaux ministères. Aparicio y a inséré un plancher et une dalle de plafond constituant un pavillon ouvert, ainsi qu'un mur vertical qui délimite une partie du jardin. Les arbres poussent droit à travers le plancher et le plafond, comme si ceux-ci n'existaient pas. Des éléments superposés modifient les vues que l'on découvre à travers le pavillon et établissent de nouvelles relations entre les espaces au fur et à mesure qu'on le contourne. D'un blanc pur, c'est un sanctuaire de silence et de contemplation. Le projet a été réalisé en collaboration avec Héctor Fernández Elorza.

Exterior, left, and interior views, right

Links Außenansicht, rechts die Innenräume

Vues de l'extérieur (à gauche) et de l'intérieur (à droite)

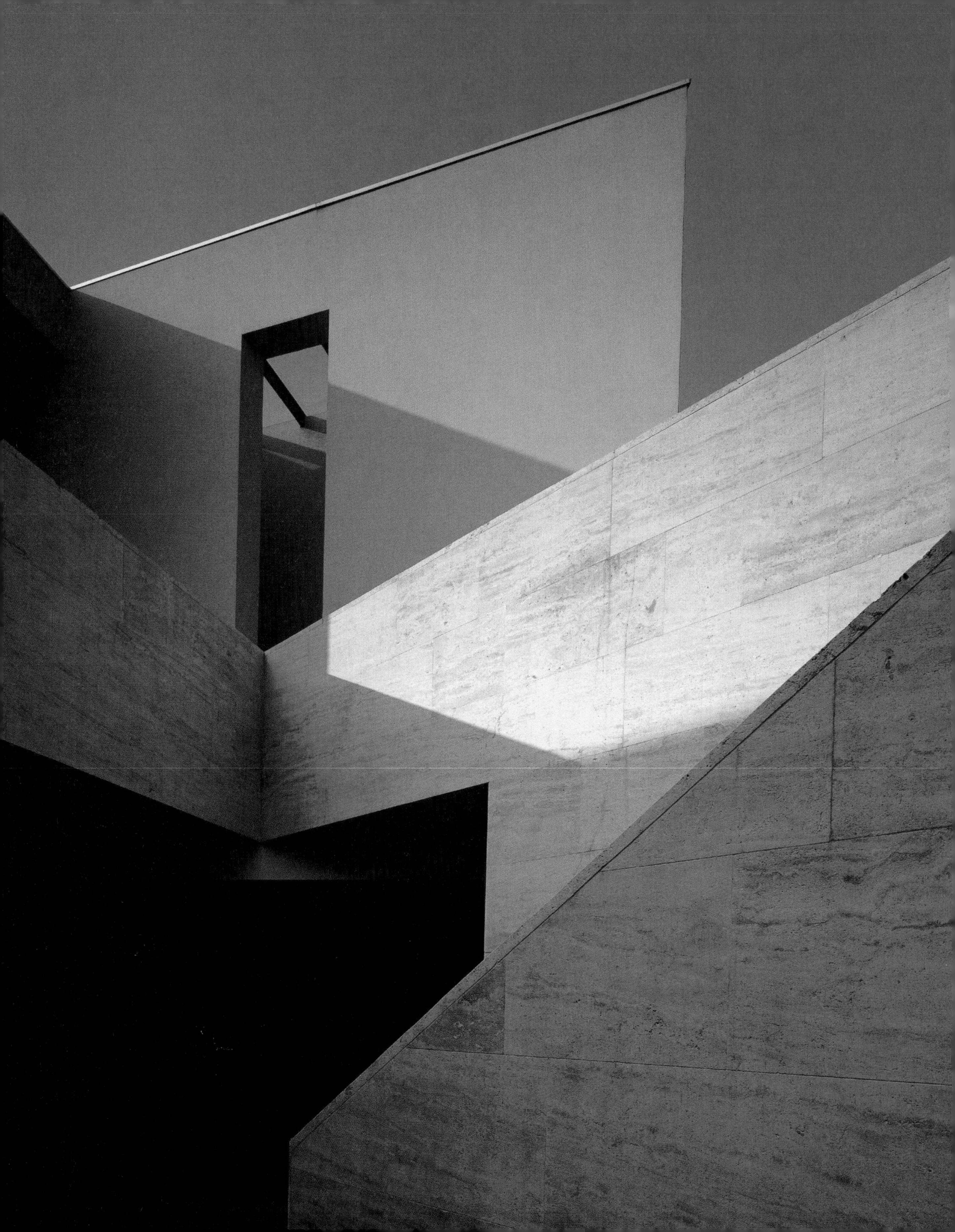

Studio Archea

Via della Fornace 30/R, 50125 Florence, Italy tel +39 055 685 202 fax +39 055 6810 850 e-mail staff@archea.it

Laura Andreini

born	1964	Florence, Italy
studied	1990	Florence University
	1994	PhD Florence University
practice	1988	co-founded Studio Archea

Marco Casamonti

born	1965	Florence, Italy
studied	1990	Florence University
	1992	PhD Florence University
practice	1988	co-founded Studio Archea

Giovanni Polazzi

born	1959	Florence, Italy
studied	1986	Florence University
practice	1988	co-founded Studio Archea

Selected projects

Galleria d'Arte Tornabuoni, Lungarno Cellini	1993	Florence, Italy
Centro Uffici, Via Pier Capponi	1995	Florence, Italy
Stop Line recreation centre	1995	Curno, near Bergamo, Italy
Urban planning for the Mons Natale Basilico district	1996	Merate (Lecco), Italy
Library and auditorium	1996	Bergamo, Italy
Single family house	1997	Leffe, near Bergamo, Italy
Nuovo Opificio d'Avenza	1998	Massa, Italy
Commercial centre	1998	Nembro (Bergamo), Italy
Single family house	1999	Bergamo, Italy

Laura Andreini, Marco Casamonti and Giovanni Polazzi founded studio Archea intending to create "a laboratory of architecture where they can experiment with design". Their work ranges from small-scale architectural projects and interiors to larger public buildings and urban planning.
Research plays an important part in their work, and they see their buildings as an opportunity for experimentation with different materials and geometrical

Laura Andreini, Marco Casamonti und Giovanni Polazzi gründeten Studio Archea in der Absicht, »ein Architekturlabor für experimentelles Entwerfen« zu schaffen. Ihre Aufträge reichen von kleinformatigen Architekturprojekten und Interieurs bis zu größeren öffentlichen Gebäuden und urbanistischen Projekten.
Dabei macht Forschung einen bedeutenden Teil ihrer Arbeit aus, und sie verstehen ihre Bauten als Gelegenheit, mit verschiedenen Materialien und geometrischen Gestal-

Laura Andreini, Marco Casamonti et Giovanni Polazzi ont fondé le Studio Archea dans l'intention d'en faire « un laboratoire d'architecture pour le design expérimental ». Leurs réalisations vont de projets architecturaux à petite échelle et d'aménagement d'intérieurs à des édifices publics plus importants et à des projets d'urbanisme.
La recherche constitue un important secteur de leur activité ; ils considèrent leurs constructions comme des occasions d'expérimenter divers matériaux et composi-

compositions. Materials, particularly metals, are left exposed rather than disguised by paint, and often they are treated in a way that speeds up the weathering process.
All born and educated in Florence, the practice takes on board its Renaissance heritage, manifested in repetitive geometric forms and respect for the golden section.
The three partners are also members of the editorial board of the international architecture magazine "Area", edited by Marco Casamonti.

tungen zu experimentieren. Materialien, insbesondere Metall, werden dabei stets in ihrem ursprünglichen Zustand belassen und nicht etwa mit Farbe überdeckt, oder ihre Verwitterung wird sogar mit Hilfe spezieller Verfahren beschleunigt.
Alle drei Mitglieder von Studio Archea sind in Florenz geboren und ausgebildet, und mit ihrer Arbeit treten sie das Erbe der Renaissance an, was sich etwa in der Wiederholung geometrischer Formen und der Beachtung des goldenen Schnitts niederschlägt.
Die drei Partner gehören darüber hinaus der Redaktion der internationalen Architekturzeitschrift »Area« an, die von Marco Casamonti herausgegeben wird.

tions géométriques. Les matériaux, en particulier les métaux, sont toujours laissés tels quels, sans le déguisement de la peinture, ou font l'objet de traitements spéciaux destinés à accélérer le vieillissement.
Tous ses membres étant nés à Florence et y ayant fait leurs études, le bureau s'appuie sur l'héritage de la Renaissance, comme en témoignent les formes géométriques répétitives et le respect de la section d'or.
Les trois partenaires font également partie du comité de rédaction de la revue d'architecture internationale « Area », éditée par Marco Casamonti.

Careful juxtaposition of planes in a reworking of a 70s villa. Facade, left, and outdoor staircase, below.

Wohl durchdachtes Nebeneinander von Flächen bei der umgestalteten Villa aus den 70er-Jahren. Links die Fassade, unten das äußere Treppenhaus.

Une intéressante juxtaposition de plans pour cette rénovation d'une villa des années 70. A gauche, la façade principale ; ci-dessous, l'escalier extérieur.

1999 **Bergamo, Italy**

Single family house

This residence is an elegant reworking of a 70s villa. The emphasis of the design is on the vertical, with long narrow slits for doors and windows, and angled walls terminating in sharp points, a counterpoint to the low horizontal features of the two-storey house. An Escher-like treatment of the staircase as it moves up the side of the building and across stepping stones, and a careful angling of planes, has set up a series of curious views and routes through the house. Though detailing is painfully precise, and a rich palette of marble and smooth stones predominates, there is little additional ornament to detract from the sculptural qualities of the building itself.

Dieses zweigeschossige Einfamilienhaus in Bergamo ist die elegante Überarbeitung einer Villa aus den 70er-Jahren. Der Entwurf betont die Vertikale mit langen, schmalen Schlitzen für Türen und Fenster und spitz zulaufenden, abgewinkelten Wänden – ein Gegengewicht zu den niedrigen, horizontalen Formen des Hauses. Die an Escher erinnernde Gestaltung der Treppe, die an der Seite des Hauses über Trittsteine nach oben führt, und der durchdachte Einsatz schräger Flächen ließen im Haus eine Reihe ungewöhnlicher Ausblicke und Durchgänge entstehen. Die Details sind äußerst präzise gearbeitet, und obwohl viele verschiedene Arten von Marmor und poliertem Naturstein verwendet werden, beeinträchtigt kaum zusätzliches Dekor die plastische Qualität des Baus.

Cette maison individuelle est un élégant remaniement d'une villa des années 70. Le design met l'accent sur la verticale : portes et fenêtres hautes et étroites, murs obliques formant des pignons aigus qui contrastent avec les lignes horizontales et basses de la maison à deux niveaux. Un escalier traité à la Escher tient un des côtés de la maison ; plusieurs paliers et une pente savamment calculée créent une série de vues inattendues et de couloirs traversant la maison. La qualité sculpturale de l'ensemble ne souffre pas d'ornements superflus, en dépit des finitions très soignées et d'une riche palette de marbres et de pierres polies.

Left, indoor pool looks on to the garden. Below, outdoor stair is continued as stepping stones.

Links: Vom Schwimmbecken im Haus ergeben sich Ausblicke in den Garten; unten: Trittsteine führen die Außentreppe fort.

A gauche, la piscine intérieure avec vue sur le jardin. Ci-dessous, l'escalier extérieur, prolongé par une allée pavée de larges dalles.

Secondary entrance by way of two glazed bridges over moat.

Der Nebeneingang: zwei verglaste Brücken überqueren einen Wassergraben.

L'entrée secondaire, avec ses ponts vitrés enjambant le fossé.

1995 **Curno (near Bergamo), Italy**

Stop Line recreation centre

A dramatic 60 m-long facade of rusty Corten steel acts as a giant billboard on the main road between Como and Lecco. By day it is a fortress, a seemingly impenetrable blank sheet, broken only by a narrow slit for the entrance and reached across a glazed bridge over a narrow moat. At night it becomes a wall of stars as light from behind shines through the perforations in the steel.

The new leisure centre is a reworking of an abandoned concrete warehouse. Arranged over four levels, it includes a performance arena, night-club, ice rink, bowling alley and roof-terrace. The interior displays youthful exuberance with illuminated signs, raw industrial materials, glass stairs, vast conical concrete beams supporting thick girders, and a sea of broken green glass sunk into the floor of the entrance hall.

Die auffällige 60 m lange Fassade des Freizeitzentrums Stop Line aus Cortenstahl fungiert an der Hauptstraße zwischen Como und Lecco als riesige Reklamewand. Bei Tag macht die scheinbar undurchdringliche leere Fläche, die nur von einem engen Schlitz für den Eingang durchbrochen wird, den Bau zu einer Festung, zu der eine verglaste Brücke über einen schmalen Wassergraben führt. Bei Nacht, wenn von der Rückseite Licht durch die Öffnungen im Stahl dringt, wird die Fläche zur sternenübersäten Wand.

Der Bau entstand als Umnutzung eines aufgelassenen Lagerhauses aus Beton. Auf vier Ebenen enthält er eine Theaterbühne, einen Nachtclub, eine Eisbahn, eine Bowlingbahn und eine Dachterrasse. Die Innenräume vermitteln mit ihren Leuchtzeichen, den unbehandelten Industriematerialien, der gläsernen Treppe, den riesigen konischen Betonbalken, die dicke Träger stützen, und einem in den Boden der Eingangshalle versenkten Meer aus grünen Glasscherben einen jugendlich ungestümen Eindruck.

La spectaculaire façade en acier Corten oxydé, longue de 60 m, fait l'effet d'un gigantesque panneau d'affichage sur la route reliant Côme à Lecco. De jour, le centre de loisir est une forteresse, un pan apparemment impénétrable percé uniquement par l'étroite ouverture servant d'entrée, que dessert un pont vitré jeté sur un fossé. De nuit, la façade devient un mur d'étoiles, la lumière passant par les multiples perforations de l'acier.

Le nouveau centre de loisirs est né du remaniement d'un entrepôt en béton désaffecté. Disposé sur quatre niveaux, il comprend un espace scénique, un night-club, une patinoire, un bowling et un toit-terrasse. L'intérieur, d'une exubérance toute juvénile, présente des panneaux lumineux, des matériaux industriels bruts, des escaliers en verre, d'énormes piliers coniques en béton surmontés de lourdes solives, et une étendue de verre brisé formant une mer verte dans le sol du hall d'entrée.

Main entrance, right, leading straight into foyer, below. Floor panels contain crushed green glass.

Rechts: Der Haupteingang führt geradewegs ins Foyer (unten). In den Bodenplatten zerstoßenes Glas.

A droite, l'entrée principale, donnant sur le foyer (ci-dessous). Le sol du foyer avec ses panneaux emplis de verre brisé.

Blank street facade, left, and concertinaed facade set back from neighbours, far left

Links die geschlossene Straßenfront; ganz links die von den Nachbargebäuden zurückgesetzte gefaltete Fassade

A gauche, la façade aveugle donnant sur la rue. Page de gauche : la façade en accordéon isole la maison du voisinage.

1997 **Leffe (near Bergamo), Italy**

Single family house

Keeping the facade back from neighbouring buildings has resulted in a concertinaed wall, squashed from either side. Overlooked by its neighbours, the front is completely closed except for a sequence of narrow slits in the masonry letting light pass through. The irregular floor plan stretched over five floors creates a series of exciting spaces inside, deep vertical voids, a double-height living space and an enclosed stair tower.
On the other side of the building, a narrow strip squeezed between two buildings of different heights, the street line is given coherence by the introduction of a simple rectilinear glazed facade. A system of shutters made of stainless steel and oxidised copper-plate covers the entire rear facade as a single unifying plane.

Der Wunsch, das Einfamilienhaus hinter die benachbarten Gebäude zurücktreten zu lassen, führte zu einer gedrängten, gefalteten Fassade. Die hofseitige Front ist bis auf Reihen schmaler Schlitze im Mauerwerk, durch die Licht eindringen kann, vollständig geschlossen. Durch den unregelmäßigen Grundriss entsteht im Innern auf fünf Ebenen eine Folge ungewöhnlicher Räume. So gibt es tiefe, vertikale Hohlräume, einen zwei Geschosshöhen umfassenden Wohnbereich und einen geschlossenen Treppenturm.
Die andere Seite des Hauses, ein zwischen zwei Nachbarbauten unterschiedlicher Höhe eingezwängter schmaler Streifen, gibt der Straße mit ihrer schlicht-geradlinigen, verglasten Fassade logischen Zusammenhang. Ein System von Jalousien aus Edelstahl und oxidiertem Kupfer bedeckt die gesamte Rückfront und schafft so eine einheitliche Fläche.

Afin d'isoler la maison individuelle des constructions avoisinantes qui la dominent, le mur de façade est en accordéon, complètement fermé à l'exception d'une série de fentes étroites laissant entrer la lumière. Le plan au sol irrégulier se répète sur les cinq niveaux, créant une succession d'espaces intérieurs surprenants, de profonds puits verticaux, un espace de vie à double hauteur et une tour-escalier fermée.
De l'autre côté de l'étroite maison enserrée entre deux bâtiments de hauteurs différentes, le niveau de la rue est indiqué par une simple façade vitrée rectiligne. Un système de volets en acier inoxydable et tôle de cuivre oxydée recouvre entièrement l'arrière, en faisant un seul plan qui unifie cette façade.

Architectus

Architectus Bowes Clifford + Thomson
1 Centre Street, PO Box 90621, Auckland, New Zealand
tel +64 9 307 5970 fax +64 9 307 5972 e-mail e-mail@architectus.co.nz web www.architectus.co.nz

Malcolm Bowes

born	1956 Wanganui, New Zealand
studied	1981 University of Auckland, Auckland, New Zealand
previous practice	Cook Hitchcock and Sargisson Architects, Auckland; John Spence and Partners, London; Archiplan, London

Patrick Clifford

born	1956 Wellington, New Zealand
studied	1981 University of Auckland, Auckland, New Zealand
previous practice	New Zealand Government Architects, Wellington; John Spence and Partners, London; Archiplan, London; Michael Sorkin Studio, New York

Michael Thomson

born	1955 Wellington, New Zealand
studied	1983 University of Auckland, Auckland, New Zealand
previous practice	Cook Hitchcock and Sargisson, Auckland; Terry Farrell Partnership, London

Selected projects

Grace House	1990	Auckland, New Zealand
Jones House	1993	Titirangi, New Zealand
FHE Gallery	1994	Auckland, New Zealand
Te Horo House	1995	Wellington, New Zealand
Medland Beach House	1997	Great Barrier Island, New Zealand
Mathematics & Statistics and Computer Sciences building	1997	University of Canterbury, Christchurch, New Zealand
Clifford/Forsyth House	1999	Auckland, New Zealand
Teacher Support Services building	2000	Auckland College of Education, Auckland, New Zealand

The three partners met when studying at the University of Auckland. After having expanded their experience by travelling and working for architects in London, they designed a series of beautifully constructed award-winning houses in New Zealand, pursuing an interest in materials.
Their breakthrough came when they won all three parts of the 1994 competition for the University of Canterbury: Masterplan, Mathematics & Statistics and Computer Sciences Building and Science Library,

Die drei Partner von Architectus lernten sich beim Studium an der University of Auckland kennen. Nach Reisen und Tätigkeiten für Architekten in London entwarfen sie eine Reihe schön gestalteter, preisgekrönter Häuser in Neuseeland, bei denen sie ihr Interesse an Materialien vertieften.
Der Durchbruch gelang ihnen 1994 mit dem Sieg ihres Wettbewerbsbeitrags für die University of Canterbury, Neuseeland in allen drei Bereichen: Masterplan, Gebäude für Mathematik & Statistik und Computerwissenschaften

Les trois associés se sont rencontrés pendant leurs études à l'université d'Auckland. Après avoir acquis de l'expérience en parcourant le monde et en travaillant pour des architectes londoniens, ils ont dessiné en Nouvelle-Zélande une série de superbes édifices souvent primés, qui témoignent de leur intérêt constant pour les matériaux.
La grande percée eut lieu en 1994, lorsqu'ils remportèrent les trois parties du concours pour la construction de l'université de Canterbury : Plan d'ensemble, Mathema-

after a near miss in the earlier competition for the Te Papa Tongarewa Museum, Wellington, New Zealand's best-known contemporary landmark. The University of Canterbury project gave them the chance to experiment with form and structure on a large scale, combining a straightforward functional floor plan with a bold, expressive facade that revels in its honeycomb of bare concrete.
"We are passionately concerned about how things are made and the way that making expresses the spirit and intent of the architecture."

und naturwissenschaftliche Bibliothek. Zuvor hatten sie einen Erfolg beim Wettbewerb für Neuseelands inzwischen bekanntestes zeitgenössisches Bauwerk, das Te Papa Tongarewa Museum in Wellington, nur knapp verfehlt. Die Bauten für die University of Canterbury gaben Architectus Gelegenheit, mit Form und Konstruktion in großem Maßstab zu experimentieren und dabei einen streng funktionalen Grundriss mit einer kühnen, expressiven Fassade zu kombinieren, die in der Wabenstruktur ihres Sichtbetons schwelgt.
»Es ist für uns von großer Bedeutung, wie Dinge gemacht sind und wie dieses Machen Geist und Intention der Architektur zum Ausdruck bringt.«

tics & Statistics and Computer Sciences Building, et Bibliothèque scientifique, après avoir failli remporter le concours pour le musée de Te Papa Tongarewa à Wellington, la réalisation contemporaine la plus célèbre de Nouvelle-Zélande. Le projet de l'université de Canterbury leur permit de réaliser une expérience formelle et structurelle à grande échelle, alliant un plan simple et fonctionnel à une façade hardie et expressive constituée d'un nid d'abeille de béton brut.
« Notre passion, c'est la manière dont les choses sont réalisées, et la façon dont cette mise en œuvre exprime l'esprit et l'intention de l'architecture. »

Aerial view showing the three teaching towers, far left, and, left, their facades in detail

Ganz links: Luftaufnahme mit den drei Unterrichtstürmen, links ein Fassadendetail

Vue aérienne des trois tours (page de gauche) et détails des façades (à gauche)

1997 **University of Canterbury, Christchurch, New Zealand**

Mathematics & Statistics and Computer Sciences building

Slotted into the 1960s campus of predominantly dour rectilinear buildings, the new building relates to the more brutalist end of this spectrum with an unabashed enjoyment of bare concrete. The floor plan separates working and teaching space with a seven-storey glazed atrium comprising services and circulation. To the south, communal computer labs are contained in a standard four-storey glazed box overlooking the river, a solid anchor for the building, while three towers containing quieter, more intimate, tutorial rooms project from the north-east side of the atrium. Arranged in groups, offices are clustered around double-height core spaces which the tutors requested for informal meetings. Adding a dramatically sculptural element to the building, these towers are characterised by huge concrete blade walls, which appear to be twisted away from the perpendicular facing the sun in the north. Sheer walls appear unsupported, giving depth to the construction, and the pattern of light and shade created by recesses and repetitive warm timber shutters sets up a rhythm that plays across the facades, changing throughout the day.
The new Sciences Library, won at the same time as the Mathematics & Statistics and Computer Sciences Building, has yet to be built.

Eingefügt in einen Campus im Stil der 60er-Jahre mit streng rechtwinkligen Gebäuden, erinnert der kühne Neubau für Mathematik & Statistik und Computerwissenschaften mit seiner unbekümmerten Freude am Sichtbeton an die Architektur des Brutalismus. Der Grundriss trennt Arbeits- und Unterrichtsräume und sieht ein siebengeschossiges, verglastes Atrium für Serviceeinrichtungen und Erschließung vor. Auf der Südseite sind Computerarbeitsräume für Gruppen mit Blick auf den Fluss in einem vierstöckigen Standard-Glaskasten untergebracht, der dem Bauwerk optisch Halt gibt; drei Türme mit ruhigeren, intimeren Unterrichtsräumen schließen sich an die Nordostseite des Atriums an. Büros in Zehnergruppen umgeben zentrale Räume von doppelter Höhe, die auf Wunsch der Tutoren für informelle Treffen zur Verfügung stehen. Die riesigen Flügelwände dieser Türme, die aus dem Lot gekippt scheinen, um sich der im Norden stehenden Sonne zuzuwenden, lassen das Gebäude dramatisch plastisch wirken. Scheinbar frei stehende, durchscheinende glatte Wände geben dem Bau Tiefe, und das von Rücksprüngen geschaffene Muster aus Licht und Schatten erzeugt zusammen mit dem warmen Holzton der sich wiederholenden Jalousien den im Laufe des Tages ständig wechselnden Rhythmus der Fassade.
Die neue Science Library, deren Wettbewerb Architectus ebenfalls für sich entscheiden konnte, ist noch nicht gebaut.

Insérée dans un campus composé en majeure partie d'austères bâtiments rectilignes des années 1960, la nouvelle structure architecturale évoque une architecture brutaliste puisque l'on y a employé le béton brut avec un plaisir non dissimulé. Les espaces de travail et d'enseignement sont séparés par un atrium vitré de sept étages abritant les aires de services et assurant la circulation. Au sud, les laboratoires d'informatique sont contenus dans une boîte vitrée standard à quatre étages dominant le fleuve, qui ancre solidement le bâtiment, tandis que trois tours abritant des salles d'enseignement plus intimes s'avancent du côté nord-est de l'atrium. Disposés par groupes, les bureaux sont répartis autour d'espaces centraux à double hauteur que les enseignants avaient demandés pour y tenir des réunions en petit comité. Ajoutant un élément sculptural spectaculaire à l'ensemble, ces tours sont caractérisées par d'énormes lames de béton qui semblent arrachées à la perpendiculaire, face au soleil, donc orientées au nord. Des murs verticaux sans support apparent donnent de la profondeur à la construction, et le jeu d'ombres et de lumière créé par des renfoncements et par le motif répétitif de chaleureux volets en bois imprime aux façades un rythme changeant selon l'heure du jour. La nouvelle Bibliothèque scientifique n'est pas encore construite.

Computer labs are housed in a glazed block on the southern side of the building, below left, while the balconies of the teaching rooms enjoy the sun of the northern facade, above left. Right, the internal circulation core between the two blocks.

Links unten: Die in einem verglasten Bau untergebrachten Computerräume befinden sich auf der Südseite des Gebäudes, während die Balkone der Unterrichtsräume an der sonnigen Nordfassade liegen (links oben). Rechts: Das Treppenhaus zwischen den beiden Bauteilen.

Les laboratoires d'informatique occupent un bloc vitré du côté sud du bâtiment (en bas à gauche). Sur la façade nord, les balcons des salles de cours sont généreusement ensoleillés (en haut à gauche). A droite, l'espace assurant la circulation entre les deux blocs.

The three-storey house sits among the treetops.

Das dreigeschossige Haus liegt inmitten der Baumwipfel.

Les trois niveaux de la maison sont insérés dans la végétation.

1999 **Auckland, New Zealand**

Clifford/Forsyth House

Though essentially urban in context, Patrick Clifford's own family house is built on a steep wooded site in a narrow river valley. The architects have inserted a strong geometric form to bring order into the chaos, deliberately using symmetry and a series of bays based on a 1.2-m grid. The house rises through three storeys: entrance and main living room are located on the middle level with the guest rooms below and the family bedrooms above. Full-height wings of concrete blocks, set at a 45° angle to the floor plan, are dramatic insertions into the otherwise very natural timber and glass box. Structurally, they serve to support the outer corners of the V-shaped roof and to create sheltered balconies off either end of the living room. Glazed walls, external folding doors and cantilevering balconies link the interior of the house to its surroundings. Through the height of the building and the sloping terrain on the first floor one is among the treetops. Inside materials are kept natural and the colour scheme neutral. Exposed timbers bring warmth into the open-plan spaces. Translucent glass panels offer privacy to the bedrooms and cut down on solar gain. White-lacquered storage and service units form the few partitions between rooms, a suitably simple solution.

Das Haus für Patrick Cliffords Familie entstand – obwohl dem Kontext nach eigentlich urban – auf einem steilen, bewaldeten Hang in einem engen Flusstal. Um Ordnung in die chaotische Bausituation zu bringen, verwendeten die Architekten für den Grundriss eine prägnante, geometrische Form, die die Raumeinheiten auf einem 1,2-m Raster bewusst symmetrisch gruppiert. Eingang und Hauptwohnraum liegen auf der mittleren Ebene, die Gästezimmer darunter und die Schlafzimmer der Familie im Obergeschoss. Flügelwände aus Betonblöcken erstrecken sich über die gesamte Höhe und stehen im Winkel von 45° zum Grundriss – spannende Akzente in dem im übrigen sehr naturnah gestalteten Kasten aus Holz und Glas. Konstruktiv stützen sie die äußeren Ecken des V-förmigen Dachs und schaffen geschützte Balkone zu beiden Seiten des Wohnraums. Glaswände, außenliegende Falttüren und vorkragende Balkone verbinden das Haus mit seiner Umgebung. Dank seiner Höhe und des abfallenden Terrains befindet man sich im ersten Stock auf Höhe der Baumkronen. Im Innern hat man sich auf natürliche Materialien und ein neutrales Farbschema beschränkt. Unbehandelte Hölzer setzen in den offenen Räumen warme Akzente. Transluzente Verglasungen gewährleisten die Intimität der Schlafräume und begrenzen die Sonneneinstrahlung. Wenige weiß lackierte Stau- und Funktionselemente dienen als Raumteiler – eine adäquat schlichte Lösung.

Bien que son contexte soit essentiellement urbain, la propre maison de Patrick Clifford est construite sur un site boisé en forte pente, dans une étroite vallée où coule une rivière. Les architectes ont inséré une puissante forme géométrique qui ordonne le chaos grâce à une symétrie rigoureuse et à une série de baies de 1,2 m de long. La maison comporte trois niveaux; l'entrée et le séjour principal sont à l'étage intermédiaire, les chambres d'amis en bas, et les chambres des membres de la famille en haut. De massives ailes en béton prenant toute la hauteur forment un angle à 45° avec le bâtiment principal, ajout dramatique à la boîte en bois et verre, par ailleurs très simple. Structurellement, elles servent à soutenir les angles de la toiture en V, tout en créant des balcons abrités aux deux extrémités du séjour. Des murs vitrés, des portes extérieures pliantes et des balcons en saillie relient la maison à son environnement. Du fait de sa hauteur et de la pente du terrain, les étages supérieurs sont de niveau avec le sommet des arbres. A l'intérieur, les matériaux sont naturels et les couleurs, neutres. Des poutres apparentes donnent un aspect chaleureux aux espaces ouverts. Des panneaux de verre translucide assurent l'intimité des chambres et réduisent l'intensité de la lumière. Des espaces de rangement et de services laqués de blanc forment les rares cloisons entre les pièces, solution simple et rationnelle.

Living room, left, which opens on to outdoor balconies. Bedrooms are hidden behind transluscent glass, right.

Links: Wohnraum mit Durchgang zu den vorkragenden Balkonen. Die Schlafräume sind durch opakes Glas abgeschirmt (rechts).

Le séjour s'ouvre sur de vastes balcons (à gauche). Les chambres sont isolées par des pans de verre dépoli (à droite).

Artto Palo Rossi Tikka

Arkkitehtityöhuone Artto Palo Rossi Tikka Oy,
Lastenkodinkuja 1, 00180 Helsinki, Finland

tel +358 9 2709 1470 fax +358 9 2709 1476 e-mail akprt@nettilinja.fi

Aaro Artto

born	1964 Helsinki, Finland
studied	1993 Helsinki University of Technology
previous practice	"Arkkitehti", The Finnish architectural magazine; Heureka, The Finnish Science Centre; The Museum of Finnish Architecture
	1994 co-founded Artto Palo Rossi Tikka

Teemu Palo

born	1962 Helsinki, Finland
studied	1993 Helsinki University of Technology
previous practice	worked with different architects in Helsinki (Pekka Salminen, Reijo Lahtinen, Harris-Kjisik, Aarne von Boehm, Nurmela-Raimoranta-Tasa, Raili and Reima Pietilä, Kosti Kuronen)
	1994 co-founded Artto Palo Rossi Tikka

Yrjö Rossi

born	1961 Eno, Finland
studied	1993 Helsinki University of Technology
previous practice	worked with different architects in Helsinki (Pekka Salminen, Mauri Tommila, Huhtiniemi-Söderholm, Laiho-Pulkkinen-Raunio) and in Turku with Benito Casagrande
	1994 co-founded Artto Palo Rossi Tikka

Hannu Tikka

born	1960 Helsinki, Finland
studied	1993 Helsinki University of Technology
previous practice	Pekka Salminen Architects, Helsinki; Studio Daniel Libeskind, Berlin; Harris-Kjisik Architects, Helsinki; Aarne von Boehm Architects, Helsinki; Nurmela-Raimoranta-Tasa Architects, Helsinki
	1994 co-founded Artto Palo Rossi Tikka

Selected projects

Raisio Library Auditorium	1999 Raisio, Finland
Trivium	1999 Turku, Finland
Lappeenranta University of Technology, 5th phase	2000 Lappeenranta, Finland
Töölönlahti Parks	2000 Helsinki, Finland
Helsinki-Gardenia environmental information centre	2000 Viikki, Helsinki, Finland
Sibelius Congress and Concert Hall	2000 Lahti, Finland
Joutsa Cultural Centre	2002 Joutsa, Finland

As for many young architects, much of Artto Palo Rossi Tikka's work has originated from competitions that have allowed them to flex their architectural muscle on prominent public buildings including concert halls, auditoriums, and cultural centres.
Urban planning is an important aspect in their work. Artto Palo Rossi Tikka and their Danish partner KHRAS are currently engaged in a continuous urban development master plan for the Ørestad area of Copenhagen, former state-owned green fields that the government hopes to develop into a new urban centre. Artto Palo Rossi Tikka are conceiving their projects from a grand scale, allotting areas of land for specific uses, down to detailed design of the pavements. This approach to urban planning is also evident in their buildings, which they treat as miniature cities. In their design for the library and auditorium complex at Raisio, for example, different uses were given separate buildings, all linked by a communal glazed foyer. In the Gardenia environmental information centre in Helsinki, plants are zoned in spaces displaying varying degrees of openness.

Wie bei vielen ihrer jungen Kollegen gingen zahlreiche Arbeiten von Artto Palo Rossi Tikka aus Wettbewerbsbeiträgen hervor, in denen sie ihr Können an markanten öffentlichen Bauten wie Konzerthallen, Auditorien und Kulturzentren erproben konnten.
Stadtplanung macht einen wichtigen Teil ihrer Arbeit aus. Artto Palo Rossi Tikka und ihr dänischer Partner KHRAS sind derzeit an einem Entwicklungsplan für den Kopenhagener Stadtteil Ørestad beteiligt, wo die Regierung auf ehemals staatlichen Grünflächen ein neues urbanes Zentrum entstehen lassen will. Die Architekten konzipieren ihre Projekte vom großen Maßstab bis ins Detail, d. h. von der Zuordnung bestimmter Nutzungen für einzelne Flächen bis hin zum Entwurf des Straßenbelags. Diese urbanistische Herangehensweise charakterisiert auch ihre Bauten, die sie wie Miniaturstädte behandeln. So werden in ihrem Entwurf für den Bibliotheks- und Auditoriumskomplex in Raisio unterschiedliche Nutzungen separaten Gebäuden zugewiesen, die ein gläsernes Foyer miteinander verbindet. Das Umwelt-Informationszentrum Gardenia in Helsinki ordnet Pflanzen in unterschiedlich offenen Räumen an.

Comme nombre de jeunes architectes, Artto Palo Rossi Tikka ont pu réaliser une grande partie de leur œuvre grâce à des concours, ce qui leur a permis d'exercer leurs talents architecturaux sur d'importants édifices publics tels que salles de concert, auditoriums et centres culturels.
La planification urbaine est un aspect important de leur activité. Artto Palo Rossi Tikka et leur partenaire danois KHRAS sont actuellement responsables du développement du quartier d'Ørestad à Copenhague : des terres agricoles appartenant à l'Etat, dont le gouvernement espère faire un nouveau centre urbain. Ils suivent ce projet de développement depuis l'affectation des parcelles à des usages spécifiques jusqu'au design détaillé du pavement. Leur optique urbanistique est également manifeste dans leurs édifices, qu'ils traitent comme des villes miniatures. Dans leur projet pour le complexe bibliothèque-auditorium de Raisio, par exemple, les divers bâtiments consacrés à des fonctions spécifiques sont reliés par un foyer vitré commun. Au centre d'information environnemental Gardenia de Helsinki, les plantes sont répartis dans des zones autorisant divers degrés d'ouverture et de contact.

Sibelius Congress and Concert Hall

Built on the site of a former factory, the complex seeks to restore the different layers of the old building and the poetic atmosphere of its halls. Executed predominantly in various types of Finnish wood, it celebrates the country's traditional craftsmanship, which is well known for its high-quality finishes.
A vast hall, with a glazed facade and tall wooden pillars, contains the new conference centre, concert hall and the old carpentry factory like massive wooden structures inside a metaphorical pine forest. The concert hall is built like a boat, a laminated wooden skin supported on wooden girders. The conference wing is also built of wood, its much heavier forms echoing the machinery in the harbour that the building overlooks. The building was designed in cooperation with Kimmo Lintula.

Der Komplex auf dem Gelände einer ehemaligen Fabrik oberhalb des Hafens versucht, die verschiedenen Schichten des alten Bauwerks und die poetische Atmosphäre seiner Hallen zu bewahren. Überwiegend aus verschiedenen finnischen Hölzern errichtet, stellt das Gebäude gleichsam eine Reverenz an die traditionelle Handwerkskunst des Landes dar, die für ihre hohe Qualität bekannt ist.
Die riesige Halle mit verglaster Fassade und hohen hölzernen Stützen bietet dem neuen Konferenzzentrum, der Sibelius-Konzerthalle und einer alten Zimmerei Platz, die sich wie massive Holzbauten in einem metaphorischen Kiefernwald ausnehmen. In Anspielung auf den nahegelegenen Hafen ist die Konzerthalle gebaut wie ein Schiffsrumpf, dessen Außenhaut aus Schichtholz von hölzernen Trägern gestützt wird. Der Konferenzflügel, der mit seinen schwereren Formen die Sprache der Maschinen im Hafen aufnimmt, ist ebenfalls aus Holz errichtet. Der Bau entstand in Zusammenarbeit mit Kimmo Lintula.

Construit sur le site d'une usine désaffectée, ce complexe s'efforce de respecter les différents niveaux de l'ancien bâtiment ainsi que l'ambiance poétique de ses salles. Exécuté en majeure partie en diverses essences de bois finlandaises, il célèbre l'artisanat traditionnel du pays, connu pour la finesse de sa facture.
Un vaste hall pourvu d'une façade vitrée et de hauts piliers en bois abrite le nouveau centre de conférences, la salle de concerts et l'ancien atelier de charpenterie, massives structures en bois évoquant une forêt de sapins. Faisant allusion au port situé non loin, la salle de concert est construite comme un bâteau dont la coque de bois laminé soutenue par une ossature en bois. L'aile des salles de conférences est également construite en bois ; ses formes plus robustes font écho aux machines du port, que l'édifice surplombe. Le bâtiment a été conçu en association avec Kimmo Lintula.

The wooden structure is enveloped in glass, left. Right, the reverberation chamber between the auditorium and its outer skin, which amplifies music.

Links der glasumhüllte Holzbau. Rechts: Zwischen dem Auditorium und der Glasfassade verstärkt ein Resonanzraum den Klang.

A gauche, la structure en bois et son enveloppe de verre. A droite : la chambre à échos placée entre l'auditorium et la peau de l'édifice amplifie le son.

Foyer connecting auditorium with administration block. Wooden columns and beams represent a forest.

Das Foyer verbindet Auditorium und Verwaltungsbau. Hölzerne Stützen und Balken bilden einen Wald.

Le foyer relie l'auditorium au bloc administratif. Les colonnes et poutres en bois évoquent une forêt.

Inside the 1250-seat auditorium, left. Right, the glazed facade reveals the view of the different wooden elements.

Links: Innenansicht des Auditoriums mit 1250 Plätzen; rechts: Die gläserne Fassade gibt den Blick auf die verschiedenen hölzernen Elemente frei.

A gauche, vue partielle de l'auditorium de 1250 places et de la scène. A droite, la façade de verre permet la vue sur les diverses structures en bois.

1999 **Raisio, Finland**

Raisio Library Auditorium

In response to the original competition brief entitled "Vesipiha" or "Water Garden", Artto Palo Rossi Tikka conceived a multi-faceted building broken down into a series of pavilions, sheltering a landscaped garden between its wings.
The architects describe the complex as "a collage of masses: a small village where the different functions each have their own house." These essentially separate buildings are linked by a spacious central spine or street used as a covered foyer and exhibition space. The largest mass is the library, a blue box running along the northern edge of the site. Its most striking aspect is its northern facade, a completely glazed slanting wall through which protrude larch-boarded reading cubicles at ground level. The red-rendered auditorium provides a vibrant contrast, its curved wall adding drama to the northern entrance, and the corner window looking out like a giant eye.
The southern side of the building dispenses with bright colour, using more natural monochromes to give a softer edge to the garden. The newspaper room is a light board-clad pavilion that hovers between the lobby and the garden, stuck in the glass wall, and the wedge-shaped music department is clad in corrugated black Minerit sheet.

Der Titel der ursprünglichen Ausschreibung für diesen Komplex aus Bibliothek und Auditorium lautete »Vesipiha« oder »Wassergarten«. Artto Palo Rossi Tikka konzipierten ein differenziertes Gebäude aus einer Reihe von Pavillons, das eine Grünanlage zwischen seinen Flügeln birgt.
Die Architekten beschreiben den Komplex als »eine Collage aus Baukörpern: ein kleines Dorf, in dem die verschiedenen Funktionen alle ihr eigenes Haus haben.« Die im Grunde separaten Gebäude sind durch eine breite zentrale Achse oder Straße miteinander verbunden, die als überdachtes Foyer oder Ausstellungsraum genutzt wird.
Der größte Baukörper, die Bibliothek, zieht sich als blauer Kasten am Nordrand des Geländes entlang. Ihr auffallendstes Merkmal ist die vollständig verglaste schräge Wand der Nordseite, aus der mit Lärchenholz verkleidete Lesekabinen auf Erdgeschosshöhe herausragen. Das in Rot gehaltene Auditorium bildet dazu einen lebhaften Kontrast; seine geschwungene Wand und das einem riesigen Auge gleichende Eckfenster geben dem nördlichen Eingang eine gewisse Dramatik.
Die Südseite verzichtet auf starke Farben zugunsten natürlicher wirkender Töne, um einen sanfteren Übergang zum Garten zu schaffen. Der Zeitschriftenraum, ein leichter, holzverkleideter Pavillon, steckt in der Glaswand und schwebt zwischen Foyer und Garten; die keilförmige Musikabteilung ist mit geriffelten schwarzen Mineritplatten verkleidet.

Le thème original du concours pour la bibliothèque-auditorium de Raisio était « Vesipiha », ou « jardin d'eau ». Artto Palo Rossi Tikka ont conçu un bâtiment à multiples facettes constitué d'une série de pavillons, qui abritent entre leurs ailes un jardin paysagé.
Les architectes décrivent le complexe comme « un collage de masses : un petit village au sein duquel les différentes fonctions ont chacune leur maison ». Ces bâtiments séparés sont reliés par une large épine dorsale, sorte d'allée couverte servant de foyer et d'espace d'expositions.
La masse la plus importante est la bibliothèque, boîte bleue s'étendant à la limite nord du site. Sa caractéristique la plus remarquable est la façade nord, mur oblique complètement vitré dont émergent au niveau du sol des box de lecture lambrissés de mélèze. L'auditorium de couleur rouge fournit un contrepoint vibrant ; ses murs incurvés donnent un caractère dramatique à l'entrée nord, dont la fenêtre d'angle est pareille à un œil géant.
Le côté sud de l'édifice n'est pas traité en couleurs vives ; ses monochromes plus naturels et plus doux mettent mieux en valeur le jardin. La salle des périodiques est un pavillon revêtu de boiseries claires ; suspendu entre le hall d'entrée et le jardin, il est comme fiché dans le mur vitré. Le département de musique en forme de coin est revêtu de plaques de Minerit ondulé noir.

The complex is broken down into distinct volumes: above, the library (blue), the auditorium (red); left the newspaper room (right of picture), which penetrates the glazed foyer.

Der Komplex ist in unterschiedliche Baukörper gegliedert: oben die Bibliothek (blau) und das Auditorium (rot); links der Zeitschriftensaal (rechts im Bild), der das verglaste Foyer durchstößt.

Le complexe est composé de plusieurs volumes spécifiques. Ci-dessus, la bibliothèque (bleue), l'auditorium (rouge) ; à gauche (à droite de la photo), la salle des périodiques, insérée dans le foyer vitré.

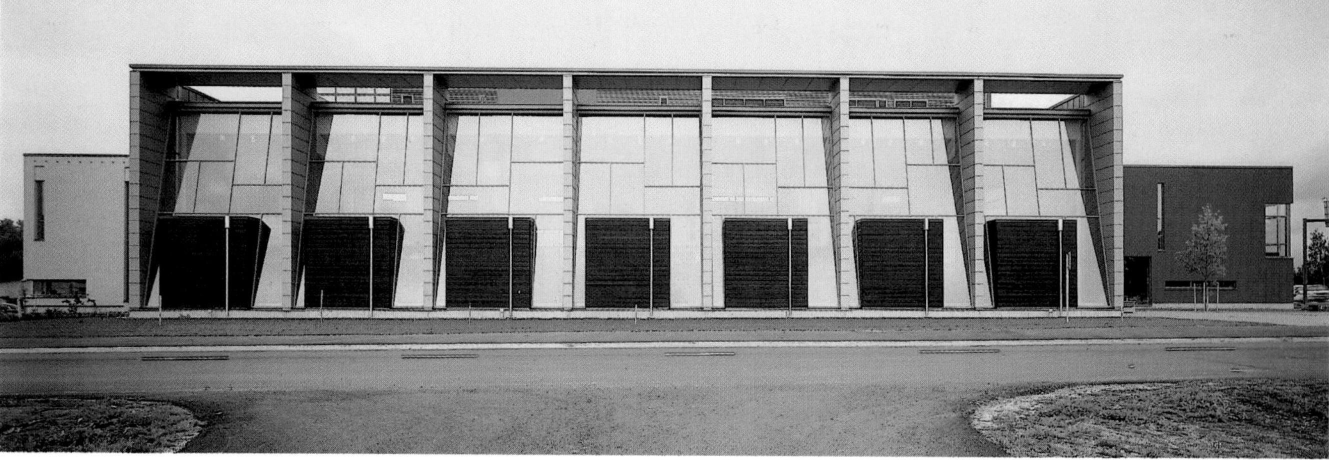

Above, the southern facade looks out on to a garden framed by the black wall of the music department. Left, the sloping glazed facade of the library.

Oben: Vor der Südfassade liegt ein Garten, der von der schwarzen Wand der Musikabteilung gerahmt wird. Links die geneigte Glasfassade der Bibliothek.

En haut : la façade sud donne sur un jardin délimité par le mur noir du département de musique. A gauche, les vitrages obliques de la bibliothèque.

Asymptote

561 Broadway 5a, New York, NY 10012, USA   tel +1 212 343 7333   fax +1 212 343 7099   e-mail info@asymptote.net   www.asymptote.net

Lise Anne Couture

born	1959	Montreal, Canada
studied	1996	Yale University
previous practice	1989	co-founded Asymptote

Hani Rashid

born	1958	Cairo, Egypt
studied	1985	Cranbrook Academy of Art, Bloomfield, Michigan, USA
previous practice	1989	co-founded Asymptote

Selected projects

Steel Cloud	1989	Gateway to Los Angeles, USA (still seeking funding)
Multimedia research facility	1996	Kyoto, Japan
Univers Multimedia Theatre	1997	Århus, Denmark
Kyoto Edutainment Centre	1998	Kyoto, Japan
Trading Floor and Virtual Trading Floor	1998	New York Stock Exchange, NY, USA
Dodger Stadium	1999	Los Angeles, USA (conceptual project)
Technology Culture Museum	2005	New York, USA

If the digital revolution is the single thing that has had the most profound effect on architecture in the late 20th and early 21st centuries, few have speculated as fully on its potential as multidisciplinary practice Asymptote. In an attempt to challenge the conventional boundaries of architecture and embrace new technology, they expand their work beyond the design of buildings to include installation art and digital environments. This has included a virtual trading floor for the New York Stock Exchange and a virtual museum for the Guggenheim. Always seeking to experiment with concepts of space and our experience of it, the partners also have a high academic profile that gives them the opportunity to explore more theoretical projects. Couture is a professor in the Department of Architecture at Parsons School of Design, New York, while Rashid leads an advanced digital design research programme at Columbia University, New York.

Wenn es stimmt, daß die digitale Revolution der stärkste Faktor in der Architektur des ausgehenden 20. und frühen 21. Jahrhunderts ist, haben sich nur wenige so konsequent ihres Potentials bedient wie Asymptote.
In dem Bemühen, die gewohnten Grenzen von Architektur in Frage zu stellen und sich neue Technologien anzueignen, erweitern sie ihre Tätigkeit über den Entwurf hinaus auf Installationen und digitale Environments. Dazu gehören das virtuelle Handelsparkett der New Yorker Börse und ein virtuelles Gebäude für das New Yorker Guggenheim Museum. Immer bemüht, mit Konzepten und Erfahrungen von Raum zu experimentieren, haben die Partner auch einen ausgeprägt akademischen Hintergrund, der es ihnen ermöglicht, eher theoretische Projekte auszuloten: Couture ist Professorin am Fachbereich Architektur der Parsons School of Design in New York, während Rashid ein digitales Forschungsprogramm an der New Yorker Columbia University leitet.

Si la révolution informatique est le facteur qui a le plus profondément affecté l'architecture de la fin du XXe et du début du XXIe siècle, peu d'architectes ont autant misé sur son potentiel que le bureau multidisciplinaire Asymptote. Dans leur volonté de repousser les limites conventionnelles de l'architecture et d'embrasser une technologie nouvelle, ils ont étendu leurs activités à l'art de l'installation et aux environnements informatisés. Ils ont notamment réalisé une salle de transactions numériques pour la Bourse de New York et un musée virtuel pour le Musée Guggenheim. Poursuivant toujours leurs explorations des concepts spatiaux et de notre perception de ceux-ci, les associés ont également des qualifications universitaires qui leur permettent d'aborder des projets plus théoriques. Couture est professeur au département d'architecture de la Parsons School of Design de New York, et Rashid dirige un cours avancé de design sur ordinateur à l'université Columbia dans la même ville.

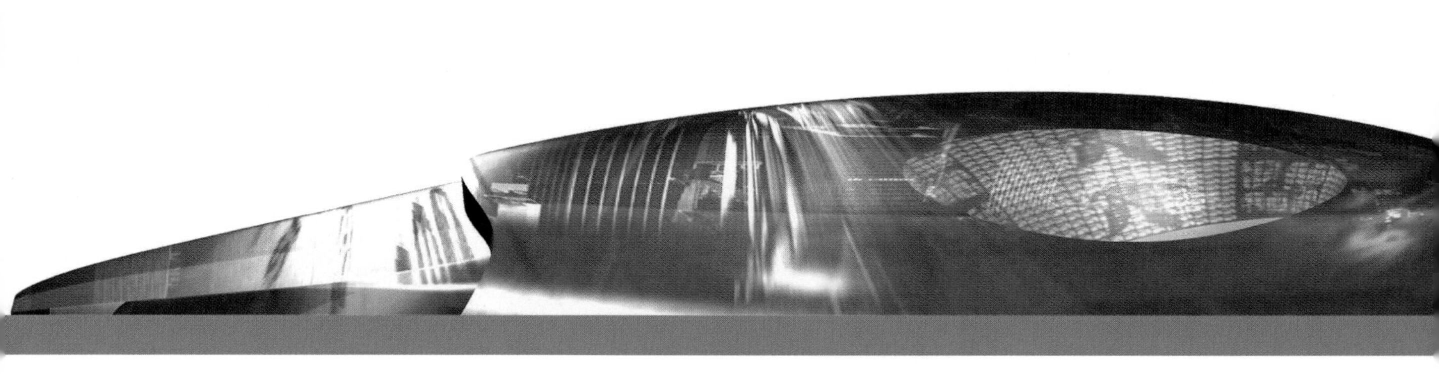

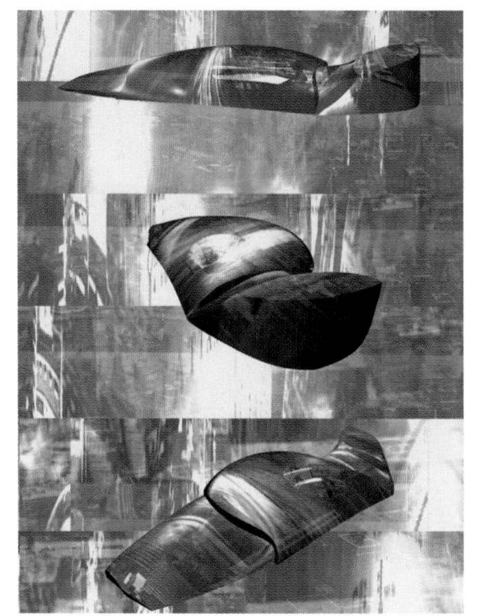

The vast building would be wrapped in a skin of high-tech cladding screening digital video images.

Der riesige Bau soll eine Hülle aus High-tech-Materialien erhalten, auf der digitale Videobilder visualisiert werden können.

L'immense édifice sera enveloppé d'une peau high-tech permettant de visualiser des images et vidéos numériques.

Asymptote's artwork is included in the collections of the Museum of Modern Art, New York, the San Francisco Museum of Modern Art, The Canadian Center for Architecture, Montreal, and the Fonds régionale d'art contemporain du centre (Frac), Orleans, France. More conventional architectural projects include the Univers Multimedia Theatre in Århus, Denmark, a sail-like structure erected annually, its ca. 2800 m² white tensile roof pulled into a series of planes that define irregular spaces underneath while doubling as projection screens. Their competition-winning "Steel Cloud", a design for a gateway to Los Angeles to rival New York's Statue of Liberty, ran into funding problems but images of its wild form made a remarkable impact - a 500 m-long web of trusses, galleries, screens and walkways that spanned the freeway.

Asymptotes künstlerische Arbeiten sind in den Sammlungen des Museum of Modern Art, New York, des San Francisco Museum of Modern Art, des Canadian Center for Architecture, Montreal und des Fonds régionale d'art contemporain du centre (Frac) im französischen Orléans vertreten. Zu ihren »konventionell« architektonischen Werken zählt das Univers Theater in Århus, Dänemark, ein jährlich neu errichteter segelartiger Bau, dessen ca. 2800 m² großes weißes Spanndach in eine Abfolge von Flächen unterteilt ist, die die unregelmäßigen Räume markieren und als Projektionsleinwände dienen. Ihr siegreicher Wettbewerbsbeitrag »Steel Cloud« – ein Entwurf für ein »Gateway« für Los Angeles als Konkurrenz zur New Yorker Freiheitsstatue – stieß auf Finanzierungsprobleme, aber schon die Bilder der komplexen Struktur waren sehr eindrucksvoll: ein 500 m langes Netz aus Trägern, Galerien, Bildschirmen und Laufstegen, das eine achtspurige Schnellstraße überspannen sollte.

Les œuvres d'art d'Asymptote figurent dans les collections du Museum of Modern Art de New York, du San Francisco Museum of Modern Art, du Centre canadien d'Architecture de Montréal et du Fonds régional d'art contemporain (Frac) d'Orléans. Leurs réalisations architecturales plus « conventionnelles » comprennent le Théâtre Univers d'Århus, au Danemark, structure évoquant une voile qui est érigée annuellement ; sa toiture extensible blanche d'environ 2800 m² forme une série de plans définissant les espaces irréguliers qu'elle recouvre, et peut servir d'écrans de cinéma. Leur « Steel Cloud » (« nuage d'acier »), projet qui a remporté un concours visant à doter Los Angeles d'une « porte » rivalisant avec la Statue de la Liberté de New York, a connu des problèmes de financement, mais les images de sa forme extravagante ont eu un énorme impact : un enchevêtrement d'armatures, de galeries, d'écrans et de passages pour piétons enjambe l'autoroute sur 500 m de long.

2005 **New York, USA**

Technology Culture Museum

An original idea by Asymptote, the museum charts the rise of information technology and examines its relation to the human condition at the turn of the millennium. The building is a hybrid structure that merges convention centre typology with the utility of an aeroplane hangar. The 300 m-long structure is located off piers 9 and 11 on the East River in Lower Manhattan and will include an 8-storey education and administration block.

A vast internal space - the largest container of public events and exhibitions in the world, capable of hosting large-scale expositions, media events and public spectacles - is framed by a lightweight steel structure designed and constructed using computer modelling and fabrication techniques. The skin of the building will utilise cutting-edge cladding technologies to create a building envelope capable of broadcasting digital video signals across its surface, giving the building an ephemeral, liquid presence.

"The Technology Culture Museum is an architecture where the convergence of art, technology, culture and commodity is articulated and made explicit" say the architects. "Visitors will be able to experience the 'beauty' and cultural relevancy of technological innovation in much the same manner that we have become accustomed to experiencing art, objects, performance and even science in museum settings throughout the later part of the 20th century."

Forward-looking backers are invited.

Das Technology Culture Museum ist eine Idee von Asymptote. Es stellt den Aufstieg der Informationstechnologie dar und untersucht ihre Beziehung zur Situation des Menschen am Anfang des neuen Jahrtausends. Der Bau verbindet die Typologie des Kongresszentrums mit der Funktionalität eines Flugzeughangars. Der 300 m lange Bau mit achtgeschossigem Lehr- und Verwaltungsblock soll in Lower Manhattan vor den Piers 9 und 11 in den East River ragen.

Ein riesiger Innenraum – der weltweit größte öffentliche Raum für Veranstaltungen und Ausstellungen, der großen Exponaten, Medienereignissen und öffentlichen Vorführungen Platz bieten soll – wird von einer leichten Stahlkonstruktion überfangen, die mit Hilfe computergestützter Entwurfs- und Fertigungsverfahren entstand. Innovative Verkleidungstechniken schaffen eine Gebäudehülle, auf deren Oberfläche digitale Videosignale gesendet werden können. So erhält der Bau ein flüchtig-fließendes Erscheinungsbild.

»Das Technology Culture Museum«, so die Architekten, »ist eine Architektur, die die Konvergenz von Kunst, Technologie, Kultur und Kommerz ausführt. Die Besucher werden die ›Schönheit‹ und kulturelle Relevanz technischer Innovation ebenso erfahren können, wie wir es im ausgehenden 20. Jahrhundert gewohnt sind, Kunst, Objekte, Performance und sogar Wissenschaft in Museumsräumen zu erleben.« Zukunftsorientierte Förderer sind willkommen.

Ce musée est une idée d'Asymptote. Il retrace l'évolution foudroyante de la technologie informatique et examine ses effets sur la condition humaine au tournant du millénaire. Le bâtiment est une structure hybride alliant la typologie des palais des congrès au caractère utilitaire d'un hangar d'aéroport. Long de 300 m, il s'étend entre les quais 9 et 11 de l'East River, dans Lower Manhattan, et comportera un bloc pédagogique et administratif de sept étages.

L'immense volume intérieur – le plus grand espace public du monde, pouvant accueillir des expositions et salons, des spectacles et événements médiatiques de grande ampleur – est délimité par une légère structure en acier dessinée et calculée sur ordinateur. L'enveloppe de l'édifice, faisant appel à des technologies de pointe, pourra diffuser des informations et images vidéo sur toute sa surface, ce qui donnera à l'édifice un aspect changeant et éphémère.

« Le Museum of Technology », disent les architectes, « est une architecture dans laquelle la convergence de l'art, de la technologie, de la culture et de l'utilité est articulée avec éloquence. Les visiteurs pourront faire l'expérience de la ‹ beauté › et de la pertinence culturelle des nouvelles technologies, de la même manière que nous nous sommes habitués depuis quelques décennies à voir réunis dans un cadre muséal œuvres d'art, objets, performances et même phénomènes ou appareils scientifiques. »

Les sponsors tournés vers l'avenir sont les bienvenus.

Ramps spiral up through the exhibition space.

Spiralförmige Rampen durchziehen den Ausstellungsraum.

Des rampes en spirale s'élèvent dans l'espace d'expositions.

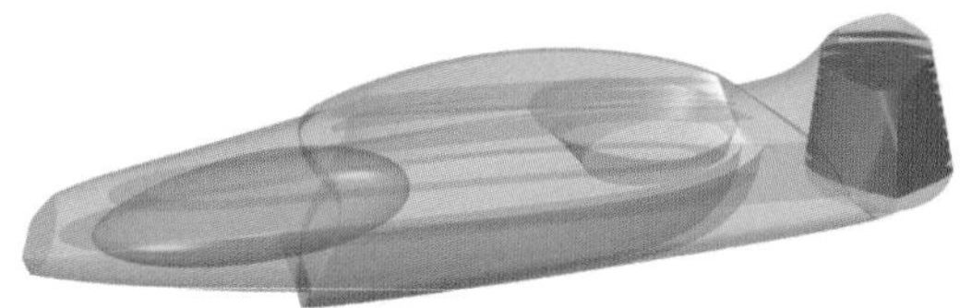

1 Offices/Archive/Education

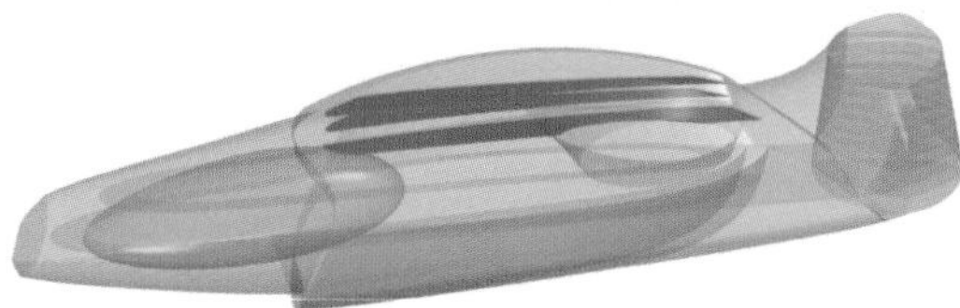

4 Galleries

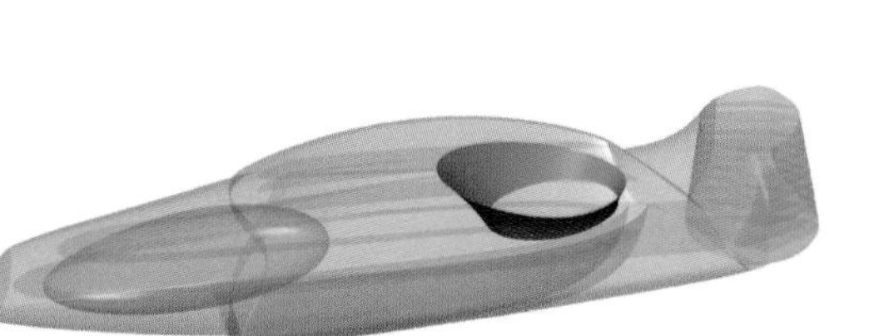

2 Virtual theatre

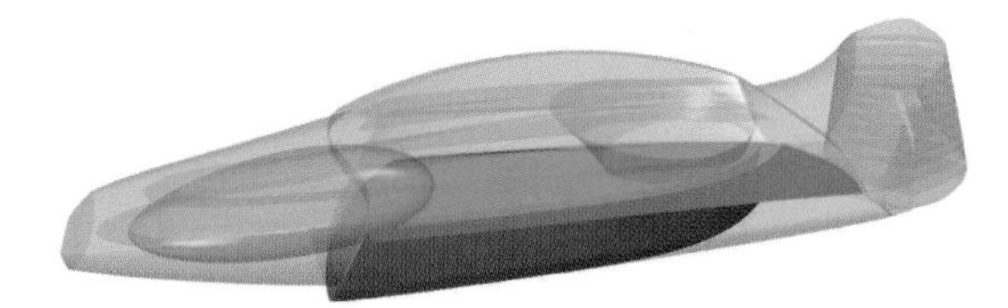

5 Exhibition hall

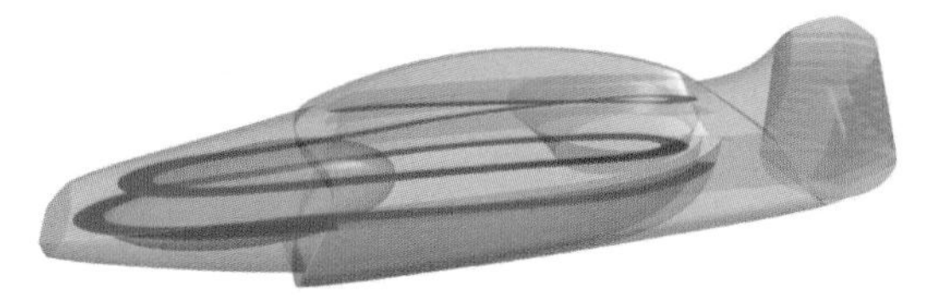

3 Ramps

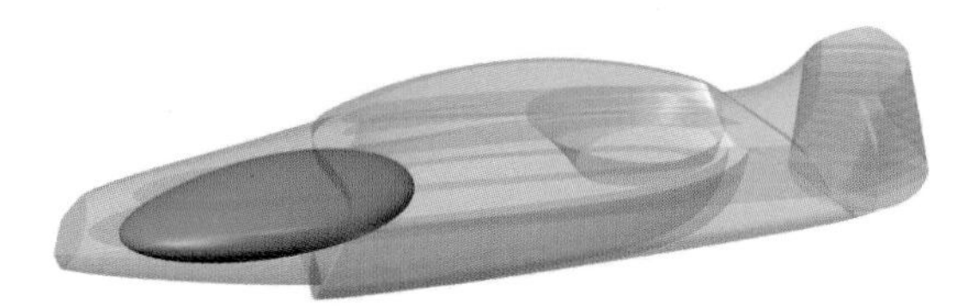

6 Cinema/Theatre

Photomontage of the building as it would look projecting into the East River.

Fotomontage des in den East River hinein ragenden Gebäudes.

Photomontage montrant la situation de l'édifice sur l'East River.

The new Dodger Stadium would be covered in a pneumatic roof, and a moving vessel would run around the outside of the stadium.

Das neue Dodger-Stadion soll ein pneumatisches Dach erhalten; ein Schienenfahrzeug soll es außen umrunden.

Le nouveau stade Dodger sera couvert d'une toiture pneumatique, et un vaisseau mobile en fera le tour.

1999 **Los Angeles, USA**

Dodger Stadium

The conceptual project is a response to an invitation by "Esquire" magazine issued in 1999 as part of their "21 people to watch in the 21st century" series. New polymers and PVC fabrics provide a fully reconfigurable pneumatic roofing that not only provides protection from rain and weather but by adjusting the nature of the air infiltration into the inflatable structure can also achieve different levels of transparency. Daylight can be modulated, and at night the roof can become completely transparent so that television cameras can obtain aerial views while circling above in helicopters. The stadium itself contains a digital display board circumscribing the entire interior space, which shows all game information in real-time including batting averages, speed of pitch and other statistics. Text and video would run simultaneously using state-of-the-art imaging technology and could be seen from anywhere in the stadium. A "moving vessel" would circulate the stadium on tracks providing full access to various shops and cafes throughout the game.
Couture and Rashid are in fact Mets fans.

Diese Studie für das Baseballstadion der Dodgers entstand als Reaktion auf eine Einladung der Zeitschrift »Esquire« 1999 im Rahmen ihrer Serie »21 people to watch in the 21st century«. Neuartige Polymere und PVC-Gewebe machen eine innovative pneumatische Dachlösung möglich, die nicht nur Schutz vor der Witterung bietet, sondern durch Veränderung der Luftzufuhr in der aufblasbaren Konstruktion auch unterschiedlich transparent sein kann. Tageslicht lässt sich dämpfen, und bei Nacht kann das Dach vollständig transparent werden, so dass Fernsehaufnahmen von Helikoptern aus möglich sind.
Im Stadion umzieht ein elektronisches Display den gesamten Innenraum, das in Echtzeit sämtliche Informationen zum Spiel, wie den Schlagdurchschnitt pro Spieler, die Schlaggeschwindigkeit und andere Daten anzeigt. Dank neuester Technik können Text und Videobilder gleichzeitig ablaufen und von überall im Stadion zu sehen sein. Während des gesamten Spiels soll ein Schienenfahrzeug den Bau umrunden, um Läden und Cafés zugänglich zu machen.
Couture und Rashid sind übrigens Fans der Mets.

L'étude du projet du Stade Dodger a été conçu suite à une invitation du magazine « Esquire », dans le cadre de la série « 21 personnes à suivre au 21e siècle ». De nouveaux tissus en polymères et PVC ont permis de réaliser une couverture « pneumatique » à configuration variable, qui protège non seulement de la pluie et du vent, mais qui permet d'obtenir divers degrés de transparence selon la quantité d'air admise dans la structure gonflable. De jour, l'intensité de la lumière peut être modulée, tandis que de nuit, il est possible d'obtenir une transparence totale permettant de réaliser pour la télévision des prises de vues aériennes depuis des hélicoptères.
Le stade lui-même est entouré d'une bande d'affichage électronique indiquant en temps réel toutes les informations et statistiques concernant le match en cours ; textes et images vidéo sont projetés simultanément grâce à une technologie state of the art, et sont visibles de tous les points du stade. Pendant le match, un « vaisseau sur rails » parcourt le stade, permettant au public d'accéder à tout moment aux cafés et autres magasins.
Couture et Rashid sont d'ailleurs des supporters des « Mets ».

Shigeru Ban

5-2-4 Matsubara, Setagaya, Tokyo 156-0043, Japan tel +81 3 3324 6760 fax +81 3 3324 6789 web www.dnp.co.jp/millennium/SB/VAN.html

Shigeru Ban	
born	1957 Tokyo, Japan
studied	1980 Southern California Institute of Architecture, Los Angeles; 1982/84 Cooper Union School of Architecture, New York
previous practice	1982-83 Arata Isozaki, Tokyo
	1985 set up own practice

Selected projects	
Odawara Pavilion	1990 Kanagawa, Japan
Paper Gallery	1994 Tokyo, Japan
Paper House	1995 Lake Yamanaka, Yamanashi, Japan
Paper Church	1995 Kobe, Hyogo, Japan
Curtain Wall House	1995 Tokyo, Japan
2/5 House	1995 Nishinomiya, Hyogo, Japan
Consultant to the United Nations High Commissioner for Refugees	1995-99
Wall-less House	1997 Karuizawa, Nagano, Japan
9-Square Grid House	1997 Kanagawa, Japan
Japanese Pavilion, Expo 2000	2000 Hanover, Germany

In what he has self-consciously dubbed his "Case Study" series in homage to the 50s Californian programme of the same name, Ban is constantly reinventing the single family house. Each of his private houses can be seen as an intellectual exercise, whether to create the ultimate wall-less house, a house based entirely on a noughts and crosses grid of nine cubic rooms where walls can be moved along the lines to change the dimension of the spaces, or a three-storey house enveloped in a giant white curtain. These houses are terrifyingly open spaces that leave no place to hide. External walls are no more than near-invisible planes of floor-to-ceiling glazing, and internal walls are avoided.
But Ban also has humanitarian concerns. He takes his responsibility as an architect seriously, recognising his role as a provider of shelter. He is keenly aware of the impact of buildings on the environment. This has

Mit seiner »Case Study«-Reihe – benannt in selbstbewusster Anspielung auf das gleichnamige kalifornische Bauprogramm der 50er-Jahre – ist Ban beständig mit der Neuerfindung des Einfamilienhauses befasst. Jedes seiner Privathäuser lässt sich als intellektuelle Übung verstehen, ob es um das ultimative wandlose Haus geht – ein Haus, das aus einem quadratischen Raster von neun Raumkuben besteht, deren Wände sich entlang der Rasterlinien verschieben lassen – oder um ein dreigeschossiges Wohngebäude, das in einen riesigen weißen »Vorhang« gehüllt ist. Diese Häuser sind beängstigend offen und bieten dem Bewohner keine Möglichkeit, sich zu verstecken. Außenwände sind auf nahezu unsichtbare, raumhohe Glasflächen reduziert, Innenwände möglichst vermieden.
Ban hat jedoch auch humanitäre Anliegen. Er nimmt seine Verantwortung als Architekt, der für Obdach sorgt, ernst.

Dans le cadre d'une série qu'il a baptisée « Case Study » en hommage au programme californien du même nom lancé au cours des années 50, Shigeru Ban ne cesse de réinventer l'habitat individuel. Chacune de ses maisons peut être considérée comme un exercice intellectuel – qu'il s'agisse de l'ultime maison sans murs, entièrement basée sur une grille de neuf unités le long desquelles des cloisons peuvent être déplacées de sorte à changer la disposition de l'espace, ou d'une maison à trois niveaux enveloppée d'un gigantesque rideau blanc. Ces maisons sont de terrifiants espaces ouverts n'offrant aucune cachette ou protection. Les murs extérieurs ne sont que des pans de verre pratiquement invisibles tenant toute la hauteur, tandis que les cloisons intérieures sont quasi inexistantes.
Ban a également des préoccupations humanitaires. Il prend très au sérieux la responsabilité de l'architecte,

led to his development of cardboard tubes as a low-cost, recyclable building material, and his nickname "the paper architect". Cardboard tubes have been used to create easy-to-build log cabins for the victims of the Kobe earthquake of 1995, refugee shelters that can be used by the United Nations in response to humanitarian disasters, an undulating screen in his Paper House, and the recyclable vaulted Japanese Pavilion at Expo 2000 in Hanover. More importantly, he achieves these noble aims without compromising his rigorous aesthetic ideals.

Zudem ist er sich der gravierenden Auswirkungen des Bauens auf die Umwelt bewusst. Dieses Bewusstsein führte zu der Entwicklung von Pappröhren als billiges, recycelbares Baumaterial, was ihm die Bezeichnung »Papierarchitekt« eintrug. Solche Pappröhren verwendete er bei den leicht zu errichtenden Blockhäusern für die Opfer des Erdbebens von Kobe im Jahre 1995, für Flüchtlingsunterkünfte, wie sie die UN bei Katastropheneinsätzen brauchen, für den gewellten Raumteiler in seinem Paper House und für den Japanischen Pavillon der Expo 2000 in Hannover. Ban gelingt es, noble Ziele zu verwirklichen, ohne seine strikten ästhetischen Ideale preiszugeben.

dont le rôle premier est de fournir un abri. Il a également une vive conscience de l'impact de ses constructions sur l'environnement. Cela l'a conduit à utiliser comme matériau de construction des tubes en carton, à la fois recyclables et peu coûteux, – et lui a valu le surnom d'« architecte du papier ». Ces tubes ont permis de réaliser des bungalows de construction facile pour les victimes du tremblement de terre de Kobe en 1995, des abris pour réfugiés dont l'ONU peut disposer en cas de catastrophe humanitaire, ainsi que l'écran ondoyant de sa Maison de Papier et le Pavillon japonais à coupole de l'Expo 2000 de Hanovre. Détail qui a son importance, il réalise ces nobles objectifs sans renier le moins du monde ses rigoureux idéaux esthétiques.

Wall-less House

The eighth in Ban's series of "Case Study" houses in which he pushes his theories of a "universal floor" (a single open-plan space) to their limits. The 60-m² floor slab curls up the back wall and flows into the steel roof so that the house is a sandwich of air between these two white planes. Structural elements are limited to imperceptibly thin roof supports, and glass walls can be slid back so that the room dissolves into the surrounding trees. A cantilevered kitchen worktop is treated as a sculptural element floating in the space. The only concession to privacy is sliding screens that can be pulled around areas such as the bathroom.

Bans Wall-less House, das »Haus ohne Wände«, ist das achte seiner »Case Study«-Reihe, in der er seine Vorstellungen vom »universal floor«, einem einzigen, offenen Raum, an ihre Grenzen führt. Die 60 m² große Bodenplatte biegt sich an der Rückseite aufwärts und geht in das Metalldach über, so dass das Haus einem »Luftsandwich« zwischen zwei weißen Flächen gleicht. Konstruktive Elemente beschränken sich auf verschwindend dünne Stützen; die Glaswände lassen sich zurückschieben, so dass der Raum mit den umgebenden Bäumen verschmilzt. Eine vorkragende Arbeitsfläche im Küchenbereich wird als im Raum schwebendes plastisches Element aufgefasst. Das einzige Zugeständnis an die Privatsphäre sind verschiebbare Raumteiler, die sich um Bereiche wie das Bad ziehen lassen.

Dans cette « Maison sans murs », huitième maison de la série « Case Study », Ban va jusqu'au bout de sa théorie du « plan universel », espace unique sans séparations. La dalle de plancher de 60 m² se relève pour former le mur arrière que prolonge une toiture en acier, de sorte que la maison est en fait une couche d'air prise entre ces deux plans d'une blancheur immaculée. Les éléments structurels sont limités aux fins piliers presque invisibles qui soutiennent la toiture et à des murs en verre escamotables, la pièce se dissolvant alors dans les arbres qui l'entourent. Le plan de travail en porte-à-faux de la cuisine est traité comme un élément sculptural suspendu dans l'espace. Unique concession à l'intimité, des écrans coulissants peuvent isoler des aires telles que la salle de bains.

The floor plane continues up the back wall and out across the roof. The remaining glass facades are open.

Die Bodenfläche setzt sich über Rückwand und Dach fort; die Glasfassaden sind offen.

La dalle formant le sol se poursuit par le mur du fond, avant de constituer la toiture. Les autres façades sont entièrement vitrées.

The interior takes open-plan living to extremes, although sliding screens can be pulled around the bathroom area.

Der Innenraum führt das Konzept des offenen Grundrisses an seine Grenzen, auch wenn der Badezimmerbereich mit Schiebewänden geschlossen werden kann.

L'intérieur est un exemple extrême du plan ouvert, bien que l'espace contenant baignoire et toilettes puisse être isolé par des écrans coulissants.

Built-in items of furniture become isolated elements in the space.

Einbaumöbel verwandeln sich in isolierte Raumobjekte.

Les meubles intégrés deviennent des éléments sculpturaux dans l'espace intérieur.

The church is defined by an ellipse of cardboard tubes and sheltered by a tensile roof.

Der Kirchenraum ist von einer Ellipse aus Pappröhren umschlossen und mit einem Spanndach gedeckt.

L'église est délimitée par une ellipse en tubes de carton ; la toiture se déploie comme un parapluie.

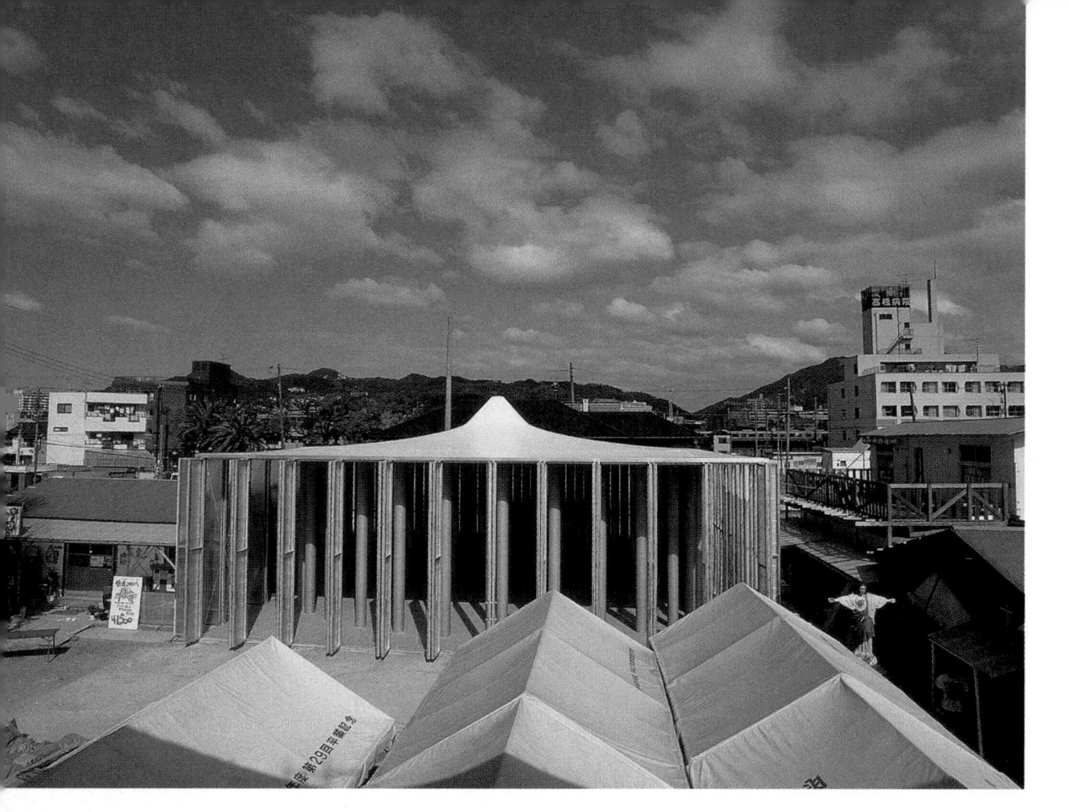

1995 **Kobe, Hyogo, Japan**

Paper Church

Influenced by Gian Lorenzo Bernini's baroque church designs, an ellipse of paper tubes cocoons the congregation, densely packed at the front of the church, gradually opening out at the rear to allow the congregation access. The ellipse sits within a square box of corrugated polycarbonate sheeting with a tensile roof that opens up like an umbrella.
Quick and cheap to erect, the structure was designed in response to the Kobe earthquake and built by volunteers of the Roman Catholic congregation in just five weeks. In all, 58 cardboard tubes were used, 330 mm in diameter and 5 m high. "Even in disaster areas I want to create beautiful buildings, to move people and to improve people's lives. If I did not feel that way, it would not be possible to create works of architecture and make a contribution to society at the same time."

Die von Gian Lorenzo Berninis barocken Kirchenentwürfen inspirierte, elliptisch gestaltete Papierkirche umhüllt die Gemeinde mit an der Vorderseite dicht stehenden Pappröhren, die sich im hinteren Teil allmählich öffnen, um der Gemeinde Zugang zu gewähren. Die Ellipse befindet sich im Innern eines quadratischen Kastens aus gewelltem Polykarbonat mit einem gespannten, schirmähnlichen Dach.
Der preiswerte und leicht zu errichtende Bau entstand nach dem Erdbeben in Kobe und wurde von Freiwilligen der katholischen Gemeinde in nur fünf Wochen errichtet. Insgesamt wurden 58 Pappröhren mit 330 mm Durchmesser und 5 m Höhe verwendet. »Auch in Katastrophengebieten möchte ich schöne Bauten errichten, um die Leute zu inspirieren und ihr Leben zu verbessern. Wenn ich daran nicht glauben würde, wäre es nicht möglich, Architektur zu gestalten und zugleich einen gesellschaftlichen Beitrag zu leisten.«

Influencée par les églises baroques du Bernin, cette ellipse en tubes de papier entourant douillettement l'assemblée des fidèles s'ouvre progressivement à l'arrière pour permettre l'accès à l'« Eglise de papier ». Elle occupe le centre d'une boîte carrée en polycarbonate ondulé, surmontée d'un toit extensible qui s'ouvre comme un parapluie. D'une construction rapide et peu coûteuse, la structure, conçue à la suite du tremblement de terre de Kobe, avait été assemblée par des volontaires de la communauté catholique. Elle comporte en tout 58 tubes en carton de 330 mm de diamètre et de 5 m de haut. « Même dans les régions sinistrées, je tiens à créer de belles constructions, susceptibles d'émouvoir les gens et d'améliorer leur vie. Si je n'avais pas cette conviction, il ne serait pas possible de créer des œuvres architecturales tout en contribuant au bien-être de la société. »

Above, spacing between tubes increases to allow access. Right, a service in the church.

Oben: Am Eingang ist der Abstand zwischen den Röhren größer. Rechts: eine Messe in der Kirche.

Ci-dessus : les tubes de carton sont plus espacés à l'endroit de l'entrée. A droite, une messe dans la nouvelle église.

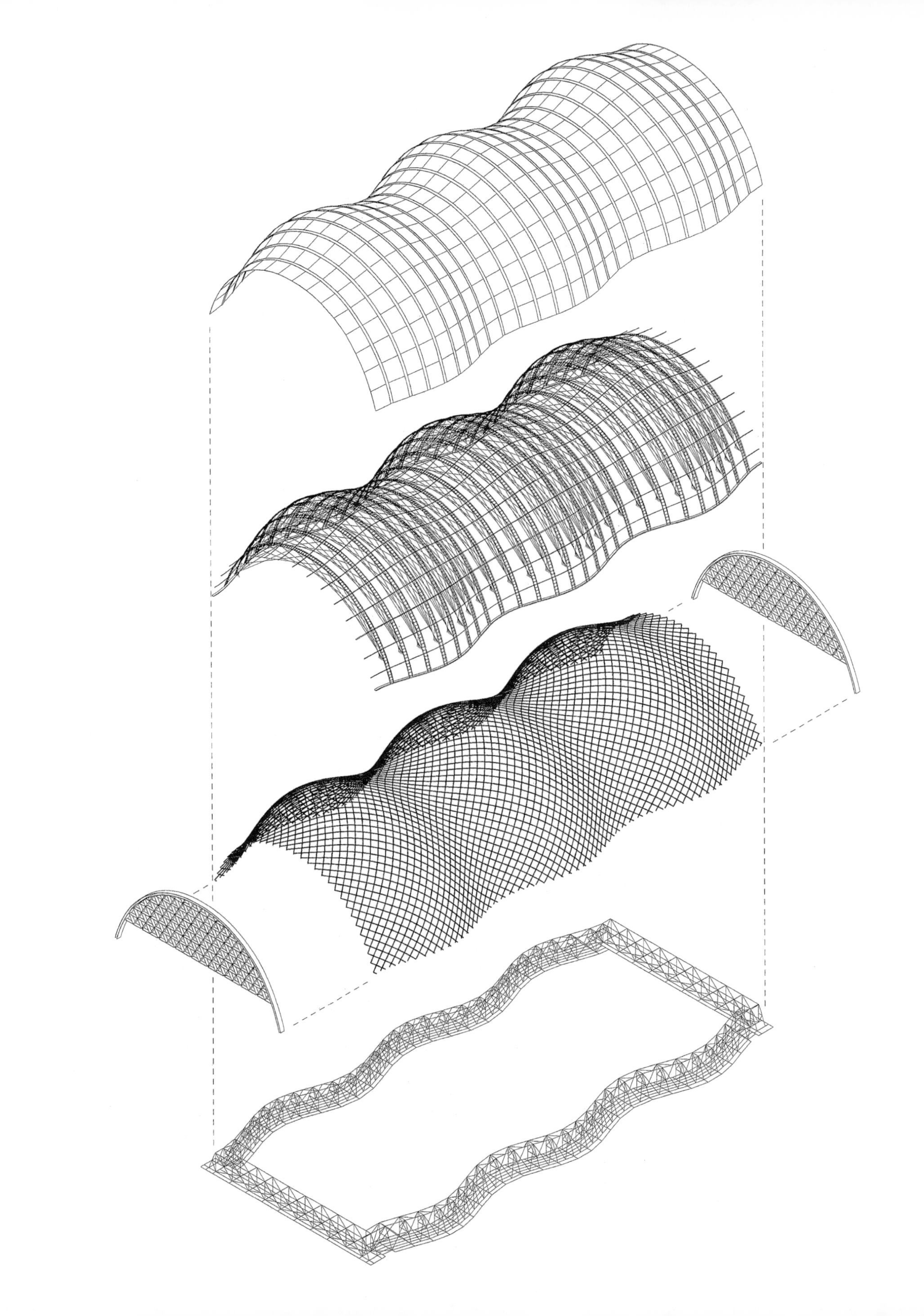

Far left, a framework of cardboard tubes is covered with a paper membrane. The entire pavilion is recyclable. Left, view of the interior.

Ganz links: Das Pappröhrengitter ist mit einer Papiermembran überzogen. Der gesamte Pavillon ist wiederverwertbar. Links: Innenansicht der Konstruktion.

Page de gauche : l'ossature en tubes de carton est couverte d'une membrane de papier ; le pavillon est entièrement recyclable. Ci-contre : une partie du toit vu de l'intérieur.

2000 **Hanover, Germany**

Japanese Pavilion, Expo 2000

Ban addresses the paradox between the theme of Expo 2000 - sustainable development - and the inevitable waste of building pavilions to last only half a year. Using recycled and reusable building materials for the construction of the pavilion as much as possible, Ban intends its components to be reused after the building is dismantled. The main hall is a hybrid of a paper tube grid (which Ban likens to a basket weave) and a laminated timber arch, which form an undulating roof. The waterproof and fireproof paper membrane was developed in Japan especially for the pavilion. It is combined with a transparent PVC membrane that lets natural light filter through the paper. As structural supports for the roof he uses steel frames and scaffold boards filled with sand (minimising the use of concrete, which cannot be recycled); container units are used for the office building.

Bans Entwurf für den Japanischen Pavillon geht auf den Widerspruch ein zwischen dem Thema der Expo 2000 – nachhaltige Entwicklung – und der unvermeidlichen Verschwendung beim Errichten von Bauten, die nur ein halbes Jahr lang benutzt werden. Er verwendet vorwiegend recycel- und wiederverwendbare Materialien, die nach der Demontage weiter genutzt werden sollen. Die Haupthalle besteht aus einem Pappröhrengitter, das Ban mit einem Korbgeflecht vergleicht, und Schichtholzbögen, die gemeinsam die gewölbte Dachform bilden. Die wasserdichte und feuerfeste Papierhaut wurde in Japan eigens für den Pavillon entwickelt. Kombiniert mit einer transparenten PVC-Membran lässt sie Tageslicht durch das Papier dringen. Als Stützen für das Dach werden Stahlträger und mit Sand gefüllte Verschalungen verwendet und der Einsatz von nicht recycelbarem Beton minimiert. Container beherbergen den Bürotrakt.

Ban aborde ici le paradoxe né de l'incompatibilité entre le thème d'Expo 2000 – le développement durable – et l'inévitable gâchis qu'entraîne la construction de pavillons qui ne durent que six mois. Utilisant principalement pour la construction du pavillon des matériaux recyclés et réutilisables, Ban tient à ce qu'ils soient réutilisés après le démantèlement de l'édifice. Le hall principal est un hybride alliant une grille en tubes de papier (que Ban compare à un ouvrage de vannerie) à un arc en bois laminé formant une toiture ondoyante. La membrane en papier ignifugé et imperméable a été spécialement développée au Japon pour le pavillon. Elle est doublée d'une enveloppe en PVC transparent qui permet à la lumière du jour de filtrer à travers le papier. La toiture est soutenue par une ossature en acier reposant sur des caissons emplis de sable, de sorte à minimiser l'usage du béton, matériau non recyclable. Le bâtiment abritant les bureaux est constitué de conteneurs.

Marc Barani

27 Boulevard Joseph Garnier, 06000 Nice, France tel +33 4 9351 0810 fax +33 4 9351 5311 e-mail atelier.Barani@wanadoo.fr

Marc Barani

born	1957	Menton, France
studied	1984	UP Marseilles-Luminy, architectural degree; 1990 Ecole Pilote Internationale d'Art et de Recherches, Nice, set-designer degree

Selected projects

Extension to Saint-Pancrace Cemetery	1992	Roquebrune-Cap-Martin, France
Water filtration plant	1995	Roquebrune-Cap-Martin, France
Multi-purpose space	1996	La Gaude, France
Offices for Gregoire Gardette Editions	1996	Nice, France
Motorway A75	1996	Lodève, France
Extension to San Michele Cemetery	1997	Venice, Italy (competition)
Centre for Applied Arts and Studios	1997	Mouans-Sartoux, France
Town hall and housing	1998	Saint-Jacques de la Lande, France (under construction)
Extension to Picasso Museum	1999	Antibes, France
Tramway	2000	Nice, France
Arts Centre	2000	Crestet, France

A student of anthropology, landscape architecture, set design and fine art as well as architecture, Barani brings a richness to his work drawn from these other disciplines. The dramatic topography of his native Côte d'Azur is confronted with sensitivity but equal force: the deep gashes into the hillside at the Saint-Pancrace Cemetery; an open courtyard addressing the valley and the sky for the Crestet Arts Centre. His wife, set-designer Birgitte Fryland, plays an important role in his practice and Barani has worked with artists James Turrell (on Crestet Arts Centre), Bernard Pagès (on an office and exhibition space for Gregoire Gardette Editions in Nice) and Eric Benqué, and with the philosopher Jean-Marc Ghitti.

Mass, depth and opacity have become recurring themes in Barani's work, often manifested as vast thick walls of textured concrete that enclose a space and control one's experience of it. The effect is of monumental sculptures in the landscape, havens of calm waiting to be explored.

Barani lässt Erfahrungen aus Anthropologie, Landschaftsarchitektur, Bühnenbild und Kunst in seine Arbeit einfließen. Der spektakulären Topographie seiner Heimat, der Côte d'Azur, begegnet er mit Sensibilität und ebenbürtiger Kraft zugleich: tiefe Einschnitte in den Abhang beim Friedhof Saint-Pancrace, ein offener Hof, der beim Kunstzentrum in Crestet Tal und Himmel einbezieht. Seine Frau, die Bühnenbildnerin Birgitte Fryland, spielt für Baranis Arbeit eine wichtige Rolle. Beim Kunstzentrum Crestet hat er mit dem Künstler James Turrell zusammengearbeitet, bei einem Büro- und Ausstellungskomplex für Gregoire Gardette Editions in Nizza mit Bernard Pagès und Eric Benqué sowie mit dem Philosophen Jean-Marc Ghitti. Masse, Tiefe und Opazität wurden in Baranis Werk zu gängigen Themen, häufig in Form mächtiger Wände aus strukturiertem Beton. Die Wirkung ist die monumentaler Skulpturen in der Landschaft, Oasen der Ruhe, die darauf warten, erkundet zu werden.

Cultivant également l'anthropologie, l'architecture de paysage, la scénographie et les beaux-arts, Barani enrichit sa pratique architecturale des apports de ces autres disciplines. Il affronte la topographie tourmentée de sa Côte d'Azur natale avec autant de sensibilité que de force : les profondes entailles dans la colline du cimetière Saint-Pancrace, la cour s'ouvrant sur la vallée et sur le ciel du Centre d'art de Crestet, la salle longue et basse de La Gaude s'insérant tout naturellement dans la colline. Sa femme, la scénographe Birgitte Fryland, joue un rôle important dans sa pratique. Barani a travaillé avec les artistes James Turrell (pour le Centre d'Art de Crestet), Bernard Pagès (pour un espace de bureaux et d'expositions réalisé à Nice pour les éditions Grégoire Gardette) et Eric Benqué, ainsi qu'avec le philosophe Jean-Marc Ghitti. La masse, la profondeur et l'opacité sont devenus des thèmes récurrents de son œuvre, souvent sous la forme de massifs murs en béton texturé délimitant un espace et contrôlant notre perception de celui-ci.

Extension to Saint-Pancrace Cemetery

One of Barani's earliest projects, and one that displays shades of Louis Kahn, was an extension to the cemetery where Le Corbusier is buried on a steep promontory overlooking the sea.
The burial space is cut deep into the steep wooded slope, encased in thick high walls of white concrete that frame the views, creating order and rigidity in a wild landscape. Individual tombs line the walls and are sealed with squares of Carrara marble.
The vast structure is beyond human scale, and the narrow staircase leading up the hillside (the width of a man with outstretched arms) masks the terraces and the tombs from view so that the structure is always in control of the visitor. The high walls of the crevasses shut out daily life, yet leave the space wide open to the landscape and the sea. Powerful and peaceful, Saint-Pancrace Cemetery captures a sense of the spiritual and provides a space for solitary contemplation.

Eines von Baranis frühesten, an Louis Kahn erinnernden Projekten ist die Erweiterung des Saint-Pancrace Friedhofs, auf dem u. a. Le Corbusier auf einer steilen Klippe hoch über dem Meer bestattet ist. Die Grabstätte ist tief in den steilen, bewaldeten Abhang eingeschnitten und von dicken weißen Betonmauern umschlossen, die Ausblicke rahmen und damit in einer wilden Landschaft Ordnung und Strenge schaffen. Die Mauern werden von Einzelgräbern gesäumt, die mit quadratischen Platten aus Carraramarmor verschlossen sind.
Die riesige Anlage orientiert sich nicht am menschlichen Maßstab; die den Abhang hinauf führende Treppe, deren Breite den ausgestreckten Armen eines Menschen entspricht, verdeckt den Blick auf Terrassen und Gräber, so dass die Anlage den Besucher stets unter Kontrolle hat. Die hohen Mauern der Einschnitte sperren das alltägliche Geschehen aus, erlauben jedoch weite Ausblicke auf Landschaft und Meer. Mächtig und friedvoll zugleich, ist der Friedhof Saint Pancrace geprägt von einer spirituellen Atmosphäre und lädt zur Kontemplation ein.

Une des premières réalisations de Barani, qui n'est pas sans évoquer Louis Kahn, fut l'extension du cimetière Saint-Pancrace où est enterré Le Corbusier, sur un promontoire abrupt dominant la mer.
Le cimetière proprement dit, profonde entaille dans la colline boisée, est pris entre de hauts et épais murs de béton blanc qui encadrent la vue, créant ordre et rigueur dans le paysage sauvage. Les tombes bordant les murs sont scellées par des plaques de marbre de Carrare.
La composition dépasse l'échelle humaine : de l'étroit escalier d'accès grimpant la colline (de la largeur d'un homme étendant les bras) les terrasses et les tombes ne sont pas visibles, de sorte que la structure exerce un contrôle permanent sur le visiteur. Les hautes murailles excluent la vie quotidienne, mais s'ouvrent largement sur le paysage et la mer. A la fois puissant et paisible, le cimetière Saint-Pancrace atteint au spirituel et crée un espace propice à la contemplation.

Vast concrete walls create a crevasse looking out to sea.

Hohe Betonwände rahmen eine »Gletscherspalte« mit Blick aufs Meer.

Les hauts murs en béton sont percés d'une « crevasse » donnant sur la mer.

Individual tombs are sealed with squares of Carrara marble.

Quadratische Platten aus Carraramarmor verschließen die Einzelgräber.

Les tombes sont scellées par des plaques en marbre de Carrare.

The Saint-Pancrace Cemetery takes advantage of its natural site on the Côte d'Azur.

Der Friedhof Saint-Pancrace ist eingebettet in die Hänge an der Côte d'Azur.

Le cimetière Saint-Pancrace est niché dans les collines de la Côte d'Azur.

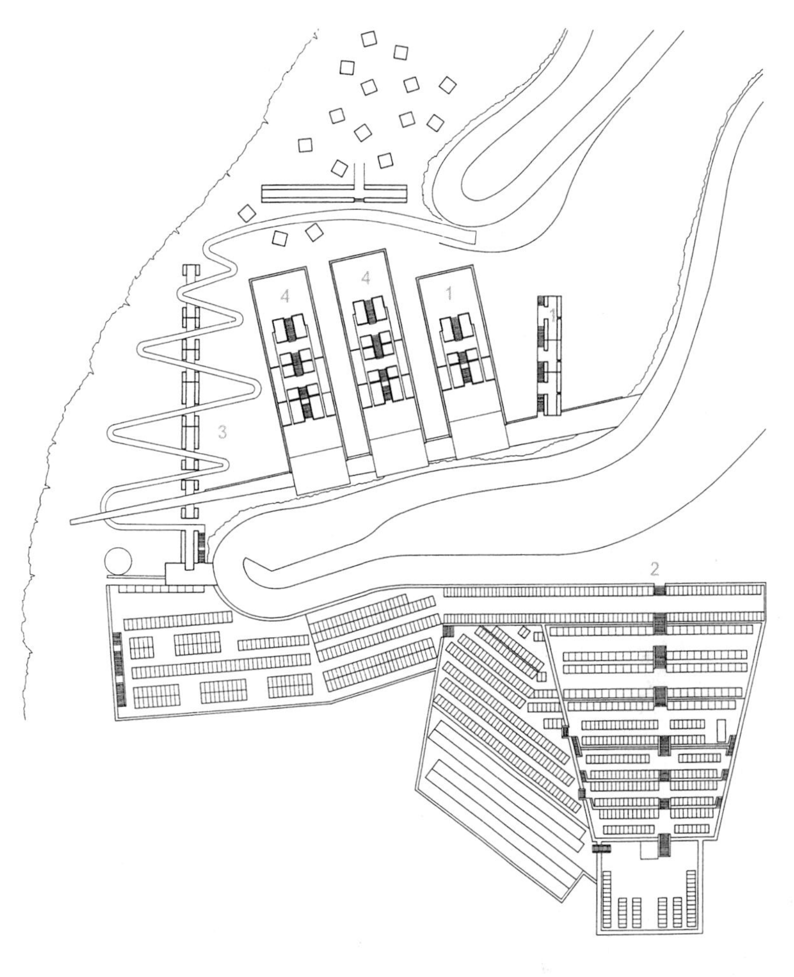

Site plan/ Plan der Anlage/ Plan général du site

1 **first phase/** erste Phase/ première phase

2 **existing cemetery/** bestehender Friedhof/ ancien cimetière

3/4 **second phase (proposed)/** zweite Phase (geplant)/ deuxième phase (en projet)

Centre for Applied Arts and Studios

The teaching space and workshops are located in the grounds of the château Mouans-Sartoux, and complement the triangular footprint of the chateau with two more geometric shapes - a drum-shaped amphitheatre and a square building housing workshops.
Dug deep into the side of a hill, the workshop building is partially submerged and does not impinge upon the historic chateau. The composition of closed and open areas on the entrance facade strikes a harmonious balance while the woodland facade presents an austere wall of rough concrete. Countering this is the open amphitheatre, a sunken concrete circle that continues the procession of buildings down the slope.

Die Unterrichtsräume und Lehrateliers des Zentrums für angewandte Kunst befinden sich auf dem Gelände des Château Mouans-Sartoux und ergänzen den dreieckigen Grundriss des Schlosses durch zwei weitere geometrische Formen – ein kreisrundes Amphitheater und ein rechteckiges Gebäude, in dem die Ateliers untergebracht sind.
Das tief in einen Hang eingeschnittene, zum Teil unter Planum liegende Ateliergebäude beeinträchtigt das historische Schloss in keiner Weise. Die Anordnung geschlossener und offener Partien an der Eingangsfront wirkt ausgewogen, während sich die dem Wald zugewandte Seite als schmucklose, rauhe Betonwand präsentiert. Ein Gegengewicht dazu bildet das offene Amphitheater, ein abgesenkter Betonkreis, mit dem sich die Abfolge von Bauten den Hang hinunter fortsetzt.

L'Espace de l'art concret et les ateliers pédagogiques sont situés dans le parc du château de Mouans-Sartoux, ajoutant à la forme triangulaire de ce dernier deux autres formes géométriques : un amphithéâtre cylindrique et un édifice carré abritant les ateliers.
Construit à flanc de colline, le bâtiment des ateliers est en partie enterré, de sorte à ne pas interférer avec le château historique. La composition de la façade principale, alternance d'aires ouvertes et fermées, est harmonieuse et équilibrée, tandis que la façade donnant sur la forêt présente un austère mur de béton brut. En contrepoint, l'amphithéâtre ouvert, cercle de béton enfoncé dans le sol, prolonge la ligne des bâtiments se succédant sur la pente.

The workshop block is set below the level of the historic chateau, left. A rough concrete wall, right, responds to the adjacent woodland.

Links: Der Block mit den Werkstätten respektiert das alte Schloss. Rechts: Eine rauhe Betonwand nimmt Bezug auf den angrenzenden Wald.

A gauche : le bloc bas abritant les ateliers ne cache pas le château historique. A droite : un mur en béton brut, en harmonie avec la forêt environnante.

Workshop space, left. Above, the roof terrace of the arts centre with the chateau behind.

Links der Werkstattraum, oben die Dachterrasse des Kunstzentrums mit dem Schloss.

A gauche, vue d'un atelier. Ci-dessus, le toit-terrasse du centre d'arts et le château.

Section/ Schnitt/ Coupe

1 **amphitheatre/** Amphitheater/ amphithéâtre
2 **workshop and teaching space/** Werkstatt und Lehratelier/ ateliers et salle de cours
3 **roof terrace/** Dachterrasse/ toit-terrasse

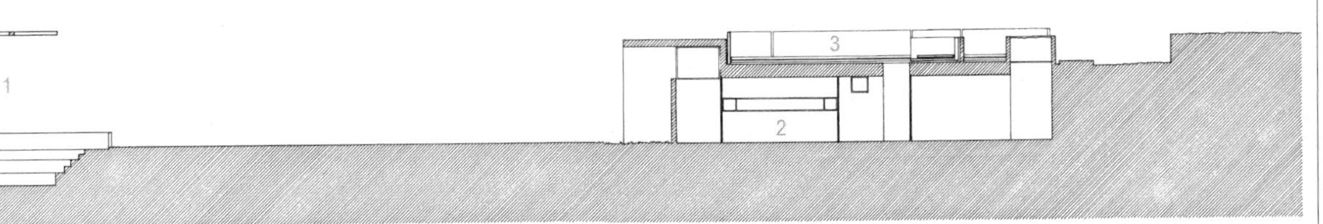

2000 Crestet, France

Arts Centre

An extension of the existing Maison Stahly, the centre is designed to house artists in residence, exhibition space and a small cafe. The building is as much about the open courtyard as about the three blocks that enclose it. Routes through, over and around the building immediately invite exploration. A sculpture in the landscape, the complex is continuously encouraging one to look away from it up to the sky and out across the valley.

Das als Erweiterung der bestehenden Maison Stahly gedachte Kunstzentrum soll Unterkünfte für Stipendiaten, Ausstellungsflächen und ein kleines Café aufnehmen. Bei dem Komplex spielt der offene Innenhof eine ebenso große Rolle wie die drei ihn umgebenden Gebäudeteile. Wege durch, über und um den Bau herum wecken unmittelbar die Lust auf Entdeckungen. Der wie eine Skulptur in der Landschaft wirkende Bau fordert gleichwohl ständig dazu auf, den Blick von ihm weg hinauf in den Himmel und über das Tal zu lenken.

Extension de la Maison Stahly préexistante, le Centre d'ar abrite résidences d'artistes, des espaces d'expositions et un petit café. La cour ouverte a une importance égale à celle des trois blocs qui l'entourent. Des itinéraires traversant, contournant ou passant par-dessus l'ensemble encouragent l'exploration. Sculpture posée dans le paysage, le complexe invite constamment à s'en détourner pour regarder le ciel et la vallée.

Model showing the situation of the building, far left. Artist's impressions of how the building will look, above and left.

Das Modell zeigt die Einbettung des Gebäudes in seine Umgebung (ganz links).
Künstlerische Darstellungen der künftigen optischen Wirkung des Gebäudes (oben und links)

Modèle montrant l'édifice dans son environnement (page de gauche).
Dessins d'artistes montrant divers aspects de l'édifice (en haut et à gauche).

Berger + Parkkinen

Fillgradergasse 16, 1060 Vienna, Austria
tel +43 1 581 4935 fax +43 1 581 4937 e-mail info@berger-parkkinen.com web www.berger-parkkinen.com

Alfred Berger

born	1961	Salzburg, Austria
studied	1983	Technische Universität, Vienna; 1989 Akademie der Bildenden Künste, Vienna
previous practice	1990	co-founded Berger & Krismer, 1992 Penttilä - Berger - Krismer, 1995 Berger + Parkkinen Architekten, Vienna-Helsinki

Tiina Parkkinen

born	1965	Vienna, Austria
studied	1994	Akademie der Bildenden Künste, Vienna
previous practice	1995	co-founded Berger + Parkinen Architekten, Vienna-Helsinki

Selected projects

Ice Stadium	1994	Vienna, Austria
Akademie der Bildenden Künste renovation	1998	Vienna, Austria
MUMUT Music Theatre	1998	Graz, Austria (Project)
Nordic Embassies, masterplan and Felleshus	1999	Berlin, Germany
NORDEN (design exhibition) Kunsthalle	2000	Vienna, Austria
Biomedical Research Centre	2000	Vienna, Austria (Project)
Court House Complex	2000	Leoben, Austria (Project)

An Austro-Finnish collaboration between Alfred Berger and Tiina Parkkinen, the practice maintains offices in both Vienna and Helsinki. Like many young practices their bread and butter comes from small private commissions and teaching, while they plug away at international competitions looking for that big break.
For Berger and Parkkinen, that break came in 1995 when they were selected from 222 entries to design the master plan for the combined residence of the Nordic Embassies in Berlin. Inaugurated in October 1999, it has been acclaimed as architecturally one of the most exciting of the new embassies to be built in the capital.
Competition entries for the opera house in Linz (1998) and the Court House Complex in Leoben (1999) in Austria have been runners up, and the next big commission cannot be far away.

Das österreichisch-finnische Architektenteam Alfred Berger und Tiina Parkkinen unterhält Büros in Wien und Helsinki. Wie viele junge Büros beziehen sie einen Großteil ihrer Einkünfte aus kleinen Privataufträgen und Lehrverpflichtungen, während sie sich gleichzeitig in der Hoffnung auf den entscheidenden Durchbruch an internationalen Wettbewerben beteiligen.
Für Berger und Parkkinen kam dieser Durchbruch 1995, als sie unter 222 Teilnehmern am Wettbewerb um den Entwurf des Masterplans für die gemeinsame Botschaft der Nordischen Länder in Berlin ausgewählt wurden. Der im Oktober 1999 eingeweihte Bau fand große Anerkennung als eine der architektonisch gelungensten neuen Botschaften der Hauptstadt.
Wettbewerbsbeiträge für das Linzer Opernhaus und das Justizzentrum in Leoben belegten zweite Plätze – der nächste große Auftrag ist gewiss nicht fern.

Fruit d'une coopération austro-finlandaise entre Alfred Berger et Tiina Parkkinen, leur bureau est implanté à Vienne et à Helsinki. Comme beaucoup de jeunes architectes, ils tirent leurs principaux revenus de petites commandes privées et de l'enseignement, tout en participant à des concours internationaux dans l'espoir de décrocher une commande prestigieuse.
Pour Berger et Parkkinen, cette percée est venue en 1995, lorsqu'ils ont été sélectionnés parmi 222 candidats pour concevoir le schéma directeur du complexe regroupant les ambassades des divers pays scandinaves à Berlin. Inauguré en 1999, l'édifice a été salué comme une des plus belles réussites architecturales parmi les nouvelles ambassades construites dans la capitale allemande.
Ils ont participé aux concours concernant l'opéra de Linz (1998) et un Palais de Justice à Leoben, Autriche (1999); une autre commande importante ne saurait tarder.

Nordic Embassies, masterplan

In an unprecedented display of international cooperation, the Nordic countries chose to house their five embassies in the new German capital on a communal site. Berger + Parkkinen's competition-winning solution for the compound was to wrap a copper band around the site. Within this, five individual embassies have been designed by different architects: Nielsen, Nielsen & Nielsen (Denmark), VIIVA Arkkitehtuuri OY (Finland), Palmar Kristmundson (Iceland), Snøhetta a. s. (Norway), Wingårdh Arkitektkontor AB (Sweden), with one communal reception and information building, the "Felleshus", designed by Berger + Parkkinen.
Measuring 226 m long and 15 m high, the copper band or wall consists of 4000 individual louvres. Strategically placed openings allow light and air to pass to the buildings and streets behind and provide a rhythm and urban scale to the exterior facade. The soft green tones of the prepatinated metal act as a transition between the embassy complex and the surrounding Tiergarten.
The ground plan is based on a horseshoe shape, defined by the copper band, which is then cut up by intersecting paths, as if the remaining six volumes, of uniform height, have been carved out of a solid whole. The facades of the buildings define the edge of the negative space so that the voids between them become both separation and connection. Between Sweden and Finland, and Iceland and Denmark, these spaces are expressed as ponds.
From the main entrance on Rauchstrasse, the wide glazed opening makes the complex appear very open, but in fact the "Felleshus" is the only building accessible from outside the main piazza.

In einem beispiellosen Akt internationaler Zusammenarbeit beschlossen die nordeuropäischen Staaten, ihre fünf Botschaften in der neuen deutschen Hauptstadt auf einem gemeinsamen Gelände anzusiedeln. Der siegreiche Entwurf von Berger + Parkkinen sah vor, den gesamten Komplex mit einem Kupferband zu umgeben. Innerhalb dieses Bandes entstanden fünf eigenständige Bauten von verschiedenen Büros: Nielsen, Nielsen & Nielsen (Dänemark), VIIVA Arkkitehtuuri OY (Finnland), Palmar Kristmundson (Island), Snøhetta a. s. (Norwegen), Wingårdh Arkitektkontor AB (Schweden) sowie das »Felleshus«, das von Berger + Parkkinen entworfene gemeinsame Empfangs- und Informationsgebäude.
Die 226 m lange und 15 m hohe kupferne Wand besteht aus 4000 einzelnen Lamellen. Geschickt platzierte Öffnungen lassen Licht und Luft zu den dahinter liegenden Bauten und Straßen zirkulieren, rhythmisieren die Außenansicht und geben ihr urbanes Maß.
Der hufeisenförmige Grundriss der Anlage wird von dem Kupferband umgrenzt und von sich kreuzenden Wegen durchschnitten, so als seien die sechs etwa gleich hohen Gebäude aus einem massiven Block gehauen. Die Fassaden der Bauten markieren den Rand des negativen Raumes, so dass die Zwischenräume zugleich trennend und verbindend wirken. Zwischen den Botschaften Schwedens und Finnlands und auch zwischen denen Islands und Dänemarks werden diese Zwischenräume von kleinen Wasserflächen eingenommen.
Vom Haupteingang an der Rauchstraße lässt eine große Glastür den Komplex sehr offen erscheinen – tatsächlich ist das »Felleshus« jedoch das einzige Gebäude, das von außerhalb der zentralen Piazza zugänglich ist.

Témoignant d'une coopération internationale sans précédent, les pays scandinaves décidèrent de regrouper leur cinq ambassades sur le même site. La solution proposée par Berger + Parkkinen consistait à entourer le site d'une bande de cuivre. A l'intérieur de cette enceinte, cinq ambassades ont été dessinées par autant d'architectes : Nielsen, Nielsen & Nielsen (Danemark), VIIVA Arkkitehtuuri OY (Finlande), Palmar Kristmundson (Islande), Snøhetta a. s. (Norvège), Wingårdh Arkitektkontor AB (Suède), sans oublier un bâtiment commun regroupant les services d'accueil et de renseignements, le « Felleshus », conçu par Berger + Parkkinen.
Long de 226 m et haut de 15 m, ce « ruban » ou mur de cuivre consiste en 4000 éléments, dans lesquels des ouvertures disposées stratégiquement laissent passer l'air et la lumière, tout en donnant à la façade extérieure un rythme à l'échelle urbaine. Les tons vert pâle du métal pré-patiné constituent une transition entre le complexe des ambassades et les pelouses et plantations du Tiergarten.
Le plan d'ensemble est basé sur une forme en fer à cheval déterminée par la bande de cuivre, puis découpée par des sentiers qui s'entrecroisent, comme si les six volumes restants, de hauteur uniforme, avaient été taillés dans un seul bloc. Les façades des bâtiments définissent la limite de l'espace négatif, de sorte que les vides subsistant entre eux séparent et unissent à la fois. Entre la Suède et la Finlande, et entre l'Islande et le Danemark, ces espaces sont exprimés sous forme d'étangs.
La grande baie vitrée de l'entrée principale, sur la Rauchstrasse, donne l'impression d'un complexe très ouvert, alors qu'en fait le « Felleshus » est le seul bâtiment accessible de l'extérieur, les autres étant desservis par la piazza de l'enceinte.

Far right, entrance facade and copper wall. Right, detail of louvres in copper wall.

Ganz rechts: Eingangsfassade und Wand aus Kupfer. Rechts: Detail der aus Lamellen bestehenden Kupferwand.

Page de droite, la façade principale et le mur-ruban en cuivre. A droite, détails des contrevents de l'enceinte.

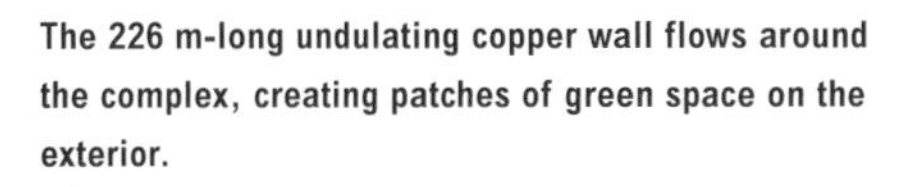

The 226 m-long undulating copper wall flows around the complex, creating patches of green space on the exterior.

Die 226 m lange geschwungene Kupferwand umspannt den Komplex und lässt auf der Außenseite Raum für kleine Grünzonen.

Vue partielle du mur de cuivre de 226 m de long qui entoure le complexe; ses ondulations créent des îlots de verdure à l'extérieur.

The plan is built up from a horseshoe dissected by channels that carve out the space to leave the five embassy blocks and the Felleshus.

Der Grundriss basiert auf einer Hufeisenform, die von Wegen durchzogen ist. Auf den so entstandenen Sektoren befinden sich die fünf Botschaftsgebäude und das Felleshus.

Le plan en fer à cheval avec les « canaux » qui divisent l'espace entre les ambassades et la « Felleshus ».

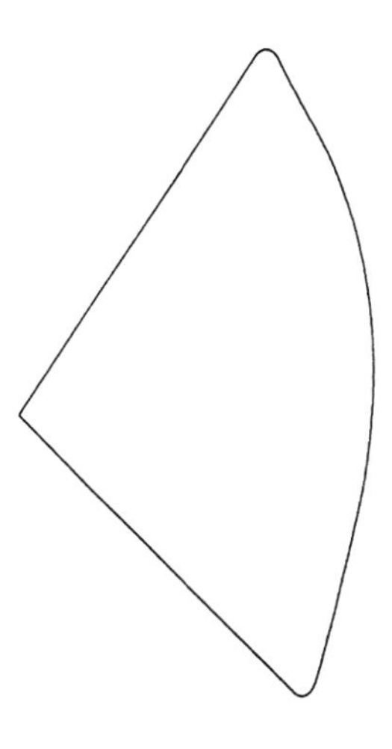

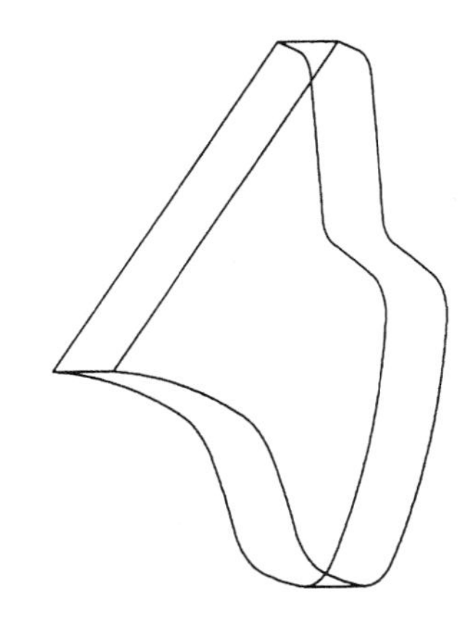

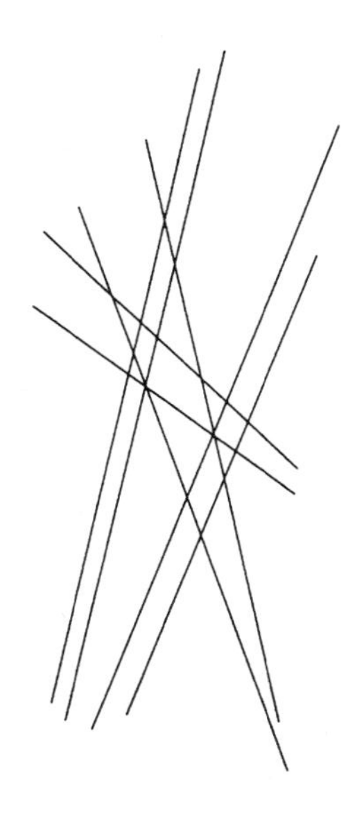

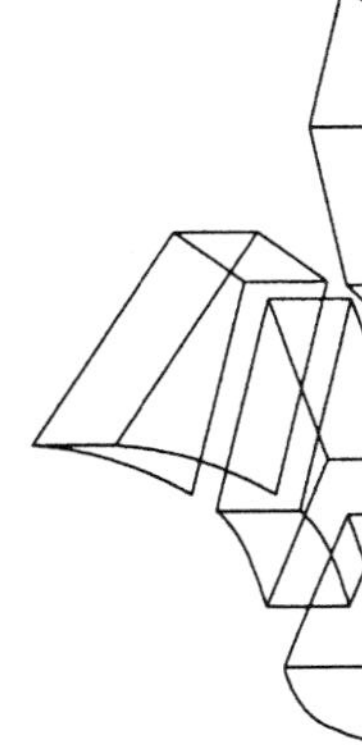

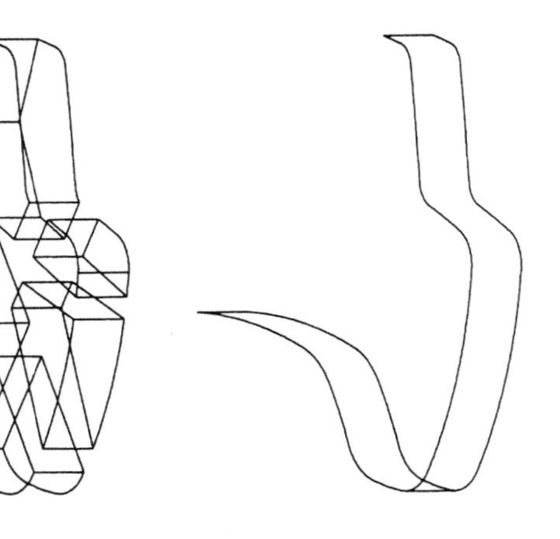

Facade of the Felleshus, left, which marks the entrance to the Nordic Embassies complex. Far left, the communal restaurant.

Links: Fassade des Felleshus am Eingang zum Botschaftskomplex der skandinavischen Länder. Ganz links das gemeinsame Restaurant.

A gauche, la façade du Felleshus, qui donne accès au complexe des ambassades scandinaves. Page de gauche, vue du restaurant.

1999 Berlin, Germany

Nordic Embassies, Felleshus

The Felleshus or "House for All" contains shared facilities such as conference rooms, an information centre, consulates and a restaurant, and serves as a main reception and security area for the complex. Closed wooden facades oppose the open spaces of the building's interior. The horizontal banding and narrow glazed strips inbetween give the impression of a single hollow volume enclosed in a wooden crate. Inside, the focus turns in on the full-height atrium, which splits the building in two. Glazed front and back covered with a steel and glass roof, it is a veritable void and even the staircase attempts to deny its own mass by being constructed of glass. Throughout the building, materials are kept plain and simple in quintessentially Nordic manner.

Das Felleshus oder »Haus für Alle« dient dem Komplex als Hauptempfangs- und Sicherheitsbereich. Es bündelt gemeinsam genutzte Einrichtungen wie Konferenzräume, ein Informationszentrum, Konsulate sowie ein Restaurant. Geschlossene Holzfassaden kontrastieren mit offenen Innenräumen. Die horizontalen Bänder mit den dazwischenliegenden schmalen Glasstreifen erzeugen den Eindruck eines großen, von einer hölzernen Kiste umschlossenen Hohlraums. Im Innern konzentriert sich alles auf das gebäudehohe Atrium, das den Bau in zwei Hälften teilt. Die verglaste Vorder- und Rückseite sowie die Dachkonstruktion aus Glas und Stahl lassen es nahezu als Leerstelle erscheinen, und selbst die ebenfalls gläserne Treppe versucht, ihre eigene Substanz zu verleugnen. Die schlichten Materialien im Haus entsprechen dem typischen Stil der skandinavischen Länder.

Le Felleshus ou « maison pour tous » abrite des services collectifs tels que salles de conférences, bureaux d'information et consulats ainsi qu'un restaurant, et constitue le principal centre d'accueil et de sécurité du complexe. Des façades en bois aveugles contrastent avec des espaces intérieurs très ouverts. Les bandeaux horizontaux séparés par des baies vitrées longues et étroites donnent l'impression d'un unique volume creux enfermé dans une boîte en bois. A l'intérieur, le principal centre d'intérêt est le hall prenant toute la hauteur, qui coupe le bâtiment en deux. Vitré à l'avant et à l'arrière et couvert d'une toiture en verre et acier, il constitue à proprement parler un vide; même l'escalier semble nier sa propre masse du fait qu'il est en verre. Dans l'ensemble du bâtiment, les matériaux sont simples et naturels, dans un style typiquement scandinave.

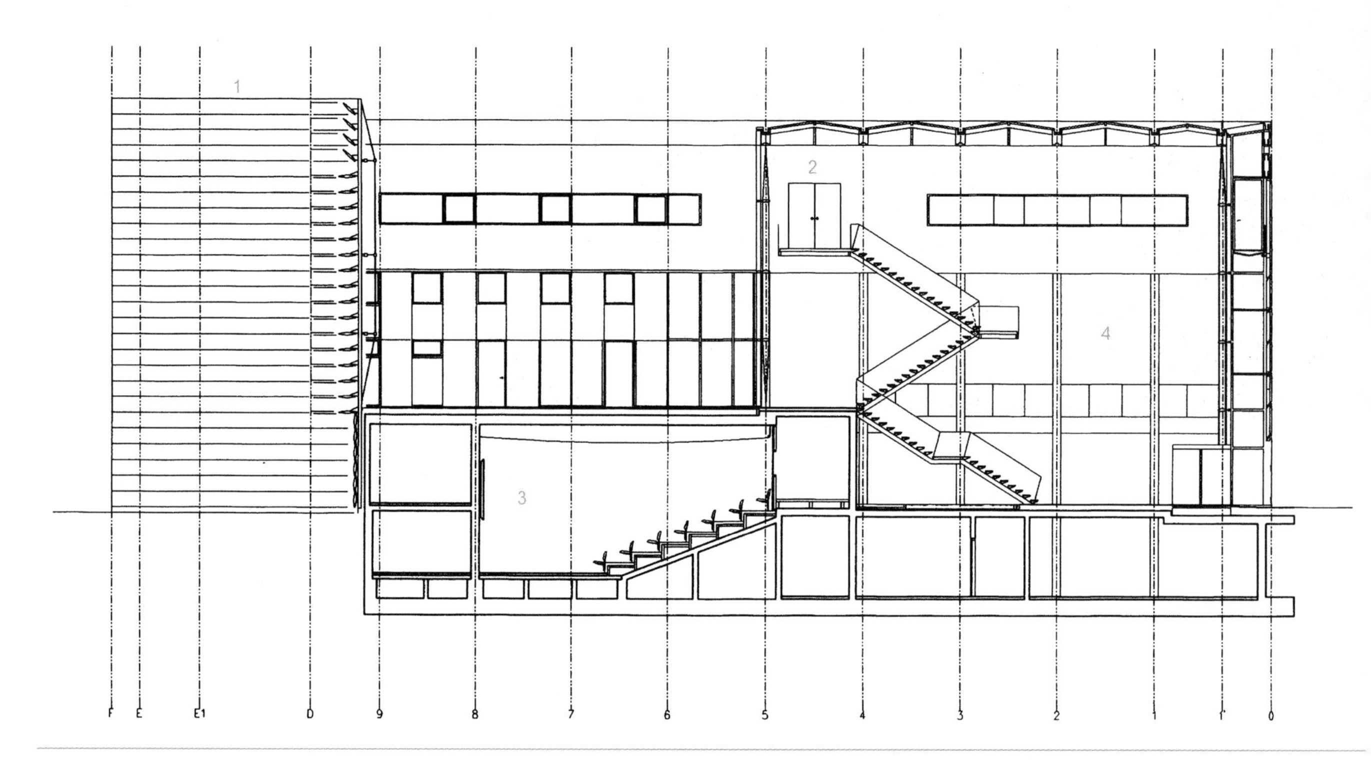

Section/ Schnitt/ Coupe

1 **copper wall/** Kupferwand/ mur de cuivre

2 **penthouse flat/** Penthousewohnung/ appartement du penthouse

3 **auditorium/** Auditorium/ auditorium

4 **atrium/** Atrium/ atrium

Glazed atrium and staircase

Verglastes Atrium und Treppenhaus

L'atrium vitré et cage d'escalier

Ice Stadium

Designed by Alfred Berger with Werner Krismer and Sepp Müller, the ice hockey stadium sits like an iceberg in downtown Vienna. Cold and grey during the day, every element from the external steel frame to the raked seating is washed in icy hues. At night, it is a bright ice palace whose glow can be seen for miles around.
Nothing about this building is concealed. The main supporting structure is on the outside, the pitched roofline follows the line of the banks of seating, and the transparent facades allow views of the activity within.

Das von Alfred Berger in Zusammenarbeit mit Werner Krismer und Sepp Müller entworfene Eishockeystadion liegt einem Eisberg gleich in der Wiener Innenstadt. Tagsüber erscheint es kalt und grau; sämtliche Elemente, angefangen beim außen liegenden Tragrahmen aus Stahl bis hin zu den schräg angeordneten Tribünenplätzen, sind in eisigen Farbtönen gehalten. Bei Nacht wird es zum hell erleuchteten Eispalast, dessen Schein kilometerweit zu sehen ist.
Nichts an diesem Bauwerk ist verdeckt. Der Haupttragrahmen liegt außen, das geneigte Dach folgt den Konturen der Sitzreihen, und die transparente Fassade gestattet Einblicke in das Geschehen im Stadion.

Dessiné par Alfred Berger avec Werner Krismer et Sepp Müller, le stade de hockey sur glace se dresse comme un iceberg au centre de Vienne. Froid et gris de jour, tous ses éléments, de l'ossature d'acier extérieure aux gradins, sont lavés de tons de glace. De nuit, il devient un lumineux palais de glace visible à des kilomètres à la ronde.
Dans cet édifice, rien n'est caché. La principale structure portante est à l'extérieur, la toiture inclinée suit la pente des gradins, et les façades transparentes donnent un aperçu de ce qui se passe à l'intérieur.

The stadium interior, left, and the soaring roof, far left

Das Innere des Stadions (links) und das aufragende Dach (ganz links)

L'intérieur du stade (à gauche) et sa toiture qui s'élève hardiment (page de gauche)

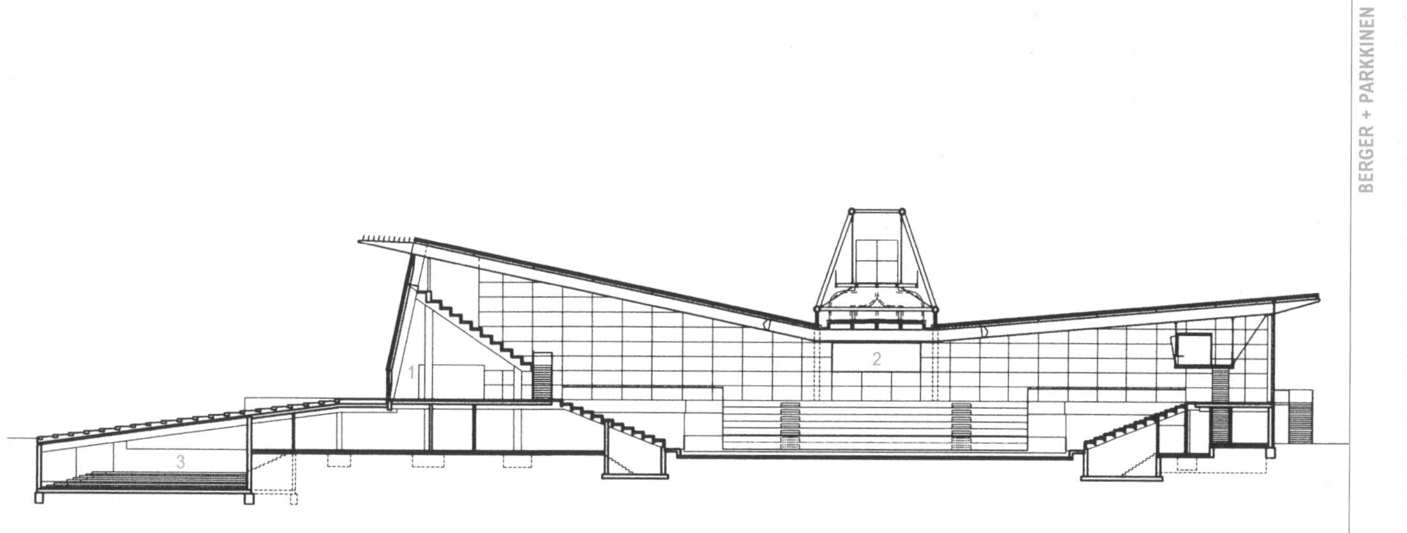

Section/ Schnitt/ Elévation

1 **entrance hall/** Eingangshalle/ hall d'entrée

2 **main ice arena/** Eissporthalle/ partinoire

3 **bowling arena/** Bowlingbahn/ bowling

Wendell Burnette

9830 North 17th Street, Phoenix, Arizona, USA tel +1 602 395 1091 fax +1 602 395 0839 e-mail burnette@azlink.com

Wendell Burnette

born	1962 Nashville, Tennessee, USA
studied	1980-83 Apprenticeship at Taliesin West, Scottsdale, Arizona
previous practice	William Mims Associates, Nashville, Tennessee; Taliesin West, Scottsdale, Arizona; William P Bruder Architect, New River, Arizona; 1996 established Wendell Burnette Architects

Selected projects

New Phoenix Central Library (with William Bruder)	1995	Phoenix, Arizona, USA
Burnette Studio/Residence	1995	Phoenix, Arizona, USA
Offices for David Michael Miller Associates	1999	Scottsdale, Arizona, USA
ASU Desert Arboretum Park	unbuilt	Tempe, Arizona, USA
Schall Residence	1999	Phoenix, Arizona, USA
Tocker Residence	2000	Phoenix, Arizona, USA
Nicholas Residence	unbuilt	Paradise Valley, Arizona, USA

Largely self-taught through extensive travel in Europe, the USA and Mexico, Burnette spent three years at the Frank Lloyd Wright Foundation at Taliesin West and eleven years in the Arizona office of William Bruder. His architecture responds to the specifics of a site and the client, and his buildings relate to the landscape. The desert, omnipresent in Arizona life, is a guiding force that Burnette both respects and learns from, resulting in houses that are cool and tranquil, even in urban settings. Water features, landscaping and careful planting, designed in association with Debra Burnette Landscape Design, keep residents cool, while careful screening of urban clutter focuses attention on stunning views.
Burnette approaches building as a craft, making the most out of a tight budget. Even when he uses inexpensive or industrial materials, he treats them in a way that brings out their beauty.

Wendell Burnette, der sich seine Kenntnisse auf ausgedehnten Reisen in Europa, den USA und Mexiko weitgehend autodidaktisch aneignete, verbrachte drei Jahre in der Frank Lloyd Wright-Stiftung in Taliesin West und elf Jahre im Büro von William Bruder in Arizona.
Seine in Beziehung zur Landschaft stehende Architektur geht stets auf die Besonderheiten des Geländes und auf den Bauherrn ein. Die in Arizona allgegenwärtige Wüste, die Burnette respektiert und von der er lernt, spielt dabei eine leitende Rolle; selbst in einem städtischen Umfeld entstehen so kühle, ruhige Häuser. Der Einsatz von Wasser und wohl überlegter Bepflanzung, geplant in Zusammenarbeit mit Debra Burnette Landscape Design, sorgt für größtmögliche Kühle, während die effektive Abschirmung vom urbanen Chaos den Blick auf eindrucksvolle Aussichten lenkt.
Burnette betrachtet Bauen als Handwerk und ist bemüht, ein begrenztes Budget optimal auszunutzen. Selbst wenn er preiswerte oder industrielle Materialien verwendet, bringt er ihre Schönheit zum Vorschein.

En grande partie autodidacte, Burnette s'est formé au cours de ses voyages à travers l'Europe, les Etats-Unis et le Mexique. Il a passé trois ans à la Fondation Frank Lloyd Wright à Taliesin West, et onze ans en Arizona dans les bureaux de William Bruder.
Son architecture répond aux spécificités du site et aux besoins du client, et ses constructions sont toujours reliées au paysage. Le désert, omniprésent dans l'Arizona, est une force que Burnette respecte et qui le guide. Il en résulte des maisons fraîches et paisibles, même dans un environnement urbain. L'utilisation de l'eau, le dessin des jardins et les plantations soigneusement conçues (le tout réalisé en association avec Debra Burnette Landscape Design) donnent de la fraîcheur aux habitants, tandis qu'une protection minutieuse contre le chaos urbain tourne l'attention vers des panoramas surprenants.
Burnette aborde la construction comme un métier artisanal, tirant un parti maximum d'un budget serré. Même lorsqu'il utilise des matériaux industriels ou bon marché, il sait révéler leur beauté intrinsèque.

Burnette Studio/Residence

Burnette describes this house built for himself and his wife Debra as a Band-Aid for the ca. 3 m-wide scar that splits the desert site, a man-made canyon. The house blocks out views of surrounding houses and focuses on the horizon, creating a sense of isolation in a suburban setting. Parallel rows of post-tensioned cantilevered masonry monoliths form a screen up either side of the building, supporting concrete floor and ceiling slabs that span the gorge. On the north side, posts are 1.2 m wide leaving wide glass slots between them, creating a disjointed view of the landscape and flooding the interior with north light; on the south side posts are twice the width, forming a sun screen.
Decoration is minimal, but a rich palette of materials, enhanced by natural lighting effects, enlivens the space: the screen casts a sundial effect across the floor; wooden shuttering used for the in situ concrete is recycled back into the building; concrete formwork has been deliberately rendered a deep reddish brown by a water-based form release agent; concrete panels have been sealed and buffed to a reflective silvery finish.
Below the studio floor, a fully shaded evaporation pool emits water via a trough, similar to a desert canyon seep, which trickles down the slope, creating a cool microclimate in the interior courtyard.

Burnette beschreibt das Atelier- und Wohnhaus für sich und seine Frau Debra als Pflaster für die etwa 3 m breite Narbe, die das Baugelände in der Wüste in Form eines künstlichen Canyons durchzieht. Parallele Reihen vorgespannter, vorkragender Mauerblöcke bilden an beiden Seiten des Gebäudes Schutzwände, die den die Schlucht querenden Betonboden und die Deckenplatten tragen. Auf der Nordseite sind die weiten Zwischenräume zwischen den 1,20 m breiten Stützen verglast, wodurch sich zergliederte Ausblicke auf die Landschaft bieten und das Innere Licht von Norden erhält; auf der Südseite sind die Stützen doppelt so breit und bilden einen wirksamen Sonnenschutz.
Schmuckformen sind auf ein Minimum beschränkt, aber eine differenzierte Materialvielfalt belebt den Raum: die Schatten der Pfeilerwand wirken auf dem Boden wie eine Sonnenuhr; die Holzverschalung, die für den in situ gegossenen Beton benutzt wurde, wird im Gebäude wiederverwendet; durch den bewussten Einsatz eines Entschalungsmittels verfärbte sich der Beton tief rotbraun; die Oberfläche der Betonplatten wurde versiegelt und erhielt durch Politur einen silbrigen Schimmer.
Ähnlich wie in einem Wüstencanyon an den Wänden Sickerwasser herunterrinnt, fließt unterhalb des Atelierbodens aus einem vollständig im Schatten liegenden Verdunstungsbecken Wasser durch eine Rinne, was im Innenhof ein kühles Mikroklima erzeugt.

Burnette décrit la maison et atelier qu'il a dessinée pour lui-même et pour sa femme Debra comme un emplâtre sur une cicatrice de 3 m de large qui traverse le site désertique, canyon fait de main d'homme. La maison, visuellement coupée des constructions environnantes, est axée sur l'horizon, suscitant une impression d'isolement dans un cadre urbain. Des rangées parallèles de monolithes en porte-à-faux, formant écran des deux côtés du bâtiment, soutiennent les dalles de plafond et le plancher en béton qui enjambent le ravin. Au nord, des piliers larges de 1,20 m séparés par de vastes pans de verre offrent une vue discontinue du paysage et éclairent généreusement l'intérieur. Du côté sud, des piliers deux fois plus larges font office de pare-soleil.
La décoration est minimale, mais une riche gamme de matériaux, mise en valeur par des effets d'éclairage naturels, anime l'espace : les écrans projettent sur le sol un effet de cadran solaire; le coffrage en bois du béton coulé in situ est réutilisé à l'intérieur, délibérément teinté en brun-rouge foncé par un agent de décoffrage à base aqueuse; les panneaux en béton ont été stabilisés et polis de sorte à prendre un aspect argenté et réfléchissant.
Sous le plancher de l'atelier, une nappe d'évaporation émet par un « entonnoir » semblable à un canyon du désert de l'eau qui coule lentement sur la pente, créant un microclimat frais dans le patio.

Side walls are formed by slabs of masonry, right. Left, the oasis that helps to cool the house.

Rechts: Die Seitenwände setzen sich aus gemauerten Platten zusammen. Links: Die »Oase« trägt zur Kühlung des Hauses bei.

Les murs latéraux en maçonnerie (page de droite), et l'« oasis » qui rafraîchit la maison (à gauche).

View into the living room at night

Blick in den Wohnraum bei Nacht

Le séjour tel qu'il apparaît la nuit

Visitors enter the house over stepping stones through the oasis, left as seen from above. Below, view straight through the house from main bedroom at the rear.

Links: Besucher betreten das Haus über Trittsteine in der »Oase« (von oben gesehen). Unten: Blick durch das gesamte Haus vom hinten gelegenen Hauptschlafraum.

A gauche : pour entrer dans la maison, les visiteurs doivent franchir l'« oasis » sur de hautes marches (vue d'en haut). Ci-dessous, vue nocturne à travers la maison ; au premier plan, la chambre principale.

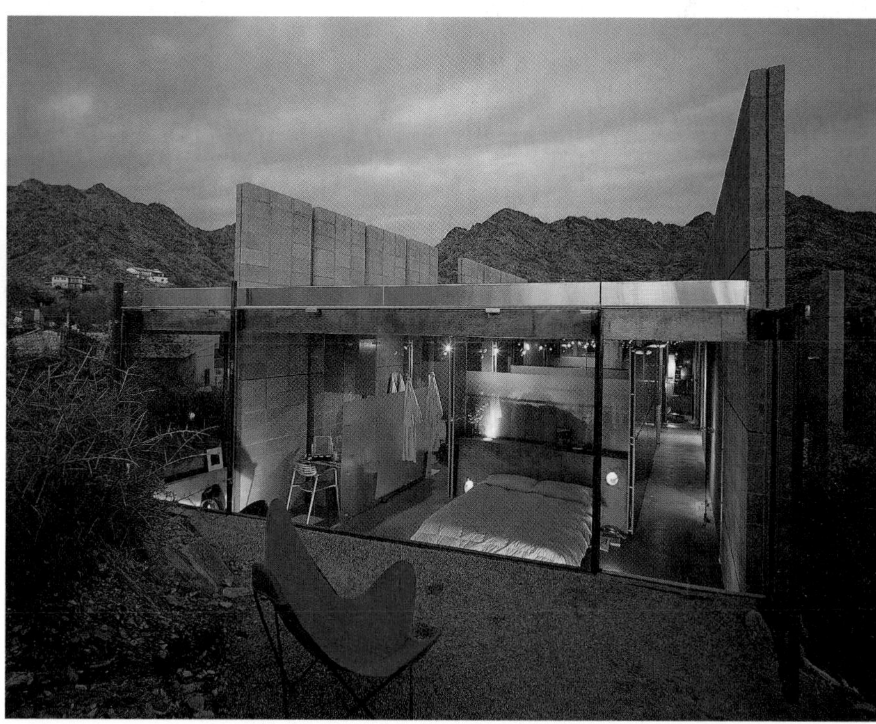

The high wall of the Schall Residence encloses house and courtyard.

Die hohe Wand des Hauses Schall umschließt Haus und Innenhof.

Le haut mur de la résidence Schall enveloppe la maison et sa cour-jardin.

1999 **Phoenix, Arizona, USA**

Schall Residence

Heavily influenced by the architecture of North Africa, the Schall Residence sits in a courtyard enclosed by a high wall, setting it apart from its environment atop Phoenix's main thoroughfare, Central Avenue. The house is conceived as a ship's hull, a swollen wooden structure finished in grey cement mortar wash. The living room projects from the top like a crow's nest enjoying the views in peace.
Outside, cooling evaporation towers, the sound of running water, and the fragrance of blooming citrus pamper the senses and take the mind off the urban sprawl on the other side of the wall.

Das stark von nordafrikanischer Architektur beeinflusste Haus Schall steht in einem von einer hohen Mauer umgebenen Hof isoliert von seinem Umfeld am oberen Ende der Central Avenue, der Hauptdurchgangsstraße von Phoenix. Die mit grauem Mörtelüberzug verkleidete, abgerundete Holzkonstruktion ähnelt einem Schiffsrumpf. Einem Mastkorb gleich ragt das Wohnzimmer hervor und bietet großartige Ausblicke.
Im Außenbereich betören kühlende Verdunstungstürme, das Geräusch fließenden Wassers und der Duft blühender Zitruspflanzen die Sinne und lassen die Stadtlandschaft auf der anderen Seite der Mauer vergessen.

Fortement influencée par l'architecture d'Afrique du Nord, la résidence Schall est construite dans une cour entourée d'un haut mur, qui l'isole de son environnement, en haut de la Central Avenue de Phoenix. La maison est conçue comme une coque de bateau, structure en bois renflée, revêtue d'un enduit de mortier gris. Du séjour perché en haut du bâtiment comme un nid de corbeau, la vue est spectaculaire.
A l'extérieur, des tours d'évaporation rafraîchissent l'air, le clapotis de l'eau et le parfum des agrumes en fleurs flattent les sens et détournent l'esprit de la ville qui s'étend anarchiquement de l'autre côté de l'enceinte.

Landscaped outdoor spaces, fragrant planting and water features create a pleasant internal environment.

Landschaftsgärtnerisch gestaltete Außenflächen, duftende Pflanzen und Wasseranlagen schaffen ein angenehmes Binnenklima.

Des espaces paysagés plantés d'espèces odorantes et des plans d'eau créent un cadre plaisant.

Windows cut into the wall create interest on the outer skin, above, and frame the views, right.

In die Mauern eingeschnittene Fenster gestalten die Außenwand abwechslungsreich (oben) und rahmen die Ausblicke (rechts).

Les baies découpées dans le mur animent la façade (ci-dessus) et encadrent le paysage (page de droite).

Computer-generated images of the Tocker Residence, conceived as "a box of light".

Computerbilder des Hauses Tocker, das als »Lichtkasten« konzipiert wurde.

Images informatisées de la résidence Tocker, conçue comme un « caisson lumineux ».

Tocker Residence

Built on an abandoned site on the southern tip of a volcanic mountain ridge known locally as Echo Mountain Foothills, the residence offers spectacular views across downtown Phoenix to the South Sierra Estrella mountain ranges, but is also right next to a busy road. Burnette has created a haven for the residents by pushing the house back into the north-west corner of the site and putting all the main living spaces on the second level. Structurally the building is a very simple, single volume, which was cost-effective and quick to erect. Conventional framing and a one-coat stucco system are supported on a lateral pin-wheel brace of charcoal masonry walls. Load-bearing planes extend out into the site. The effect, according to Burnette, is "from the street, a five-sided box of light with no apparent thickness floating above and within the dark landscape".
A quarter of the budget is dedicated solely to hardscape and landscape designed by his wife Debra Burnette. A lush forest of Mesquite is punctured with the colour of Ironwood in bloom (a cherry blossom colour), while night-blooming cacti create a moonlight garden.

Das Haus Tocker steht auf der Südspitze eines als Echo Mountain Foothills bekannten vulkanischen Bergrückens auf einem aufgelassenen Gelände und bietet weite Blicke über die Innenstadt von Phoenix bis hin zum Höhenzug der South Sierra Estrella Bergen – dennoch liegt es an einer stark befahrenen Straße.
Indem er das Haus in die nordwestliche Ecke des Geländes zurückschob und sämtliche Wohnräume auf die zweite Ebene legte, schuf Burnette einen Zufluchtsort für die Bewohner. In konstruktiver Hinsicht ein sehr schlichter Baukörper, ließ sich das Haus kosteneffektiv und schnell errichten. Eine herkömmliche Rahmenkonstruktion und einlagiger Putz kommen auf gemauerten Wänden zu liegen. Tragende Flächen setzen sich in die Landschaft hinein fort. Burnette zufolge ist die Wirkung »von der Straße aus die eines fünfseitigen Lichtkastens ohne erkennbare Tiefe, der über und in die dunkle Landschaft driftet«.
Ein Viertel des Budgets ist ausschließlich für die von seiner Frau Debra Burnette geplante landschaftsgärtnerische Gestaltung vorgesehen. Mesquitbäume formieren sich zu einem Dickicht, gesprenkelt von den kirschblütenfarbigen Blüten des Eisenbaum, während nachtblühende Kakteen einen »Garten im Mondlicht« bilden.

Construite sur un site abandonné à la pointe sud d'une arête volcanique localement connue sous le nom d'Echo Mountain Foothills, la résidence Tocker offre des vues spectaculaires sur le centre de Phoenix et sur les montagnes de la South Sierra Estrella, tout en étant proche d'une route très fréquentée.
Burnette a créé un îlot protégé pour les résidents en repoussant la maison dans l'angle nord-ouest du site, et en mettant les pièces d'habitation à l'étage. Structurellement, c'est un volume unique très simple, dont la construction fut rapide et peu coûteuse : une ossature conventionnelle, un système de stuc monocouche sur des murs latéraux en maçonnerie au charbon de bois, des murs porteurs se prolongeant dans le site. Selon Burnette, l'effet produit est « vu de la rue, un caisson lumineux à cinq faces sans épaisseur apparente flottant au-dessus du sombre paysage ».
Un quart du budget fut consacré exclusivement au jardin paysagé, conçu par sa femme Debra Burnette. Une luxuriante forêt de mesquites est parsemée de taches de couleurs du bois de fer en pleine floraison (couleur des fleurs du cerisier), tandis que des cactées à floraison nocturne créent un jardin lunaire.

Camenzind Gräfensteiner

Samariterstrasse 5, 8030 Zurich, Switzerland
tel + 41 1 253 9500 fax + 41 1 253 9510 e-mail info@camenzindgrafensteiner.com
web www.camenzindgrafensteiner.com

Stefan Camenzind

born	1963 Zurich, Switzerland
studied	1987 Technikum Winterthur, Switzerland; 1992 University of North London
previous practice	Nicholas Grimshaw and Partners, London; Renzo Piano Building Workshop, Paris
	1995 co-founded Camenzind Gräfensteiner

Michael Gräfensteiner

born	1964 Zurich, Switzerland
studied	1987 Technikum Winterthur, Switzerland
previous practice	Atelier Cube Architects, Lausanne; Angélil/Graham Architecture, Zurich/Los Angeles
	1995 co-founded Camenzind Gräfensteiner

Selected projects

Buchholz sports centre	1998 Uster, Switzerland
Drusberg apartments	2001 Zurich, Switzerland
Hasenacker sports centre	2001 Männedorf, Switzerland
Siemens Communications Centre	2001 Zurich, Switzerland
22 Prestige Houses	2001 Zollikon, Switzerland

Most of the practice's work has been won through international competitions; Stefan Camenzind and Michael Gräfensteiner launched their practice on the foundation of the Buchholz sports centre commission which they were awarded in 1994. Unlike other Swiss architects, they have avoided the Herzog + de Meuron school of sleek modernist minimalism. Camenzind Gräfensteiner's buildings are more rough and ready, delighting in quirky shapes, bright colours, and exposed structure. "The process of design begins with us freeing ourselves from preconceived ideas by engaging in a wide collaboration with both the design team, potential users and occupants. We encourage everyone in the development of their own concepts and ideas which flow into our holistic analysis of the project, emerging patterns and recurring structure. This process evolves into design."

Das Duo errang einen Großteil seiner Aufträge bei internationalen Wettbewerben. Stefan Camenzind und Michael Gräfensteiner gründeten ihr Büro, nachdem sie 1994 den Auftrag zum Bau des Sportzentrums Buchholz erhielten. Im Gegensatz zu anderen Schweizer Architekten folgen sie nicht dem Beispiel des glatten, modernistischen Minimalismus von Herzog + de Meuron. Ihre Bauten sind ungeschliffener, erfreuen durch ungewöhnliche Formen, leuchtende Farben und sichtbar gelassene Konstruktion. »Der Entwurfsprozess beginnt damit, dass wir uns von vorgefassten Ideen befreien, indem wir auf breiter Basis mit dem Entwurfsteam und möglichen Nutzern und Bewohnern zusammenarbeiten. Wir ermuntern alle, ihre eigenen Konzepte und Ideen zu entwickeln, die in unsere umfassende Analyse des Projekts einfließen, wodurch sich Muster und wiederholende Strukturen ergeben. Dieser Prozess führt schließlich zum Entwurf.«

Le bureau doit la majeure partie de ses réalisations à des concours internationaux. Stefan Camenzind et Michael Gräfensteiner ont lancé leur bureau grâce à la construction du centre sportif de Buchholz, qui leur fut confiée en 1994. Contrairement à d'autres architectes suisses, ils évitent le style moderniste minimaliste de l'école Herzog + de Meuron. Les constructions de Camenzind Gräfensteiner sont plus brutes et vigoureuses ; ils aiment les formes contournées, les couleurs vives et les structures visibles. « Nous commençons le processus de projet en nous libérant des idées préconçues grâce à une large coopération avec l'équipe de design et les occupants ou utilisateurs potentiels. Nous les encourageons à développer leurs propres idées et concepts, qui viennent enrichir notre analyse globale du projet. Des schémas et structures récurrentes finissent par émerger, et ce processus aboutit au design. »

Buchholz sports centre

Awarded in a competition in 1994, the SF 9 million project was the financial foundation of the practice. The 48 x 46-m sports centre houses three sports fields and can accommodate up to 1 000 spectators on retractable seating. Though constructed on a tight budget using mass-produced industrial materials, the building manages to convey a sense of occasion. All walls are glass - transparent on the north and south facades, translucent on the east and west - creating a light, spacious interior. The building is entered on an upper level above the changing rooms, the floor level then dropping back down with the tiers of seating revealing the 11 m-high arena, dominated by a full-length glazed wall and soaring angular I-beams.

The entrance hall contains the ticket office, an independent volume penetrating the glazed wall, rendered a warm red inside the main building and clad in wood where it pushes through the glazed wall to the outside. Reducing the number of elements and making them multifunctional (for instance, light fittings housed in the perforated steel decking roof, glazing with high U-value for insulation) has kept the cost down and maintained the clarity of the structure. Since completion, the building has been awarded the Prix fédéral suisse des Beaux-Arts 1998, the German Bauwelt Award 1999, and the American Institute of Architects International Design Award 2000.

Der 1994 bei einem Wettbewerb gewonnene Auftrag für das Sportzentrum Buchholz mit einem Budget von 9 Millionen SF verhalf dem Büro zu einer finanziellen Grundlage. Das 48 x 46 m messende Sportzentrum umfasst drei Spielfelder und kann auf einer Teleskoptribüne bis zu 1 000 Zuschauer unterbringen. Obwohl der Bau mit einem begrenztem Budget unter Verwendung serienmäßig produzierter Industriematerialien errichtet wurde, gelingt es ihm, die Besucher zu beeindrucken. Sämtliche Wände bestehen aus Glas – transparent auf der Nord- und Südseite, transluzent auf der Ost- und Westseite – wodurch ein lichter, weiter Innenraum entsteht. Man betritt das Gebäude auf einer höher liegenden Ebene oberhalb der Umkleidekabinen. Von hier senkt sich der Boden mit den Sitzreihen ab und gibt den Blick frei auf den 11 m hohen Innenraum, der von einer raumhohen Glaswand und aufragenden Doppel-T-Trägern beherrscht wird.

In der Eingangshalle ist die Kasse als eigenständiger, die Glaswand durchbrechender Baukörper untergebracht. Er bringt einen warmen Rotton in den Hauptbau und ist an der Stelle, an der er die Glaswand nach außen durchstößt, mit Holz verkleidet.

Die Beschränkung auf wenige, multifunktionale Elemente (Beleuchtungskörper in der perforierten Stahlbedachung oder Verglasung mit transparenter Wärmedämmung), trug zur Reduzierung der Kosten bei und bewahrte die konstruktive Klarheit. Der Bau erhielt 1998 den Prix fédéral suisse des Beaux-Arts, den Bauwelt Preis 1999 und den American Institute of Architects International Design Award 2000.

Camenzind Gräfensteiner ayant remporté le concours organisé en 1994, ce projet de 9 millions SF a été le fondement financier du bureau. Le centre sportif de 48 sur 46 m abrite trois terrains de sport et peut accueillir jusqu'à 1 000 spectateurs sur des sièges rétractables. Bien que construit avec un budget très serré, en faisant appel à des matériaux industriels fabriqués en série, le bâtiment évite la banalité. Tous les murs sont en verre – transparent sur les façades nord et sud, translucide à l'est et à l'ouest –, créant un espace intérieur clair et aéré. L'entrée se fait par le niveau supérieur, au-dessus des vestiaires ; le plancher descend ensuite vers les gradins, révélant l'arène haute de 11 m, dominée sur toute sa longueur par un mur entièrement vitré et d'impressionnants poteaux en I.

Le hall d'entrée contient la billetterie, volume indépendant qui perce le mur vitré ; traitée en rouge soutenu à l'intérieur du bâtiment principal, elle est revêtue de bois dans la partie située à l'extérieur.

La réduction du nombre d'éléments et leur utilisation multifonctionnelle (par exemple dispositifs d'éclairage logés dans la toiture en acier perforé, vitrages à haut indice d'isolation …), ont permis de limiter le coût de la construction tout en assurant la transparence structurelle. Achevé en 1998, l'édifice a reçu le Prix fédéral suisse des Beaux-Arts, le prix allemand de Bauwelt 1999 et l'American Institute of Architects International Design Award 2000.

The building is supported by vast I-beams, left. Above, the ends of the sports centre are transparent, allowing views into the sports hall.

Links: Der Bau wird von riesigen Doppel-T-Trägern gehalten. Oben: Die verglasten Seitenwände gestatten Einblicke in die Sporthalle.

A gauche : le bâtiment est porté par de massives poutres en I. Ci-dessus : les façades transparentes permettent de voir la salle de l'extérieur.

Entrance facade of the sports hall, above. Changing rooms are tucked below the main foyer. Right, spectators' seating.

Oben: Eingangsfassade der Sporthalle; unterhalb der Zugangsrampe zum Foyer befinden sich die Umkleiden. Rechts: Zuschauertribüne.

Ci-dessus, la façade d'entrée de la salle de sport ; les vestiaires sont aménagés sous le foyer. A droite, vue partielle de l'intérieur et des gradins.

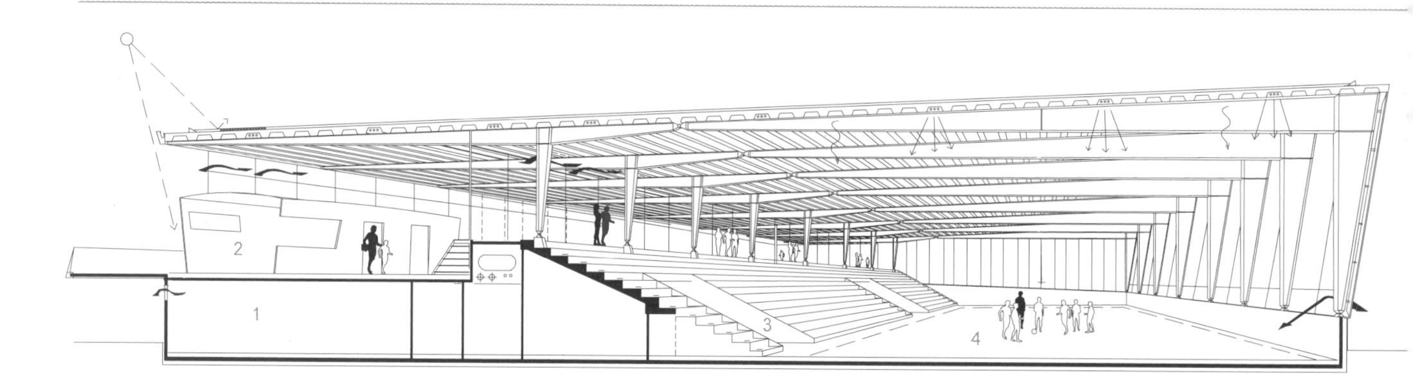
2
1
3
4

3D section/ Perspektivischer Schnitt/ Coupe-perspective tridimensionnelle

1 **changing rooms/** Umkleiden/ vestiaires
2 **entrance hall/** Eingangshalle/ foyer
3 **retractable seating for spectators/** einziehbare Zuschauertribüne/ gradins repliables
4 **sports pitch/** Spielfeld/ terrain

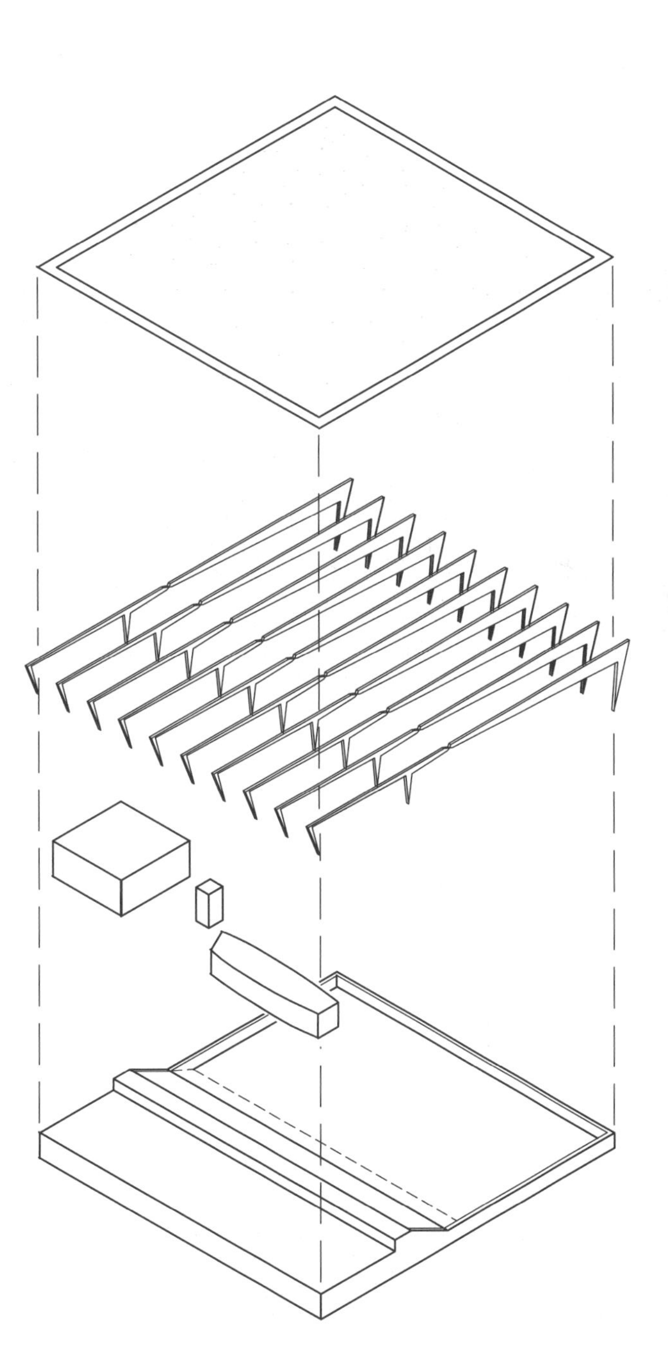

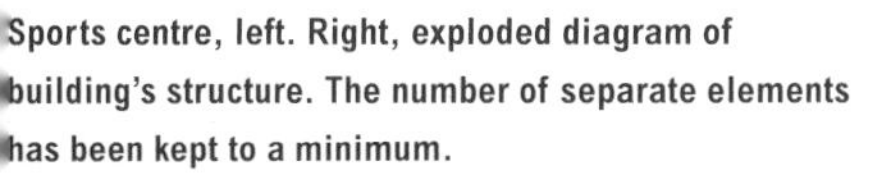

Sports centre, left. Right, exploded diagram of building's structure. The number of separate elements has been kept to a minimum.

Links: Sporthalle; rechts: Konstruktionsdiagramm. Die Zahl der Einzelelemente ist so gering wie möglich gehalten.

A gauche, le terrain et les gradins. A droite, diagramme éclaté de l'édifice ; la structure a été réalisée avec un nombre minimal d'éléments spécifiques.

Facade, far right, and central circulation core, above

Rechts die Fassade, oben das zentrale Atrium mit interner Erschließung

La façade (page de droite) ; le foyer et l'espace central de circulation (ci-dessus)

2001 **Zurich, Switzerland**

Siemens Communications Centre

Another project won in competition, the SF 15 million Siemens Communications Centre in Zurich will house offices for 1 000 staff, two restaurants, a cafeteria, exhibition space and a 190-seat auditorium. Camenzind Gräfensteiner conceived the building as being as transparent as possible, with visual links between floors and interior spaces opened up. This is achieved through a structure that is essentially a three-storey oval ring, the three floors seeming to float above each other around a glazed atrium and circulation space.

Auch das Siemens Communications Centre in Zürich ging aus einem Wettbewerb hervor, den Camenzind Gräfensteiner für sich entscheiden konnten. Für ein Budget von 15 Millionen SF entstehen Büros für 1 000 Mitarbeiter, zwei Restaurants, eine Cafeteria, Ausstellungsflächen und ein Auditorium mit 190 Sitzplätzen. Die Architekten bemühten sich um maximale Transparenz und gestalteten die optischen Verbindungen zwischen den Geschossen und Innenräumen so offen wie möglich. Diese Offenheit wird durch einen dreigeschossigen ovalen Baukörper erreicht, dessen drei Ebenen ein verglastes Atrium und Verbindungswege umschließen und übereinander zu schweben scheinen.

Autre projet ayant fait l'objet d'un concours, le Centre de communications Siemens de Zurich, représentant 15 millions SF, comporte des bureaux pour 1 000 personnes, deux restaurants, une cafétéria, un espace d'exposition et un auditorium de 190 places. Camenzind Gräfensteiner ont conçu un édifice aussi transparent que possible, avec des liens visuels entre les niveaux et des espaces intérieurs très ouverts. Ce résultat est obtenu grâce à une structure qui est essentiellement un anneau ovale à trois niveaux, les trois planchers semblant suspendus l'un au-dessus de l'autre autour d'un atrium vitré et de l'espace de circulation.

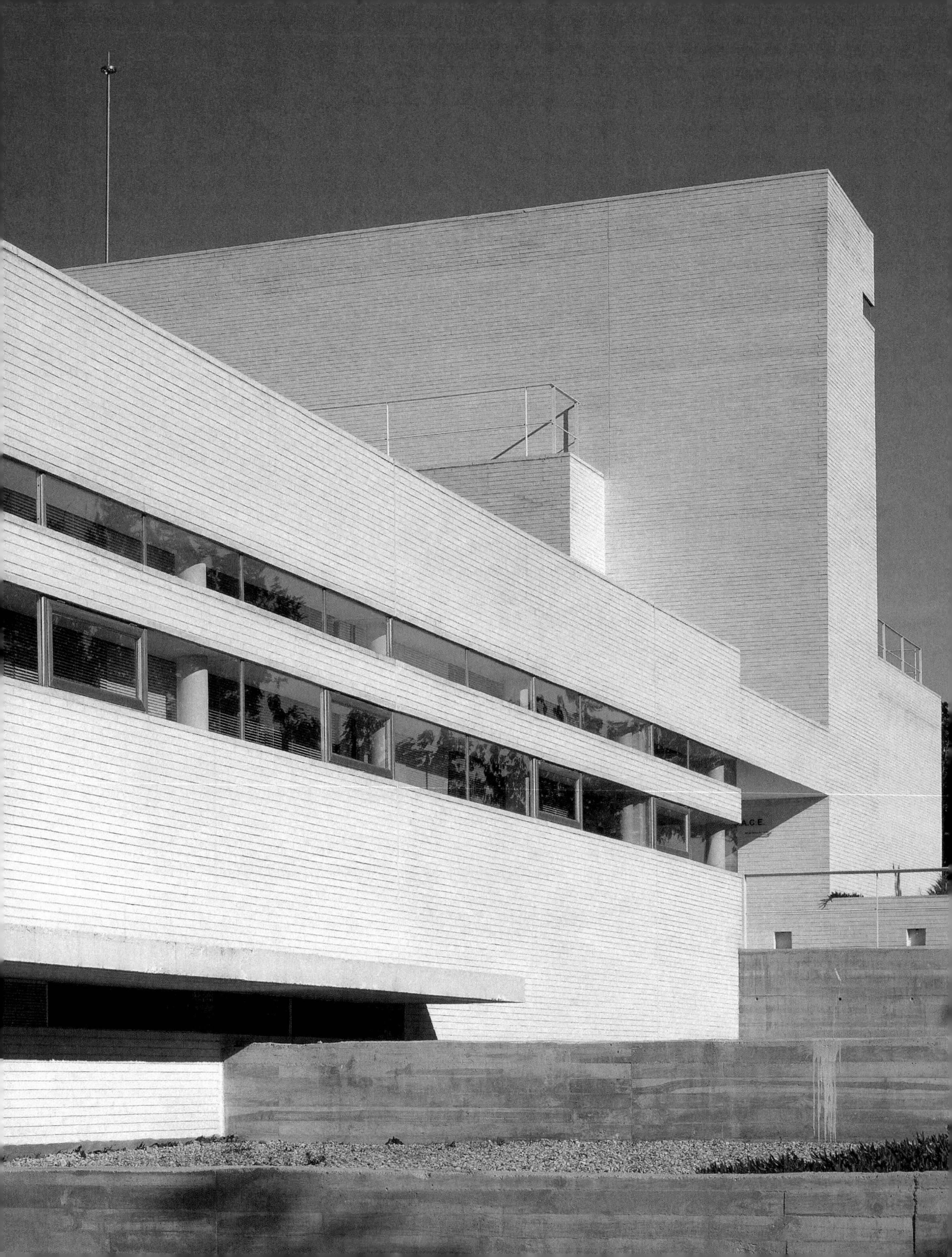

Estudio Cano Lasso

alle Guecho 27, 28023 Madrid, Spain | tel +34 91 307 7073 fax +34 91 307 7789 e-mail canolasso@nexo.es

ego Cano Pintos		
rn	1954	Santiago de Compostela
udied	1978	Escuela Técnica Superior de Arquitectura de Madrid

onzalo Cano Pintos		
rn	1956	Madrid
udied	1985	Escuela Técnica Superior de Arquitectura de Madrid

fonso Cano Pintos		
rn	1960	Madrid
udied	1986	Escuela Técnica Superior de Arquitectura de Madrid

cía Cano Pintos		
rn	1965	Madrid
udied	1992	Escuela Técnica Superior de Arquitectura de Madrid

elected projects		
ouse	1994	Ames, Galicia, Spain
ACE laboratories	1998	University of Murcia, Spain
overed swimming pool	1999	La Coruña, Spain
ousing development	2000	Vallecas, Spain
oorts complex	2000	Molinos, Madrid, Spain
useum for the Royal Collections	2000	Madrid, Spain (Project)

ne Cano Pintos are the children of the Madrid archi-ct Julio Cano Lasso, best known for the Spanish avilion at Expo '92, Seville, the Technical University, meria (1974), and the Galicia Auditorium, Santiago e Compostela (1986). Each began working in their ther's practice after graduating and have been in arge of operations since his death in 1996. Diego, onzalo, Alfonso and Lucía have inherited their father's ecision, appreciation of craftsmanship, and respect r the site. They believe that the roots of good archi-cture lie in the equilibrium between form, function, chnology and the coherent correspondence of struc-re, materials and construction.

Die Cano Pintos sind Kinder des Madrider Architekten Julio Cano Lasso, dessen bekannteste Werke der Spanische Pavillon auf der Expo '92 in Sevilla, die Technische Universität Almería (1974) und das Galicia Auditorium in Santiago de Compostela (1986) sind. Seit Abschluss ihrer Ausbildung arbeiten alle vier im Büro ihres Vaters, daß sie nach seinem Tod 1996 auch leiten. Diego, Gonzalo, Alfonso und Lucía haben von ihrem Vater die Präzision, die Wertschätzung handwerklicher Arbeit und den Respekt vor dem Standort übernommen. Sie sind davon überzeugt, dass die Wurzeln guter Architektur im Gleichgewicht von Form, Funktion und Technik sowie der Kohärenz von Konstruktion, Materialien und Bauwerk liegen.

Les Cano Pintos sont les enfants de l'architecte madrilène Julio Cano Lasso, dont les réalisations les plus connues sont le pavillon de l'Espagne à l'Expo '92 de Séville, l'Université technique d'Almeria (1974), et l'Auditorium Galicia à Saint-Jacques-de-Compostelle (1986). Après avoir passé leur diplôme, tous ont commencé par travailler dans le bureau de leur père, avant de prendre la relève après le décès de celui-ci en 1996. Diego, Gonzalo, Alfonso et Lucía ont hérité des qualités de leur père : précision, goût du travail bien fait et respect du site. Ils sont convaincus qu'une bonne architecture repose sur l'équilibre entre forme, fonction et technologie, et sur l'harmonisation de la structure, des matériaux et de la mise en œuvre.

However, theirs is not a cold scientific approach; they also bring to the basic architectural ideas sensitivity, emotion and meaning. A major competition-win to build a museum for the Royal Collections in Madrid has established them as important architects in their own right. "Since our father died, the practice has continued to work with the same spirit that was transmitted to us. The ideas evolve continuously and will continue to do so, but the essential core, our way of seeing architecture, will always remain the same as our father taught us."
Alfonso Cano Pintos has also distinguished himself by representing Spain at pole vault in the Los Angeles Olympics of 1984.

Dennoch sind Estudio Cano Lasso keine Vertreter einer kalten wissenschaftlichen Methodik, sondern sie komplettieren den zu Grunde liegenden architektonischen Gedanken durch Sensibilität, Emotion und Bedeutung. Ihr erfolgreiches Abschneiden im bedeutenden Wettbewerb für einen Museumsbau für die Königlichen Sammlungen in Madrid etablierte sie als eigenständige Architekten von Rang. »Seit dem Tod unseres Vaters konnten wir das Büro in seinem Geist weiterführen. Es entwickeln sich kontinuierlich neue Ideen, und das wird auch weiterhin so bleiben, aber der Kern, die Art, wie wir Architektur verstehen, wird sich immer an dem orientieren, was unser Vater uns beigebracht hat.«
Alfonso Cano Pintos machte sich darüber hinaus einen Namen als Stabhochspringer in der spanischen Mannschaft bei den Olympischen Spielen 1984 in Los Angeles.

Leur approche n'est pas pour autant froidement scientifique, car l'idée architecturale de base, traitée avec sens bilité et émotion, est dotée de signification. Un importar concours leur a permis d'établir leur réputation personnelle en construisant à Madrid un musée destiné à accueillir les collections royales. « Depuis la mort de no père, le bureau a poursuivi son activité dans l'esprit qu'i nous avait légué. Les idées ont changé et continueront à évoluer, mais l'essentiel, à savoir notre conception de l'a chitecture, restera toujours telle que notre père nous l'a enseignée. »
Alfonso Cano Pintos s'est également distingué en représentant l'Espagne au saut à la perche lors des Jeux Olympiques de 1984 à Los Angeles.

1998 **University of Murcia, Spain**

SACE laboratories

Responding to a brief that required a range of laboratory spaces - some dark, some light - the architects have used the project to experiment with contrasts of light and dark. Built on uneven terrain the building takes advantage of its topography, half burying itself into the ground allowing some rooms to be totally blacked out. The staggered building sits on the slope like two separate volumes linked by a double-height entrance hall with floor-to-ceiling glazing. The floor plan is based on a rigorously geometric grid carefully inserting modular courtyards between laboratory blocks to bring light into the building.
The plan has the harmony of a Mondrian painting. Looking out into a courtyard one is drawn into "a game of transparencies, reflection and the flow of light" gazing through a series of buildings and courtyards and eventually out over the Murcia Sierra. White walls formed of concrete tiles the size of bricks, and white roofs covered with crushed concrete, continue the play of light.

Entsprechend der Ausschreibung für die SACE laboratories, die sowohl gut belichtete als auch verdunkelbare Laborräume verlangte, nutzten die Architekten das Projekt, um mit Hell-Dunkel-Kontrasten zu experimentieren. Der Bau macht sich das unebene Gelände zunutze und schiebt sich zur Hälfte in den Boden, wodurch sich einige Räume vollständig verdunkeln lassen. Das auf dem Abhang versetzt angeordnete Gebäude besteht aus zwei separaten Baukörpern, die eine zweigeschossige, raumhoch verglaste Eingangshalle verbindet.
Der Grundriss hat die Harmonie eines Mondrian-Bildes. Blickt man in einen der Patios und durch eine Folge von Bauten und Höfen schließlich hinaus auf die Sierra von Murcia, wird man in »ein Wechselspiel von Transparenz, Reflexion und Licht« gezogen, während man durch eine Folge von Bauten und Höfen und schließlich hinaus über die Sierra von Murcia schaut. Die weißen Mauern, die mit backsteingroßen Betonkacheln verkleidet sind, und die mit Betonschotter bedeckten weißen Dächern setzen die Lichtreflexe fort.

Comme le cahier des charges prévoyait divers laboratoires, en partie clairs et en partie obscurs, les architectes ont décidé d'explorer dans leur projet les contrastes lumière/obscurité. Edifié sur un terrain accidenté, le bâtiment tire parti de cette topographie ; il est partiellement enterré, ce qui crée des salles totalement obscures. Etagé sur la pente, il se présente sous la forme de deux volumes distincts reliés par un haut hall d'entrée entièrement vitré. Le plan est basé sur une grille rigoureusemen géométrique ; des cours modulaires insérées entre les blocs abritant les laboratoires assurent un éclairage généreux. L'ensemble est aussi équilibré qu'un tableau de Mondrian. L'utilisateur est pris dans « un jeu de transparences, de réflexions et de circulation de la lumière », car le regard porte, à travers une succession de constructions et de cours, jusqu'à la Sierra de Murcia. Des murs blancs, construits en « briques » de béton et des toits blancs recouverts de béton poursuivent ces jeux de lumière.

White walls are covered in concrete tiles the size of bricks.

Die Wände sind mit backsteingroßen weißen Betonkacheln verkleidet.

Les murs sont revêtus de « briques » de béton blanc.

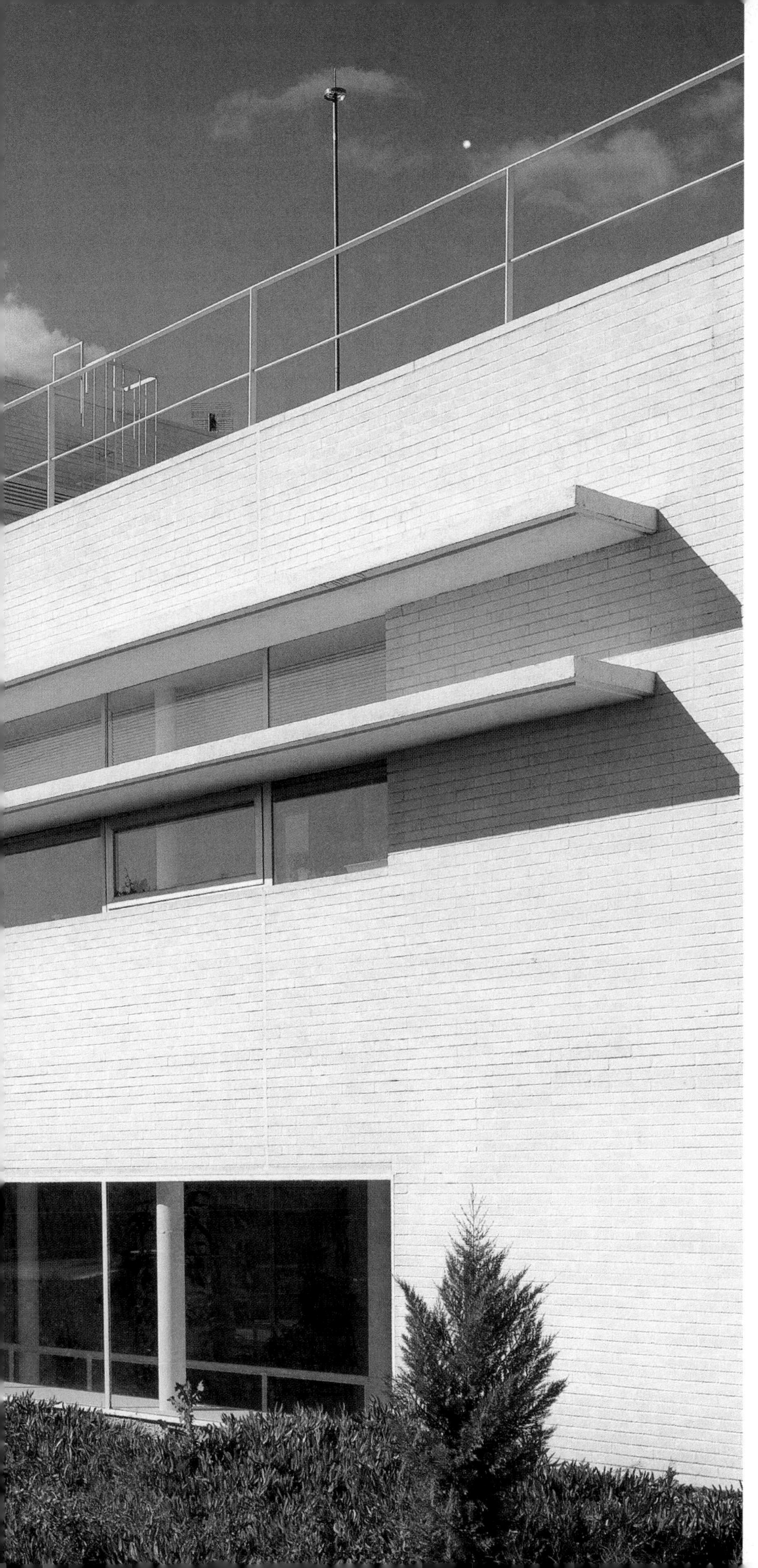

The two blocks are of different heights, and are separated by a tall entrance tower.

Ein hoher Eingangsturm trennt die beiden unterschiedlich hohen Gebäudeblöcke.

Les deux blocs, de hauteurs différentes, sont reliés par la haute « tour » abritant le hall d'entrée.

Facade and roof of the higher block. The roof is covered with crushed concrete.

Fassade und Dach des höheren Bauteils. Das Dach ist mit Betonschotter bedeckt.

Façade et toit du bloc le plus élevé. Le toit est recouvert de béton concassé.

Ground floor plan/ Erdgeschossgrundriss/ Plan du rez-de-chaussée

1 **entrance/** Eingang/ entrée
2 **courtyards/** Innenhöfe/ cours
3 **lower block/** flacher Bauteil/ bloc bas
4 **higher block/** höherer Bauteil/ bloc haut

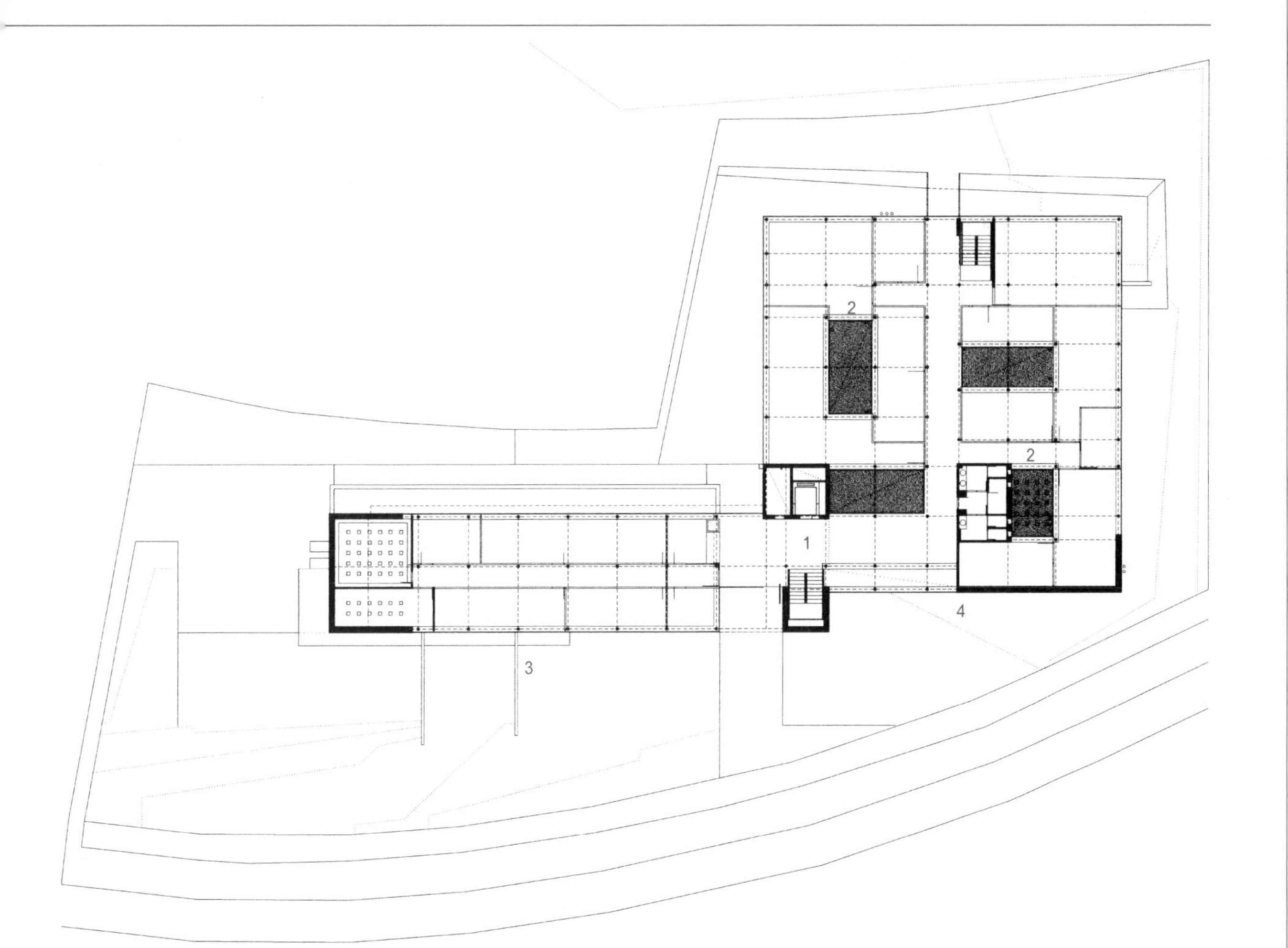

1994 **Ames, Galicia, Spain**

House

Built in a rural setting in the wilds of Galicia, the house is about sanctuary and protection within which the architects have tried to combine the language of Modernism with regional traditions. A low aspect, heavy stone walls and a mono-pitch roof rising towards the south keep the house firmly anchored to the site. An exploded floor-plan creates a series of patios, pergolas, passages and sheltered gardens between rooms forming an organic relationship between indoors and outdoors. A glazed "galeria" or conservatory (a typical feature of Galician houses) forms a buffer between the harsh outdoors and the cosy living room. A series of staggered bedrooms are set apart from the public areas of the house, oriented east so that it is impossible to see the rest of the building from the windows. The house is intended to weather over time, and plants will begin to grow over it until it becomes part of the environment.

Das Haus in der ländlichen Umgebung von Ames im galicischen Hinterland will ein Ort der Zuflucht und des Schutzes sein und versucht, Stilmittel der Moderne mit regionalen Traditionen zu kombinieren. Der flache Baukörper, schwere Steinmauern und ein nach Süden aufragendes Pultdach verankern das Haus optisch fest mit dem Terrain. Der aufgebrochene Grundriss lässt zwischen den Räumen eine Reihe von Patios, Pergolen, Passagen und geschützten Gartenflächen entstehen, die Innen- und Außenraum organisch verbinden. Eine verglaste »Galeria« oder Wintergarten (typischer Bestandteil galicischer Häuser) bildet eine Pufferzone zwischen der unwirtlichen Umgebung und dem behaglichen Wohnraum. Die gestaffelt angeordneten Schlafräume sind von den allgemein zugänglichen Bereichen des Hauses abgesetzt und nach Osten ausgerichtet, so dass es unmöglich ist, von den Fenstern aus das übrige Haus zu sehen. Mit der Zeit soll das Haus Patina ansetzen und von Pflanzen überwuchert werden, um schließlich Teil seiner Umgebung zu werden.

Edifiée dans le cadre sauvage de la campagne galicienne, la maison d'habitation, dont les thèmes sont sanctuaire et protection, s'efforce d'allier le vocabulaire du modernisme aux traditions locales. De massifs murs en pierre et une toiture monopan s'élevant vers le sud ancrent solidement dans le site la maison, d'apparence basse. Le plan éclaté crée une série de patios, de pergolas, de couloirs et de jardins abrités entre les pièces, établissant une relation organique entre intérieur et extérieur. Une « galeria » (élément typique des habitations galiciennes), sorte de jardin d'hiver vitré, constitue un tampon entre le rude paysage et le séjour douillet. Une série de chambres échelonnées est nettement séparée des « espaces collectifs » de la maison ; les fenêtres orientées à l'est les isolent visuellement du reste du bâtiment. La maison évoluera avec le temps ; lorsqu'elle sera couverte de plantes grimpantes, elle s'intégrera complètement à son environnement.

Left, public rooms including the traditional glazed "galeria". Right, the staggered series of bedrooms. Below, main entrance

Links die öffentlichen Räume mit der traditionellen verglasten »Galeria«. Rechts die gestaffelten Schlafräume, unten der Haupteingang

A gauche : les pièces communes, avac la traditionnelle « galeria » vitrée. A droite, les chambres forment des unités décalées. Ci-dessous, l'entrée principale.

A courtyard separates the "wet" pool to the left and the "dry" cafeteria to the right. Above right, the pool.

Eine Freifläche trennt den Nassbereich zur Linken von der »trockenen« Cafeteria zur Rechten (oben). Rechts das Schwimmbecken.

Une cour gazonnée sépare la piscine, zone « humide » (à gauche), de la cafétéria, zone « sèche ». Page de droite, une vue de la piscine.

1999 La Coruña, Spain

Covered swimming pool

Built in collaboration with Luis Pancorbo and Monica J. Denia for the municipal authority of La Coruña, the pool building is an exercise in simplicity and purity. Large concrete walls form a clear and ordered geometry strictly modulated by a 5-m grid. Between this strong horizontal geometry one can make out the two parallel halves of the building - one housing a cafe, gym and first aid room (activities done with shoes on), and one containing the pool (used barefoot) - linked by a transitional block of changing rooms. Vast windows look out onto patio-like spaces between the pavilions, planted with bright flowers, bringing colour, light and fresh air into the building. The pool pavilion is a simple box lined with bleached wood (chosen both for aesthetic reasons and because it is easy to maintain and stands up to humid conditions) with a glazed gallery that filters light, sunshine, air and views through from outside.

Das im Auftrag der Stadtverwaltung von La Coruña in Zusammenarbeit mit Luis Pancorbo und Monica J. Denia entstandene Hallenbad ist ebenso schlicht wie klar. Großflächige, durch ein 5 m-Raster strukturierte Betonwände geben klar geordnete geometrische Proportionen vor. Innerhalb dieser stark horizontal ausgerichteten Geometrie lassen sich zwei parallel angeordneten Gebäudehälften ausmachen: in der einen sind die mit Schuhen zu betretenden Bereiche wie Café, Fitnessraum und Sanitätsstation untergebracht, in der anderen das nur barfuß zugängliche Schwimmbecken. Ein Block mit Umkleidekabinen verbindet die beiden Bereiche. Große Fenster geben den Blick frei auf die terrassenartigen Areale zwischen den Pavillons. Diese mit bunten Blumen bepflanzten Bereiche bringen Farbe, Licht und Luft ins Innere. Der schlichte, kastenförmige Pavillon mit dem Schwimmbecken ist mit gebleichtem Holz verkleidet, ein Material, das ästhetischen Ansprüchen Stand hält und selbst in Feuchträumen leicht zu pflegen ist; eine verglaste Galerie lässt Licht, Sonne, Luft und Blicke von außen ein.

Commandée par la municipalité de La Corogne en collaboration avec Luis Pancorbo et Monica J. Denia, cette piscine couverte est un exercice de simplicité et de pureté. Les grands pans de murs en béton sont strictement modulés par une grille de 5 m sur 5. Entre ces rigoureuses formes géométriques horizontales, apparaissent les deux moitiés parallèles de l'édifice – l'une abritant un café, un gymnase et un service de premiers secours (lieux où l'on peut garder ses chaussures), et l'autre, la piscine (qui n'est accessible que pieds nus) – reliées par un bloc transversal où se trouvent les vestiaires. De grandes baies vitrées s'ouvrent sur les espaces séparant les bâtiments ; pareils à des patios, ceux-ci sont plantés de fleurs et amènent non seulement la lumière et l'air, mais aussi de joyeuses notes de couleur. L'aile de la piscine est une simple boîte revêtue de bois blanchi, matériau choisi pour des raisons esthétiques mais aussi parce qu'il est d'un entretien facile et résiste à l'humidité ; elle comporte également une galerie vitrée assurant l'éclairage et l'aération, tout en permettant de voir à travers le bâtiment.

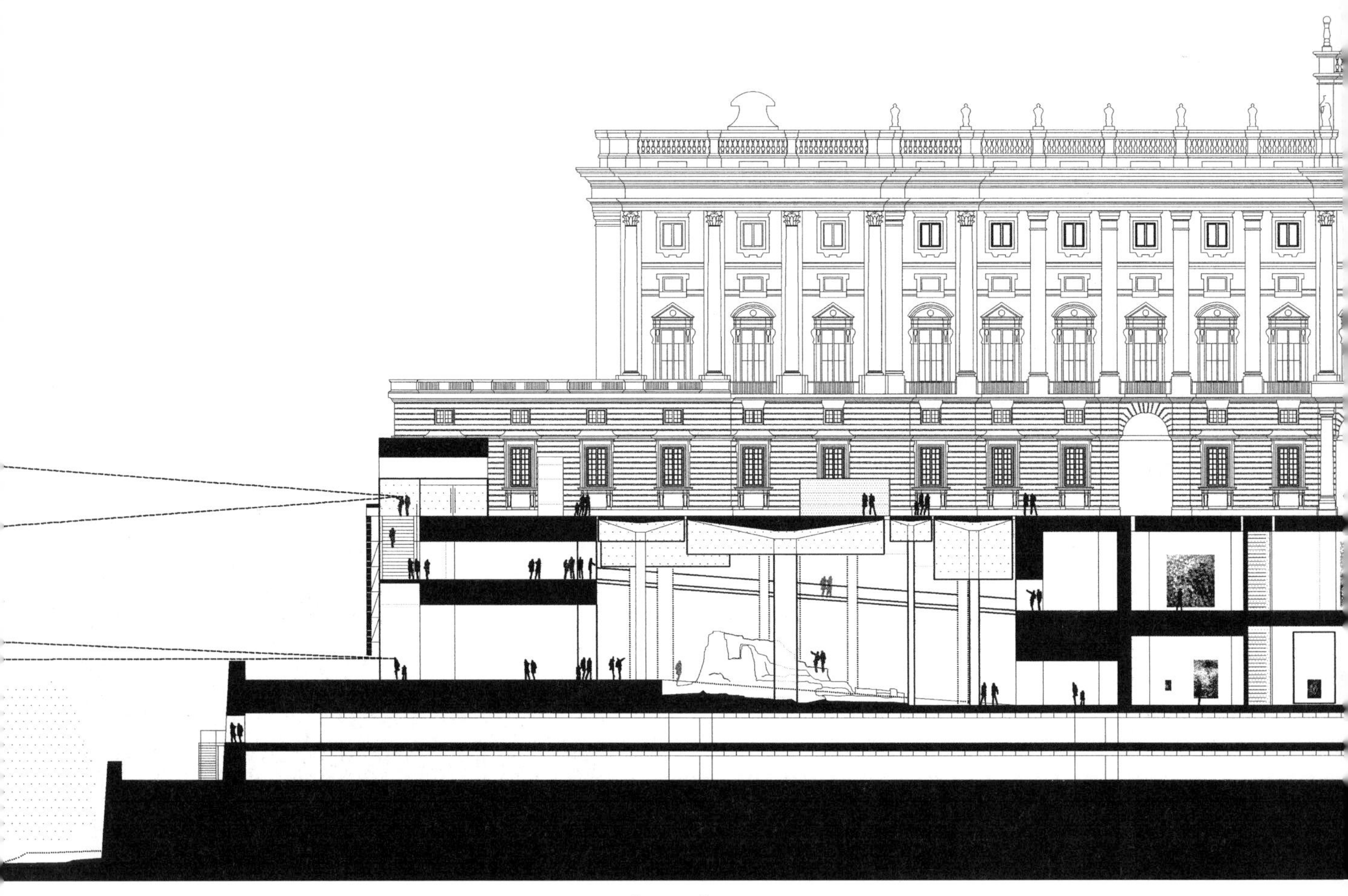

2000 **Madrid, Spain (Project)**

Museum for the Royal Collections

The new intervention to house the Royal Collections incorporates itself in the context created by the Palacio Real and the Almudena Cathedral, resulting in a "void" tensed between the two blocks that form part of the Madrid skyline. The building converts itself as a main stepped retaining platform in the urban composition. The stone mass is broken down by a horizontal lattice, through which light filters into the museum. The simple, neutral style is respectful of the historic context. A US$ 38 million-project won at an international competition, this is the first opportunity for Julio Cano Lasso's children to assert their own identity on a grand scale.

Das Museum für die Königlichen Sammlungen in Madrid tritt zwischen Palacio Real und Almudena-Kathedrale und schafft einen spannungsreichen Raum zwischen diesen Komplexen, die die Madrider Skyline prägen. Der Bau fügt sich als terrassierte Plattform ins urbane Umfeld ein; seine Mauerfläche wird durch ein horizontales Spalier gegliedert, das Licht ins Innere fallen lässt.
Die schlichte, neutrale Formgebung zollt dem historischen Kontext Respekt. Dieser im Rahmen eines internationalen Wettbewerbs errungene Auftrag mit einem Budget von 38 Millionen Dollar ist für Cano Lasso die erste Gelegenheit zur Bewährung in einem Großprojekt.

Ce musée est destiné à accueillir les collections royales : situé entre le Palacio Real et la cathédrale de l'Almudena, il crée un espace empli de tension entre ces complexes qui marquent de leur empreinte la ligne d'horizon de la capitale. L'édifice est intégré dans l'environnement urbain sous forme de plate-forme en terrasse, les architectes ont brisé cette masse compacte par un treillage horizontal qui laisse pénétrer la lumière.
Le style simple et neutre respecte le contexte historique. Ce chantier de 38 millions de dollars remporté à l'issue d'un concours international donnera pour la première fois aux enfants de Julio Cano Lasso la possibilité d'affirmer leur identité sur une grande échelle.

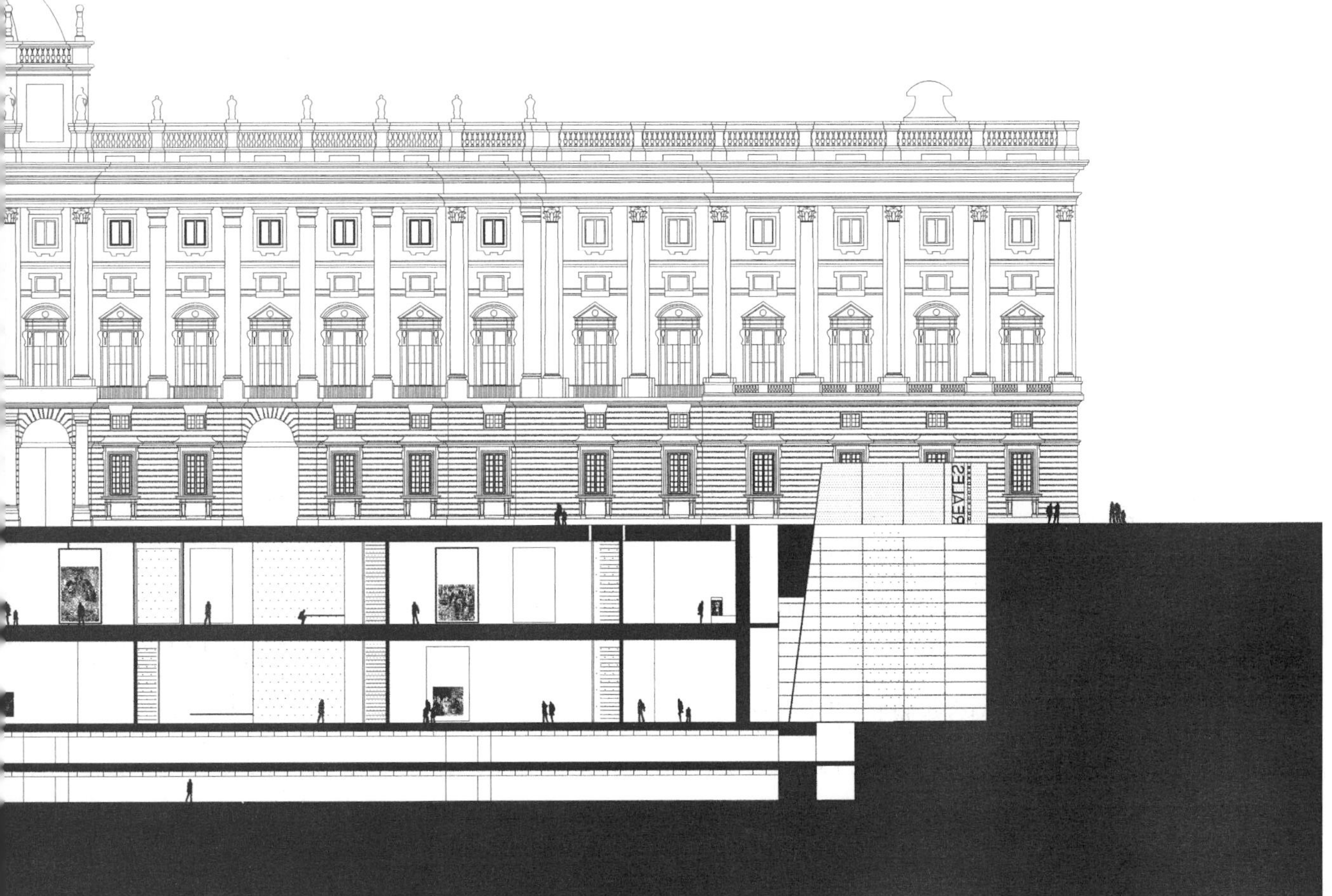

The ambitious project of the extension of the Royal Collections connects the Palacio Real with the Almudena Cathedral.

Das ambitionierte Projekt der Erweiterung der Königlichen Sammlungen verbindet den Palacio Real mit der Almudena-Kathedrale.

L'ambitieux projet d'extension des collections royales, reliant le Palacio Real à la cathédrale de l'Almudena.

Claesson Koivisto Rune

Sankt Paulsgatan 25, 118 48 Stockholm, Sweden
tel +46 8 644 5863 fax +46 8 644 5883 e-mail arkitektkontor@claesson-koivisto-rune.se
www.scandinaviandesign.com/claesson-koivisto-rune

Mårten Claesson

born	1970	Lidingö, Sweden
studied	1992	Parsons School of Design, New York; 1994 Konstfack, Stockholm

Eero Koivisto

born	1958	Karlstad, Sweden
studied	1992	Parsons School of Design, New York; 1994 Konstfack, Stockholm; 1995 University of Art & Design, Helsinki

Ola Rune

born	1963	Lycksele, Sweden
studied	1989	Southwark College of Art & Design, London; 1992 The Royal Academy of Art, Copenhagen; 1994 Konstfack, Stockholm

Selected projects

Offices for A3 advertising agency	1995	Stockholm, Sweden
One Happy Cloud restaurant	1997	Stockholm, Sweden
No Picnic offices	1997	Stockholm, Sweden
Museum shop, Liljevalchs Konsthall	1998	Stockholm, Sweden
Wallinder Apartment	1999	Stockholm, Sweden
Interiors of Swedish ambassador's residence	1999	Berlin, Germany

One of CKR's main considerations is the experience of moving through spaces. One Happy Cloud restaurant plays with the senses through carefully positioned screens and mirrors, creating the impression of infinite space. No Picnic industrial design studio sets up intriguing glimpses between public and private space as one progresses up a long, enclosed flight of stairs. A recurring motif is a concealed surface such as the underside of a table or upper surface of a hole cut into a wall painted in a vibrant colour so that a faint glow emerges to be reflected by ubiquitous white environs. White walls are not minimal but merely surfaces that are a starting point for textural interventions - a frosted glass panel, punched-out squares, hidden spots of colour. In some cases they break away to become free

Eines der Hauptanliegen von CKR ist die Erfahrung der Bewegung im Raum. Das Restaurant One Happy Cloud spielt mit den Sinnen durch geschickt positionierte Wandschirme und Spiegel, die den Eindruck eines endlosen Raumes schaffen. In der Industriedesign-Agentur No Picnic bietet eine lange, geschlossenen Treppe beim Hinaufgehen faszinierende Einblicke in öffentliche und private Räume. Ein immer wiederkehrendes Motiv stellen Blicke auf verborgene Oberflächen dar: die Unterseite eines Tisches oder der Ansatz einer Öffnung, die in eine mit leuchtender Farbe gestrichene Wand geschnitten ist, so dass ein schwacher Glanz sichtbar wird, den die allgegenwärtigen weißen Wände reflektieren.
Diese sollen nicht Minimalismus suggerieren, sondern sind bloße Oberflächen, die als Ausgangspunkt für struk-

Un des principaux centres d'intérêt de CKR est la perception du mouvement dans l'espace architectural. Le restaurant One Happy Cloud joue avec les sens, des écrans et miroirs ingénieusement disposés donnant une impression d'espace infini. En montant le long escalier de l'atelier de design industriel No Picnic, le visiteur aura de surprenants aperçus sur les espaces publics et privés. Un motif souvent utilisé est une surface cachée – dessous d'une table, partie supérieure d'un orifice pratiqué dans un mur, etc. – peinte d'une couleur vibrante, qui projette une lueur colorée sur l'environnement d'une blancheur omniprésente.
Les murs blancs ne témoignent pas d'une volonté minimaliste, ce sont des surfaces autorisant des effets de texture : panneaux de verre dépoli, carrés découpés dans

planes, screens between spaces with carefully located cuts controlling views, setting up complex internal landscapes in the most confined of volumes.
In addition to architectural work, Claesson Koivisto Rune have had increasing success with their furniture designs, many of which are manufactured for the Swedish company David Design, the broad, low "Bowie" plywood chair (easily identified by the slit across its back) being perhaps the best-known.
Much of their work to date has been restricted to interiors, an impressive list of private homes, offices, exhibitions, advertising agencies, shops and restaurants for wealthy and usually fashionable clients. In 1999 a prestigious commission to style the interior for the Swedish ambassador's residence in Berlin "to epitomise modern Swedish design" provided official recognition as one of their country's leading young practices.

turierende Eingriffe dienen – eine Mattglasscheibe, ausgestanzte Quadrate, verborgene Farbflecke. Bisweilen verselbständigen sie sich und werden zu freien Flächen, Wandschirme zwischen Räumen mit überlegt platzierten Einschnitten, die Durchblicke bestimmen und auf sehr begrenztem Raum komplexe, innere Landschaften entstehen lassen.
Neben ihrer architektonischen Arbeit haben Claesson Koivisto Rune zunehmend Erfolg mit ihren Möbelentwürfen, von denen zahlreiche von der schwedischen Firma David Design hergestellt werden; der breite Sperrholzstuhl »Bowie«, leicht erkennbar am Schlitz quer über der Rückenlehne, ist vielleicht das bekannteste Stück.
Ein Großteil ihrer Arbeit ist bis dato Innenarchitektur: eine lange Liste von Privathäusern, Büroräumen, Ausstellungsarchitekturen, Werbeagenturen, Läden sowie Restaurants für wohlhabende und in der Regel fortschrittlich gesinnte Auftraggeber. Im Jahre 1999 verhalf ihnen der prestigeträchtige Auftrag »zur Darstellung des modernen schwedischen Designs« die Innenräume der Residenz des schwedischen Botschafters in Berlin zu entwerfen, zu offizieller Anerkennung als eins der führenden jungen Architekturbüros ihres Landes.

des cloisons, notes de couleur dissimulées. Dans certains cas, ils se détachent pour devenir des plans autonomes séparant des espaces, écrans percés d'ouvertures soigneusement localisées de sorte à créer des paysages internes complexes au sein de volumes extrêmement restreints.
Outre leurs réalisations architecturales, Claesson Koivisto Rune connaissent un succès croissant grâce à leurs modèles de meubles, fabriqués en majeure partie par la société suédoise David Design, et dont le plus connu est sans doute le fauteuil « Bowie » large et bas, en contreplaqué, aisément reconnaissable à la fente pratiquée dans le dossier.
Jusqu'à présent, l'activité de CKR est surtout limitée à l'architecture d'intérieur – une liste impressionnante de résidences privées, espaces de bureaux, expositions, agences de publicité, magasins, restaurants fréquentés par une clientèle aisée et « dans le vent ». En 1999, une commande prestigieuse – l'aménagement intérieur de la résidence de l'ambassadeur de Suède à Berlin, « condensé de design suédois moderne » – a confirmé officiellement la valeur d'un des jeunes bureaux d'architectes les plus intéressants du pays.

1997 **Stockholm, Sweden**

No Picnic offices

Offices and workshops for the successful industrial design agency No Picnic. The main feature is a centrally located staircase that runs along the building's axis, narrowing slightly towards the top to make it appear even longer. To one side is the double-height public space, to the other are single-storey offices and meeting rooms. Despite being just 450 m², the space is labyrinthine. Claesson Koivisto Rune's complex interlocking planes manipulate public and private spaces in a series of screens and views that create a deceptive visual complexity.

Das Gebäude beherbergt Büros und Werkstätten für die erfolgreiche Industriedesign-Agentur No Picnic. Kernstück ist die zentral angeordnete Treppe entlang der Gebäudeachse, die sich am oberen Ende leicht verjüngt, um noch länger zu wirken. Auf einer Seite befindet sich ein zweigeschossiger, öffentlich zugänglicher Raum, auf der anderen eingeschossige Büro- und Konferenzräume. Trotz seiner begrenzten Fläche von nur 450 m² wirkt der Bau labyrinthisch, da Claesson Koivisto Rune mit ihren komplex ineinandergreifenden Ebenen öffentliche und private Räume durch eine Folge von Wandschirmen und Durchblicken derart manipulieren, dass der trügerische Eindruck optischer Komplexität entsteht.

L'élément le plus frappant des bureaux et ateliers de l'agence de design industriel No Picnic est un escalier central qui suit l'axe de l'édifice ; il est légèrement plus étroit dans sa partie supérieure, ce qui le fait paraître encore plus long. D'un côté, un espace public à double hauteur ; de l'autre, des bureaux et salles de réunion sur un seul niveau. En dépit de ses modestes 450 m², l'espace est un vrai labyrinthe. Les complexes plans qui se recoupent, imaginés par Claesson Koivisto Rune, manipulent les espaces publics et privés grâce à une succession d'écrans et d'ouvertures créant une trompeuse complexité visuelle.

White planes conceal the main staircases.

Weiße Flächen verbergen die zentrale Treppe.

L'escalier central, entouré de plans d'une blancheur immaculée.

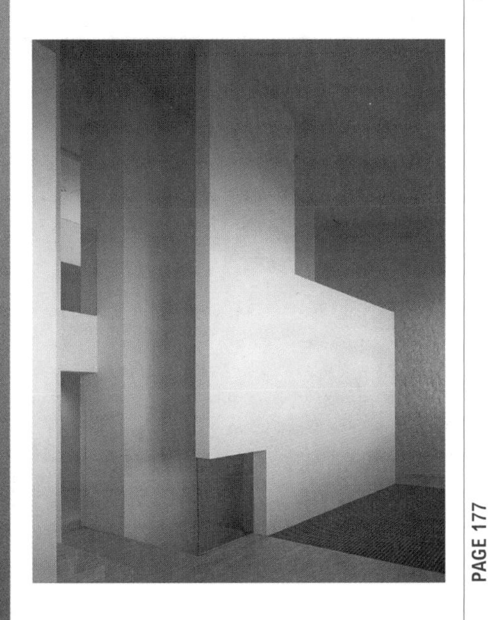

Disjointed wall planes add complexity to the space, left, and splashes of colour come as a surprise, far left.

Links: Zergliederte Wandflächen lassen den Raum komplexer wirken. Ganz links: Farbflecke schaffen überraschende Effekte.

A gauche: les découpes des cloisons génèrent un espace complexe. Page de gauche: des touches de couleur créent un effet de surprise.

The main bar. The blackboard picture changes monthly.

Die Bar; das Bild auf der Tafel wechselt monatlich.

Le bar ; l'image tracée sur le tableau noir change tous les mois.

1997 **Stockholm, Sweden**

One Happy Cloud restaurant

Japanese and Scandinavian cultural traditions complement each other in this Japanese restaurant in Stockholm. Colours and materials are tranquil - white, concrete, oiled beech wood furniture, galvanised steel fittings, acid-etched glass panels, and a blackboard paint on the walls with ever-changing artworks.
The horizontal axis of the restaurant is emphasised with a regimented row of tables and chairs following the wall, divided by full-height screens, and carefully positioned mirrors at either end of the space that draw the room out into infinity in their reflections.

In dem japanischen Restaurant One Happy Cloud in Stockholm ergänzen sich japanische und schwedische Traditionen. Farben und Materialien strahlen Ruhe aus – Weiß, Beton, Möbel aus geöltem Buchenholz, verzinkte Stahlbeschläge, säuregeätzte Glaspaneele und mit Tafelfarbe gestrichene Wände für ständig wechselnde Kunstwerke.
Die Längsachse des Restaurants wird durch die Reihe von Tischen und Stühlen parallel zur Wand betont, die durch deckenhohe Wandschirme unterbrochen ist; geschickt platzierte Spiegel an gegenüber liegenden Enden des Restaurants verlängern den Raum mit ihren Reflexionen ins Unendliche.

Dans ce restaurant japonais de Stockholm, les traditions culturelles japonaise et scandinave se complètent harmonieusement. Les couleurs et les matériaux sont discrets : blanc, béton, mobilier en hêtre huilé, accessoires en acier galvanisé, pans de verre gravés à l'acide, murs d'un noir mat ornés d'œuvres d'art qui sont régulièrement changées.
L'axe horizontal du restaurant est souligné par l'alignement rigoureux des tables et des chaises, séparées par de hauts écrans, et par des miroirs disposés aux deux extrémités de l'espace et dans lesquels la salle se reflète à l'infini.

Carefully positioned screens and mirrors make the room appear longer, right. Above, plywood furniture was also designed by the architects.

Rechts: Geschickt platzierte Zwischenwände und Spiegel lassen den Raum länger wirken. Oben: Die Sperrholzmöbel sind ebenfalls Entwürfe der Architekten.

A droite : un jeu d'écrans et de miroirs fait paraître la salle plus longue. Ci-dessus : les sièges en contreplaqué ont été dessinés par les architectes.

Wallinder Apartment

The 65-m² apartment was refurbished for a businessman who wanted a serene home in which to recharge between long hours in the office and trips abroad.
One half of the apartment has been kept in a traditional 19th-century Swedish style of wooden floors and white walls while the other - bathroom, bedroom and kitchen - is completely modern and painted a light grey for contrast.
A series of aligned glass slits runs through the modern rooms, rhythmically alternating between the horizontal and vertical, connecting the spaces. Vertical dimmed glass in the door between the entrance and the bathroom, a horizontal dimmed glass between bathroom and kitchen, a vertical clear glass between dining and bedroom, and a horizontal acid-etched mirror glass sunk into the end wall for the bedroom create the illusion of continuing space.
Much of the furniture selected for the apartment is designed by the architects.

Das 65 m² große Wallinder Apartment wurde für einen Geschäftsmann umgestaltet, der einen Zufluchtsort braucht, an dem er sich zwischen langen Stunden im Büro und Geschäftsreisen erholen kann.
Eine Hälfte der Wohnung wurde mit Holzböden und weißen Wänden im traditionellen schwedischen Wohnstil des 19. Jahrhunderts belassen, während die andere Hälfte mit Badezimmer, Schlafraum und Küche im Gegensatz dazu hellgrau gestrichen und modern gestaltet ist.
Eine gerade Reihe verglaster Schlitze zieht sich, rhythmisch zwischen horizontal und vertikal wechselnd, durch den modernen Teil der Wohnung und schafft so eine Verbindung zwischen den Räumen. Eine vertikale, opake Glasscheibe in der Tür zwischen Diele und Bad, eine horizontale zwischen Bad und Küche, eine vertikale, transparente Scheibe zwischen Esszimmer und Schlafraum und eine horizontale, säuregeätzte Spiegelglasscheibe in der Stirnwand des Schlafraums schaffen die Illusion eines fortlaufenden Raumes.
Viele der für das Apartment ausgewählten Möbelstücke wurden von den Architekten selbst entworfen.

Cet appartement de 65 m² a été réaménagé à l'intention d'un homme d'affaires souhaitant se détendre après les longues heures de bureau ou entre deux voyages.
Une moitié de l'appartement a conservé le style suédois traditionnel du XIXᵉ siècle, planchers en bois et murs blancs, tandis que l'autre – salle de bains, chambre et cuisine – est complètement moderne, et peinte en gris pour fournir un contraste.
Une succession d'étroites baies vitrées alternant de façon rythmique l'horizontale et la verticale ponctuent les pièces « modernes » et relient les divers espaces : un pan de verre opaque vertical entre l'entrée et la salle de bains un pan de verre opaque horizontal entre cette dernière et la cuisine, un pan de verre transparent vertical séparant la salle à manger de la chambre, et un miroir horizontal gravé à l'acide encastré dans le mur opposé de la chambre donnent l'illusion d'un espace continu.
Un grande partie du mobilier de l'appartement a été dessinée par les architectes.

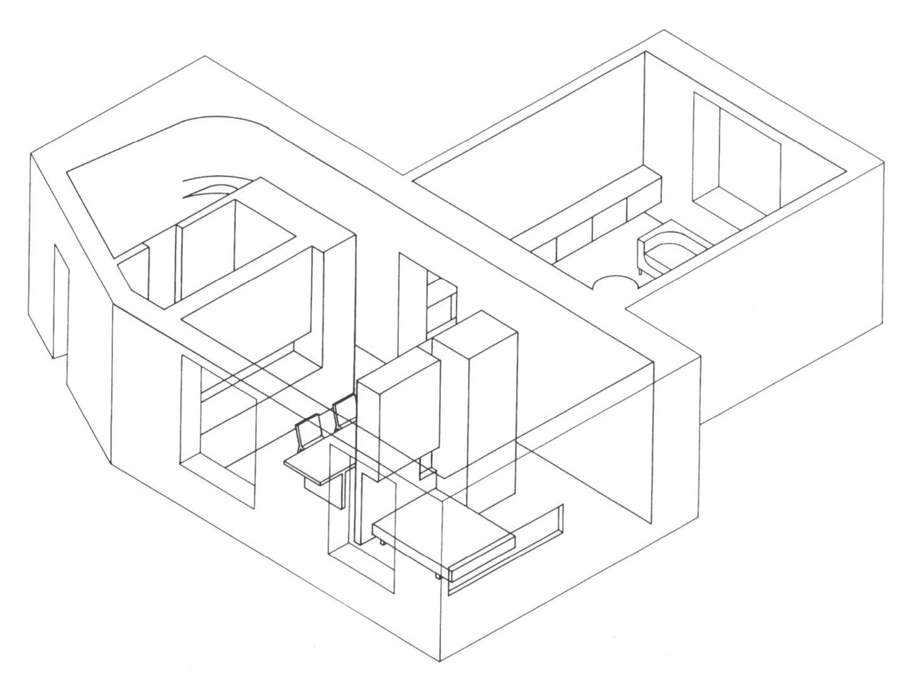

Kitchen/diner, right, with horizontal dimmed glass pane through to the bathroom

Rechts: Küche/Essbereich mit getönter horizontaler Glasscheibe zum Badezimmer

La salle à manger-cuisine ; le pan de verre opaque horizontal donne sur la salle de bains.

Kitchen/diner with vertical window through to bedroom, right. Bedroom, above, with false horizontal window for continuity.

Rechts: Küche/Essbereich mit vertikalem Fenster zum Schlafraum. Oben: Schlafraum mit blindem horizontalem Fenster (eingefügt, um die Kontinuität zu wahren).

A droite, la chambre, avec sa fausse fenêtre horizontale assurant une continuité visuelle. Page de droite : la salle à manger avec la fenêtre verticale donnant sur la chambre.

Henri Comrie + 'Ora Joubert

4 Wild Ave, Clydesdale, Pretoria
O Box 11998, Hatfield, 0028, South Africa
tel/fax +27 12 3466 390 e-mail henricomrie.pia@saia.org.za

enri Comrie

orn	1965 Pretoria, South Africa
tudied	1991 B.Arch. University of Pretoria; 1995 M. Urban Design University of the Witwatersrand
revious practice	Michael Haskoll Associates, London; Erhard Roxin Architects, Namibia; Taljaard Carter Architects, Johannesburg/Pretoria
	1996 established own office

)ra Joubert

orn	1959 Pretoria, South Africa
tudied	1982 B.Arch University of Pretoria; 1984 MScArch Pennsylvania State University, Philadelphia, USA
	1999 PhD University of Natal, Durban, South Africa
revious practice	GAPS Architects, Johannesburg; in-house architect for Get Ahead Foundation, Pretoria
	1986 sets up 'Ora Joubert Architect
	1996 association with Henri Comrie

elected projects

wabou Headquarters	1995	Windhoek, Namibia
FG Glass Centre	1995	Midrand, South Africa (in association with TC Design Group)
uis Laubscher	1996	Pretoria, South Africa
ouse Steyn	1999	Pretoria, South Africa
ordon Institute of Business Science	2000	Illovo, Johannesburg, Gauteng, South Africa (in association with TC Design Group)

rchitects Comrie and Joubert collaborate as Henri omrie + 'Ora Joubert but also practice under their wn names, combining resources on larger projects nd exploring their own ideas on smaller ones. An come from teaching has allowed them to keep their ork experimental and avoid becoming too commer- al. They are also keen to avoid what they see as a urocentric approach by many clients and architects their country, preferring to explore the architectural emands of post-apartheid South Africa.
omrie describes his philosophy as "one of inclusion nd open-endedness which results in fragmented and patially diverse form. Once having fragmented form rough an inclusive process I take great joy in stitch-

Comrie und Joubert vereinen ihre Ressourcen für große Projekte und arbeiten als Henri Comrie + 'Ora Joubert zusammen; bei kleineren Aufträgen dagegen verfolgen sie unter je eigenem Namen ihre eigenen Ideen. Ihre Lehrtätigkeit erlaubt beiden, experimentelle Ansätze zu verfolgen und nicht allzu kommerziell zu werden. Zudem sind sie darauf bedacht, sich dem zu entziehen, was sie als eurozentrischen Ansatz vieler Bauherren und Architekten ihrer Heimat sehen. Statt dessen erforschen Comrie und Joubert die architektonischen Bedürfnisse Südafrikas nach dem Ende der Apartheid.
Comrie beschreibt seine Philosophie als »eine, bei der es um Inklusion und Unbegrenztheit geht, was zu fragmentierten und räumlich diversifizierten Formen führt.

Les architectes Comrie et Joubert se sont associés sous l'étiquette de Henri Comrie + 'Ora Joubert, tout en continuant à exercer sous leurs propres noms, alliant leurs ressources pour les commandes importantes et explorant leurs idées personnelles dans le cadre de projets plus modestes. Des revenus provenant de l'enseignement leur ont permis de préserver l'aspect expérimental de leur travail et de ne pas devenir trop commerciaux. Ils tiennent également à éviter l'approche selon eux trop eurocentrique de nombreux clients et architectes de leur pays, préférant explorer les besoins architecturaux de l'Afrique du Sud d'après l'apartheid.
Comrie décrit sa philosophie comme un mélange d'« inclusion et d'indétermination, produisant des formes

ing the parts together in a way which contributes towards the experience of the whole." Comrie is strongly influenced by the work of Charles Correa in India and Riccardo Legoretta in Mexico, while both Comrie and Joubert aim for a rich spatial architecture that acknowledges the constraints of a low-tech building industry by using simple construction methods and everyday materials, then enriching them through the use of light and texture.

Joubert's work includes a series of award-winning private houses that celebrate and advance indigenous architecture. Her work aims at "the development of a regionally South African architecture in terms of the use of materials, climatic conditions and building techniques, whilst respecting the spatial integrity and plastic inventory of heroic Modernism". As in-house architect for the Get Ahead Foundation in the late 1980s, she designed and implemented many projects in the townships of Gauteng.

Habe ich die Form durch einen Prozess der Inklusion fragmentiert, macht es mir großen Spaß, die Teile in einer Weise zusammenzuheften, die zur Erfahrung des Ganzen beiträgt.« Comrie ist stark vom Werk Charles Correas in Indien und Riccardo Legorettas in Mexiko beeinflusst, während beide eine Architektur räumlicher Vielfalt anstreben, die sich zu den Beschränkungen einer »low-tech«-Bauindustrie bekennt, indem sie einfache Konstruktionsverfahren und alltägliche Materialien verwendet und sie dann mittels Licht und Struktur optimiert.

Jouberts Œuvre umfasst eine Reihe preisgekrönter Privathäuser, die sich heimischer Architekturformen bedienen und sie weiterentwickeln. Ihre Arbeit hat »die Entwicklung einer im Hinblick auf die Verwendung von Materialien, klimatische Bedingungen und Bauverfahren regionalen südafrikanischen Architektur zum Ziel, die gleichwohl die räumliche Integrität und plastische Vielfalt der Moderne respektiert.« Während ihrer Zeit als Architektin bei der Get Ahead Foundation zeichnete Joubert Ende der 80er-Jahre für zahlreiche Projekte in den Townships von Gauteng verantwortlich.

fragmentées et spatialement diversifiées. Après avoir fragmenté la forme, je prends un énorme plaisir à recoller les parties d'une manière qui contribue à la perception du tout. » Si Comrie est très influencé par le travail de Charles Correa en Inde et de Riccardo Legoretta au Mexique, Comrie et Joubert recherchent tous deux une architecture d'une grande richesse spatiale, tout en tenant compte des possibilités d'une industrie du bâtiment rudimentaire. Ils utilisent des méthodes de construction simples et des matériaux courants, ensuite enrichis par le maniement de la lumière et des textures.

L'œuvre de Joubert comprend une série de maisons privées qui célèbrent l'architecture indigène tout en la faisant évoluer; plusieurs ont été primées. Son objectif est de « développer une architecture sud-africaine régionaliste en ce qui concerne les matériaux et les techniques de construction, sans oublier les conditions climatiques, tout en respectant l'intégrité spatiale et le vocabulaire plastique du modernisme héroïque ». En sa qualité d'architecte en résidence à la Get Ahead Foundation, elle a conçu et réalisé à la fin des années 80 de nombreux projets dans les townships de Gauteng.

2000 **Illovo, Johannesburg, Gauteng, South Africa**

Gordon Institute of Business Science

The specifications stipulated that the building should have an "African feel" and, at the same time, the client wanted the MBA students to learn from the process to be creative in finding their unique solutions in their business life.

The influence of Charles Correa and Riccardo Legoretta is particularly strong in this project. Layered spaces open to the sky and strongly juxtaposed forms and bold colours create a vibrant series of spaces that are constantly changing as one moves through the building. Rendered facades define the courtyards and give the impression that the building is carved out of a solid block. The facade is consciously layered to create changing views through it, suggesting the spatial experience that lies beyond. The series of open courtyards terminates in a large lawned quadrant, designed in classic campus tradition as the main gathering place. The building was designed in association with TC Design Group.

Der Ausschreibung zufolge sollte das Gordon Institute of Business Science eine »afrikanische Identität« haben; gleichzeitig sollten die angehenden Betriebswirte nach dem Willen des Bauherrn aus dem Verfahren lernen, eigene Lösungen im Geschäftsleben kreativ zu entwickeln.

Der Einfluss Charles Correas und Riccardo Legorettas ist bei diesem Projekt besonders augenfällig. Geschichtete Räume öffnen sich zum Himmel; harsch nebeneinandergestellte Formen und kräftige Farben schaffen eine sprühende Folge von Räumen, die sich beim Gang durch das Gebäude beständig wandeln. Putzfassaden umgeben die Innenhöfe und lassen den Bau wirken, als sei er aus einem massiven Block geschnitten. Die Fassade ist bewusst gestaffelt, um wechselnde Ausblicke zu schaffen und die hinter ihr liegenden Räume anzudeuten. Die Folge offener Innenhöfe mündet in eine Rasenfläche, die nach klassischer Campustradition als Haupttreffpunkt dienen soll. Der Bau entstand in Zusammenarbeit mit der TC Design Group.

Le cahier des charges stipulait que le bâtiment devait avoir un « aspect africain »; parallèlement, le client souhaitait que les étudiants préparant la MBA (maîtrise de gestion) y apprennent à devenir créatifs et à trouver des solutions originales dans leur vie professionnelle.

L'influence de Charles Correa et de Riccardo Legoretta est particulièrement manifeste dans ce projet. Espaces stratifiés s'ouvrant sur le ciel, formes juxtaposées avec force et couleurs vives créent une succession d'espaces vibrants qui changent d'aspect au fur et à mesure que l'on parcourt le bâtiment. Des façades enduites délimitant des cours intérieures donnent l'impression que le bâtiment est taillé dans un seul bloc. La façade principale délibérément ajourée permet de voir les espaces intérieurs selon des perspectives sans cesse changeantes. La succession de cours à ciel ouvert s'achève sur une grande pelouse carrée – principal lieu de réunion, dans la tradition des campus universitaires. Le bâtiment a été conçu en association avec le TC Design Group.

The rich colours and shaded cloisters of the business school are influenced by the work of Charles Correa.

Die lebhaften Farben und schattigen Innenhöfe der Wirtschaftsschule sind vom Werk Charles Correas beeinflusst.

Les allées ombragées et les couleurs chaudes de l'Ecole de commerce portent la marque de Charles Correa.

bove, sunken seating in the main courtyard intended s a gathering point. Use of light and shade, right, esponds to the South African climate.

ben: Abgesenkte Sitzbänke im zentralen Hof sind als reffpunkt gedacht. Rechts: Der Einsatz von Licht und chatten entspricht dem Klima Südafrikas.

-dessus : dans la grande cour, des gradins en partie nterrés servent de point de rencontre. A droite: les jeux 'ombre et de lumière sont conçus en fonction du climat ud-africain.

open to sky
court (small)
1

he facade is simple yet monumental, above. Left, the ollege is designed as a series of open-air courtyards.

)ben: Die Fassade ist schlicht und monumental zugleich. inks: Das College ist als Abfolge offener Innenhöfe onzipiert.

'i-dessus : en dépit de sa simplicité, la façade possède n caractère monumental. Page de gauche : l'école est tructurée autour d'une série de cours à ciel ouvert.

Henri Comrie's Glass Centre displays shades of Zaha Hadid's fire station for Vitra.

Henri Comries Glass Centre erinnert entfernt an Zaha Hadids Feuerwehrhaus für Vitra.

Le Glass Centre de Henri Comrie n'est pas sans évoquer le poste d'incendie de Zaha Hadid pour Vitra.

1995 **Midrand, South Africa**

PFG Glass Centre

This building was the product of an open competition won by Comrie from 122 entries. Influenced by Zaha Hadid's Vitra Fire Station in Weil am Rhein, Germany, which was completed around the time of the competition, the PFG Glass Centre is conceived as a dynamic collection of shards of glass protruding from a calm central mass that would engage with the movement of traffic on the adjacent highway. Acute angles and tilted planes are kept sharp and crisp, as any crystalline structure should, through an absence of detail. In the interior a spiralling floor plan achieves a logical flow of spaces despite the spatially complex volumes contained within. This building was designed in association with TC Design Group.

Comries Entwurf ging als Sieger aus einem Wettbewerb mit 122 Teilnehmern hervor. Unter dem Einfluss von Zaha Hadids Feuerwehrhaus für Vitra in Weil am Rhein, die um die Zeit des Wettbewerbs fertiggestellt wurde, ist das PFG Glass Center als dynamische Ansammlung von Glasscherben konzipiert, die aus einem ruhenden zentralen Baukörper herausragen, als wollten sie in den Verkehr des benachbarten Highways eingreifen. Wie bei jeder kristallinen Struktur fehlen Details – spitze Winkel und geneigte Flächen bleiben scharf und klar. Der spiralförmige Grundriss sorgt für einen logischen Fluss der komplexen Innenräume. Der Bau entstand in Zusammenarbeit mit der TC Design Group.

Ce projet est le résultat d'un concours gagné par Comrie parmi 122 participants. Influencé par le Poste d'incendie de Vitra à Weil am Rhein, Allemagne, dû à Zaha Hadid, achevé à l'époque, le PFG Glass Centre est caractérisé par un assemblage d'éclats de verre ornant une paisible masse centrale, dont le dynamisme rivalise avec l'animation de la rue adjacente. Les angles aigus et les plans inclinés sont durs et nets comme il convient à une structure cristalline, sans le moindre détail superflu. A l'intérieur, un plan au sol en spirale assure une circulation rationnelle en dépit de la forme complexe des espaces. Le bâtiment a été conçu en association avec le TC Design Group.

Windows emerge where planes meet.

Wo Flächen aufeinandertreffen, kommen Fenster zum Vorschein.

Les pans de murs et les baies vitrées sont rigoureusement imbriqués.

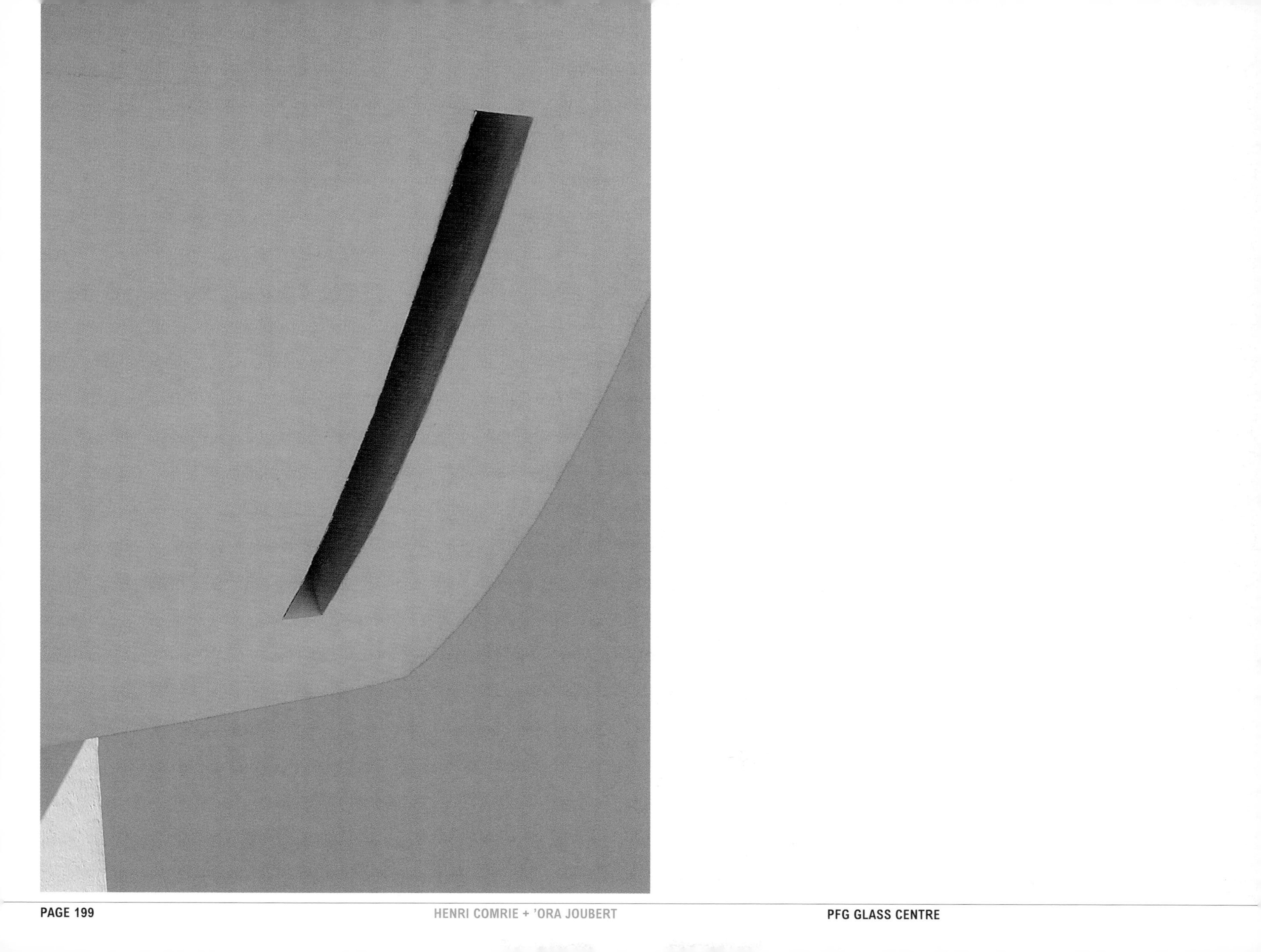

Huis Laubscher

'Ora Joubert's house for Cornelius Laubscher is built on the site of a mid-century thatched house built by Bauhaus-trained architect Helmut Stauch. A simple double-height structure of a neat thatch supported by rough wooden posts provides simple shelter for open-plan living. Beneath, and making no attempt to disguise or glamorise this barn-like construction, areas of brick and glass enclose the living quarters.

'Ora Jouberts Haus für Cornelius Laubscher entstand auf dem Gelände eines um die Jahrhundertmitte vom Bauhausschüler Helmut Stauch erbauten Reetdachhauses. Das schlichte, zwei Geschosshöhen umfassende Bauwerk besitzt ebenfalls ein Reetdach, das hier von roh behauenen Holzpfosten getragen wird. Der weitgehend unstrukturierte Wohnbereich wird von Backstein- und Glasflächen umschlossen; jeder Versuch, das an eine Scheune erinnernde Äußere zu kaschieren oder zu veredeln, unterbleibt.

La maison conçue par 'Ora Joubert pour Cornelius Laubscher est construite sur le site d'une maison à toit d chaume, construite au milieu du siècle par l'architecte Helmut Stauch, formé au Bauhaus. Une structure en chaume à deux niveaux, soutenue par des piliers en bois brut, constitue un abri d'une grande simplicité pour un habitat à plan ouvert. Au niveau inférieur, sans tenter le moins du monde de déguiser ou d'embellir cette construction semblable à une grange, des surfaces en brique et verre délimitent les pièces d'habitation.

'Ora Joubert's house for Cornelius Laubscher strives to create a new South African vernacular using rough materials such as timber and brick.

'Ora Joubert verwendet bei ihrem Haus für Cornelius Laubscher rohe Materialien wie Holz und Backstein, um einen neuen südafrikanischen Landesstil zu schaffen.

La maison dessinée par 'Ora Joubert pour Cornelius Laubscher, faite de matériaux bruts (brique, bois ...) cherche à renouveler l'architecture traditionnelle sud-africaine.

Exposed timber rafters dominate the double-height living space. Views from the sleeping platform, right and below.

Frei liegende hölzerne Dachsparren beherrschen den zweigeschossigen Wohnraum. Rechts und unten: Blicke von der Schlafebene.

Le séjour à double hauteur est dominé par de massives poutres apparentes (vues prises depuis la mezzanine).

Crosson Clarke Architects

8 Augustus Terrace, Parnell, Auckland, New Zealand   tel +64 9 302 0222   fax +64 9 302 0234   e-mail arch@cca.net.nz

Ken Crosson

born	1957 Ashburton, New Zealand
studied	1976 University of Auckland Architectural School
previous practice	Covell Matthews Wheatley Architects, London, England
	1987 set up Crosson Architects
	1999 became Crosson Clarke Architects

Paul Clarke

born	1967 Dunedin, New Zealand
studied	1990 University of Auckland Architectural School, Auckland, New Zealand
previous practice	Mason and Wales, Dunedin, New Zealand; Hannah Wallace Architects, Auckland, New Zealand; Crosson Architects, Auckland, New Zealand
	1999 made partner of Crosson Clarke Architects

Selected projects

Stevenson Concrete administration building	1994 Auckland, New Zealand
Edendale Primary School	1996 Auckland, New Zealand
Crosson Architects office building	1996 Auckland, New Zealand
Wilson House	1998 Remuera, Auckland, New Zealand
Long Drop Cafe	1998 Titirangi, New Zealand
Beach House	1999 Waiheke Island, New Zealand

Crosson Clarke has established itself as a practice with a wide portfolio ranging from houses, shops, interiors and offices to educational, commercial and industrial buildings. Their business-like approach is focused on budgets and deadlines. They are less interested in imposing a "house-style" on their buildings as getting to know the client and devising individual and widely differing solutions. The result could be a primary school made of odd shapes and colours, a light and airy house or an austere office block. Yet through all this diversity an architectural rigour can be traced that never over-embellishes. The palette of materials is always restricted, and the outline form keeps its coherence through simple straightforward relationships between the elements of the building.

Crosson Clarke konnte sich mit einer großen Bandbreite von Aufträgen, angefangen bei Wohnhäusern über Läden, Inneneinrichtungen und Büros bis hin zu Schul-, Geschäfts- und Industriebauten, etablieren. Ihre pragmatische Arbeitsweise ist auf die Einhaltung von Budgets und Terminen ausgerichtet. Sie sind weniger daran interessiert, ihren Bauten einen stilistischen Stempel aufzudrücken als ihre Auftraggeber kennenzulernen und für sie individuelle und höchst unterschiedliche Lösungen auszuarbeiten. Das Ergebnis kann eine in herkömmlichen Formen und Farben errichtete Grundschule sein, ein lichtes, luftiges Wohnhaus oder ein nüchternes Bürogebäude.
Bei aller Verschiedenheit der einzelnen Bauten bleibt eine gewisse architektonische Strenge erkennbar, die nie ein Zuviel an Schmuckformen zulässt. So ist etwa die Materi-

Crosson Clarke est un bureau, dont le portefeuille important et varié comprend aussi bien des maisons individuelles que des magasins et aménagements d'intérieurs, des bureaux et des bâtiments scolaires, commerciaux et industriels. Leur approche pragmatique est axée sur le respect des budgets et des délais. Ils cherchent moins à donner à leurs réalisations un « style maison » qu'à comprendre les besoins du client et à leur trouver des solutions extrêmement variées. Le résultat peut être aussi bien une école primaire aux formes et aux couleurs inhabituelles qu'une maison claire et aérée, ou un austère bloc de bureaux.
En dépit de cette diversité, leurs constructions témoignent d'une rigueur architecturale qui évite toujours l'esthétisme gratuit. La gamme des matériaux reste

Such simplicity makes their work refreshingly unpretentious.
In 1997 Ken Crosson was made one of the youngest Fellows of the New Zealand Institute of Architects at the age of 39. He was joined as a partner in 1999 by Paul Clarke.

alpalette stets beschränkt, und der Zusammenhang der umrissbildenden Formen bleibt durch schlichte, geradlinige Beziehungen zwischen Teilen gewahrt, was die Bauten erfreulich unaufdringlich erscheinen lässt.
1997 wurde Ken Crosson mit 39 Jahren zum jüngsten Mitglied des New Zealand Institute of Architects berufen. 1999 schloss sich ihm Paul Clarke als Partner an.

toujours limitée, et les contours maintiennent leur cohérence grâce à des relations simples et évidentes entre les divers éléments du bâtiment, ce qui donne à leurs réalisations une absence de prétention rafraîchissante.
En 1997, Ken Crosson est devenu, à l'âge de 39 ans, un des plus jeune membres du New Zealand Institute of Architects. En 1999, Paul Clarke devenait son associé.

1996 **Auckland, New Zealand**

Crosson Architects office building

Perched on a cliff top overlooking Waitemata Harbour, Crosson Clarke's own architectural offices have a lightness of touch and structure commensurate with their fragile but dramatic site. Quite predictably, the north-facing harbour facade is completely glazed, though Crosson Clarke have pushed a red box housing the conference room out through the facade, an unexpected surprise.
Though the building presents a fairly closed street facade, the main mass is lifted up, allowing passers-by a view straight through to the harbour almost unaware of the mass hovering above. A tall thin stair tower rises up the side, glazed at both sides, leaving the red treads hanging precariously in space. This strong vertical element provides a powerful counterpoint to the black horizontal facade. The structure is held together visually by sheer side walls of anodised aluminium sheets.
Using a limited palette of materials and an exposed frame, the architects have created a simple, unpretentious building that is easy to read from its exterior alone.

Hoch auf einer Klippe mit Blick über dem Waitemata Harbour erbaut, zeichnet sich Crosson Clarkes eigenes Architekturbüro durch plastische und konstruktive Leichtigkeit aus, die mit dem heiklen und zugleich spektakulären Standort harmoniert. Wie zu erwarten, besteht die nördliche, dem Hafen zugewandte Fassade ganz aus Glas, mit Ausnahme eines roten Kastens, dem Konferenzraum, den Crosson Clarke als überraschendes Element durch die Fassade geschoben haben.
Obgleich das Gebäude der Straße eine eher geschlossene Fassade zuwendet, können Passanten direkt auf den Hafen schauen, nahezu ohne sich des erhöhten Hauptvolumens des Gebäudes recht bewusst zu werden. An der Seite erhebt sich ein hoher, dünner, auf beiden Seiten verglaster Treppenturm, dessen rote Stufen bedenklich in der Luft zu hängen scheinen. Dieses ausgeprägt vertikale Element stellt ein kräftiges Gegengewicht zur schwarzen, horizontalen Fassade dar. Als visuelle Klammer des Gebäudes fungieren glatte Seitenwände aus eloxiertem Aluminiumblech.
Durch die begrenzte Zahl von Materialien und den sichtbaren Tragrahmen gelang den Architekten ein schlichtes, zurückhaltendes Gebäude, dessen Konstruktion sich von außen leicht erschließt.

Perché au sommet d'une falaise qui domine le port de Waitemata, le propre bureau de Crosson Clarke possède une légèreté de design et de structure en rapport avec le caractère à la fois précaire et dramatique du site. Comme il était prévisible, la façade nord donnant sur le port est entièrement vitrée, mais une boîte rouge abritant la salle de conférences perce la façade, créant la surprise.
Bien que la façade sur rue soit presque aveugle, la masse principale est surélevée, de sorte que les passants en ont à peine conscience car la vue porte jusqu'au port. Une haute et étroite tour-escalier s'élève sur le côté; comme elle est vitrée sur deux côtés, les marches rouges semblent flotter dans l'espace. Cet élément vertical fournit un puissant contrepoint à la façade sombre et horizontale. Les murs latéraux en plaques d'aluminium anodisé assurent la cohésion visuelle de la structure.
Utilisant une gamme de matériaux limitée et une ossature apparente, les architectes ont réalisé un bâtiment simple et sans prétentions, qu'il est facile de lire de l'extérieur.

**Above, the penthouse office and roof terrace of Crosson Clarke's Auckland office building.
Left, the black southern facade of the office building with ground floor left open, maintaining views through to Waitemata Harbour.**

Oben: Penthousebüro und Dachterrasse des Bürogebäudes in Auckland. Links: Die schwarze Südfassade, deren offenes Erdgeschoss Durchblicke auf den Waitemata Harbour zulässt.

Ci-dessus : le « penthouse » bureaux et terrasse de l'immeuble de bureaux. A gauche : la façade noire, dont le rez-de-chaussée entièrement vitré préserve la vue sur le port de Waitemata.

8

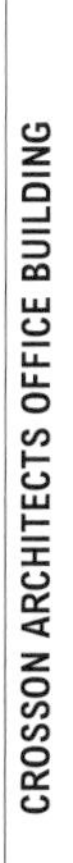

Elements of the office building are clearly defined: stair tower to the left, exaggerated rainwater channel to the right, black mass for the main office floors, and the glazed penthouse.

Die Elemente des Bürogebäudes sind klar erkennbar: links der Treppenturm, rechts das markante Regenrohr, der schwarze Baukörper mit den Hauptbüroetagen und das verglaste Penthouse.

Les éléments de l'immeuble sont nettement définis : à gauche, la cage d'escalier ; au centre, la masse noire abritant les bureaux ; à droite, un chéneau surdimensionné ; sur le toit, le « penthouse » entièrement vitré.

The building is sandwiched between two blank walls of anodised aluminium.

Die Seitenwände des Gebäudes bestehen aus eloxiertem Aluminium.

Le bâtiment est enserré entre deux murs aveugles en aluminium anodisé.

oor plans/ Grundrisse der Etagen/
ans des divers niveaux

car deck/ Parkdeck/ garage
street entrance/ Eingang/ entrée principale
office/ Büro/ bureau
conference room/ Konferenzraum/ salle de conférences
roof terrace/ Dachterrasse/ terrasse

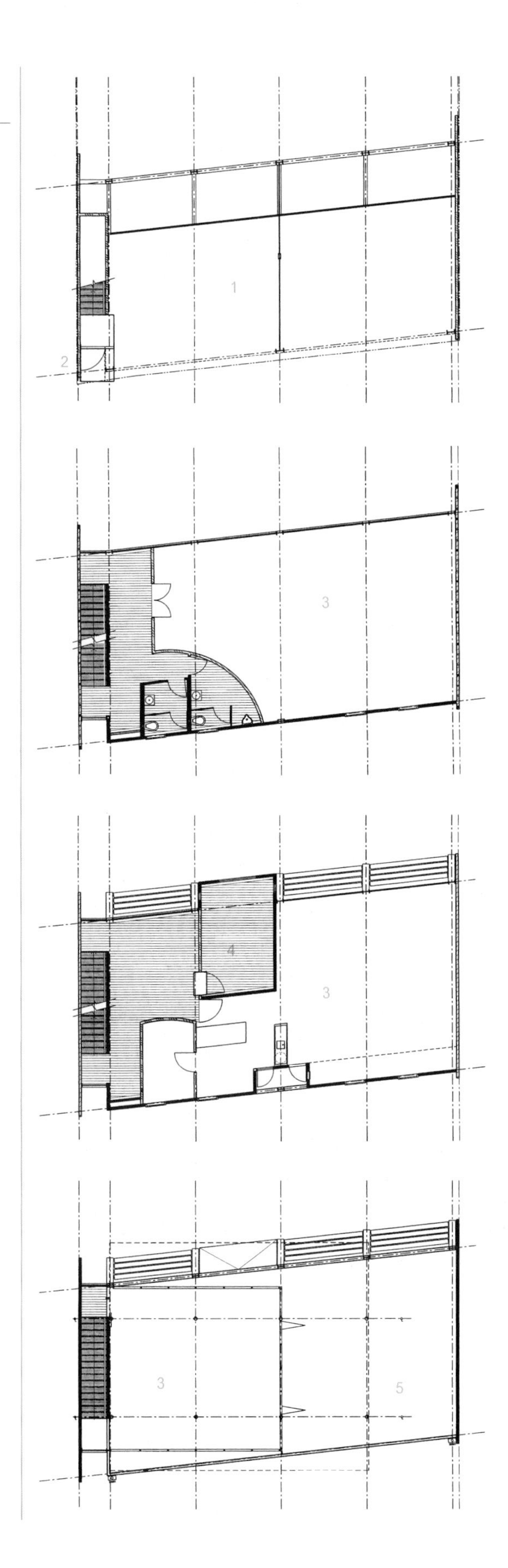

The Wilson House is essentially two rectangular boxes crashing through each other.

Das Haus Wilson setzt sich im Wesentlichen aus zwei einander durchstoßenden rechtwinkligen Kästen zusammen.

La maison Wilson est structurée par l'interpénétration de deux boîtes rectangulaires.

998 Remuera, Auckland, New Zealand

Wilson House

terior and exterior have a degree of ambiguity in the ilson House. Floor-to-ceiling glass doors disappear to the wall cavities so that the living area can flow amlessly on to the patio, the transition made even ore gradual by the erection of a canvas awning over e outdoor space. Likewise the dining room stops ort of the end of the building's floor plan, leaving indoor-outdoor space for a barbecue terrace that en flows out into the patio adjoining the living room. e house is essentially two rectangular units, a lower at-roofed unit clad in plywood stained black and a ghtly taller unit clad in Zincalume cutting through e middle, its gently sloping roof and broad eaves nbracing its neighbour. The use of rough materials ves a makeshift feel that echoes rural Australasian ildings. The tradition was perhaps most famously propriated by Glenn Murcutt and Roy Grounds, but now becoming a common theme among younger ustralasian architects, particularly in single family ouses.

Im Haus Wilson sind Innen- und Außenraum nicht streng differenziert. Raumhohe Glastüren gleiten in Hohlräume in den Wänden, so dass der Wohnbereich nahtlos in den Patio übergehen kann; eine Segeltuchmarkise über dem Außenbereich macht den Übergang noch fließender. Auch das Esszimmer endet vor der Außenkante des Grundrisses, wodurch eine überdachte Grillterrasse entsteht, die in den vor dem Wohnbereich liegenden Patio übergeht. Das Haus besteht im Wesentlichen aus zwei rechteckigen Elementen: einem niedrigeren flachgedeckten Bauteil, der mit schwarz gebeiztem Sperrholz verschalt ist und einem etwas höheren, mit verzinktem Aluminium verkleideten Teil, der die Mitte durchschneidet und mit seinem sanft geneigten Dach und den ausladenden Traufen den benachbarten Bauteil überfängt. Die Verwendung roher, unbehandelter Materialien vermittelt den Eindruck eines Provisoriums und entspricht damit ländlichen Bauten im australisch-ozeanischen Raum. Diese Tradition, die vor allem Glenn Murcutt und Roy Grounds aufgenommen haben, erfreut sich bei jüngeren australisch-ozeanischen Architekten inzwischen – besonders für Einfamilienhäuser – einiger Beliebtheit.

Dans la maison Wilson, les notions d'intérieur et d'extérieur deviennent ambiguës. Des portes en verre allant d'un seul tenant du plancher au plafond se glissent dans les murs, de sorte que la salle de séjour se prolonge insensiblement jusqu'au patio, la transition devenant encore plus graduelle lorsque des stores en tissu couvrent l'espace extérieur. De même, la salle à manger va jusqu'à l'extrême limite du plan, qui n'est pas identique avec la limite du terrain, créant un espace à la fois intérieur et extérieur pour la terrasse du barbecue, qui elle-même s'étend jusqu'au patio donnant sur le séjour.
La maison se compose pour l'essentiel de deux unités rectangulaires : un volume assez bas au toit en terrasse, revêtu de contreplaqué teinté de noir, et, le recoupant au milieu, une unité un peu plus haute revêtue de Zincalume, dont la toiture en pente douce et les larges avant-toits semblent étreindre sa voisine. L'utilisation de matériaux bruts donne une impression d'inachevé évoquant l'habitat rural d'Australasie. Ce style, mis en honneur par Glenn Murcutt et Roy Grounds, est de plus en plus utilisé par les jeunes architectes de cette aire géographique, en particulier pour les maisons individuelles.

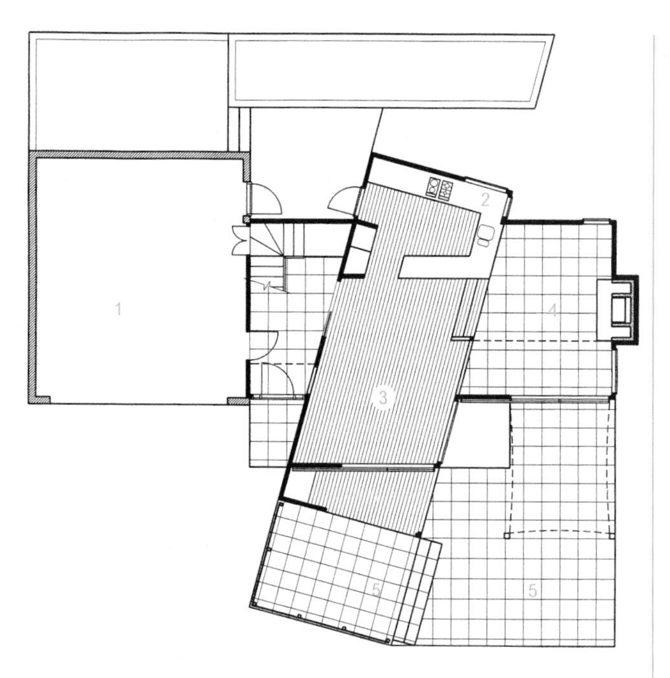

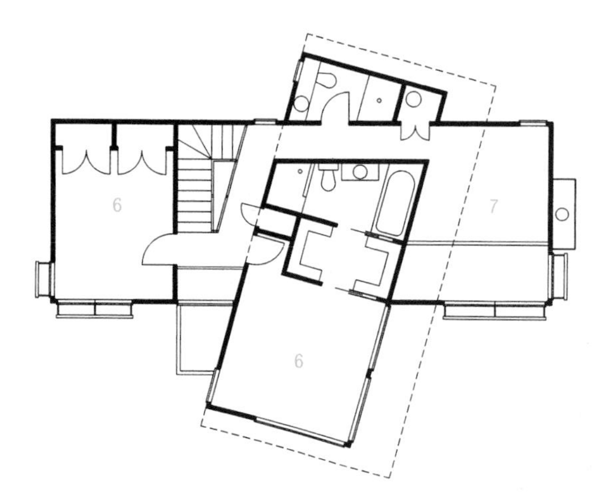

Floor plans/ Grundrisse/ Plans

1 **garage/** Garage/ garage
2 **kitchen/** Küche/ cuisine
3 **dining/** Esszimmer/ salle à manger
4 **living/** Wohnzimmer/ séjour
5 **terrace/** Terrasse/ terrasse
6 **bedroom/** Schlafraum/ chambre
7 **study/** Arbeitszimmer/ bureau

:ooking, living and dining spaces, left, are defined ›ut open-plan. The exterior of the house is clad in ':incalume, above.

inks: Koch-, Wohn- und Essbereich sind klar umrissen, ber offen. Oben: der Außenbau ist mit verzinktem \luminium verkleidet.

'age de gauche : bien que nettement définis, la cuisine, a zone-repas et le séjour sont réunis dans un seul espace ı plan ouvert. Ci-dessus, les façades revêtues de ':incalume.

Vincent Van Duysen

ɔmbardenvest 34, 2000 Antwerp, Belgium   tel +32 3 205 9190   fax +32 3 227 2265   e-mail vincent.vanduysen@skynet.be

ncent Van Duysen	
ɔrn	1962 Lokeren, Belgium
udied	1980-85 Higher Institute of Architecture, Sint Lucas, Ghent, Belgium
evious practice	1990 set up practice
	collaborations with several architects and interior architects in Belgium and abroad

elected projects		
B V.D House	1995	St. Amandsberg, Belgium
H Residence	1995	Lokeren, Belgium
ɔpyright bookshop	1996	Antwerp, Belgium
ames Van Damme Art Gallery	1996	Brussels, Belgium
ne Capital Markets Company, offices	1998	Antwerp, Belgium; London, UK; New York, USA
elfridges, 2nd floor	1998	London, UK
portmax shops	1999	Milan, Italy; Paris, France; Tokyo, Japan
oncordia offices	2000	Waregem, Belgium
.H B.H Loft	2000	New York, USA

is minimalist style has attracted a string of high-rofile fashionable clients, but Van Duysen's work s really more profound, than the reputation from these hain stores might suggest.
he has a penchant for bare walls or stark interiors, is only because they serve to focus attention on the xciting spaces they contain. He inspires an awareness f the shape of a wall and its featureless doors and vindows as they become positive or negative shapes n its surface. Furniture is kept to simple sculptural ɔrms, architectural objects in the space.
fften behind this apparently blinding simplicity is unning deception. A house that might seem very onventional is, in fact, a complete subversion of onvention. A wide open space can suddenly become ery intimate thanks to a few carefully positioned ieces of furniture.

Sein minimalistischer Stil wirkte anziehend auf eine Reihe bekannter, trendbewusster Auftraggeber, aber Van Duysens Arbeiten sind tatsächlich differenzierter als es der Ruf dieser Kettenläden vermuten lässt.
Wenn er eine Neigung zu kahlen Wänden oder schlichten Interieurs hat, dann deshalb, weil sie die Aufmerksamkeit auf die reizvollen Räume lenken sollen. Van Duysen regt zur bewussten Wahrnehmung einer Wand und ihrer undekorierten Türen und Fenster an, die auf der Oberfläche zu positiven oder negativen Formen gerinnen. Möbel reduziert er auf einfache, plastische Formen und macht sie zu architektonischen Objekten im Raum.
Hinter dieser Schlichtheit verbirgt sich jedoch ein geschicktes Täuschungsmanöver. Bei einem höchst konventionell erscheinenden Haus kann es sich tatsächlich um eine völlige Umkehrung der Konvention handeln.
Ein weiter, offener Raum kann mittels einiger weniger geschickt platzierter Möbelstücke plötzlich sehr intim wirken.

Son style minimaliste a séduit toute une série de clients prestigieux, mais la démarche de Van Duysen est plus approfondie que la réputation de ces chaînes de magasins à la mode ne pourrait le faire croire.
S'il a un penchant pour les murs nus et les intérieurs austères, c'est uniquement parce qu'ils attirent l'attention sur les espaces fascinants qu'ils renferment. Il fait prendre conscience de la nature d'un mur et des portes et fenêtres d'un seul tenant, qui deviennent des formes négatives ou positives à la surface de celui-ci. Le mobilier est réduit à de simples formes sculpturales, objets architecturaux dans l'espace. Cette simplicité réductrice cache toutefois une subtile subversion. Une maison qui peut paraître très conventionnelle est en fait un renversement total des conventions. Un espace largement ouvert peut faire preuve d'une grande intimité grâce à quelques meubles habilement disposés.

D.B V.D House

The D.B V.D house plays along with the conventions of a family house on a residential estate, matching the cornice height, and including a pitched roof and chimney. However, he beats the planning authorities at their own game, inverting the pitch so that the roof, in fact, dips in the middle, leaving the cornice as a stark straight edge on what appears to be a brick box.

With three of the four sides sloping down into the building, the fourth facade becomes a dramatic winged plane of brick, a purely sculptural facade supporting just three interrelating rectangles: the open oblong of the chimney, the dark recess that leads to the main entrance, and a featureless side door.

Mit dem Haus D.B V.D greift Van Duysen die Konventionen des Einfamilienhauses in einer Wohnsiedlung mit einheitlicher Traufhöhe, geneigtem Dach und Schornstein auf. Er schlägt die Bauaufsicht jedoch mit ihren eigenen Waffen, indem er etwa die Dachneigung umkehrt, so dass sich das Dach nun zur Mitte hin senkt und das Gesims als gerader Rand eines Backsteinkastens erscheint.
Während sich drei der vier Seiten in das Haus hinabsenken, gestaltete Van Duysen die vierte Front zu einer spektakulären geflügelten Backsteinfläche, einer rein plastischen Fassade, die drei aufeinander bezogene Rechtecke trägt: das offene Rechteck des Kamins, die dunkle, zum Haupteingang führende Öffnung und einen schlichten Nebeneingang.

La maison D.B V.D joue sur les conventions d'une mais individuelle dans un lotissement résidentiel. La hauteur de la corniche est conforme, le toit est en pente et il y a une cheminée. Mais la maison bat les réglementations e matière de construction sur leur propre terrain : la pente est inversée de sorte que le toit forme un V, tandis que corniche devient un rebord droit et nu qui semble posé sur un cube en brique.
Quatre des trois côtés étant inclinés vers l'intérieur du bâtiment, le quatrième devient un audacieux plan de brique, façade purement sculpturale dessinée par trois rectangles : la cheminée oblongue, le sombre renforcement qui abrite la porte d'entrée, et une porte secondai nue.

The inverted roof line gives the house a dramatic profile, right. Left, a dark hole leads to the main entrance.

Rechts: Das abgesenkte Dach gibt dem Haus ein markantes Profil. Links: Eine dunkle Öffnung führt zum Haupteingang.

Page de droite : la maison doit son profil caractéristique à sa toiture à pente inversée. A gauche : une ouverture béante donne accès à l'entrée principale.

Above, doorways are featureless. Right, the house opens up round the corner, where the ground-floor living room opens on to the garden.

Oben: Die Türen sind profillos eingeschnitten. Rechts: Der Wohnbereich öffnet sich zum Garten.

Ci-dessus : les portes sont des rectangles d'une neutralité absolue. A droite, le côté ouvert de la maison, avec le séjour donnant sur le jardin.

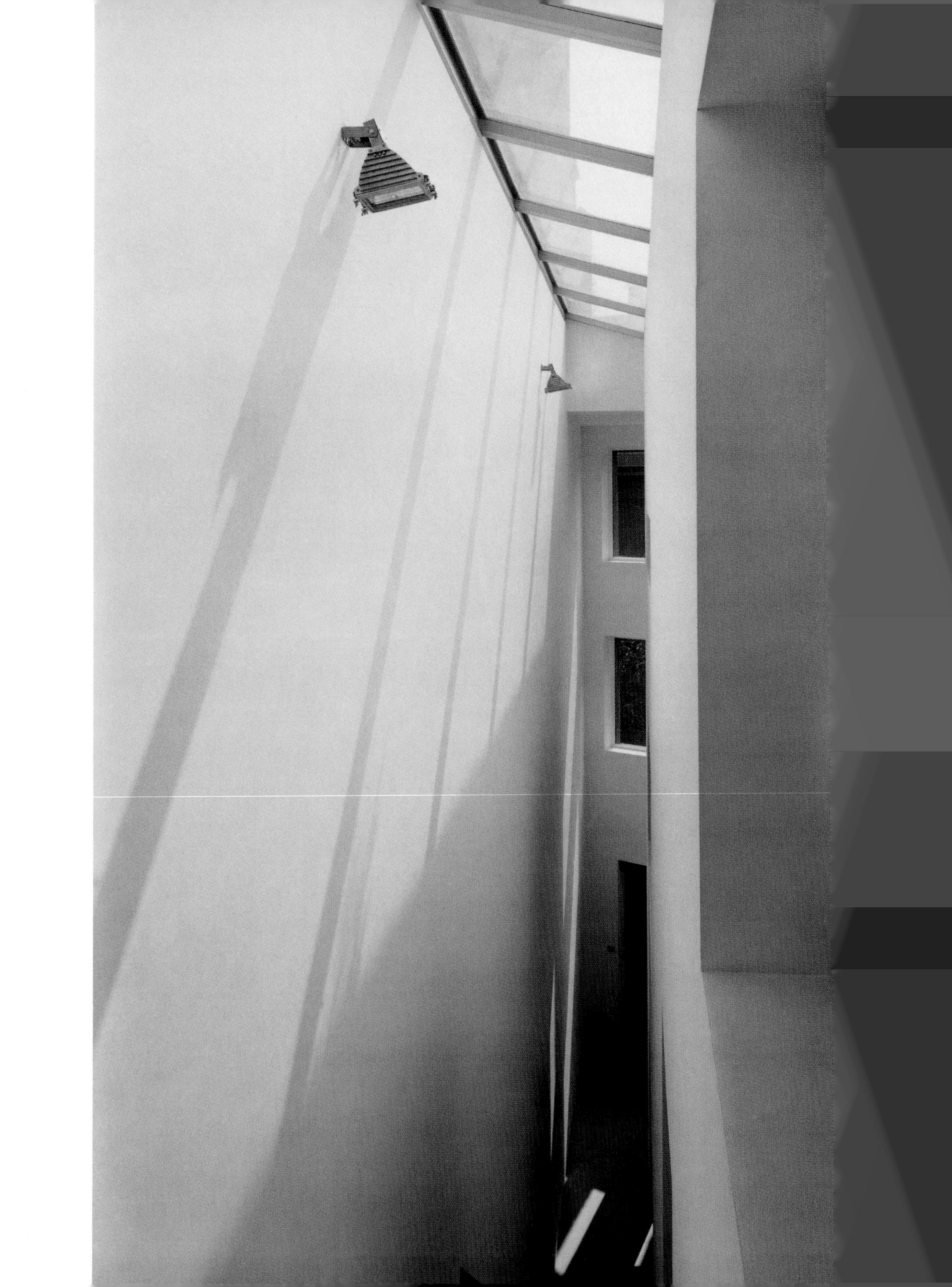

llleries open on to the deep stairwell, lit by the long ip of roof light.

e Galerieräume sind zum Treppenschacht offen, der rch ein langes Oberlicht erhellt wird.

profonde cage d'escalier éclairée d'en haut par un g bandeau vitré donne sur des espaces ouverts.

196 **Brussels, Belgium**

James Van Damme Art Gallery

reworking of an early 20th-century Brussels town use spread over five storeys and an adjacent three-orey block. A long narrow staircase has been inserted connect the two buildings, beginning in the three-orey block that houses the gallery and continuing in a aight line undaunted past vast openings on to the llery floor. At the top of the stair where it meets the wn house, a frosted glass door marks the transition tween new and old, hard and soft, public and private. om the old part of the house, a long strip of glazing the edge of the roof terrace marks the line of the llery staircase below so that the two parts of the velopment are intrinsically linked but never impinge on each other.

Die James van Damme Art Gallery in Brüssel umfasst den Umbau eines fünfgeschossigen Brüsseler Stadthauses aus dem frühen 20. Jahrhundert und eines angrenzenden dreistöckigen Blocks. Um beide Gebäude zu verbinden, wurde eine lange, schmale Treppe eingezogen, die in dem dreistöckigen Block beginnt, in dem die Galerie untergebracht ist und sich vorbei an großformatigen Öffnungen in gerader Linie gewagt bis auf die Galerieebene fortsetzt. Am oberen Ende der Treppe, wo sie auf das Stadthaus trifft, markiert eine Milchglastür den Übergang zwischen neu und alt, hart und weich, öffentlich und privat. Ausgehend vom alten Teil des Hauses zeigt ein langer Glasstreifen am Rand der Dachterrasse den Verlauf der darunterliegenden Galerietreppe an, so dass die beiden Teile der Baumaßnahme zwar aufeinander bezogen sind, einander jedoch nie beeinträchtigen.

Remodelage d'une maison de ville du début du siècle comportant cinq niveaux, à laquelle vient s'ajouter un bloc de trois étages. Un escalier long et étroit, inséré pour relier les deux bâtiments, commence dans le bloc de trois étages où se trouve la galerie. Partant du rez-de-chaussée de celle-ci, il monte en ligne droite, en passant par de larges ouvertures, jusqu'à la maison de ville. Une porte en verre dépoli marque la transition entre le neuf et l'ancien, le dur et le doux, le public et le privé. Dans la partie ancienne, une longue bande vitrée bordant le toit-terrasse indique le trajet de l'escalier situé en-dessous. Les deux parties du bâtiment sont donc intimement reliées sans jamais empiéter l'une sur l'autre.

ng narrow stair connecting the two parts the house.

ne lange, schmale Treppe verbindet die beiden Teile s Gebäudes.

escalier long et étroit relie les deux parties bâtiment.

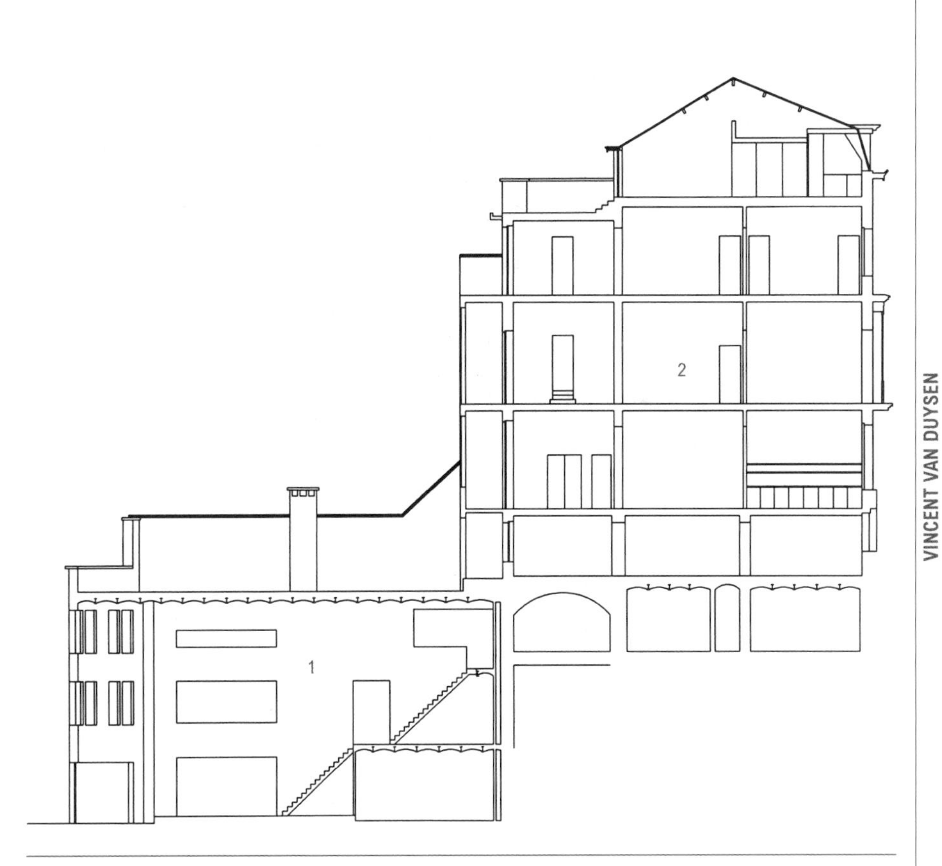

Section/ Schnitt/ Coupe

1 **new gallery/** neue Galerie/ nouvelle galerie

2 **existing house/** vorhandenes Haus/ maison

Van Duysen has created boutiques for Sportmax in Tokyo, Milan (shown), Paris and London.

Van Duysen gestaltete Sportmax-Boutiquen in Tokio, Mailand (hier abgebildet), Paris und London.

Van Duysen a dessiné des magasins pour Sportmax à Tokyo, Milan (photos), Paris et Londres.

1999 **Milan, Italy**

Sportmax

"A naked space where infinity is emphasised by the repetition of materials and colours." Bare brickwork walls, sandwiched between a light grey concrete tiled floor and ceiling with repetitive light grey beams, carry straight through the shop, stretching its dimensions. In this minimal space, the clothes stand out as the main feature, displayed on free-standing monovolumes (clothing containers), which create more intimate areas as a counterpoint to the openness of the main space. This is one of a series of boutiques created for Sportmax in major international cities.

Sportmax ist »ein kahler Raum, in dem durch die Wiederholung von Materialien und Farben auf die Unendlichkeit verwiesen wird.« Zwischen einem Fußboden aus hellgrauen Betonfliesen und der Decke mit ihrer Reihung hellgrauer Balken eingespannt, strecken unverputzte Backsteinwände optisch die Abmessungen des Ladens. In dem kleinen Raum fallen die auf freistehenden Displays dekorierten Kleider ins Auge. Als Gegengewicht zur Offenheit des Hauptraums entstehen durch diese Displays abgeteilte, intimere Räume.
Der Laden ist beispielhaft für eine Kette von Boutiquen in internationalen Großstädten, die Van Duysen für Sportmax konzipierte.

« Un espace nu indiquant l'infini par la répétition des matériaux et des couleurs. » Des murs en briques apparentes, pris entre un sol de dalles de béton gris clair et un plafond aux poutres répétitives gris clair, s'étendent d'un bout à l'autre du magasin, étirant ses dimensions. Dans cet environnement minimaliste, les vêtements tiennent la vedette, disposés sur des volumes isolés (conteneurs à vêtements) créant des îlots d'intimité en contrepoint avec l'ouverture de l'espace principal. Il s'agit d'un des magasins dessinés pour Sportmax dans des grandes villes de divers pays.

The light industrial building has been stripped back and remodelled.

Das lichte Industriegebäude wurde rückgebaut und erweitert.

Le bâtiment industriel a été entièrement remodelé et agrandi.

2000 **Waregem, Belgium**

Concordia offices

An existing office for the Belgian weaving company Concordia has been stripped back and expanded. Van Duysen's new monolithic shell is conceived as three giant light boxes, inspired by the technical additions on the roofs of industrial buildings. Executed in planes of glass and concrete, which can be read as opposing positive and negative planes, the building is a powerful presence externally, and a light airy space internally.

Das bestehende Bürogebäude der belgischen Weberei Concordia wurde rückgebaut und erweitert. Inspiriert von den technischen Aufbauten auf Dächern von Industriegebäuden, konzipierte Van Duysen die neue, monolithische Schale in Form dreier überdimensionaler Lichtkästen. Das Gebäude besteht aus Glas- und Betonflächen, die als gegenüberliegende positive und negative Flächen verstanden werden können; nach außen behauptet es sich mit seiner kraftvollen Formensprache, das Innere ist hell und luftig.

L'immeuble de bureaux existant de l'entreprise de tissage Concordia a été entièrement rénové et agrandi. La nouvelle coque monolithique de Van Duysen prend la forme de trois énormes boîtes, inspirées par les superstructures techniques construites sur le toit de bâtiments industriels. Réalisé en pans de verre et béton, qui peuvent êtres lus comme des images positives ou négatives, l'édifice affirme une présence puissante, tout en étant clair et lumineux à l'intérieur.

oom 1706-08, 663 King's Road,
orth Point, Hong Kong, China

tel +852 2802 6212 fax +852 2802 6213 e-mail edgeltd@netvigator.com web www.edge.hk.com

ary Chang

orn	1962 Hong Kong
udied	1987 University of Hong Kong
revious practice	P&T Architects and Engineers (HK) Ltd., Hong Kong
	1994 set up Edge with Michael Chan
	1998 set up EDGE (HK) LTD as principal director

elected projects

roadway Cinematheque	1995 Yaumatei, Hong Kong, China (with Michael Chan as Edge)
gilvy & Mather Asia-Pacific	1997 Quarry Bay, Hong Kong, China (with Michael Chan as Edge)
ong Kong Institute of Architects	1997 Causeway Bay, Hong Kong, China (with Michael Chan as Edge)
ary's Apartment	1998 Island East, Hong Kong, China
ong Kong Pavilion	1999 Beijing, China
roadway Cineplex	1999 Tin Shui Wai, Hong Kong, China
enovation of Hong Kong Arts Centre	2000 Wanchai, Hong Kong, China
lega Advantage Data Centre	2000 Chaiwan, Hong Kong, China

nlike many of his contemporaries who rode the devel-ment wave in Asia's boom period during the early 0s, Chang refused to be caught by the commercial ndertow. Though inescapably urban, his portfolio is ot one of huge uninspiring office towers for big cor-orate clients, but concentrates on quality of space precious commodity on such a cramped island) or hat he terms "Interiorscape", challenging the bound-ries that define an interior. Elements traditionally und on the exterior of Hong Kong buildings are brought side (striped tarpaulins, window cages, corrugated lastic and metal), injecting them with new meaning. his is a response to the crowded conditions of Hong ong, where a labyrinthine network of pedestrian treets runs between and often through buildings, ometimes open, sometimes covered, some even with oving walkways, connecting the entire city as one ontinous indoor-outdoor space.

Im Gegensatz zu vielen seiner Altersgenossen, die in den frühen 90er-Jahren auf der Welle des asiatischen Baubooms ritten, geriet Gary Chang nicht in die kommerzielle Unterströmung. Obgleich sein Schaffen urban geprägt ist, finden sich unter seinen Bauten keine belanglosen Bürotürme für Firmenkunden. Chang konzentriert sich auf die Qualität des Raums – kostbares Gut auf einer so dicht besiedelten Insel wie Hongkong – oder dessen, was er als »Interiorscape« bezeichnet. Er betrachtet Architektur als Herausforderung an die Begrenzungen, die den Innenraum definieren. Elemente, die sich in Hongkong traditionell an Fassaden befanden, werden ins Innere verlegt (gestreifte Planen, Fensterkörbe, geriffelter Kunststoff oder Wellblech). Damit reagiert Chang auf die beengten Verhältnisse der Insel, wo sich ein labyrinthisches Netz von Fußwegen zwischen den Gebäuden und häufig auch durch sie hindurch zieht. Diese mal offenen, mal überdachten und bisweilen mit Laufbändern ausgestatteten Wege verbinden die ganze Stadt zu einem einzigen Innen-Außenraum.

Contrairement à nombre de ses contemporains portés par le boom économique asiatique du début des années 90, Gary Chang a refusé de céder au mercantilisme. Bien qu'inévitablement urbain, son portefeuille ne consiste pas en gigantesques et banales tours de bureaux destinées à de grosses sociétés. Chang met l'accent sur la qualité de l'espace, denrée précieuse dans cette île surpeuplée – il parle à ce propos d'« Interiorscape », paysage intérieur.
A ses yeux, l'architecture est un défi aux limites ou frontières qui définissent un intérieur. Des éléments traditionnellement présents à l'extérieur des édifices de Hong Kong (bâches rayées, fenêtres-cages, plastique ou métal ondulé ...) sont transférés dans l'espace intérieur et investis d'une signification nouvelle.
Cette démarche répond à l'environnement de Hong Kong, où un dédale de rues piétonnes en partie couvertes, parfois même équipées de tapis roulants, serpente entre les immeubles et souvent les traverse, transformant la ville en un unique espace intérieur-extérieur.

Broadway Cineplex

The eight-screen multiplex cinema is a series of pairs, using light and colour to give individual salons a distinctive identity. The four twins are located in two different buildings on either side of the thoroughfare of a shopping mall, therefore needing a sense of unity. Conceived as glowing objects, they are floating within the shell of the reflective curtain-wall glass buildings. By day, the glass is visually impenetrable, but when lit from behind after dark, the interior emerges on to the street. The audience is drawn in by the illuminated ticket booth and a wall of flickering video monitors, then follows a translucent wall round to a glowing bar. Giant mosaics numbers set into the floor suggest a cinematic countdown.

Das Multiplexkino besitzt acht Säle, die in Zweiergruppen angeordnet sind und durch Licht und Farbe unverwechselbaren Charakter erhalten. Die insgesamt vier Saalpaare sind in zwei verschiedenen Gebäuden untergebracht, die sich an der Hauptachse eines Einkaufszentrums gegenüberstehen und daher eines verbindenden Elements bedürfen. Als Leuchtobjekte konzipiert, schweben sie in der Hülle der reflektierenden Glasbauten mit Vorhangfassaden. Bei Tag erscheint das Glas undurchsichtig; nach Einbruch der Dunkelheit jedoch, wenn er von innen erleuchtet ist, wird der Innenraum von der Straße aus sichtbar. Das Publikum wird durch die beleuchtete Kasse und eine Wand flimmernder Videomonitore angezogen und folgt im Innern einer durchscheinenden Wand bis zu einer glitzernden Bar. Riesige, in den Boden eingelassene Mosaikzahlen erinnern an einen Film-Countdown.

Ce multiplexe comporte huit salles de cinéma, disposées deux par deux, l'éclairage et la couleur donnant à chaque ensemble son identité spécifique. Les quatre salles jumelles étant situées dans deux bâtiments distincts, de part et d'autre de l'artère principale d'un centre commercial, il importait de leur donner une unité. Conçues comme des objets lumineux, elles flottent dans une coque formée par des murs-rideaux en verre réfléchissant. De jour, le verre est absolument opaque, mais lorsque les cinémas sont éclairés la nuit, l'intérieur est comme projeté dans la rue. Le public est attiré par la caisse baignée de lumière et par un mur de moniteurs vidéo, puis le regard suit une cloison translucide qui s'incurve vers un bar à l'éclairage plus intime. Une mosaïque de chiffres géants incrustés dans le sol évoque un compte à rebours cinématographique.

Left, walls are decorated with light; right, the ticket hall.

Links: Die Wände werden durch Lichteffekte belebt; rechts der Kassenraum.

A gauche : les murs au décor de lumière; a droite : le hall du multiplex et les caisses.

Above and right, the cafe. The glowing circular bar draws people towards it.

Das Café. Die leuchtende runde Theke zieht das Publikum an.

Deux vues du café. Le bar circulaire éclairé de l'intérieu attire le regard – et les clients.

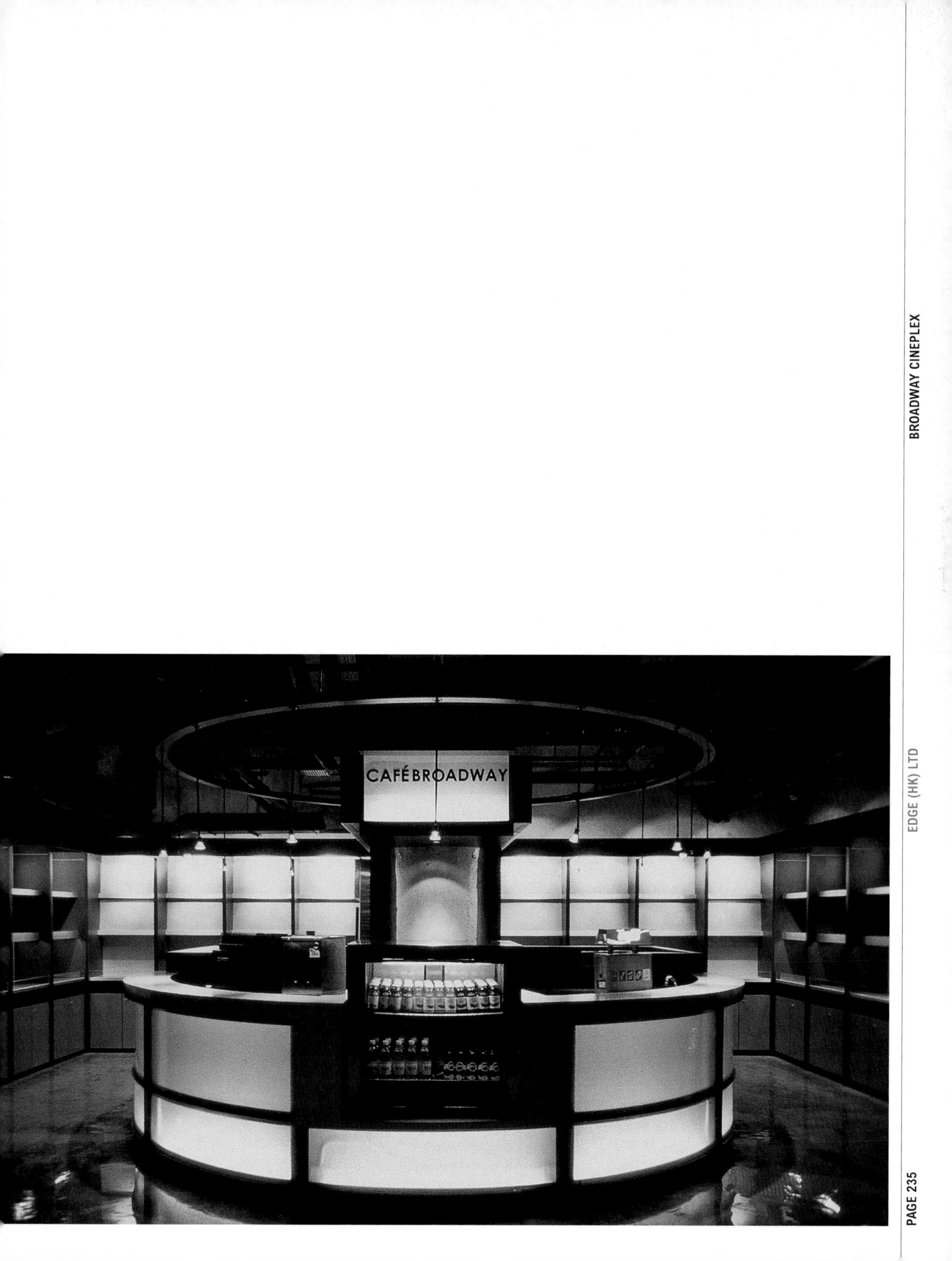
CAFÉBROADWAY

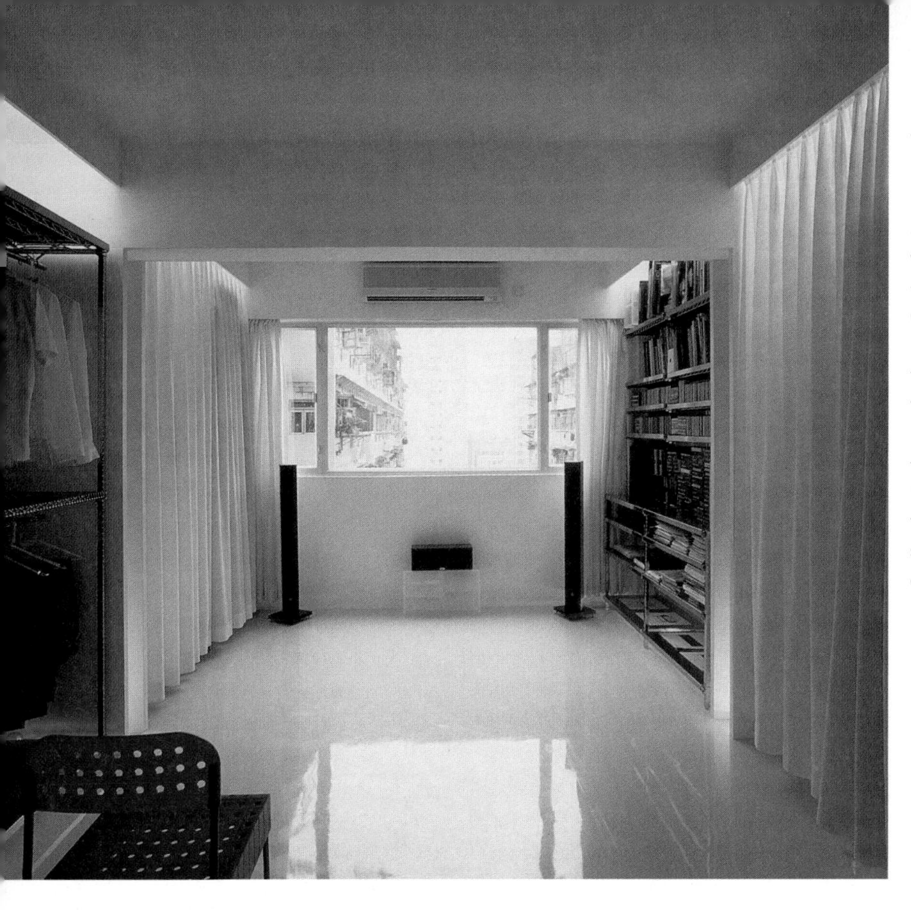

The bijou apartment is essentially a single room with kitchen and bathroom facilities concealed, far left. Left, curtains give the room a nebulous edge. A screen can be pulled down in front of the window for viewing films.

Ganz links: Changs eigenes Apartment besteht aus einem Raum, der auch die verdeckten Küchen- und Badeinrichtungen enthält. Links: Vorhänge lassen die Raumgrenzen verschwimmen. Vor dem Fenster lässt sich eine Leinwand zum Betrachten von Filmen herunterziehen.

Le propre studio de Chang est un petit bijou ; des tentures filtrent la lumière ; au fond à gauche, une structure en merisier abrite cuisine et bains ; un écran de cinéma peut être déroulé devant la fenêtre.

1998 **Island East, Hong Kong, China**

Gary's Apartment

A bijou bachelor studio measuring just 31 m² (generous by Hong Kong standards), Gary Chang's own apartment required careful planning and flexible use of space. By minimising the number of individual elements not an inch has been wasted.
White translucent curtains hang around the main room, giving a soft edge to the space, concealing storage and diffusing light. Blue fluorescent tubes wash the floor with an eerie light while up-lighters accentuate structural members. Folding furniture and pull-down screens allow the studio to be bedroom, dining room, office, lounge, and cinema. A cherrywood tower stands out from the glowing white interior and incorporating all of the services for the studio - refrigerator, cooker, sink, washing machine and film projector.
The fact that the studio was originally occupied by Chang's family of six when he was growing up highlights the cramped conditions on this Asian island.

Das mit nur 31 m² für Hongkongs Verhältnisse großzügige Apartment Gary Changs erforderte sorgfältige Planung und flexible Nutzung des Raums. Bei einer minimalen Anzahl einzelner Elemente blieb kein Quadratzentimeter ungenutzt.
Weiße, lichtdurchlässige Vorhänge ziehen sich an den Wänden des Hauptwohnbereichs entlang und verhüllen den Stauraum in den Randzonen. Blaue Neonröhren tauchen den Boden in ein geisterhaftes Licht, während Deckenfluter konstruktive Elemente hervorheben. Klappmöbel und herunterziehbare Wandschirme machen die Wohnung als Schlafraum, Esszimmer, Büro, Wohnzimmer und Kino nutzbar. Ein Turm aus Kirschbaumholz hebt sich vom gleißend weißen Interieur ab und enthält die gesamte Haustechnik – Kühlschrank, Kochgelegenheit, Spüle, Waschmaschine und Filmprojektor.
Die Tatsache, dass die Wohnung in Changs Jugend von seiner sechsköpfigen Familie bewohnt wurde, wirft ein Licht auf die beengten Wohnbedingungen der Insel.

Ravissant studio pour célibataire, de tout juste 31 m² (surface généreuse pour Hong Kong), le logement personnel de Gary Chang exigeait une planification rigoureuse et une utilisation très souple de l'espace. La réduction drastique du nombre d'éléments a permis de ne pas perdre un seul centimètre carré.
Des voilages blancs entourant le volume principal rendent les limites imprécises, dissimulent les espaces de rangement et diffusent la lumière. Des tubes fluorescents bleus baignent le sol d'une lumière irréelle, tandis que des sources d'éclairage dirigées vers le haut soulignent les éléments structurels. Des meubles pliants et des écrans escamotables permettent au studio de faire fonction de chambre à coucher, de salle à manger, de salon et même de salle de projection. Une colonne en merisier se détachant du volume blanc et lumineux regroupe tous les services : réfrigérateur, appareils de cuisson, évier, machine à laver et projecteur de cinéma.
Le studio était primitivement habité par la famille de Chang – six personnes au total, ce qui donne une bonne idée de la surpopulation de cette île d'Asie.

Far left, the sofa folds out into a bed at night.
Left, the bath and toilet are hidden from view.

Ganz links: Nachts lässt sich das Sofa in ein Bett verwandeln; links: Bad und Toilette bleiben den Blicken verborgen.

Page de gauche : le canapé transformable en lit. A gauche, la salle de bains et les toilettes sont cachées par des écrans.

Shuhei Endo

OAN, 1-7-13, Edobori, Nishi-ku, Osaka 550-0002, Japan tel +81 6 6445 6455 fax +81 6 6445 6456 e-mail endo@tk.airnet.ne.jp web www2c.airnet.ne.jp/endo/

huhei Endo	
orn	1960 Shiga Prefecture, Japan
udied	1986 Kyoto City University of Art
revious practice	Osamu Ishii & Biken Associates, Osaka
	1988 established Shuhei Endo Architect Institute, Osaka

elected projects		
yclestation M	1994	Maihara-cho, Shiga, Japan
kintecture I	1996	Singu-cho, Hyogo, Japan
ealtecture K	1996	Takatsuki, Osaka, Japan
ranstation O	1996	Sakai-cho, Fukui, Japan
alftecture F	1997	Fukui, Japan
pringtecture H	1998	Singu-cho, Hyogo, Japan
oofftecture O	1998	Oomori, Fukui, Japan
oofftecture Y	1999	Yamasaki-cho, Hyogo, Japan
oofftecture B	2000	Biwa-cho, Shiga, Japan
oofftecture K	2000	Nishinomiya, Hyogo, Japan

was in his search for an agile architecture that would reak away from the rectilinear block that Shuhei Endo egan experimenting with the material that has become is calling card. Corrugated metal, which is easy to end but strong enough to form a self-supporting memrane, provided the opportunity to create continuous culptural skins for his buildings and spaces that are either indoors nor out, a structure he describes as Halftecture". Working with non-Euclidean geometry e has fashioned his structures into fluid shapes: the urling roof and spiralling floor plan of his public amenies in the national park at Singu-cho (Springtecture); looping shelters for the rail platform in Fukui (Halfecture F); the more restrained single-curved roof of he bike park at Maibara rail station, Shiga (Cycletation M); and perhaps his best-known project, the hythmic arcade of Transtation O. He has been comared stylistically to the deconstructionists, but he is n original thinker with a style of its own.

In seinem Bemühen um eine bewegliche Architektur begann Shuhei Endo mit dem Material zu experimentieren, das zu seinem Markenzeichen wurde: Wellblech, leicht zu formen und doch stark genug, um daraus selbsttragende Teile zu fertigen, bot ihm Gelegenheit, seine Bauten, die weder eindeutig Innen- noch Außenraum sind und die er daher als »Halftecture« bezeichnet, mit durchgehenden plastischen Außenwänden zu versehen. Er fasst seine Bauten als im Fluss befindliche Formen auf: das gewellte Dach und der spiralförmige Grundriss der öffentlichen Einrichtungen im Nationalpark von Singu-cho (Springtecture H); Unterstände für den Bahnsteig in Fukui (Halftecture F); das einfach gebogene Dach des Fahrradparks am Bahnhof von Maibara, Shiga (Cyclestation M) sowie die rhythmische Arkade der Transtation O.
Obgleich man sein Werk in stilistischer Hinsicht mit den Dekonstruktivisten verglichen hat, ist Endo zweifellos ein unabhängiger Denker, dessen Arbeiten sich durch einen individuellen Stil auszeichnen.

En quête d'une architecture très souple, en rupture avec le bloc rectiligne, Shuhei Endo commença à faire des expériences avec le matériau qui est devenu sa signature. Le métal ondulé, facile à plier et suffisamment solide pour constituer une membrane autoporteuse, lui permit de créer des peaux sculpturales continues et des espaces qui ne sont ni intérieurs, ni extérieurs, des structures qu'il a baptisées « Halftecture ». Travaillant sur une géométrie non-euclidienne, il donne à ses constructions des formes fluides : toiture ondoyante et plan en spirale pour les services publics du parc national de Singu-cho (Springtecture H); abris sinueux pour les quais de la gare de Fukui (Halftecture F); toiture plus sage à courbe unique pour l'abri à vélos de la gare de Maibara, Shiga (Cyclestation M); et sans doute son projet le plus connu, l'arcade rythmée de la Transtation O.
Bien que son œuvre ait été comparée au déconstructivisme, Endo est un esprit original dont les réalisations très personnelles sont immédiatement identifiables.

1998 Oomori, Fukui, Japan

Rooftecture O

Designed to host an annual Shinto fertility rite, the form of the building is dictated by the ritual procession. The roof rises out of the ground in the north-west corner and soars out over the south-west entrance point, supported by a forest of tall slender columns, with a circular hole to let in the sun, a vital component of the fertility rite. The main ceremony hall is marked by a suspended ceiling of wooden slats and a floating wooden floor. For non-ceremonial days, the building also contains multi-purpose rooms, a kitchen, and a tatami room.

Die Form der Rooftecture O, entworfen für einen alljährlich stattfindenden Shinto Fruchtbarkeitsritus, wird von der zeremoniellen Prozession bestimmt. An der nordwestlichen Ecke steigt das Dach vom Boden auf und schwingt sich empor über den Eingang im Südwesten; es wird von einer Vielzahl hoher, schlanker Stützen getragen und öffnet sich kreisförmig zur Sonne – ein zentraler Bestandteil des Fruchtbarkeitsritus'. Die Haupthalle hat eine abgehängte Decke aus Holzleisten und einen schwimmenden Holzboden. Für die Zeit außerhalb der Feierlichkeiten bietet der Bau zudem Mehrzweckräume, eine Küche und einen Tatamiraum.

La forme de la Rooftecture O, construction destinée à accueillir un rite de fertilité shintoïste annuel, est dictée par la procession rituelle. La toiture surgit du sol à l'angl nord-ouest pour se dresser au-dessus du point d'entrée, au sud-ouest, soutenue par une forêt de minces colonnes ; une ouverture circulaire laisse entrer le soleil, élément essentiel du rite de fertilité. La grande salle de céré monie est caractérisée par un plafond suspendu en lame de bois et un plancher flottant du même matériau. Pour les jours ordinaires, l'édifice comporte également des salles multifonctionnelles, une cuisine et un local au sol couvert de tatamis.

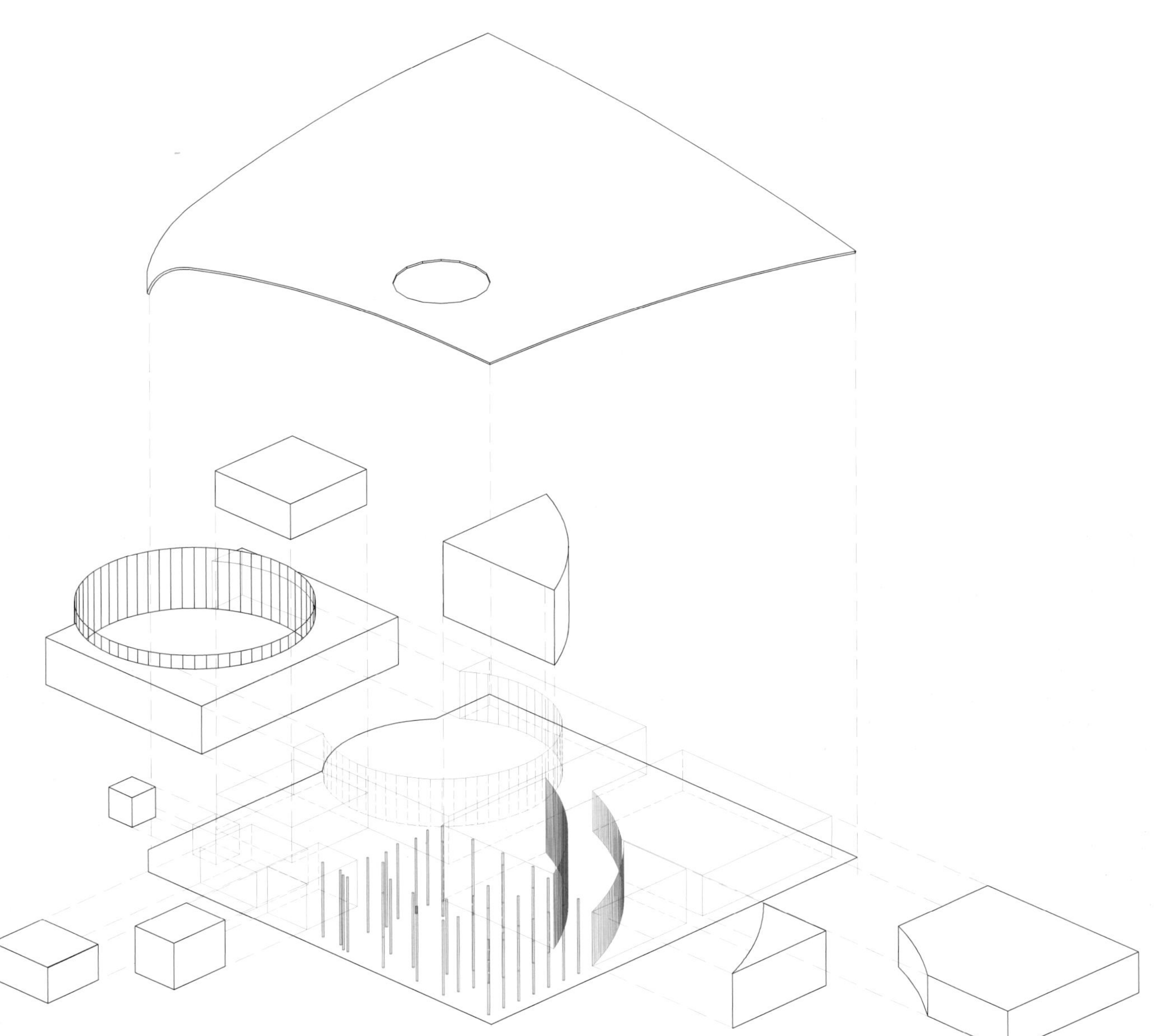

xploded diagram, above, showing the main compo-ents of the building. At the entrance, left, the roof is upported by a forest of slender posts, and a symbolic ole in the roof lets the sun in.

ben: Zerlegtes Diagramm mit den wichtigsten Elemen-en des Gebäudes. Links: Am Eingang wird das Dach von iner Vielzahl schlanker Stützen getragen und öffnet sich ymbolisch zur Sonne.

i-dessus : diagramme éclaté montrant les principaux léments de l'édifice. La toiture du hall d'entrée (à auche) est soutenue par une forêt de minces piliers, t percée d'un orifice symbolique qui s'ouvre au soleil.

The roof wraps right over the building.

Das markante Dach überzieht das gesamte Gebäude.

La toiture d'un seul tenant enveloppe entièrement le bâtiment.

The main ceremonial hall

Die Haupthalle für die Zeremonien

La grande salle servant aux cérémonies

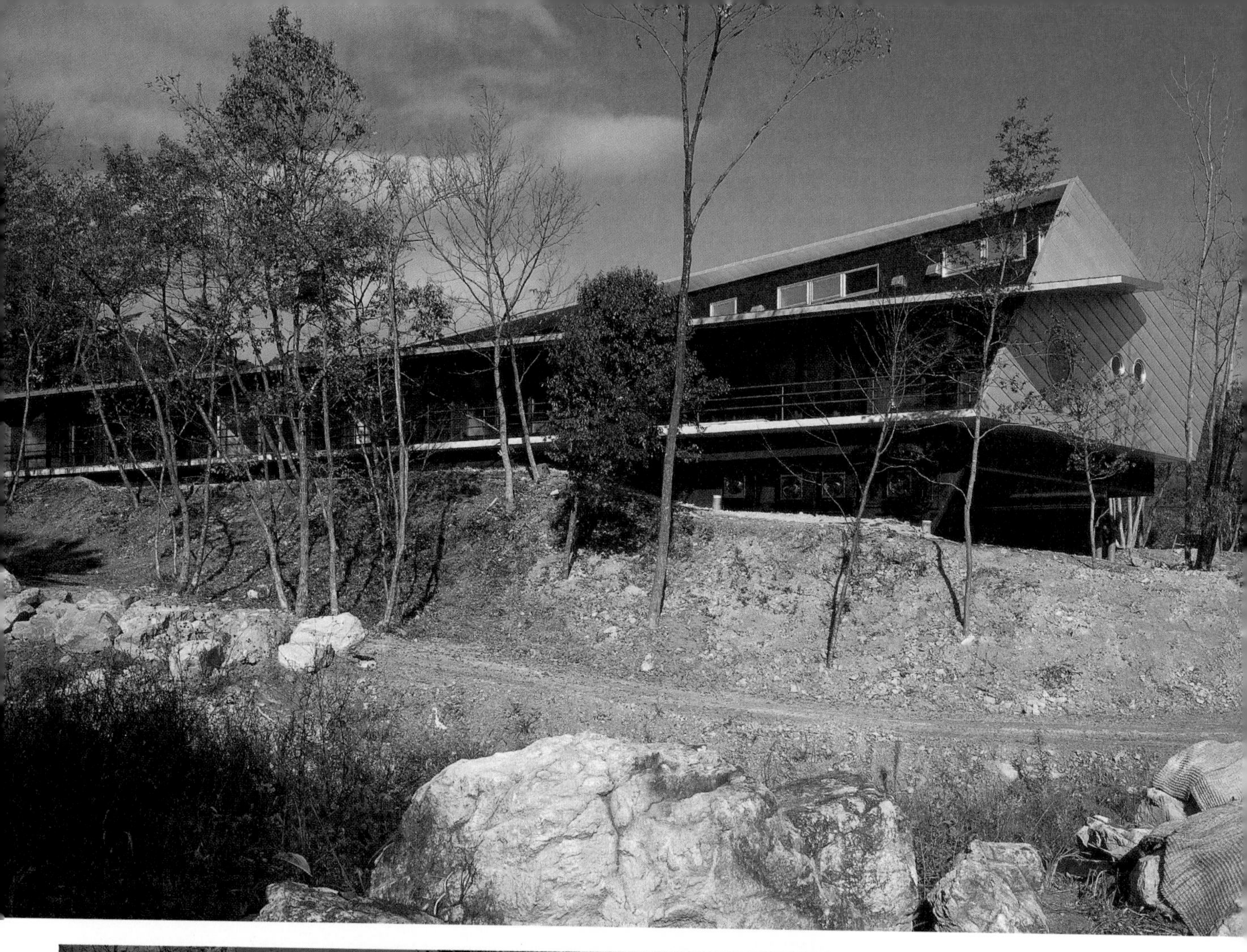

The spa at Yoi. The two wings of the building are set at a V in plan. A continuous "belt" wraps around them, beginning as the roof of the lower wing, then finishing as the end wall of the higher wing.

Das Badehaus in Yoi. Zwei Gebäudeflügel stehen auf einem V-förmigen Grundriss und werden von einem durchgehenden Gurt umzogen, der als Dach des flacheren Flügels beginnt und als Abschlussmauer des höheren endet.

Les thermes de Yoï. Les deux ailes disposées en V sont entourées d'une « ceinture » continue, qui s'étend de la partie basse de la toiture au mur latéral de l'aile la plus élevée.

999 **Yamasaki-cho, Hyogo, Japan**

Rooftecture Y

spa in the small mountain village of Yoi, about an our's drive from Osaka. The facility consists of two uildings combined and integrated with each other to a belt-like structure; one building houses bath-oms for men, women and the physically handi-apped, the other contains offices and public spaces. art of Endo's "Rooftecture" series - a name he coined describe his architectural style of creating a building integrating interior and exterior spaces - the two uildings are joined together by a corridor, and inter-ect with each other to form the entrance and lounge rea. A belt-like structure of corrugated steel wraps ound the steel skeleton of the building, linking all the rooms and spaces.
he complex is orientated to the south and, as a con-equence, protrudes slightly from its narrow ridge at s eastern end. A generous strip of windows along the outh facade capitalises on sunlight allowing visitors enjoy the natural landscape from the bathrooms. ndo explains his concept: "In this structure, partial pace sharing by the constituent buildings enables reation of various additional spaces. Covered by a ee-standing roof, the structure secures necessary pace for each room."

Die Rooftecture Y ist ein Badehaus in dem kleinen Bergdorf Yoi, etwa eine Stunde von Osaka entfernt. Zwei Gebäude sind zu einem gurtförmigen Komplex vereint und miteinander verbunden; das eine enthält Bäder für Männer und Frauen sowie für körperbehinderte Badegäste, das andere Büros und öffentliche Räume. Als Teil von Endos »Rooftecture«-Serie – von ihm so genannt, um seine Arbeitsweise zu charakterisieren, die Gebäude durch die Verbindung von Innen- und Außenräumen schafft – sind die beiden Bauteile durch einen Korridor verbunden und überschneiden sich, um einen Eingangs- und Loungebereich entstehen zu lassen. Ein gurtartiges Gebilde aus gewelltem Stahlblech umzieht das Stahlskelett des Gebäudes und verbindet sämtliche Räume miteinander.
Der Komplex ist nach Süden ausgerichtet und ragt am östlichen Ende ein wenig über den Hang vor. Das großzügige Fensterband der Südfassade lässt Sonnenlicht eindringen und gestattet den Besuchern, sich von den Bädern aus an der umgebenden Landschaft zu erfreuen. Endo erläutert seine Vorstellung: »Dadurch, dass die Gebäudeteile Räume anteilig gemeinsam nutzen, entstehen verschiedene Zusatzräume. Der von einem freistehenden Dach überfangene Komplex sichert jedem Bereich den nötigen Platz.«

Ce complexe thermal situé dans le petit village montagnard de Yoï, à environ une heure de voiture d'Osaka, consiste en deux corps de bâtiment, réunis par une structure qui les entoure comme une ceinture. L'un des bâtiments de la Rooftecture Y abrite les bains pour hommes, pour femmes et pour personnes handicapées ; l'autre, les bureaux et les espaces publics. Faisant partie de la série « Rooftecture » – nom forgé par Shuhei Endo pour désigner un style architectural intégrant intérieur et extérieur –, ils sont reliés par un couloir, et leur intersection délimite le hall d'entrée et le salon. Une structure (en tôle ondulée) s'enroule autour de l'ossature en acier, reliant toutes les pièces et espaces.
A son extrémité est, le complexe, orienté au sud, déborde légèrement de l'étroite arête sur laquelle il est construit. Les larges baies vitrées de la façade sud permettent aux visiteurs de profiter du soleil et de voir le paysage depuis les bains. Endo explique ainsi son concept : « Dans cette structure, les espaces communs aux bâtiments qui la constituent permettent de créer divers espaces supplémentaires. La toiture portée par des piliers indépendants autorise une utilisation maximale des espaces intérieurs. »

ol room, above, and entrance lobby, left

en die Schwimmhalle; links die Eingangslobby

dessus, la piscine thermale ; à gauche, le hall d'entrée

n's changing rooms, with roof of entrance wing the building cutting across

ıkleideräume der Männer, überschnitten vom Dach s Eingangsbereichs

vestiaire des hommes, coupé par le toit de l'entrée

First floor plan/ Erdgeschossgrundriss/ Plan du premier niveau

1 **entrance/** Eingang/ entrée
2 **pool/** Schwimmbecken/ piscine thermale
3 **disabled changing room/** Umkleide für Behinderte/ vestiaire pour personnes handicapées
4 **rest room/** Ruheraum/ salle de repos
5 **women's changing rooms/** Umkleide für Frauen/ vestiaire des femmes
6 **men's changing rooms/** Umkleide für Männer/ vestiaire des hommes

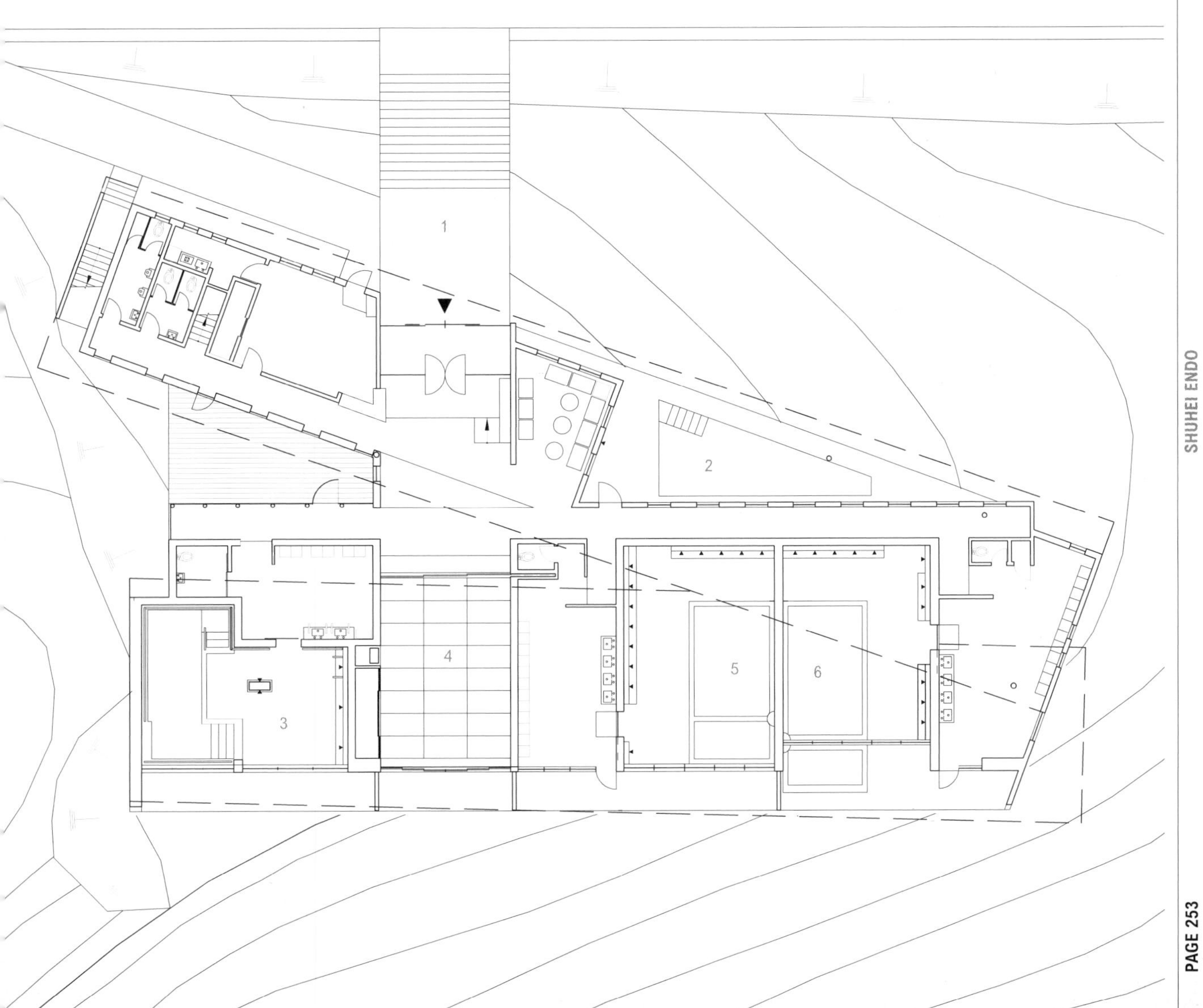

The bicycle shed is a series of curved, corrugated steel roofs.

Die Fahrradhalle besteht aus einer Reihe gebogener Dächer aus Stahlwellblech.

L'abri à bicyclettes est formé d'une succession de toits tôle ondulée.

1996 **Sakai-cho, Fukui, Japan**

Transtation O

A series of corrugated steel arcs, the shed consists of 2.7 to 7 mm sheets bent up and over, some reaching the ground at the other side, others left hanging, weighted against the wind by heavy metal tubes. Though formed from three different types of individual arc, the result is one long undulating form, at once organic and industrial. An uplifting piece of outdoor sculpture, it also shows what imagination and good design can add to the streetscape, and that even something as mundane as a train station and bike park can be a work of art.

Die aus einer Reihe gewellter Eisenbögen gebildete Transtation O besteht aus 2,7 bis 7 mm starken, nach oben und unten gebogenen Blechen, von denen einige bis zum Boden reichen; andere hängen frei und sind mittels schwerer Metallröhren gegen Winddruck gesichert. Aus drei unterschiedlichen Bogentypen ergibt sich eine einheitliche langgestreckte, gewellte Form, die organisch und technisch zugleich wirkt. Dieses rundum erfreuliche skulpturale Element demonstriert, wie Phantasie und gutes Design dem Straßenbild zuträglich sein können, und es zeigt, dass selbst etwas so banales wie ein Bahnsteig mit Fahrradhalle ein Kunstwerk sein kann.

Succession d'arcades en tôle ondulée, la « Transtation est construite en plaques faisant entre 2,7 et 7 mm d'épaisseur, pliées et repliées, dont certaines descende jusqu'au sol tandis que d'autres restent suspendues er l'air, stabilisées contre le vent par de lourds tubes méta liques. Bien que comportant trois types d'arcades distincts, l'ensemble constitue une longue forme ondoyar à la fois organique et industrielle. Cette sculpture de pl air montre ce que l'imagination et un design de qualité peuvent ajouter au paysage urbain, et que même quelq chose d'aussi banalement utilitaire qu'une gare avec ab à bicyclettes peut devenir une œuvre d'art.

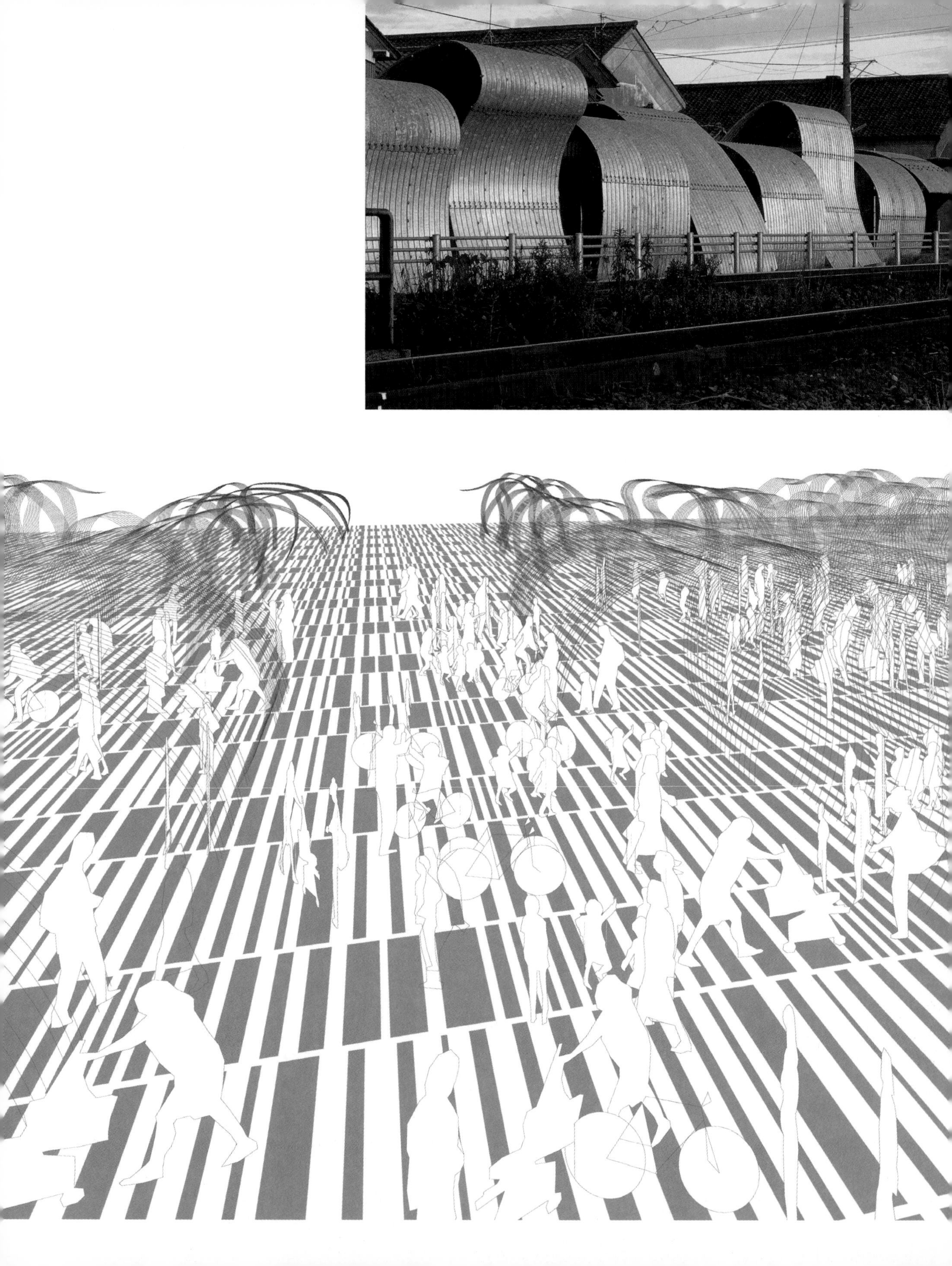

ft, the bike shed beside the tracks. Below, Endo tends his concept into a cycling utopia.

ks: Die Fahrradhalle neben den Gleisen. Unten: Endo veitert seine Idee zu einem Fahrrad-Utopia.

jauche, l'abri à bicyclettes, à côte de la voie. dessous : Endo a imaginé une « utopie vélocypédique » ur illustrer son concept.

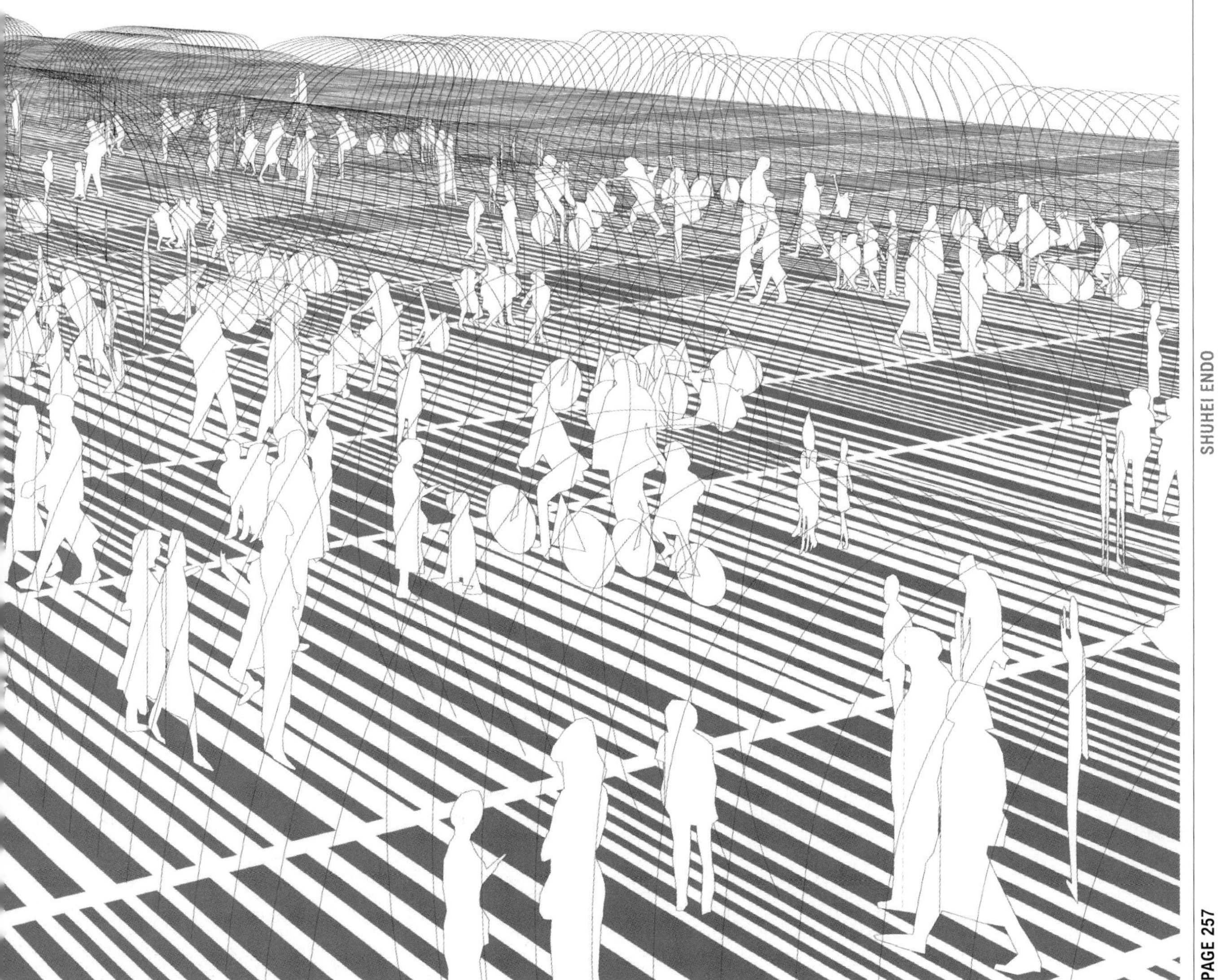

:ngelen Moore

McLachlan Avenue, Rushcutters Bay,
:dney 2011, Australia

tel +61 2 9380 4099 fax +61 2 9380 4302 e-mail architects@engelenmoore.com.au
web www.engelenmoore.com.au

a Engelen

rn	1963 Melbourne, Australia
died	1984 Sydney College of the Arts
vious practice	Partnership with Marc Newson and Danny Venlet in Sydney called Daffodil P/L
	1995 co-founded Engelen Moore

Moore

rn	1958 Warkworth, New Zealand
died	1979 Auckland Technical Institute; 1988 University of Technology, Sydney; 2000 RMIT Melbourne
vious practice	Ove Arup & Partners, London/Sidney; 1990-95 sole practice
	1995 co-founded Engelen Moore

lected projects

De Ce furniture and lighting showroom	1992	Redfern, New South Wales, Australia
ce/O'Reilly House	1995	Redfern, New South Wales, Australia
zzene/Leon House	1997	Neutral Bay, New South Wales, Australia
Cafe	1997	Sydney, Australia
se House	2000	Kiama, New South Wales, Australia
Grid apartment building	2000	Rushcutters Bay, Sydney, Australia
air apartment building	2000	Kings Cross, Sydney, Australia

/e want to do the Helmut Lang jeans and Jil Sander 't of apartments," they say, and their reputation two of the most fashionable architects in New uth Wales suggests that they have realised their bition.
lethora of elegant private residences, often on mped urban sites with budgets that belie the refined sults, have earned the duo international applause. eir simple style, honed down to one key idea per ject, subordinates decor to space - the largest pos- le space with the least possible material. Anything perfluous is discarded, and only that which is ab- utely necessary remains. The almost obligatory use louvres, a typical feature in Engelen Moore designs, vide an elegant solution to ventilation in hot coun-

»Wir wollen die Helmut Lang Jeans und Jil Sander Kostüme der Apartments bauen«, sagen Engelen Moore, und ihr Ruf als modischste Architekten von Neusüdwales lässt vermuten, dass sie ihr Vorhaben verwirklichen konnten. Eine Fülle eleganter Privathäuser brachte den beiden Partnern internationale Anerkennung. Oft auf beengten innerstädtischen Grundstücken entstanden, täuscht ihre raffinierte Ausführung über die tatsächlichen Budgets hinweg. Engelen Moores schlichter Stil, jeweils auf eine Schlüsselidee konzentriert, ordnet das Dekor dem Raum unter – größtmöglicher Raum mit möglichst wenig Material. Alles Überflüssige wird vermieden und nur das absolut Notwendige beibehalten. Die nahezu obligatorischen Jalousien, Charakteristikum des Büros, bieten in heißen Regionen eine elegante Belüftungslösung und sind deko-

« Nous voulons faire des appartements qui soient l'équivalent des jeans Helmut Lang et des costumes Jil Sander », affirment-ils. Ils sont considérés comme deux des architectes les plus « chic » de Nouvelle-Galles du Sud, ce qui laisse à penser qu'ils ont réalisé leur ambition. Une pléthore d'élégantes résidences privées, souvent construites sur d'étroits sites urbains avec des budgets que semble démentir le raffinement du résultat, leur a valu une grande réputation internationale. Leur style simple, réduit à une idée-clef par projet, subordonne le décor à l'espace – l'objectif étant d'obtenir un espace maximum avec un minimum de matériaux. Tout élément superflu est rejeté, seul ce qui est absolument nécessaire est conservé. L'utilisation presque constante de claires-voies dans tous les plans d'Engelen Moore fournit une

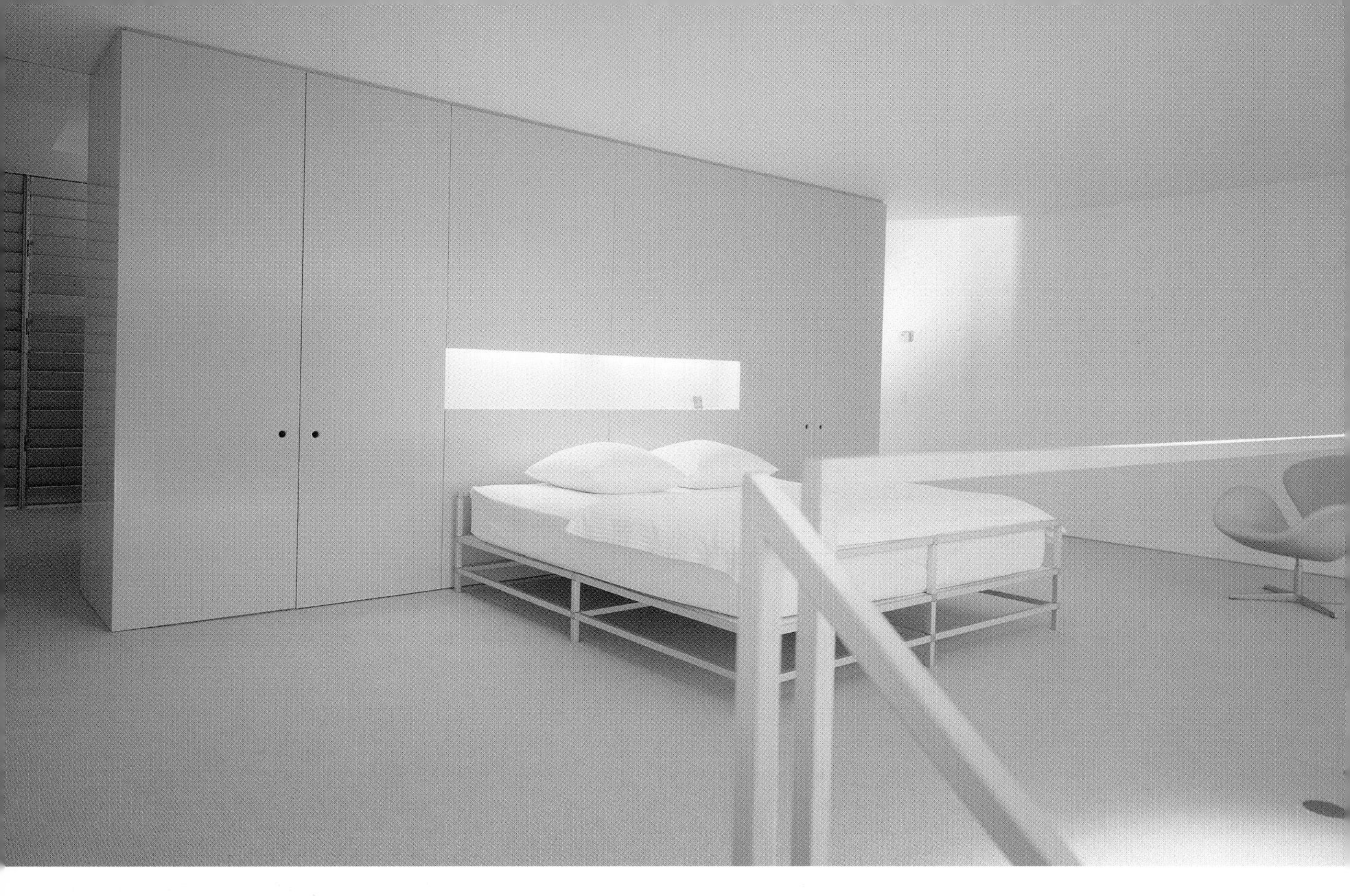

tries and function as a decorative element, adding texture to a blank glass or aluminium facade.
"The architecture of Engelen Moore seeks to build on the fine tradition of the Modern House, from the Weissenhofsiedlung, the California Case Study house program and Mies van der Rohe's Farnsworth House, producing houses of the late 20th and early 21st century which are responsive to place and climate, flexible in use, and provide a neutral background to the usually hectic lives of their occupants," say the architects.
Commissions for apartment blocks, including The Grid in Rushcutters Bay, have followed, showing that they can operate on a large scale as well as small. In addition their design shops (including one for international furniture retailer De De Ce, Engelen's family business) and cafes have endeared them to Sydney's modish urbanites.
As a partnership, the couple complement each other well - Moore's engineering background (his first degree in the late 70s before he retrained as a architect in the mid-80s) with Engelen's keen eye for design.

ratives Element, das einer glatten Glas- oder Aluminiumfassade Struktur gibt.
Den Architekten zufolge »versucht die Architektur von Engelen Moore an die gute Tradition des Modernen Hauses anzuknüpfen, wie die Weißenhofsiedlung, das Case-Study-House-Programm in Kalifornien und Mies van der Rohes Farnsworth House. Dabei entstehen Häuser des späten 20. und frühen 21. Jahrhunderts, die Rücksicht nehmen auf Ort und Klima, flexibel zu nutzen sind und einen neutralen Hintergrund für den gewöhnlich hektischen Lebensstil ihrer Bewohner bieten.«
Aufträge für Mehrfamilienhäuser wie The Grid in Rushcutters Bay folgten und zeigen, dass Engelen Moore mit großen Projekten ebenso gut umgehen können wie mit kleinen. Daneben haben ihre Designläden, darunter einer für das internationale Möbelhaus De De Ce, das Engelens Familie gehört, und Cafés ihnen die Gunst von Sydneys trendbewussten Großstädtern eingetragen.
Als Partner ergänzen sich die beiden hervorragend – Moores Hintergrund als Ingenieur (sein erster Abschluss zu Ende der 70er-Jahre, ehe er Mitte der 80er die Architektenausbildung begann) und Engelens feines Gespür für Design.

solution élégante au problème de la ventilation dans les pays chauds tout en constituant un élément décoratif et en donnant une texture aux façades nues en aluminium ou en verre.
« L'architecture d'Engelen Moore cherche à perpétuer la belle tradition de la Maison Moderne, de la Weissenhofsiedlung, du programme de la Californie Case Study et de la Farnsworth House de Mies van der Rohe, en vue d bâtir des maisons de la fin du XXe et du début du XXIe siècle, des maisons adaptées au lieu et au climat, d'une utilisation souple, fournissant un cadre neutre à l'activi habituellement fiévreuse de leurs occupants », déclarer les architectes.
Des commandes de blocs résidentiels, notamment The Grid à Rushcutters Bay, ont suivi, démontrant que la grande échelle est également dans leurs cordes. Ils des nent en outre des magasins, dont la boutique de mobili international De De Ce (appartenant à la famille d'Engelen) et des cafés, très prisés des habitants « branchés » de Sydney.
Les deux associés se complètent parfaitement : Moore avait obtenu un diplôme d'ingénieur à la fin des années 70 avant de se tourner vers l'architecture vers le milieu des années 80, et Engelen possède un sens très développé de l'architecture d'intérieur.

Price/O'Reilly House

gelen and Moore's first joint project and the one at earned them international attention. Because replaced two terraced houses, local authorities sisted that the new building read as two houses as ell. The front elevation is therefore divided into two rtical bays. Horizontal elements such as windows ign with those of neighbouring houses. The lower orey is clad in aluminium-composite sheet while the per storey is made of operable extruded aluminium uvres, which can be adjusted from transparent to paque.

the rear, the house expresses itself in a 6 x 7-m ass wall made up of six individual panels that slide d stack to one side, allowing the entire facade to be ened up.

w-cost, lightweight furniture is designed by the chitects as part of their "Easy" range.

Das Haus Price/O'Reilly, das erste gemeinsame Projekt von Tina Engelen und Ian Moore, brachte ihnen internationale Anerkennung. Es ersetzt zwei Reihenhäuser, weshalb die örtlichen Behörden darauf bestanden, dass der Neubau die Zweiteilung beibehalten sollte. Die Vorderseite ist vertikal in zwei Zonen gegliedert. Horizontale Elemente wie Fenster sind an denen benachbarter Häuser ausgerichtet. Das untere Geschoss ist mit Aluminiumverbundblech verkleidet, während die Front des oberen aus beweglichen Lamellen aus stranggepresstem Aluminium besteht, die sich von transparent bis undurchsichtig justieren lassen.

Die 6 x 7 m große Glaswand an der Rückfront des Hauses besteht aus sechs Einzelscheiben, die nach einer Seite hin übereinander geschoben werden können, um die gesamte Fassade zu öffnen.

Die kostengünstigen, leichten Möbel sind Teil der Kollektion »Easy« von Engelen Moore.

La maison Price/O'Reilly est le premier projet commun d'Engelen et de Moore, qui leur valut une attention internationale. Comme il remplaçait deux bâtiments existants, les autorités locales exigèrent que le nouvel édifice eût également l'apparence de deux maisons mitoyennes. L'élévation Est est par conséquent divisée en deux baies verticales. Les éléments horizontaux tels que les fenêtres sont alignés sur ceux des maisons voisines. Le niveau inférieur est revêtu d'un matériau composite à base d'aluminium, tandis que le niveau supérieur est fait de jalousies en aluminium extrudé, réglables de la transparence totale à l'opacité absolue.

A l'arrière, l'édifice est exprimé par un mur en verre de 6 m sur 7 composé de six panneaux coulissants qui peuvent se rabattre d'un côté, ce qui permet d'ouvrir entièrement cette façade.

Les meubles, légers et peu coûteux, ont été dessinés par les architectes eux-mêmes, dans le cadre de leur série « Easy ».

the rear of the house, right, the six panels of the m-high glazed wall slide away to the sides, xtending the living area into the courtyard. Above ft, bedroom platform.

echts: Die sechs Teile der 7 m hohen Glaswand auf r Rückseite des Hauses lassen sich zur Seite schieben d erweitern den Wohnraum in den Hof. Oben links e Schlafebene.

droite : les panneaux vitrés de 7 m de haut sont scamotables, ce qui permet de prolonger l'espace vie dans la cour. A gauche : vue de la mezzanine.

en-plan living area with mezzanine bedroom, left;
eet facade, right

nks der offene Wohnbereich mit Schlafgalerie;
chts die Straßenfassade

gauche : l'habitation à plan ouvert et sa mezzanine ;
droite : la façade sur rue

Entrance to the linear house, right, showing louvred upper facade. Left, a roof terrace sits over the kitchen/dining room.

Rechts: Eingang zum »linearen Haus« und oberer Teil c Fassade mit Jalousien. Links: Über Küche und Essberei liegt eine Dachterrasse.

A droite : l'entrée de la « maison linéaire », et le niveau supérieur vitré vu de l'intérieur. A gauche : la terrasse couvrant la cuisine-salle à manger.

1997 **Neutral Bay, New South Wales, Australia**

Ruzzene/Leon House

Part of a street of long narrow row houses, the Ruzzene/Leon House picks up on the typology of the original houses but expresses it more clearly. The main circulation still runs parallel to the boundary wall even when the house drops down one storey at the rear. A roof-terrace opening off the main bedroom follows the same module as the other rooms and brings light into the back of the building.

Once the corridor arrives at the double-height living room, the house does not stop but flows out into a walled courtyard through a glazed wall that can slide completely open in warmer weather. Though modules are deliberately repetitive, elements such as louvre wall panels, aluminium cladding and huge sliding wall panels gives the house richness and complexity.

An einer Straße mit schmalen, aber sehr tiefen Reihenhäusern greift das Haus Ruzzene/Leon die Formensprache seiner Nachbarn auf, formuliert sie jedoch klarer. Der Haupterschließungsweg verläuft nach wie vor parallel zur Begrenzungsmauer, obwohl das Haus im hinteren Bereich um ein Stockwerk abfällt. Die Dachterrasse vor dem Hauptschlafraum hat die gleichen Abmessungen wie die übrigen Räume und bringt Licht in den Rückteil des Gebäudes.

Das doppelgeschossige Wohnzimmer lässt sich bei warmer Witterung in einen ummauerten Hof erweitern, indem die Glaswand komplett zur Seite gleitet. Obwohl sich die Module bewusst wiederholen, geben Elemente wie durchbrochene Wandpaneele, Alumimiumverkleidung und große Schiebewände dem Haus Vielfalt und Komplexität.

Située dans une rue de maisons mitoyennes longues et étroites, la maison Ruzzene/Leon reprend le type de ces dernières en l'exprimant plus clairement. La circulation principale reste parallèle au mur mitoyen, bien que la maison ait un étage de moins à l'arrière. La chambre de maître donne sur un toit-terrasse du même module que les autres pièces, qui éclaire et allège l'arrière du bâtiment.

Le couloir aboutit à un séjour double hauteur, mais la maison se prolonge au-delà de celui-ci par une cour, dc il est séparé par un pan de verre qui peut complètemen disparaître par temps chaud.

Bien que les modules soient délibérément répétitifs, de éléments tels que panneaux à claire-voie, revêtements e aluminium et cloisons coulissantes donnent à la maiso une riche complexité.

View through house from rear courtyard, right, and view from living room out to the courtyard, left

Rechts: Blick vom hinteren Innenhof durch das Haus; links: Blick vom Wohnbereich in den Hof

À droite : la maison vue de la cour arrière ; à gauche : la même cour vue de la salle de séjour

Entasis Arkitekter

/lagstræde 10 c 2, 1204 Copenhagen, Denmark tel +45 3333 9525 fax +45 3333 9235 e-mail entasis@image.dk

;igne Cold

›orn	1966 Copenhagen, Denmark
;tudied	1989 Oxford Polytechnic; 1993 Kunstakademiets Arktektskole, Copenhagen
›revious practice	Blad & Thygesen, Elsinore
	1996 established Entasis Arkitekter

:hristian Cold

›orn	1966 Sønderborg, Denmark
tudied	1992 Kunstakademiets Arktektskole, Copenhagen
›revious practice	Jørn Langvad, Copenhagen; Lundgaard & Tranberg, Copenhagen
	1996 established Entasis Arkitekter

;elected projects

Row house - rebuilding	1995 Copenhagen, Denmark
:oological Gardens - entrance building	1998 Copenhagen, Denmark
Residence	1999 Alsgaarde, Denmark
›arasite (exhibition project for an ecological dwelling)	1999 Malmö/Amsterdam
3rønshøj School and Daycare Centre	2000 Copenhagen, Denmark
\cademy of Defence	2001 Copenhagen, Denmark
Housing	2002 Roskilde, Denmark

:ntasis, the Greek word for tension, manifests itself n the practice's work in what they see as a tension ›etween ideas and physical construction. The building or them is a means of architectural expression, able o educate and manipulate thoughts and emotions, ›ot just a functional shelter. Giving space priority over surface decoration, they use light, texture, rhythm, acoustics and proportion to create vibrant spaces with he power to move the spirit.

Their aim is "to give form to the Utopian vision of :lassic modern man", and their work is firmly ground- ›d in what has gone before, particularly Renaissance and Modernist architecture.

'We relate our work to the Western history of ideas 'ounded in the Renaissance, which was titanic, open- ninded and progressive. This means that we regard

Entasis, griechisch für Spannung, manifestiert sich in der Arbeit des Büros in einem Bewusstsein der Spannung zwischen Idee und ausgeführtem Bau. Für die Architekten von Entasis bedeutet Bauen über die rein schützende Funktion hinaus eine Form des architektonischen Ausdrucks, der bilden und Gedanken beeinflussen kann. Dem Raum wird Vorrang vor jeglicher Oberflächendekoration eingeräumt, und Licht, Struktur, Rhythmus, Akustik und Proportion schaffen pulsierende Räume, die das Gemüt der Bewohner beleben.

Ihr Ziel ist, »der utopischen Vision vom klassischen, modernen Menschen Form zu verleihen«, und ihre Bauten sind fest in der Tradition, insbesondere der Renaissance und klassischen Moderne, verankert.

»Wir beziehen unsere Arbeit auf die westliche Ideengeschichte, deren Ursprünge in der Renaissance liegen, die

Entasis, mot grec signifiant « tension », se réfère à la tension entre les idées et la réalisation concrète, dont les architectes sont vivement conscients. A leurs yeux, un édifice n'est pas seulement un abri fonctionnel, mais un mode d'expression architectural susceptible d'éduquer et de manipuler les pensées et les émotions. Donnant à l'espace la priorité sur la décoration, ils utilisent la lumière, la texture, le rythme, l'acoustique et les proportions pour créer des volumes capables de toucher l'esprit.

Leur objectif est de « donner forme à la vision utopique de l'homme moderne du classicisme », et leur travail est solidement ancré dans la tradition occidentale, en particulier celle de la Renaissance et du modernisme.

« Nous rattachons notre travail à l'histoire des idées issue de la Renaissance, époque titanesque et progressiste, d'une grande ouverture d'esprit. Cela signifie que nous

architecture as a political work, not in terms of old left/right-wing politics, but as a work with enormous influence on the human body and spirit.
"Our means build upon Modernism, which means open dynamic spaces, column structures, roof terraces and so on interpreted into a two-layer strategy, involving a heavy and permanent structure in large scale along with a fragile, detailed and changeable layer in the human scale. The two layers give an impression of a culture that goes back into the past with beauty and strength and stretches out towards the future with hope and vitality."

zugleich titanisch, aufgeschlossen und fortschrittlich war. Das bedeutet, dass wir Architektur als politische Arbeit auffassen, nicht im Sinne althergebrachter Rechts-Links-Kategorien, sondern als eine Arbeit von enormem Einfluss auf Körper und Geist des Menschen.«
»Unsere Stilmittel gründen in der Moderne: offene, dynamische Räume, Tragsysteme, Dachterrassen etc., die auf zwei Ebenen umgesetzt werden. Das bedeutet im großen Maßstab eine schwere, dauerhafte Bauweise neben einer den menschlichen Proportionen gemäßen fragilen, detailreichen und wandelbaren Ebene.«

considérons l'architecture comme une tâche politique, non dans le sens de la vieille politique gauche/droite, mais comme une œuvre qui exerce une influence énorm sur le corps et l'esprit de l'être humain.
« Nos méthodes s'appuient sur le modernisme, ce qui signifie espaces ouverts et dynamiques, piliers structurels, toits-terrasses etc., réinterprétés selon une stratégi à deux niveaux : à grande échelle une structure lourde et permanente, et à l'échelle humaine un niveau détaillé et modifiable. L'ensemble donne une impression de culture reliée au passé avec force et beauté, et qui s'étend vers l'avenir avec espoir et vitalité. »

he new entrance block for the zoo houses a glazed oyer and information centre, bookshop and dministration facilities.

)er neue Eingangsbau für den Zoo enthält ein verglastes oyer und ein Informationszentrum sowie eine Buchhandung und Büros für die Verwaltung.

e nouveau bâtiment d'accès au zoo comprend un foyer t centre d'information, une librairie et une aile réservée à administration.

1998 Copenhagen, Denmark

Zoological Gardens - entrance building

A long frame bordering Roskildevej road, the new entrance building is divided along its length into three spatial elements: a light glazed building for the foyer and information centre; an open, asymmetrical gateway; and a dark closed box housing a bookshop and staff facilities. The scale of the double-height entrance arch creates a sense of occasion, its timber-lined sloping walls funnelling visitors through to the zoo. Protruding from the rear of the entrance building into the zoo is the auditorium, a dark concrete box. At one end, a De Stijl-inspired rhythm of impressions turns the facade into a giant canvas. Along the side, an animated red cedar screen featuring thin vertical shutters faces into the zoo's main entrance courtyard. A low classroom unit sheltered behind an undulating cast concrete wall reduces the mass of the building as it falls away towards the adjacent pond.

Der neue Eingangsbau des Zoologischen Gartens am Roskildevej ist längs in drei räumliche Elemente unterteilt: einen hellen verglasten Teil für Foyer und Informationszentrum, ein offenes asymmetrisches Tor und einen dunklen geschlossenen Bereich, in dem eine Buchhandlung und Personalräume untergebracht sind. Die Größe des zwei Geschosshöhen umfassenden Eingangsbogens erzeugt eine besondere Atmosphäre; seine holzgetäfelten, schräg ansteigenden Wände führen die Besucher in den Zoo hinein.
Auf der Rückseite des Eingangsgebäudes ragt das Auditorium als dunkles Betonelement hervor. Auf einer Seite verwandelt eine von De Stijl angeregte Gestaltung die Fassade in ein riesiges Gemälde. Zum Haupteingangshof des Zoos bilden schmale Fensterläden aus virginischem Wacholder ein bewegtes Gitter. Ein niedriger Bereich mit Unterrichtsräumen wird von einer gekurvten Betonwand abgeschirmt und vermindert das zu einem angrenzenden Teich abfallende Volumen des Baus.

Longue structure longeant la route de Roskildevej, le nouveau bâtiment d'accueil du zoo de Copenhague est divisé dans le sens de la longueur en trois éléments spatiaux : un volume clair et vitré pour le foyer et le centre de renseignements ; une entrée ouverte de forme asymétrique ; une enceinte plus sombre abritant une librairie et les salles réservées au personnel. L'échelle de l'arcade d'accès à double hauteur frappe par son caractère exceptionnel ; ses cloisons de bois en pente forment un entonnoir dirigeant le flux des visiteurs vers le zoo.
L'auditorium, unité de béton de couleur sombre, s'avance à l'arrière du bâtiment, côté zoo. A l'une de ses extrémités, une succession d'empreintes rythmées inspirées par De Stijl transforme la façade en un tableau géant. Sur le côté, un écran en cèdre rouge percé de minces lames verticales fait face à la cour d'entrée du zoo. Une salle de classe basse, abritée par un mur de béton ondulé coulé in situ, réduit la masse de l'édifice en s'abaissant vers l'étang adjacent.

Canopy over the entranceway, left, and the red cedar shutters of the auditorium, above

Links das Vordach über dem Haupteingang; oben die hölzernen Läden des Auditoriums

Le dais couvrant l'entrée (à gauche), et les volets en cèdre rouge de l'auditorium (ci-dessus)

The teaching block extends back into the grounds of the zoo, above, defining the edge of the site. Right, the auditorium.

Oben: Auf der Rückseite ragt das Lehrgebäude ins Zoogelände hinein; rechts das Auditorium.

Le bloc pédagogique délimite le site du côté du zoo proprement dit (ci-dessus). A droite, vue extérieure de l'auditorium.

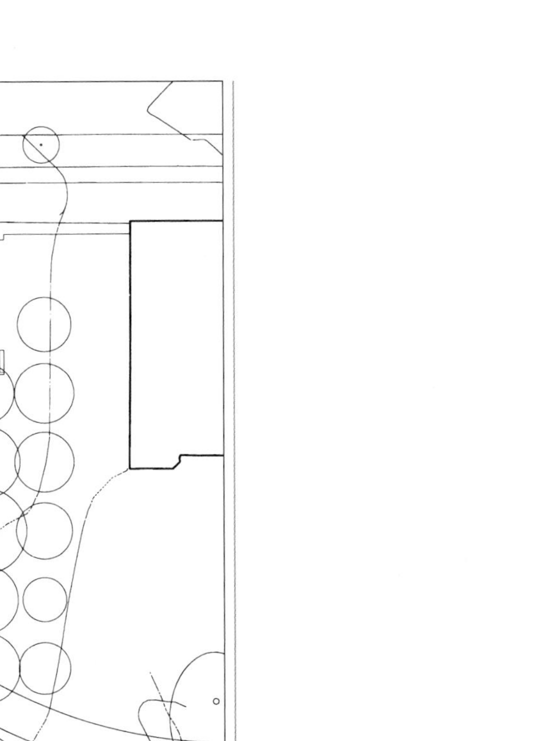

Site plan/ Lageplan/ Plan du site

1 **foyer/** Foyer/ foyer

2 **main entrance/** Haupteingang/ entrée principale

3 **bookshop and administration/** Buchhandlung und Verwaltung/ librairie et administration

4 **auditorium/** Auditorium/ auditorium

5 **classrooms/** Unterrichtsräume/ salles de cours

Signe and Christian Cold have made their home in one of Copenhagen's 19th-century worker's houses, right. Far right, the kitchen.

Rechts: Signe und Christian Cold haben sich in einem der Kopenhagener Arbeiterhäuser aus dem 19. Jahrhundert eingerichtet. Ganz rechts die Küche.

Signe et Christian Cold vivent à Copenhague, dans une maison ouvrière du XIXe siècle qu'ils ont réaménagée (à droite). Page de droite, la cuisine.

1995

Copenhagen, Denmark

Row house - rebuilding

This row house, the architects' own, grew out of Christian Cold's graduation project to transform a typical Copenhagen worker's cottage or "potato row" house, and was executed on a limited budget of KR 350 000. The house originally consisted of three apartments, and Entasis have respected its history by keeping the horizontal strata: communal living area on the ground floor, children's quarters on the first floor, adult quarters on the top floor. All non-loadbearing interior walls were torn down so that the interior is also one big open-plan volume.
Floors are organised around a core of storage, services and circulation, its outer walls covered in white porcelain mosaics to give the feeling of a monolith. Its modern materials (sandblasted glass, plywood, untreated steel) contrast with the treatment of the walls (the shell of the house), which have been covered in an extremely fine render rather than painted in order to express their heaviness and history.

Der Umbau dieses Reihenhauses, das die Architekten selbst bewohnen, ging aus Christian Colds Abschlussarbeit hervor, die die Umgestaltung eines der typischen Kopenhagener Arbeiterhäuser zum Thema hatte. Das Budget war auf 350 000 Kronen begrenzt.
Ursprünglich bestand das Haus aus drei Wohnungen; Entasis respektierte seine Geschichte, indem sie die horizontale Gliederung beibehielten: gemeinschaftlicher Wohnbereich im Erdgeschoss, Kinderzimmer im ersten, Zimmer der Erwachsenen im zweiten Stock. Sämtliche nicht-tragenden Innenwände wurden abgerissen, so dass auch im Innern große, offene Räume entstanden.
Die einzelnen Geschosse sind um einen Kern mit Stauräumen, Versorgungseinrichtungen und Verbindungswegen angeordnet, dessen Außenwände mit weißen Porzellanmosaiken bedeckt sind, wodurch der Eindruck eines monolithischen Gebildes entsteht. Seine modernen Materialien (sandstrahlmattiertes Glas, Sperrholz, unbehandelter Stahl) kontrastieren mit der Behandlung der Außenwände, der Gebäudehülle, die statt einem Anstrich einen fein strukturierten Bewurf erhielt, der ihrer Schwere und Geschichtsträchtigkeit gerecht wird.

Cette maison mitoyenne, appartenant à l'architecte luimême, est née de la thèse présentée par Christian Cold, concernant la transformation d'une maison ouvrière typique de Copenhague ; les travaux ont été exécutés avec un budget limité à 350 000 couronnes.
A l'origine, la maison était divisée en trois logements. Entasis a respecté cette histoire en préservant les strates horizontales : séjour et espaces communs au rez-de-chaussée ; espace de vie des enfants au premier étage ; logement des adultes au deuxième étage. Tous les murs intérieurs non porteurs ont été abattus, pour créer un volume unique à plan ouvert.
Chaque étage s'articule autour d'un noyau central destiné au rangement, aux services et à la circulation, dont les cloisons recouvertes d'une mosaïque de porcelaine blanche produisent un effet monolithique. Ses matériaux modernes (verre sablé, contreplaqué, acier brut), contrastent avec le traitement des murs (la coquille de la maison), couverts d'un enduit d'une grande finesse plutôt que peints, afin d'exprimer leur poids d'histoire.

R. BROBY-JOHANSEN GLÆDENS KUNST GYLDENDAL
DEN NYE KONGE
THE HISTORY OF WORLD PAINTING
PALLE NIELSEN KATALOG ATLANTIS

Floors are open-plan but have defined uses. Above, th children's floor and right, the adults' floor.

Trotz offener Grundrissgestaltung sind die Nutzungen klar verteilt: oben die Kinder-, rechts die Elternetage.

Les cloisons ont été supprimées, mais la fonction des espaces est clairement définie. Ci-dessus, le niveau des enfants. A droite, le niveau des parents.

Axonometrie/ Axonometrie/ Axonométrie

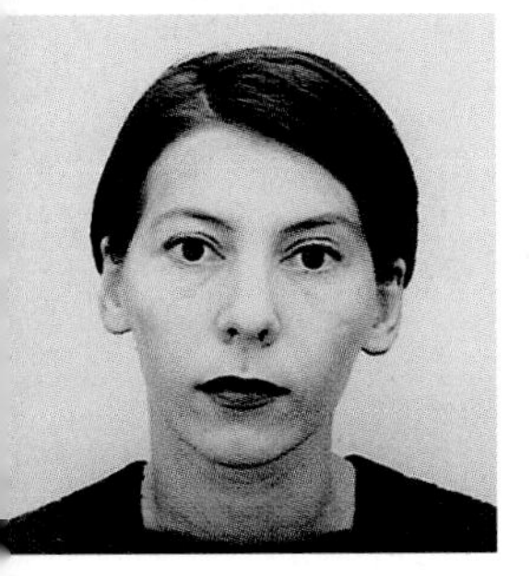

Manuelle Gautrand

, rue Lacuée, 75012 Paris, France

tel +33 1 5695 0646 fax +33 1 5695 0647 e-mail contact@manuelle-gautrand.com
web www.manuelle-gautrand.com

anuelle Gautrand

rn	1961 Marseilles, France
udied	1985 Ecole d'Architecture de Montpellier
evious practice	three years in several studios in Paris
	1991 set up "Agence Manuelle Gautrand" in Lyons; 1993 transferred office to Paris

elected projects

otbridge	1994 Lyons, France
iversity	1995 Annecy, France
aintenance building	1996 Nantes Airport, France
ver deck	1997 Fontaine-sur-Saône, France
ll stations	1998 A16 motorway, France
atering building	1998 Nantes Airport, France
eatre	1999 Béthune, France
ultural complex	2000 Saint-Louis, France

autrand originally set up practice in 1991 in Lyons here she realised her first projects, but in 1993 transrred operations to Paris. Her main concern is "connuity of urban memory", the relationship between a roject and the social and cultural history of its site. er point of departure is the context of a building hich she uses in her quest for an expressive image: e deep reds of the theatre at Béthune reflect theatre teriors from the past, and the stained glass on the 16-toll stations is inspired by the cathedrals of northrn France.

er buildings exhibit several layers, often using the kin as a canvas for eye-catching effects. Translucent olycarbonate for the maintenance building at Nantes irport creates a unit of colour, light and shadow and aux patterned brickwork is executed on a giant scale r the Béthune theatre. In the Nantes Airport catering uilding, bright blown-up images of food signal the ontents of the cold storage rooms.

Gautrand gründete ihr Büro 1991 in Lyon, wo auch ihre ersten Bauten entstanden. 1993 verlegte sie ihre Tätigkeit nach Paris. Ihr Hauptanliegen ist die »Kontinuität des urbanen Gedächtnisses«, womit sie das Verhältnis zwischen einem Bau und der soziokulturellen Geschichte seines Standorts meint. Gautrand geht stets vom Kontext aus: In den dunklen Rottönen des Theaters von Béthune spiegeln sich Theaterinterieurs der Vergangenheit, und die bemalten Glasdächer der Mauthäuschen an der A16 sind von den Kathedralen Nordfrankreichs inspiriert.
Ihre Bauten sind vielschichtig und nutzen die Außenhaut häufig für auffallende Effekte: Die Wartungshallen auf dem Flughafen von Nantes aus transluzentem Polykarbonat verbinden Farbe, Licht und Schatten zu einer Einheit, und beim Theater in Béthune kommt imitiertes Backsteinmauerwerk in riesigem Maßstab zur Anwendung. Im Cateringgebäude des Flughafens von Nantes signalisieren große Aufkleber mit farbigen Bildern von Esswaren den Inhalt der Kühlräume.

Manuelle Gautrand a commencé à exercer en 1991 à Lyon, où elle a réalisé ses premiers bâtiments. En 1993, elle a gagné Paris. Sa préoccupation principale est la « continuité de la mémoire urbaine », autrement dit la relation entre un projet architectural et l'histoire (au sens social et culturel) du site. Son point de départ est toujours le contexte d'un bâtiment, puis la recherche de ce que l'on veut qu'il exprime en termes d'image et d'expression. Les rouges profonds du théâtre de Béthune reflètent l'intérieur des théâtres anciens ; les vitrages colorés des péages de l'A16 s'inspirent des cathédrales du nord de la France.
Ses constructions révèlent plusieurs niveaux ; souvent, l'enveloppe sert de support à des effets visuels saisissants. Le polycarbonate translucide du bâtiment d'approvisionnement de l'aéroport de Nantes crée une ambiance de couleurs, de lumières et d'ombres ; des motifs imitant le briquetage traditionnel sont exécutés à une échelle gigantesque pour le théâtre de Béthune, les motifs alimentaires colorés dans le catering à Nantes signalent le contenu des chambres froides.

The toll station at Boulogne Sud: toilets, above, and the tollbooths, above right

Die Mautstation in Boulogne Sud: Toiletten (oben) und Mauthäuschen (oben rechts)

Le péage de Boulogne Sud : ci-dessus, les toilettes ; à droite, les postes de péage

98 **A16 motorway, France**

oll stations

is series of five toll stations along the A16 Amiens-ulogne motorway have been made into an event, minated by huge serigraphs across broad glazed nopies, an allusion to the stained-glass windows of e great Gothic cathedrals of northern France. Each age reflects a key aspect of the surrounding area nnecting travellers immediately with the area while ey pause briefly on their journey through.
each toll station, one colour dominates, distinguish-g it from the other toll stations, and is used as a dge for the bright bulbous toilets. The journey en-unters: Abbeville Nord (brown and red) fields of rn and poppies; Côte Picarde (light green) inspired the forest of Crécy; Etaples/Le Touquet (blue) bring-g to mind dunes and the sea; Neuchâtel/Hardelot ark green) reflecting an aerial view of the site; and ulogne Sud (yellow) inspired by fields of oilseed pe.

Die fünf Mautstationen entlang der Autobahn A16 zwischen Amiens und Boulogne wurden mit ihren riesigen Serigraphien auf breiten Glasddächern zum Ereignis – eine Reminiszenz an die Glasfenster der großen gotischen Kathedralen Nordfrankreichs. Sie sollen den Reisenden beim kurzen Halt auf der Durchreise ein charakteristisches Bild der jeweiligen Umgebung vermitteln.
Bei jeder Mautstation dominieren eine andere Farbe (die auch die runden Toiletten kennzeichnet) und unterschiedliche Motive: In Abbeville Nord sind es Braun und Rot für Mais- und Mohnfelder; an der Côte Picarde Hellgrün, angeregt vom Wald von Crécy; in Etaples/Le Touquet Blau für Dünen und Meer; in Neuchâtel/Hardelot Dunkelgrün, das an ein Luftbild der Gegend denken lässt; in Boulogne Sud schließlich Gelb, inspiriert von blühenden Rapsfeldern.

Cette série de cinq gares de péage sur l'autoroute A16 Amiens-Boulogne est traitée comme un événement. Chacune est dominée par d'énormes sérigraphies tendues sur de larges auvents vitrés, allusion aux vitraux des grandes cathédrales gothiques du nord de la France. Chaque image évoque un aspect caractéristique de la région, immergeant immédiatement dans l'environnement le voyageur qui fait une brève halte. Chaque péage est caractérisé par une couleur dominante qui le distingue des autres et personnalise les toilettes en forme de bulbe, claires et lumineuses. L'automobiliste passe successivement à Abbeville Nord : brun et rouge comme les champs de maïs et de coquelicots ; Côte Picarde : vert clair, inspiré par la forêt de Crécy ; Etaples/Le Touquet : bleu, évoquant la mer et les dunes ; Neufchâtel/Hardelot : vert foncé, reflétant une vue aérienne du site ; et Boulogne Sud : jaune, de la couleur des champs de colza.

Toll station at Abbeville Nord: tollbooths, right; toilets, below

Mautstation in Abbeville Nord: rechts die Mauthäuschen, unten die Toiletten

Le péage d'Abbeville Nord : les postes de péage (à droite), les toilettes (ci-dessous)

A field of corn and poppies reflects the surrounding countryside at Abbeville Nord, right. Below, a detail of the glass serigraph.

Rechts: In Abbeville Nord spielt ein Kornfeld mit Mohnblumen auf die umgebende Landschaft an. Unten: Detail der Glasserigraphie.

Les couleurs du péage d'Abbeville Nord reflètent les champs de céréales parsemés de coquelicots (à droite). Ci-dessous, détail du dais en verre sérigraphié.

The foyer - deep reds pay homage to cinematic and theatrical tradition.

Das Foyer – dunkles Rot knüpft an Kino- und Theatertraditionen an.

Les rouges profonds du foyer sont un hommage à la tradition du théatre et du cinéma.

1999 **Béthune, France**

Theatre

The new theatre had to preserve the facade of a 30s cinema and was restricted by adjacent buildings. However, Gautrand solves the problem with a monumental smooth round concrete box the colour of deep red that hides the existing facade. Glazed concrete carries a black diamond pattern, mimicking traditional brickwork but blown up to a giant scale, intending to link the building back into the existing urban fabric and at the same time introducing a totally different scale. Inside, a compact floor plan forces very simple circulation, and the 343-seat auditorium has a comparatively large stage area, keeping the audience close to the actors. Deep dark colours and red-purple hues dominate the womb-like interior, a homage to the cinemas of the 30s and the traditional red velvet curtain associated with the theatre.

Das neue Theater von Béthune sollte die Fassade eines Kinos aus den 30er-Jahren erhalten und seitlich angrenzende Gebäude respektieren. Gautrand löste das Problem durch eine monumentale, glatte abgerundete Betonkiste in dunklem Rot. Das schwarze Rautenmuster des glasierten Betons imitiert traditionelles Backsteinmauerwerk, wurde aber auf riesigen Maßstab vergrößert, um das Gebäude ins Stadtgefüge einzubinden und ihm dennoch einen ganz anderen Maßstab zu geben.

Im Innern erfordert ein kompakter Grundriss einfache Verkehrswege. Der Saal mit seinen 343 Sitzplätzen hat eine vergleichsweise große Bühne, was die Distanz zwischen Zuschauern und Darstellern gering hält. Tief dunkle, rot-violette Farbtöne beherrschen das höhlenartige Interieur – eine Reverenz an die Kinos der 30er-Jahre und den traditionellen roten Samtvorhang im Theater.

Le nouveau théâtre devait être construit en préservant la façade d'un cinéma des années 30, et était enserré par d'autres bâtiments. Gautrand a résolu le problème en accolant l'ancienne façade devant une monumentale boîte de béton lisse et ronde, dont la « peau » est couleur pourpre. Le béton dessine un motif de losanges noirs imitant le briquetage traditionnel à une échelle gigantesque, afin de mieux intégrer l'édifice au tissu urbain, tout en introduisant une échelle différente.

A l'intérieur, un plan compact entraîne une circulation très simple, tandis que la salle de 343 places dispose d'une scène proportionnellement très large qui rapproche les acteurs du public. Des couleurs sombres et saturées dans des tonalités rouge-violet-noir dominent l'intérieur semblable à un cocon, hommage aux cinémas des années 30 et au rideau de velours rouge associé au théâtre.

AISON B
E. LE P
OU DE
EN

OMEDIE DE B

The new building wraps around the preserved facade of a 30s cinema.

Das neue Gebäude umschließt die erhaltene Fassade eines Kinos aus den 30er-Jahren.

Le nouveau bâtiment encadre la façade d'un cinéma des années 30, qui a été préservée.

Catering building

Though this is a complex building required to provide facilities to cook and store food and drink for different airlines while meeting stringent health and safety regulations, Gautrand has simplified the catering building into two linear functions: storage and preparation.
The storage strip for non-perishable food is a 7 m-high building in blue polycarbonate with a resin floor and steel ceiling creating a cold, light atmosphere.
By contrast, the preparation strip is 5 m high, concrete (for insulation against noise from the nearby runway) and air-conditioned. It includes changing rooms, cold storage, a kitchen and a packaging area. Different floor colours mark out the different zones, and cold storages are labelled by huge colourful stickers showing the food inside blown up to giant scale. Light entering through the glass roof is diffused through transparent polycarbonate panels. These create a suspended ceiling behind which artificial light can be installed, without interfering with the smooth and easily cleaned surface.

Obgleich das komplexe Cateringgebäude des Flughafens in Nantes mehreren Fluglinien Einrichtungen zur Zubereitung und Aufbewahrung von Speisen und Getränken bietet und strengen Hygiene- und Sicherheitsvorschriften gerecht werden muss, hat Gautrand den Bau auf zwei lineare Funktionen reduziert: Vorratshaltung und Zubereitung.
Das Lager für haltbare Lebensmittel ist ein 7 m hoher Bau aus blauem Polykarbonat mit Kunststoffboden und Edelstahldecke, was für eine kühle, lichte Atmosphäre sorgt.
Die Zubereitungshalle dagegen, ein 5 m hohes, klimatisiertes Gebäude, ist zum Schutz gegen den Lärm der nahen Startbahn aus Beton errichtet und enthält auch Umkleiden, Kühlräume, eine Küche und den Verpackungsbereich. Unterschiedliche Fußbodenfarben markieren die verschiedenen Zonen; übergroße farbige Aufkleber an den Kühlräumen zeigen die darin befindlichen Lebensmittel in starker Vergrößerung. Transparente Polykarbonatscheiben filtern das durchs Glasdach einfallende Licht und bilden eine abgehängte Decke, hinter der Kunstlicht installiert werden kann. So erhält die Decke eine glatte Fläche, die leicht sauber zu halten ist.

En dépit d'une fonction complexe – préparer et conserver les repas et boissons destinés à différentes lignes aériennes en respectant de rigoureuses prescriptions sanitaires –, le bâtiment d'avitaillement de l'aéroport de Nantes est une structure simple divisée de façon linéair en deux zones : entreposage et préparation.
L'entrepôt de denrées non périssables est un bâtiment c 7 m de haut en polycarbonate bleu, avec un sol en résir et un plafond en acier, l'ensemble créant une ambiance froide et lumineuse.
L'aire de préparation est très différente : haute de 5 m, e est construite en béton (pour isoler du bruit de la piste située à proximité) et climatisée. Elle comprend des ves tiaires, un chambre froide, une cuisine et une salle de conditionnement. Chacune de ces zones est identifiée p une couleur de sol différente ; les chambres froides son en outre caractérisées par un motif adhésif différent po chacune et représentant les aliments qui y sont conservés, à une échelle démesurée. La lumière pénétrant par toit en verre est diffusée par des panneaux de polycarbo nate transparent, constituant un plafond suspendu au-dessus duquel sont installés les dispositifs d'éclairage, les surfaces restant lisses et d'un entretien facile.

e catering block, above. Inside, cold storage ambers are labelled using bold, bright graphics, ft and right.

ben: Gesamtansicht des Cateringgebäudes. Links und chts: Die Kühlräume im Innern sind mit markanten bigen Motiven beklebt.

e d'ensemble du catering (ci-dessus). A l'intérieur, le ntenu des chambres froides est indiqué par des motifs hésifs audacieux (à gauche et à droite).

MUSEUM LINER
MUSEUM LINER APPENZEL

Gigon/Guyer

ırbinenstrasse 29, 8005 Zurich, Switzerland   tel +41 1 271 7767   fax +41 1 273 0608   e-mail info@gigon-guyer.ch   web www.gigon-guyer.ch

nnette Gigon	
›rn	1959 Herisau, Switzerland
udied	1984 Eidgenössische Technische Hochschule, Zurich
evious practice	Marbach & Ruegg, Zurich; Herzog & de Meuron, Basle
	1989 co-founded Gigon/Guyer

ike Guyer	
›rn	1958 Columbus, Ohio, USA
udied	1984 Eidgenössische Technische Hochschule, Zurich
evious practice	OMA (Rem Koolhaas), Rotterdam
	1989 co-founded Gigon/Guyer

elected projects	
rchner Museum	1992 Davos, Switzerland
estaurant Vinikus	1992 Davos, Switzerland
›orts centre	1996 Davos, Switzerland
›artments Broëlberg	1996 Kilchberg, Switzerland
useum Liner	1998 Appenzell, Switzerland
skar Reinhart Collection am Römerholz	
tension and renovation	1998 Winterthur, Switzerland
gnal box	1999 Zurich, Switzerland
›using complex Susenbergstrasse	2000 Zurich, Switzerland
estaurant Rigihof, Traffic Museum	2000 Lucerne, Switzerland
chaeological museum and park	
ith Zulauf + Partner Landscape Architects)	2001 Osnabrück, Germany
iversity of Zurich, auditorium	2001 Zurich, Switzerland

nnette Gigon and Mike Guyer have achieved notable ıccess in the field of museum design, winning a num- er of competitions to create landmark buildings. In e four museums completed to date, exhibition spaces e conceived as "containers for art" - functional boxes ith good light and little decorative distraction. rchitectural exuberance is limited to the exterior which eeks to express the functions of the interior spaces ıd respond to the conditions of the site. Museum ner sets up a distinctive silhouette of an exaggerated

Annette Gigon und Mike Guyer, die eine Reihe interessanter Wettbewerbe für sich entscheiden konnten, haben vor allem im Bereich der Museumsarchitektur bemerkenswerte Erfolge zu verbuchen. Die Ausstellungsräume der bisher fertiggestellten vier Museen sind als »Behälter für Kunst« konzipiert – funktionale Kästen mit guten Lichtverhältnissen und wenig ablenkender Dekoration. Architektonische Vielfalt beschränkt sich auf den Außenbau, der die Funktionen des Inneren sichtbar machen und auf die Gegebenheiten des Standorts reagieren soll. Das

Annette Gigon et Mike Guyer ont connu un succès notable dans le domaine de l'architecture de musées. Ils ont remporté plusieurs concours concernant des édifices marquants. Dans les quatre musées qu'ils ont construits à ce jour, les espaces d'exposition sont traités comme des « containers à œuvres d'art » : des boîtes fonctionnelles offrant un éclairage de qualité et peu d'éléments décoratifs susceptibles de détourner l'attention.
La fantaisie architecturale est donc limitée à l'extérieur, qui cherche à exprimer la fonction des espaces intérieurs tout

The sawtooth roof and scaley steel facade, right, create a dramatic exterior silhouette, but the gallery spaces themselves, left, are kept deliberately neutral.

Rechts: Sheddach und schuppenartige Stahlfassade bilden eine charakteristische Silhouette, während die eigentlichen Galerieräume (links) bewusst neutral gehalten sind.

Le toit en dents de scie et la façade en « écailles » d'acier (à droite) donnent au musée une silhouette dynamique, tandis que les salles d'exposition sont d'une neutralité voulue (à gauche).

sawtooth roof and a scaly skin of chrome tiles. The extension of the galleries for the Oskar Reinhart Collection used limestone and copper in the concrete facade to create by means of an accelerated ageing process through oxidation a reference to the old existing building.
"The facade," says Annette Gigon, "can reveal more than the rooms can, especially with a museum where you must be careful not to overload the exhibition space inside with architectural flourishes. You must let the art speak for itself."
"Grammar of materials", the juxtaposition of diverse materials in a single context, has become a recurring theme in Gigon/Guyer's work, and the practice is particularly interested in exploring the different ways of processing materials. For example, a building such as the Kirchner Museum can be predominantly glass, yet the glass can feature diversity and texture depending on whether the material is smooth, etched, broken, translucent or transparent. Alternatively, their signal box in Zurich responds to its position with a mix of reddish brown iron oxide in the concrete walls, the same fine powder that in time tends to coat everything near a railway track.
"Materials are the sensual, physical element of architecture. They are what you see, what you touch, what you smell, and even what you hear."

Museum Liner zeichnet sich durch die markante Silhouette eines übersteigerten Sheddachs und eine »geschuppte« Außenhaut aus silbrigen, verchromten Schindeln aus. Bei der Erweiterung der Sammlung Oskar Reinhart verwenden die Architekten an der Betonfassade auch Kalkstein und Kupfer. Durch einen beschleunigten Alterungsprozess, in dem das Kupfer oxidiert, stellen sie so einen Bezug zum vorhandenen Bau her.
»Die Fassade«, sagt Annette Gigon, »verrät unter Umständen mehr als die Räume, insbesondere bei einem Museum, wo man sich davor hüten muss, die Ausstellungsräume mit architektonischen Schnörkeln zu überladen. Man muss die Kunst für sich selbst sprechen lassen.«
»Grammatik der Materialien«, das Nebeneinander verschiedenartiger Baustoffe in ein und demselben Kontext, wurde zum immer wiederkehrenden Thema von Gigon/Guyer, die sich besonders für die unterschiedliche Verarbeitung der Materialien interessieren. So kann etwa das Kirchner-Museum hauptsächlich aus Glas bestehen und dabei Vielfalt und Struktur aufweisen, je nachdem ob das Material glatt, geätzt, gebrochen, transluzent oder transparent ist. Das Stellwerk in Zürich reagiert auf seinen Kontext mit einer Mischung aus rotbraunem Eisenoxid in den Betonwänden, demselben feinen Staub, der früher oder später alles nahe der Bahngleise überzieht.
»Materialien sind die sinnlichen, physischen Elemente der Architektur. Man kann sie sehen, berühren, riechen und bisweilen sogar hören.«

en reflétant le contexte du site. Le musée Liner présente une silhouette caractéristique, avec sa toiture en dents de scie et une peau faite d'« écailles » de métal chromé. L'extension des galeries de la collection Oskar Reinhart insère dans sa façade en béton de la pierre calcaire et du cuivre, afin de créer par le biais d'un vieillissement accéléré dû à l'oxydation une référence à l'ancien bâtiment.
« La façade, » explique Annette Gigon, « est plus révélatrice que les salles, surtout dans un musée, où il importe de ne pas surcharger l'espace d'exposition par de grands effets architecturaux. Il faut laisser l'art s'exprimer par lui-même. »
La « grammaire des matériaux », la juxtaposition de divers matériaux dans un même contexte, est devenue un leitmotiv de l'œuvre de Gigon/Guyer, qui explorent les diverses façons de traiter les matériaux. Par exemple, le musée Kirchner est en majeure partie construit en verre, mais le verre peut prendre des aspects et textures très variés, selon qu'il est lisse, gravé, à surface irrégulière, transparent ou translucide. Autre exemple, leur cabine d'aiguillage de Zurich reflète son environnement par l'enduit à base d'oxyde de fer brun-rouge couvrant ses murs en béton : la même poudre impalpable qui finit par recouvrir tout ce qui est près de la voie ferrée.
« Les matériaux sont l'élément physique, sensuel de l'architecture. Ils sont ce que vous voyez, ce que vous touchez, ce que vous sentez et même ce que vous entendez. »

998 Appenzell, Switzerland

Museum Liner

he museum is dedicated to the permanent collection f the work of local father and son artists Carl August nd Carl Walter Liner, although it will house changing xhibitions alongside their work. Spaces must there- ore be flexible, and have been kept relatively small to reate a sense of intimacy with the works. Natural light ours in through the exaggerated sawtoothed roof, self a reference to nearby industrial buildings as well s the pitched roofs of traditional Appenzell houses. oofs are clad in sandblasted sheets of chrome steel keep the light reflected in the exhibition spaces as iffuse and undistorted in colour as possible. Facades re clad in the same material, giant overlapping hingles. The overall effect is of a single scaly beast or jagged mountain against the nearby Alpstein massif.

Das Museum Liner zeigt das Werk der einheimischen Maler Carl August und Carl Walter Liner (Vater und Sohn); daneben soll es Wechselausstellungen Raum geben. Die Räumlichkeiten müssen daher flexibel sein und wurden eher klein gehalten, um ein Gefühl der Nähe zu den Werken zu schaffen. Durch das überbetonte Sheddach, das Bezug auf nahegelegene Industriebauten wie auch auf die Satteldächer der traditionellen Appenzellerhäuser nimmt, fällt Tageslicht ein. Die Dächer sind mit sandgestrahlten Chromstahlblechen gedeckt, um das in den Ausstellungsräumen reflektierte Licht so diffus und farbrein wie möglich zu halten. Die Fronten sind mit dem gleichen Material in Form riesiger, überlappender Platten verkleidet. Der Gesamteindruck ist der eines Schuppentiers oder eines zerklüfteten Bergs vor dem Hintergrund des nahen Alpsteinmassivs.

Le musée Liner abrite une collection permanente d'œuvres des artistes locaux Liner père et fils (Carl August et Carl Walter), et accueille diverses expositions. Les espaces doivent donc être relativement souples et polyvalents, et sont délibérément assez petits afin de permettre un contact intime avec les œuvres. La lumière du jour entre à flots par la toiture en dents de scie, laquelle évoque à la fois des bâtiments industriels de la région et les traditionnelles maisons à pignon d'Appenzell. La couverture en feuilles d'acier au chrome sablé renvoie vers les espaces d'exposition une lumière aussi diffuse et neutre que possible. Les façades sont revêtues du même matériau, formant d'énormes tuiles imbriquées qui prendront en vieillissant une couleur gris argent ; l'effet d'ensemble évoque une énorme bête à écailles ou une montagne déchiquetée, se profilant sur le proche massif d'Alpstein.

40

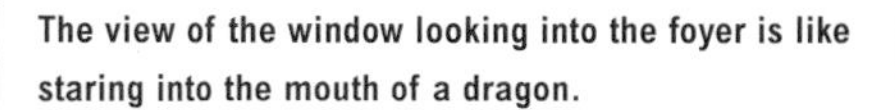

The view of the window looking into the foyer is like staring into the mouth of a dragon.

Das Fenster des Foyers erinnert an ein Drachenmaul.

La baie vitrée du foyer, béante comme une gueule de dragon.

Section/ Schnitt/ Coupe

1 **galleries/** Ausstellungsbereich/ salle d'expositions
2 **entrance/** Eingang/ entrée

The silvery facade is clad in sandblasted sheets of chrome steel, left. Below, longitudinal section showing exaggerated roof lights.

Links: Die silbrige Fassade ist mit sandgestrahlten Chromstahlplatten verkleidet. Unten: Längsschnitt mit den stark betonten Oberlichtern.

A gauche : la façade est revêtue de plaques d'acier chromé rendues mates par sablage. Ci-dessous : coupe (notez les lucarnes surdimensionnées).

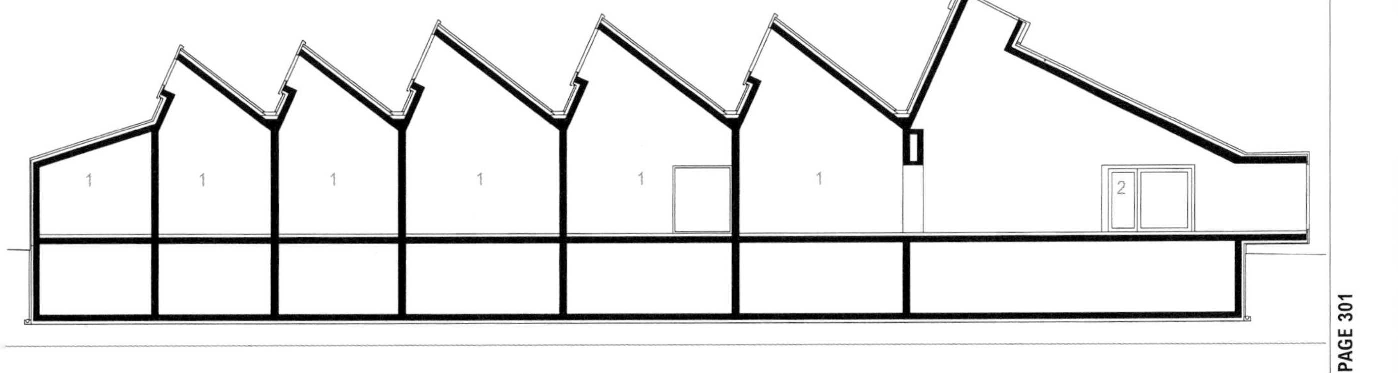

Above, the facade of the sports centre doubles as a grandstand for spectators. Right, the canteen.

Oben: Die Fassade des Sportzentrums dient zugleich als Zuschauertribüne. Rechts die Cafeteria.

Ci-dessus : la façade du centre sportif sert également de tribune pour les spectateurs. A droite, la cafétéria.

1996 **Davos, Switzerland**

Sports centre

Located next to the town's speed-skating rink, the building acts as a two-storey grandstand permeable to light and air.
The exterior is clad in a double layer of wood, giving it depth, a colourful painted pine skin behind slatted untreated larch. The use of colour, devised in collaboration with artist Adrian Schiess, continues inside the building with dark blue, strawberry, white, apricot, light green and turquoise, "a reflection of the colourful world of sports". Big bold lettering for signage is inspired by numbers and logos on athletics strips.

Das neben der Eisschnelllaufbahn gelegene Sportzentrum in Davos erscheint wie eine zweigeschossige, licht- und luftdurchlässige Tribüne.
Der Außenbau gewinnt durch eine doppelte Holzverschalung an Tiefe, bei der eine bunt bemalte Lage Kiefernholz hinter Rippen aus unbehandeltem Lärchenholz angeordnet ist. Das in Zusammenarbeit mit dem Künstler Adrian Schiess konzipierte Farbschema setzt sich mit Dunkelblau, Erdbeerrot, Weiß, Apricot, Hellgrün und Türkis im Gebäudeinnern fort und »spiegelt die farbenfrohe Welt des Sports.« Die Anregung zu den großen, augenfälligen Schriftzeichen für die Beschilderung gaben die Zahlen und Logos auf den Trikots der Sportler.

Situé à côté de la piste de patinage, le centre sportif de Davos se présente comme une tribune à deux étages perméable à la lumière et à l'air.
L'extérieur est revêtu d'une double couche de bois produisant un effet de profondeur : une peau en sapin peint de couleurs vives derrière des lattes de mélèze non traité. Cette gamme de couleurs, élaborée en collaboration avec l'artiste Adrian Schiess, se poursuit à l'intérieur du bâtiment : bleu foncé, fraise, blanc, abricot, vert clair et turquoise « reflètent le monde bigarré du sport ». Les gros caractères de la signalétique s'inspirent des chiffres et logos des pistes d'athlétisme.

Ground floor plan/ Erdgeschossgrundriss/ Plan du rez-de-chaussée

1 **canteen/** Cafeteria/ cafétéria

2 **spectator seating/** Zuschauertribüne/ gradins

he strong colour scheme has been devised with artist drian Schiess. Views into the canteen, left, and ntrance, below.

as Farbschema mit seinen starken Kontrasten wurde usammen mit dem Künstler Adrian Schiess entwickelt. inks: Blick in die Cafeteria; unten: Eingang.

a composition chromatique a été conçue avec le peintre drian Schiess. A gauche, la cafétéria ; ci-dessous, le all.

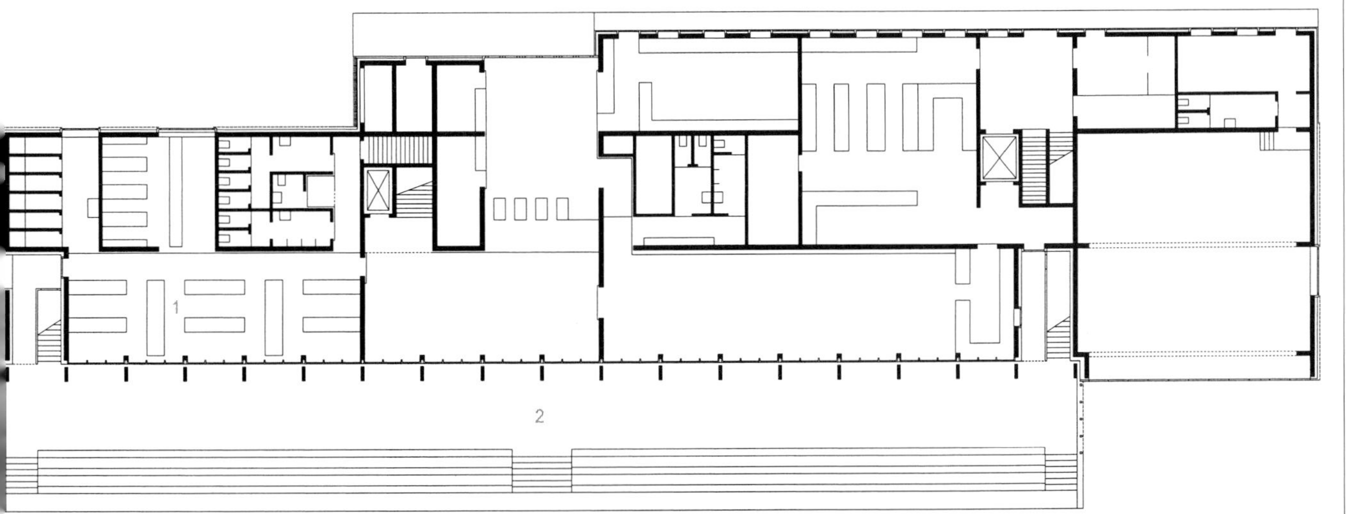

Oskar Reinhart Collection am Römerholz extension and renovation

Originally built in 1915 in the style of a French Renaissance villa, and extended in 1924, the Villa am Römerholz has housed the art collection of Oskar Reinhart. The latest series of additions and renovations includes complete replacement of two exhibition spaces, reinstating the original layout of the rooms, and the introduction of three new exhibition spaces between the former residence and the current gallery. From outside, the new rooms form a closed cube, tapering towards the top. Copper roofing matches that of the gallery, while prefabricated concrete slabs used to clad the wall have copper and Jurassic limestone, two of the predominant materials in the villa, mixed in with the cement, and will quickly weather to a similar greenish patina.

Die Villa am Römerholz, 1915 in den Formen der französischen Renaissance errichtet, wurde 1924 erweitert und beherbergt seitdem die Sammlung Oskar Reinhart. Die jüngste Folge von An- und Umbauten umfasst die komplette Neugestaltung von zwei Galerien, die Wiederherstellung der ursprünglichen Raumfolge sowie drei neue Ausstellungsflächen zwischen dem ehemaligen Wohnhaus und der heutigen Galerie. Von außen bilden die neuen Räume einen geschlossenen Kubus, der sich nach oben verjüngt. Das kupfergedeckte Dach entspricht dem der Galerie. Dem Zement der Fertigbetonplatten, mit denen die Wände verkleidet sind, wurden Kupfer und Jurakalk beigemischt, zwei der vorherrschenden Materialien der alten Villa, die dem Anbau rasch zu einer ähnlichen grünen Patina verhelfen werden.

Construite en 1915 dans le style Renaissance française, agrandie en 1924, la Villa am Römerholz abrite la collection d'art Oskar Reinhart. La récente série d'agrandissements et de rénovations inclut le renouvellement complet de deux espaces d'exposition, rétablissant la disposition primitive des salles, et l'insertion de trois nouveaux espaces d'exposition entre l'ancienne résidence et la galerie actuelle. De l'extérieur, les nouvelles salles se présentent comme un cube fermé, plus étroit au sommet. La toiture en cuivre est analogue à celle de la galerie ; les plaques de béton préfabriquées habillant les murs sont mêlées de cuivre et de calcaire du Jura, deux des principaux matériaux de la villa ; l'ensemble prendra rapidement une patine verdâtre similaire.

From outside, Gigon/Guyer's intervention is a closed concrete facade, right. Left, gallery space.

Nach außen zeigt der Erweiterungsbau eine geschlossen Betonfassade (rechts); links ein Ausstellungsraum.

De l'extérieur, l'intervention de Gigon/Guyer prend la forme d'une façade aveugle en béton (à droite). A gauche, une des salles du musée.

Elevation/ Aufriss/ Coupe

1 **1924 extension/** Erweiterung von 1924/ extension de 1924

2 **new insertion/** neue Erweiterung/ nouvelle intervention

3 **original villa/** alte Villa/ la villa primitive

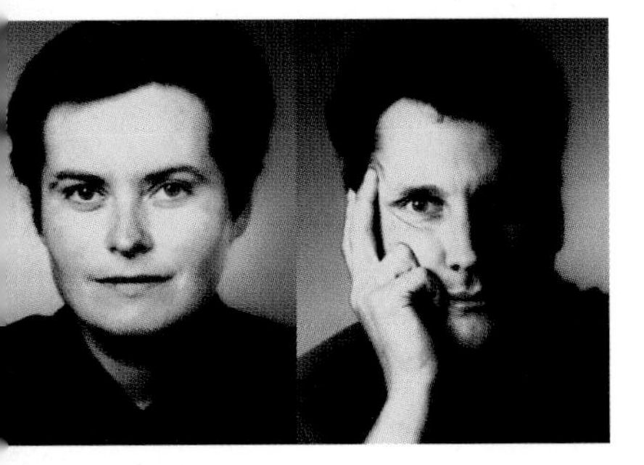

Studio Granda

nidjustigur 11b, Reykjavik IS 101, Iceland tel +354 562 2661 fax +354 552 6626 e-mail studiogranda@studiogranda.is web www.studiogranda.is

argarét Hardardóttir

rn	1959	Reykjavik, Iceland
udied	1981	Edinburgh University; Architectural Association, London
actice	1987	co-founded Studio Granda

eve Christer

rn	1960	Blackfyne, UK
udied	1981	University of Newcastle upon Tyne; Architectural Association, London
actice	1987	co-founded Studio Granda

elected projects

ty Hall	1992	Reykjavik, Iceland
ction Poliphile Houses	1992	Wiesbaden, Germany
upreme Court of Iceland	1996	Reykjavik, Iceland
inglan Car Park square and landscaping	1999	Reykjavik, Iceland (in association with artist Kristin E. Hrafnsson)
eykjavik Art Museum	2000	Reykjavik, Iceland

hough involved in a wide range of public and private rojects including housing, interiors, infrastructure, ndscaping, furniture and art installations, Studio randa established an international reputation because f its unprecedented success in designing landmark ublic buildings for Reykjavik. In only ten years they ave built the City Hall (1992), Supreme Court (1996) nd the Art Museum (2000); all projects awarded in ational competition. Their impact on the urban landcape of the Icelandic capital is evident.
rom grand-scale public projects to small-scale resiential projects or commissions to design footbridges nd car parks, Studio Granda maintains its architecral principles, carefully selecting materials (with a redilection for local volcanic stones), insisting on a gh standard of craftsmanship, relating the structure the surrounding landscape (synthetic or natural), nd creating a complex network of interior spaces. ollaborations with Icelandic artists such as Kristin E. rafnsson and Thorvaldur Thorsteinsson bring to their

Obgleich Studio Granda ein breites Spektrum öffentlicher und privater Projekte vorzuweisen hat, darunter Innenraumgestaltungen, Infrastruktur, Landschaftsgestaltung, Möbeldesign und Kunstinstallationen, beruht das internationale Renommee des Büros auf seinen beispiellosen Wettbewerbserfolgen für markante öffentliche Bauten in Reykjavik. Mit dem neuen Rathaus (1992), dem Obersten Gerichtshof (1996) und dem Kunstmuseum (2000) haben sie das Stadtbild der isländischen Hauptstadt entscheidend mit geprägt.
Angefangen bei großen öffentlichen Projekten über kleine Wohnbauten bis hin zum Entwurf von Fußgängerbrücken und Parkplätzen hält Studio Granda an seinen architektonischen Prinzipien fest: überlegte Materialwahl (mit einer Vorliebe für einheimisches Vulkangestein), hohe handwerkliche Qualitätsmaßstäbe, die Einbindung des Bauwerks in die Landschaft, sei sie künstlich oder natürlich, und die Anlage eines komplexen Netzwerks von Innenräumen. Die Zusammenarbeit mit isländischen Künstlern wie Kristin E. Hrafnsson und Thorvaldur Thorsteinsson gibt

Bien que le bureau participe à un large éventail de projets tant publics que privés – logements, intérieurs, parcs et jardins paysages, meubles et installations artistiques – sa réputation internationale est due à son succès sans précédent dans la conception de prestigieux édifices publics à Reykjavik. En l'espace de dix ans seulement, Studio Granda a construit l'Hôtel de Ville (1992), le Tribunal Suprême (1996) et le Musée des Beaux-Arts (2000), qui avaient tous fait l'objet de concours nationaux, et qui ont fortement marqué le paysage urbain de la capitale de l'Islande.
Des projets publics de grande envergure aux petites constructions résidentielles et à des commandes de ponts piétonniers ou de parkings, Studio Granda reste fidèle à ses principes architecturaux : sélection rigoureuse des matériaux (avec un goût marqué pour la pierre volcanique locale), exigence d'une mise en œuvre de haute qualité, relation à la structure du paysage (qu'il soit naturel ou artificiel), et création d'un complexe réseau d'espaces intérieurs.

projects a cerebral dimension and enliven the urban landscape. Even a car park becomes a piece of living sculpture. This is a reciprocal relationship that has led the architects to contribute to several art installation projects.

Studio Grandas Projekten eine intellektuelle Dimension und belebt die Stadtlandschaft – selbst ein Parkplatz wird so zu einer belebten Skulptur. Die Architekten ihrerseits beteiligten sich an mehreren Kunstinstallationen.

Des collaborations avec des artistes islandais tels que Kristin E. Hrafnsson et Thorvaldur Thorsteinsson donnent à leurs projets une dimension intellectuelle tout en animant le paysage urbain. Même un simple parking devient une pièce de sculpture contemporaine. Une relation réciproque a conduit les architectes à contribuer à plusieurs installations artistiques.

City Hall

on in national competition in 1987 and inaugurated 1992, this prestigious public project launched the dgling practice as an international contender.
e building is split in two north-south by a red stone- ed chasm. The city council to the north is a solid posing block anchored in the city; the lighter office ilding to the south is predominantly of glass, and ssolves into the lake. Meeting rooms panelled in rich d wood benefit from the morning sun, while the coun- chamber, usually used in the evenings, opens with glazed wall towards the evening sun.
e office building is divided into four two-storey bays, ch lit by an elliptical roof light over a central circula- n space. The vertical circulation within these areas intended to contrast with the horizontal movement ross the open ground floor public space. Along its uth facade, pillars rise from a lake to support the riegated vaulted aluminium roof, which sweeps over e building.
blic pedestrian routes lead through the building from e town centre to the west through to the east. A con- uation of the external street, materials have been osen accordingly and the passage is lit by north light om deep roof lights. A dark textured wall of black va runs 60 m across its north side, water trickling wn its surface encouraging moss growth.

Der Sieg im Wettbewerb für das Rathaus von Reykjavik, das 1992 eingeweiht wurde, verhalf dem jungen Büro 1987 zu internationaler Anerkennung.
Eine von roten Steinen gesäumte Spalte teilt den Bau in zwei Hälften: einen Bauteil mit dem Ratssaal als massiven, in der Stadt verankerten Block im Norden und einen leichteren Büroteil im Süden, bei dem Glas dominiert und der sich im See aufzulösen scheint. Die mit rötlichem Holz vertäfelten Besprechungsräume im Süden erhalten Morgensonne; in den Ratssaal, der gewöhnlich abends genutzt wird, kann das Licht durch eine Glaswand ungehindert einströmen.
Das Bürogebäude ist in vier zweigeschossige Zonen unterteilt, in die jeweils durch ein elliptisches Oberlicht über dem zentralen Treppenhaus Licht einfällt. Die vertikalen Verbindungswege innerhalb dieser Bereiche soll in Kontrast zur horizontalen Bewegung durch das öffentlich zugängliche Erdgeschoss treten. Aus dem See auf der Südseite erhebt sich eine Stützenreihe, um ein gewölbtes Aluminiumdach zu tragen, das sich über das ganze Gebäude schwingt.
Aus dem Stadtzentrum im Westen führen öffentliche Fußwege in östlicher Richtung durch das Rathaus. Die Materialien wurden entsprechend dem Charakter dieser Passage gewählt, die durch tief herab reichende Oberlichter mit Nordlicht versorgt wird. Entlang der Nordseite der Passage verläuft eine 60 m lange, dunkel strukturierte Wand aus schwarzem Lavagestein, über deren Oberfläche Wasser rieselt, das den Bewuchs mit Moos fördern soll.

Fruit d'un concours national remporté en 1987, inauguré en 1992, ce prestigieux édifice public a projeté le jeune bureau dans la compétition internationale.
Divisé en deux parties, l'Hôtel de Ville comporte au nord un bloc imposant solidement ancré dans la ville, et au sud un immeuble de bureaux plus léger, principalement en verre, qui semble se dissoudre dans le lac. Dans le sens nord-sud, l'édifice est coupé par un vide béant revêtu de pierre rouge. D'un côté, les salles de réunion lambrissées de bois aux tons chauds bénéficient du soleil matinal ; de l'autre, la salle du conseil, surtout utilisée le soir, est généreusement éclairée par un mur vitré.
L'immeuble de bureaux est divisé en quatre sections à deux niveaux ; chacune est éclairée par une grande lucarne elliptique dominant un espace de circulation central. Dans ces zones, la circulation verticale contraste délibérément avec la structure horizontale de l'espace public tenant le rez-de-chaussée. Le long de la façade sud, des colonnes surgissent d'un lac pour soutenir un toit en aluminium cintré et multicolore qui se déploie au-dessus du bâtiment.
Les voies piétonnes desservent l'édifice depuis le centre ville situé à l'ouest et continuent vers l'est après avoir traversé celui-ci. Traité comme un prolongement de la rue extérieure, avec des matériaux choisis en conséquence, le passage est éclairé du nord par de profondes ouvertures pratiquées dans la toiture. Un mur texturé en lave noire long de 60 m longe le côté nord du site ; l'eau suintant à sa surface favorise la croissance de la mousse.

bove: a footbridge leads to the office (left) and ouncil blocks (right). Right, the office block seen om the opposite side of the lake.

oen: Eine Fußgängerbrücke führt zu den Gebäudeteilen it Büros (links) und Ratssaal (rechts). Rechts: Das Bügebäude von der anderen Seite des Sees.

n haut à gauche : une passerelle conduit a l'aile administrative (à gauche) et à la salle du Conseil (à droite). droite : l'aile administrative vu de l'autre côté du lac.

ouncil chamber, right. Left, the office building issolves into the lake.

echts der Ratssaal, links das Bürogebäude, das mit em See zu verschmelzen scheint.

droite, la salle du Conseil, à gauche l'aile administrative e prolonge insensiblement vers le lac.

The moss-covered lava wall stretches 60 m along the pedestrian route that cuts through the complex.

Die Lavamauer, die den Fußweg durch den Komplex 60 m lang begleitet, ist mit Moos bewachsen.

Un mur de lave couvert de mousse et de lichens borde sur 60 m la chemin piétonnier qui traverse le complexe.

The skin of the south facade is pulled out to meet the garden.

Die aus der Senkrechten nach außen gezogene Außenhaut der Südfassade ragt in den Garten.

La « peau » de la façade sud se relève comme pour accueillir le jardin.

1996 **Reykjavik, Iceland**

Supreme Court of Iceland

Another prestigious public commission won in open competition, the building sits between the State Ministries, the former National Library and the National Theatre, with its western edge open to the Atlantic Ocean. Its northern edge is used to define the street line while to the south it shelters a public garden.
The building reflects the scale of its neighbours by starting tall and wide on the western edge and diminishing towards the east as it disappears towards the enclosed spaces, terminating in a low unit that overlooks a small square at the rear of the theatre.
Facades are clad in a rich palette of materials, each with a strong identity. The upper parts of the street facades are clad in pre-patinated copper sheet above a hewn basalt plinth. On the south facade, the copper meets the grassy incline of the garden. A sawn basalt-clad tower marks the public entrance at the south-western corner, and honed "gabbro", an indigenous metamorphic stone, emphasises other points of interest.
Public and judiciary spaces are imagined as two separate buildings united under a single enveloping skin. Daylight penetrates the interior through narrow slots, and views out of the building coincide with places of rest. The judges' offices are given kudos by their exceptional height and the open views they command over the ocean.
Throughout the interior, a limited palette of oak, plaster, polished and fair-faced concrete and steel is used with apparently simple details and an emphasis on local craftsmanship.

Der Auftrag für den Obersten Gerichtshof von Island kam ebenfalls über einen Wettbewerbserfolg zustande. Das Gebäude liegt zwischen den Ministerien, der ehemaligen Nationalbibliothek und dem Nationaltheater; im Norden bestimmt es den Straßenverlauf, im Süden umgibt es einen öffentlichen Park.
Der Bau spiegelt die Maßstäblichkeit seines Umfelds wider, indem er auf der zum Atlantik offenen Westseite breit und hoch beginnt und im Osten, wo die geschlossenen Räumen liegen, in einem flachen Gebäudeteil endet, der einen kleinen Platz hinter dem Theater überschaut.
Die Fassaden sind mit verschiedenen markanten Materialien verkleidet; so die oberen Geschosse der Straßenseiten mit vorpatiniertem Kupferblech über einem Bruchsteinsockel aus Basalt. An der Südseite treffen die Kupferverkleidung und der grasbewachsene Hang des Gartens zusammen. An der Südwestecke markiert ein mit gesägtem Basalt ummantelter Turm den öffentlichen Zugang; geschliffener »Gabbro«, ein einheimischer metamorpher Stein, hebt andere bedeutsame Punkte hervor.
Die öffentlichen und gerichtsinternen Räume sind als zwei separate Bauteile gedacht, die eine gemeinsame Außenhaut umgibt. Tageslicht dringt durch schmale Schlitze ins Innere, und aus dem Gebäude schaut man auf ruhige, erholsame Bereiche. Die Dienstzimmer der Richter sind außergewöhnlich hoch und bieten freien Blick aufs Meer.
Im Innern beschränkt sich die Auswahl der Materialien auf Eichenholz, Putz, polierten und strukturierten Beton sowie Stahl, mit scheinbar schlichten Details und einer Betonung heimischer Handwerkskunst.

Autre commande publique de prestige remportée à l'issue d'un concours, l'édifice est situé entre les ministères, l'ancienne Bibliothèque nationale et le Théâtre national, son angle ouest s'ouvrant sur l'océan. Le côté nord souligne l'alignement de la rue, tandis qu'au sud le bâtiment abrite un jardin public.
Reflétant l'échelle des constructions voisines, le Tribunal est d'abord haut et large à l'ouest, puis devient de plus en plus étroit à l'est, pour se terminer par un bâtiment bas qui donne sur une petite place à l'arrière du théâtre.
Les façades sont revêtues d'un riche choix de matériaux dont chacun affirme son identité. Les parties supérieures des façades sur rue sont habillées de feuilles de cuivre pré-patinées surmontant une plinthe en basalte taillé. Sur la façade sud, le cuivre descend jusqu'à la pelouse en pente. Une tour revêtue de basalte scié marque l'entrée principale située à l'angle sud-ouest, tandis que du « gabbro » poli (roche métamorphique locale) indique d'autres centres d'intérêt.
Les espaces public et judiciaire sont conçus comme deux bâtiments distincts enveloppés d'une seule peau. La lumière du jour pénètre par d'étroits bandeaux horizontaux, les vues sur l'extérieur coïncidant avec les aires de détente. Les bureaux des juges se distinguent par une hauteur de plafond exceptionnelle et par des baies vitrées dominant l'océan.
Tous les volumes intérieurs sont traités dans une gamme de matériaux restreinte – chêne, plâtre, béton lissé ou brut et acier –, avec des détails d'une apparente simplicité mettant l'accent sur l'artisanat local.

:reet facades are clad in copper and sit on a basalt inth.

e Straßenfassaden sind über einem Basaltsockel mit ıpferblech verkleidet.

s façades sur rue revêtues de plaques de cuivre posent sur un socle de basalte.

ild & K.

olaistraße 2, 80802 Munich, Germany tel +49 89 340 037 fax +49 89 340 049

dreas Hild		
n	1961	Hamburg
died	Technische Hochschule, Munich	
ctice	1992	co-founded Hild & Kaltwasser (with Tillmann Kaltwasser)

lected projects		
nt warehouse Kemeter	1995	Eichstätt, Germany
oftop extension	1995	Eichstätt, Germany
rlagskantine Callwey	1996	Munich, Germany
aste depot	1996	Landshut, Germany
s shelter	1997	Landshut, Germany
cial housing	1997	Kempten/Allgäu, Germany
eater im Rottenkolberstadel	1998	Landshut, Germany
ousing refurbishment	1999	Berlin, Germany
ngle family house	2000	Rudelshausen, Germany

dreas Hild is not one to worry about what is deemed shionable or tasteful. Instead he displays a maverick reak, which gives his work a welcome edge. "We are terested in all the bad things. Not in design, but in e things that are non-design. We are influenced by e ordinary world like the mahogany shelves in our arents' homes, patterned wallpaper, supermarkets, Y - our starting point is everyday culture, not the -called good taste."
ild likes to play intellectual jokes, dashing people's xpectations of what is appropriate for a given build-g type: social housing with mahogany-like panelling Kempten; an ornate rusted iron bus shelter in Land-hut; simple kitchen chairs from heavy dark oak for e canteen of Callwey Verlag in Munich; a recycling ation marked by the word "Sammeln" (collect) in rge gold letters; a paint warehouse devoid of olour.
t's not our aim that people say 'that's beautiful' or nd us unusual. I am just interested in architectural

Andreas Hild kümmert sich nicht darum, was gerade als modisch oder geschmackvoll gilt; statt dessen neigt er zu individuellen Lösungen, die seinen Bauten Prägnanz verleihen. »Wir sind an allem Schlechten interessiert. Nicht an Design, sondern an den Dingen, die Non-Design verkörpern. Wir sind beeinflusst von der normalen Welt, den Mahagoniregalen in den Wohnungen unserer Eltern, gemusterten Tapeten, Supermärkten, do-it-yourself – unser Ausgangspunkt ist die Kultur des Alltags, nicht der so genannte ›gute Geschmack.‹«
Hild liebt intellektuelle Scherze, mit denen er konterkariert, was die Öffentlichkeit für bestimmte Gebäudetypen für angemessen hält: Sozialwohnungen mit imitierter Mahagoni-Verkleidung in Kempten, ein bewusst rostiges eisernes Wartehäuschen in Landshut; einfache Küchenstühle aus schwerer dunkler Eiche für die Kantine des Callwey-Verlags in München, eine Recyclingstation, die das Wort »Sammeln« in großen goldenen Lettern ziert, ein Farbenlager ohne jegliche farbliche Gestaltung.
»Es ist nicht unser Ziel, dass die Leute sagen ›Das ist

Andreas Hild n'est pas homme à se préoccuper de modes ou de bon goût. Il a par contre un côté franc-tireur qui donne à son œuvre un mordant bienvenu.
« Nous sommes intéressés par tout ce qui est décrié. Pas par le design, mais par ce qui va à l'encontre du design. Nous sommes influencés par les objets du monde ordinaire, comme les étagères en acajou de l'appartement de nos parents, le papier peint, les supermarchés ; notre point de départ est la culture du quotidien, pas le bon goût. »
Hild adore les mystifications intellectuelles, en faisant le contraire de ce que les gens attendent d'un type de bâtiment donné : à Kempten, logements sociaux avec un revêtement mural imitation acajou ; à Landshut, abribus en fer rouillé ornementé ; pour le restaurant d'entreprise des éditions Callwey à Munich, de simples chaises de cuisine en robuste chêne foncé ; une déchetterie indiquée par le mot « Sammeln » (collecte) en grandes lettres dorées ; un entrepôt de peintures dénué de toute couleur …
« Nous ne voulons pas que les gens disent ‹ c'est beau ›,

problems. The building makes the statement, not what I am doing to it."

The untimely death of his business partner and lifelong friend Tilmann Kaltwasser in 1998 has meant changes for the practice. Meanwhile, Hild is working on large-scale projects. He is chiefly interested in the strategies and structures that lead to buildings. "I could imagine having 100 guys in my office one day."

schön‹ oder uns ungewöhnlich finden. Ich interessiere mich einfach für architektonische Fragestellungen. Das Gebäude macht die Aussage, nicht das, was ich daran tue.«

Der frühe Tod seines Geschäftspartners und Jugendfreunds Tilmann Kaltwasser 1998 bedeutete Veränderungen für das Büro, das mittlerweile auch größere Aufträge bearbeitet. Hild interessiert sich für die Strategien und Strukturen, die zu Gebäuden führen. »Ich könnte mir vorstellen, eines Tages 100 Leute in meinem Büro zu beschäftigen.«

ou que ce soit inhabituel. Ce qui m'intéresse, ce sont l problèmes architecturaux. Le bâtiment lui-même fait la déclaration, non ce que je lui fais. »

Le décès prématuré de son associé et ami de longue d Tilmann Kaltwasser en 1998 a entraîné des changeme pour le bureau qui, entre-temps, s'occupe aussi de cor mandes importantes. Hild s'intéresse aux stratégies et structures donnant lieu à des bâtiments : « Je peux ima ner qu'un jour j'emploierai 100 gars dans mon bureau.

1995 **Eichstätt, Germany**

Paint warehouse Kemeter

The absence of colour from the facade denies the building's function as a paint warehouse. Instead, white, lightweight concrete panels of varying lengths and widths create a rhythm across the facade. The windows set between the panels play along the varying lengths like notes across a musical score. During the day, the facade allows glimpses of an interior that is active and ever-changing. At night, concealed lighting highlights the vertical strips, creating a new, but equally strong pattern.

Das Fehlen jeglicher Farbe an der Fassade verleugnet die Funktion dieses Lagerhauses für Farben. Statt dessen rhythmisieren leichte weiße Betontafeln verschiedener Länge und Breite die Front, zwischen denen sich die Fenster wie Noten auf einer Partitur ausnehmen. Tagsüber gestattet die Fassade Blicke auf ein aktives, sich ständig veränderndes Inneres. Bei Nacht akzentuiert indirekte Beleuchtung die vertikalen Streifen und erzeugt ein neues, ebenfalls markantes Muster.

L'absence de toute couleur semble nier la fonction de c entrepôt de peintures. De légers panneaux en béton de couleur blanche, de longueurs et largeurs diverses, ryth ment la façade. Les baies pratiquées entre les panneau jouent sur les différences de longueur comme des note sur une partition. De jour, elles permettent d'entrevoir l'activité d'un intérieur en constant changement. De nu des sources d'éclairage cachées soulignent les ouvertu verticales, créant un rythme différent mais non moins puissant.

Main facade, right, with detail of cladding panels, lef The variation in length and thickness creates a rhythm across the facade.

Rechts die Hauptfassade; links ein Detail der Verkleidungstafeln. Die wechselnde Länge und Dicke der Tafeln rhythmisiert die Fassade.

A droite, la façade principale ; à gauche, un détail du revêtement. Les panneaux de longueur et d'épaisseur différentes rythment la façade.

ew of the paint warehouse from the road

s Farbenlager von der Straße aus

ntrepôt de peintures vu de la route

Main facade of the apartment building, left, with a close up of the faux-mahogany cladding panels, right

Links: Straßenfassade des Wohnblocks; rechts: Detail d Verkleidung aus Mahagoni-Imitat

A gauche, la façade principale de l'immeuble d'habitatioı A droite, détail des panneaux en imitation acajou.

1997 **Kempten/Allgäu, Germany**

Social housing

Standard-issue plastic cladding was specified for this social housing project, so Hild & Kaltwasser chose it in a mahogany-like finish. This gives the design a twist by using a very cheap material on a low-budget project, while alluding to a material normally associated with wealth and taste. Wonderfully kitsch, the panels are not meant to be mistaken for mahogany, but to question stereotypes.

The joke has been more fully appreciated by foreign critics, however, than by the German architectural press. "If we had done this project using a light plywood finish, everyone would have loved it", says Hild. "But that would have been too obvious, it would have taken no intellectual risks. It is too easy to do something that is fashionable. It is not that it's bad, it's just boring."

Für dieses Projekt des Sozialen Wohnungsbaus war eine Standard- Kunststoffverkleidung vorgeschrieben. Hild und Kaltwasser entschieden sich für eine Gestaltung in Mahagoni-Imitat, die wunderbar kitschig wirkt und widersprüchliche Assoziationen weckt: Bei dem knapp kalkulierten Projekt wird sehr billiges Material verwendet, das aber auf etwas anspielt, das man gemeinhin mit Reichtum und Kultiviertheit in Verbindung bringt. Die Fassade will nicht für Mahagoni gehalten werden, sondern sie soll Klischees hinterfragen.

Der Witz wurde allerdings eher von ausländischen Kritikern gewürdigt als von der deutschen Architekturpresse. Hild meint dazu: »Wenn wir diese Anlage mit einem Sperrholzimitat gebaut hätten, hätte sie allen gefallen, aber das wäre zu offensichtlich gewesen, es hätte kein intellektuelles Risiko bedeutet. Es ist zu einfach, etwas trendgerechtes zu machen. Das ist nicht unbedingt schlecht, aber langweilig.«

Des revêtements en plastique stratifié standard étant spécifiés pour cet ensemble d'habitations bon marché, Hild & Kaltwasser ont choisi une finition façon acajou. Cette utilisation d'un matériau très banal dans le cadre d'un projet à faible budget crée la surprise en faisant allusion à un matériau généralement associé à l'opulence et au bon goût. L'objectif de ce procédé merveilleusement kitsch n'est pas de faire croire que c'est de l'acajou véritable, mais de remettre en question certaines idées reçues.

La plaisanterie a été toutefois davantage appréciée par les critiques étrangers que par la presse architecturale allemande. Hild dit : « Si nous avions utilisé des finitions en contre-plaqué léger, tout le monde aurait adoré cela. Mais ç'aurait été trop évident et dénué de risques intellectuels. Il est trop facile de faire des choses à la mode. Non que ce soit mauvais en soi, mais c'est tout simplement ennuyeux. »

POLIZEI

Courtyard and balconies

Innenhof und Balkone

La cour et les balcons

Street facade of apartment building, above, with detail of the plasterwork, above right

Oben: Straßenfassade des Wohnhauses. Oben rechts: Detail der Stuckarbeiten.

La façade sur rue de l'immeuble résidentiel (ci-dessus). A droite, détail des stucs.

999 Berlin, Germany

Housing refurbishment

ather than compliantly restoring the pre-World War II ucco facade to its former splendour, the architects sisted on reflecting the apartment building's history ithout departing too far from the client's specifica- ons. The solution was an interpretation of the original etails, but executed in a planar manner. A small-scale nage of the original elevation was blown up full size, roducing a distorted image. Plastic templates were ut of the abstracted design, fixed to the facade and endered over the top. The result is a facade that is ore like a ghostly shadow of its former self.

Anstatt die ursprüngliche Pracht der Stuckfassade aus der Vorkriegszeit detailgetreu zu rekonstruieren, bestanden die Architekten darauf, die Geschichte des Wohnhauses zu respektieren, ohne sich allzu weit von den Vorgaben des Bauherrn zu entfernen. Die Lösung bestand darin, Originaldetails zu verwenden, sie jedoch in die Fläche zu übersetzen. Man vergrößerte eine kleine Abbildung der ursprünglichen Fassade auf Originalgröße, wodurch ein verzerrtes Bild entstand. Das Ergebnis gleicht eher einem gespenstischen Schatten der einstigen Fassade als ihrem alten Selbst.

Au lieu de rendre sagement sa splendeur d'antan à la façade en stuc d'avant la Deuxième Guerre mondiale, les architectes ont tenu à exprimer l'histoire de cet immeuble, sans trop s'éloigner des spécifications de leur client. La solution a consisté à réinterpréter les détails originaux, non plus en relief mais en plan. Une petite photographie de l'élévation a été agrandie à la dimension du bâtiment, avec de fortes distorsions. Des pièces en plastique ont été découpées d'après ce modèle schématique, fixées sur la façade et enduites. Il en résulte une façade qui est plutôt un fantôme de ce qu'elle était jadis.

The ornate rusted steel bus shelter in Landshut

Das ornamentale Wartehäuschen aus rostendem Stahl in Landshut

L'abribus de Landshut, au décor en fer oxydé

1997 **Landshut, Germany**

Bus shelter

Hild's bus shelter in the historic town of Landshut uses ornament in a deliberately provocative way, on a structure not normally dignified with decorative flourishes, and executed in rusty 12-mm Corten steel sheets. Playing with conventions of public versus domestic, the pattern is taken from a 19th-century wallpaper design.

Hild verwendet bei seinem Wartehäuschen in der alten Stadt Landshut Schmuckformen auf provozierende Weise an einem Gebilde, das gewöhnlich keine dekorativen Schnörkel trägt. Das Häuschen besteht aus durchbrochenen, 12 mm starken Platten aus rostigem Cortenstahl. Um das Spiel mit öffentlichen versus privaten Konventionen fortzusetzen, liegt der Gestaltung ein Tapetenmuster aus dem 19. Jahrhundert zu Grunde.

L'abribus conçu par Hild pour la ville historique de Landshut utilise l'ornementation d'une manière délibérément provocante, sur une structure d'un type rarement jugé digne d'enjolivements esthétiques. Réalisé en tôle d'acier Corten oxydée de 12 mm, il joue de surcroît sur les conventions public/privé, le motif étant emprunté à un papier peint du XIXe siècle.

ironic take on recycling

ne ironische Anspielung aufs Recycling

ne approche ironique du recyclage

996

Landshut, Germany

Waste depot

e word "Sammeln" (collect) cast in giant gilded ncrete letters is a humorous way of expressing the nction - a waste and recycling centre - with imagery rmally reserved for altogether grander associations.

Das in riesige vergoldete Betonlettern gegossene Wort »Sammeln« verweist – in einer Art, die gewöhnlich weit imposanteren Bauten vorbehalten ist – humorvoll auf die Funktion des Müll- und Recyclingzentrums.

Le mot « Sammeln » (collecte) en immenses lettres de béton doré exprime avec humeur la fonction – la collecte et le recyclage des déchets – du centre, cette imagerie étant habituellement associée à des activités plus nobles.

Gerd Jäger

·senalstraße 19, 19053 Schwerin, Germany tel +49 385 558 110 fax +49 385 558 1118 e-mail jjschwerin@uumail.de

erd Jäger

orn	1961	Kaiserslautern
udied	1987	University of Stuttgart; 1986 Eidgenössische Technische Hochschule Zurich
actice	1990	set up own practice

elected projects

el Furniture Factory	1990	Hillesheim, Germany
ouble sports hall Dammschule	1994	Wörth, Germany
ffice and apartment house	1995	Bingen, Germany
ank building	1996	Luxembourg
ports hall	1998	Saarburg, Germany
esidential housing with office	1998	Schwerin, Germany
esidential housing with art gallery, refurbishment	1999	Schwerin, Germany

fluenced indirectly by Aldo Rossi and indirectly by his rmer tutor, Austrian architect Dietmar Eberle, Jäger eeks to find value in existing culture, history, and wn planning, was profoundly influential on his work. referring to use tried and tested models of construc- on as a point of departure, he then expands them to eate structures that are new and unique for their set- ng, collaborating with artists or thinking laterally - sing materials in new and interesting ways. Jäger is fluenced by Rossi's magpie-approach and careful eo-Rationalism. Though he is not opposed to experi- enting with materials (as the aluminium mesh skin of e Saarburg sports hall indicates), he dislikes tech- ology for the sake of it or the lack of respect for sur- undings or resources. His buildings are basic without eing dull, socially and environmentally responsible, nd always economical for the client.

To place a building into its context and to shape every art and the structure as a whole accordingly are the undations of my work. I am trying to find an appropri- e prototype which I can further develop for my con- ete task."

Jäger war an der ETH in Zürich von 1990–93 als Assistent von Dietmar Eberle tätig. Diese Zeit, in der er sich mit den hergebrachten Werten von Kultur, Geschichte und Stadtplanung befasste, war für seine Arbeit von großer Bedeutung. Jäger bevorzugt erprobte Konstruktionsmethoden, die er in Zusammenarbeit mit Künstlern abwandelt. Unorthodoxes Denken führt ihn zu einem innovativen und ungewöhnlichen Materialgebrauch – wie die aus Aluminiumgeflecht bestehende Außenhaut der Sporthalle in Saarburg beweist –, um individuelle Bauten für den jeweiligen Standort zu schaffen.

Jäger ist indirekt vom eklektischen Ansatz Aldo Rossis und seinem zurückhaltendem Neo-Rationalismus beeinflusst. Seine Bauten sind elementar, ohne langweilig zu sein, sozial- und umweltverträglich und stets wirtschaftlich vertretbar für den Bauherrn. »Die Einordnung eines Gebäudes in sein städtebauliches und typologisches Umfeld und die präzise Ausformulierung jedes einzelnen Bauteiles sowie des Gebäudes als Ganzem, bilden die Grundlagen meiner Arbeit. Dabei kommt es mir weniger darauf an, neue Lösungen zu schaffen. Vielmehr versuche ich, das geeignete Vorbild zu finden, um es für meinen Zweck, meine konkrete Aufgabe weiterentwickeln zu können.«

Jäger a étudié un an sous la direction de Fabio Reinhart et Mario Campo (deux ex-assistants d'Aldo Rossi) à l'ETH de Zurich, avant de travailler dans cette ville de 1990 à 1993 comme assistant de Dietmar Eberle. Cette période de recherche et de réflexion sur la valeur des phénomènes culturels, de l'histoire et de l'urbanisme, a exercé une profonde influence sur son œuvre. Partant de modèles architecturaux éprouvés, il les enrichit de sorte à créer des structures sans précédent dans leur environnement, grâce à une pensée non conformiste et à un usage créatif des matériaux, parfois en collaboration avec des artistes. Jäger est influencé par l'approche éclectique et le prudent « néo-rationalisme » de Rossi. Ses constructions sont élémentaires sans jamais être fades, respectent l'environnement naturel et social, et sont toujours économiques pour le client. « Les bases de mon travail sont l'insertion d'un bâtiment dans son cadre architectural, urbanistique et typologique, ainsi qu'une formulation précise de chaque élément architectural et de l'édifice dans son ensemble. Inventer des solutions nouvelles est une considération secondaire. Il m'importe bien davantage de trouver un modèle approprié, afin de le développer en vue de mon objectif, de la réalisation de ma tâche concrète. »

1998 **Saarburg, Germany**

Sports hall

Jäger seeks to enclose the building in a continuous surface that wraps up the southern wall and over the roof, pinning it to the hillside. The shimmering steel skin is formed by a steel mesh on extruded steel bars held in front of roughly sawn timber boarding that has been stained dark blue. Designed in collaboration with German-Russian artist Viktoria Prischeda, it appears open or closed, shiny or matt from different angles as one moves past the building.
Built into a 35° slope, the building moves from a 6-m space along the southern side over the main hall to a single storey on the northern edge used for changing rooms and storage. Cutting across the entrance facade at an angle, it has created an inviting new plaza between the sports hall and a neighbouring school, drawing people into the tapering space between them. The monolithic black dyed concrete bench that stretches across the space was cast as a single piece.
Throughout the building, all materials are used in their pure form: concrete walls are sharp edged and smooth; glazing panels are unframed; timber is left bare and structural beams exposed; metals are untreated or galvanised; and corridors flow with dark asphalt.

Jäger überzog die Sporthalle von der Südfassade bis über das Dach mit einer einheitlichen Oberfläche, die den Bau optisch an den Hang (mit einer Neigung von 35°) anschließt, in den er eingefügt ist. Die schimmernde Edelstahlfront besteht aus einem Stahlgewebe auf stranggepressten Stahlstäben, das vor einer dunkelblau gebeizten Verschalung aus grob gesägten Hölzern hängt. Der in Zusammenarbeit mit der russisch-deutschen Künstlerin Viktoria Prischeda entworfene Bau erscheint je nach Standpunkt offen oder geschlossen, glänzend oder matt. Auf der Südseite über der Haupthalle ist das Gebäude 6 m hoch, zum nördlichen Trakt mit Umkleiden und Stauraum fällt er auf ein Geschoss ab. Durch diesen quer vor der Eingangsfassade liegenden Bauteil entstand zwischen der Sporthalle und einer benachbarten Schule ein einladender dreieckiger Platz. Eine massive schwarze Betonbank, aus einem Stück gegossen, läuft quer durch den Raum.
Sämtliche Materialien im Gebäude sind in ihrem Rohzustand belassen: Die Betonwände sind scharfkantig und glatt, Verglasungen bleiben ungerahmt und Holz unbehandelt. Träger liegen frei, Metall ist entweder unbehandelt oder feuerverzinkt, und die Flure sind durchgehend mit dunklem Asphalt belegt. Die Saarburger Sporthalle erhielt den BDA-Preis 2000.

Jäger a voulu enfermer le salle de sports de Saarburg dans une surface continue enveloppant le mur sud et se prolongeant au-dessus de la toiture, qui ancre l'ensembl à flanc de colline. Cette « peau » scintillante est constitue d'un fin grillage d'acier tendu sur des barres en acier extrudé, maintenues à l'avant par un planchéiage de boi brut coloré en bleu foncé. Conçu en collaboration avec l'artiste germano-russe Viktoria Prischeda, l'ensemble paraît ouvert ou fermé, mat ou brillant selon l'angle d'ob-servation.
Construit sur une pente à 35°, l'édifice de 6 m de haut du côté sud devient au nord un volume à un seul niveau, abritant vestiaires et placards. Formant un angle avec la façade principale, celui-ci délimite une place accueillant prise entre la salle de sports et une école adjacente. Le banc en béton noir d'un seul tenant qui traverse cet espa ce triangulaire a été coulé in situ.
D'un bout à l'autre du bâtiment, les matériaux sont utilisés sans déguisement : murs en béton lissé aux angles vifs, panneaux vitrés non encadrés, bois d'œuvre nu et poutres structurelles apparentes, métaux non traités ou galvanisés, couloirs au sol revêtu d'asphalte de couleur foncée.

himmering steel mesh skin of the building, left.
lain sports hall, above.

inks die schimmernde Außenhaut aus Stahlgewebe;
ben die Hauptsporthalle

gauche : la salle des sports est recouverte d'une
cintillante peau en maille d'acier. Ci-dessus : la salle
rincipale.

ight, materials include black asphalt flooring and are concrete walls. Street facade, above.

echts: Schwarzer Asphalt als Bodenbelag, nackte etonwände. Oben die Straßenfassade.

droite, des sols en asphalte noir, des murs en béton u. Ci-dessus, la façade sur rue.

The supporting structure is wilfully expressed, left. Right, corridor above sports hall with changing rooms leading off to the left.

Links: Die Stützkonstruktion ist bewusst sichtbar gelassen; rechts der Korridor oberhalb der Sporthalle, der zu den Umkleiden führt (links im Bild).

A gauche : les éléments structurels sont volontairement laissés à découvert ; à droite : au-dessus de la salle de sports, un passage donne accès aux vestiaires.

1994 **Wörth, Germany**

Double sports hall Dammschule

Essentially a glass box, the building sits lightly on its site, the transparency of the skin focusing attention on the structure, which protrudes from the west wall in a series of angular buttresses. It is dominated by a strong axis that cuts straight through the building, separating the sports hall from the changing rooms, then continuing out across the landscape, initially as an elegant square arch that frames views of the river, then as a low retaining wall, sheltering a garden.

Die Turnhalle Dammschule, im Wesentlichen ein Glaskasten, scheint zu schweben. Ihre transparente Haut lenkt die Aufmerksamkeit auf konstruktive Teile, die in Form winkelförmiger Stützen aus der Westwand hervortreten. Einer markanten Achse, die die Sporthalle von den Umkleideräumen trennt und sich draußen fortsetzt, durchschneidet den Bau – zunächst als eleganter, rechtwinkliger Bogen, der Ausblicke auf den Fluss rahmt, dann als niedrige Stützmauer für den Garten.

Ce gymnase consiste pour l'essentiel en une boîte en verre, assise avec légèreté sur le site. La peau transparente attire l'attention sur la structure qui sort du mur ouest pour former une succession de contreforts angulaires. Le bâtiment est dominé par un axe puissant qui le traverse de part en part ; séparant le gymnase des vestiaires, il se prolonge dans le paysage, formant d'abord une élégante arcade à section carrée qui encadre des vues sur la rivière, avant de devenir un mur de retenue qui abrite un jardin.

The building is cut in two by a long wall with the sports hall on one side and the changing rooms on the other.

Eine lange Mauer teilt den Bau in zwei Hälften: links die Sporthalle, rechts die Umkleideräume.

L'édifice est coupé par un long mur, séparant la salle des sports des vestiaires.

Just as the block steps in at the front, far right, it is pushed out at the back, right.

Den Rücksprüngen auf der Vorderseite (ganz rechts) entsprechen Vorsprünge auf der Rückseite (rechts).

L'avant du bloc s'avance hardiment (page de droite), tandis que l'arrière est en retrait (à droite).

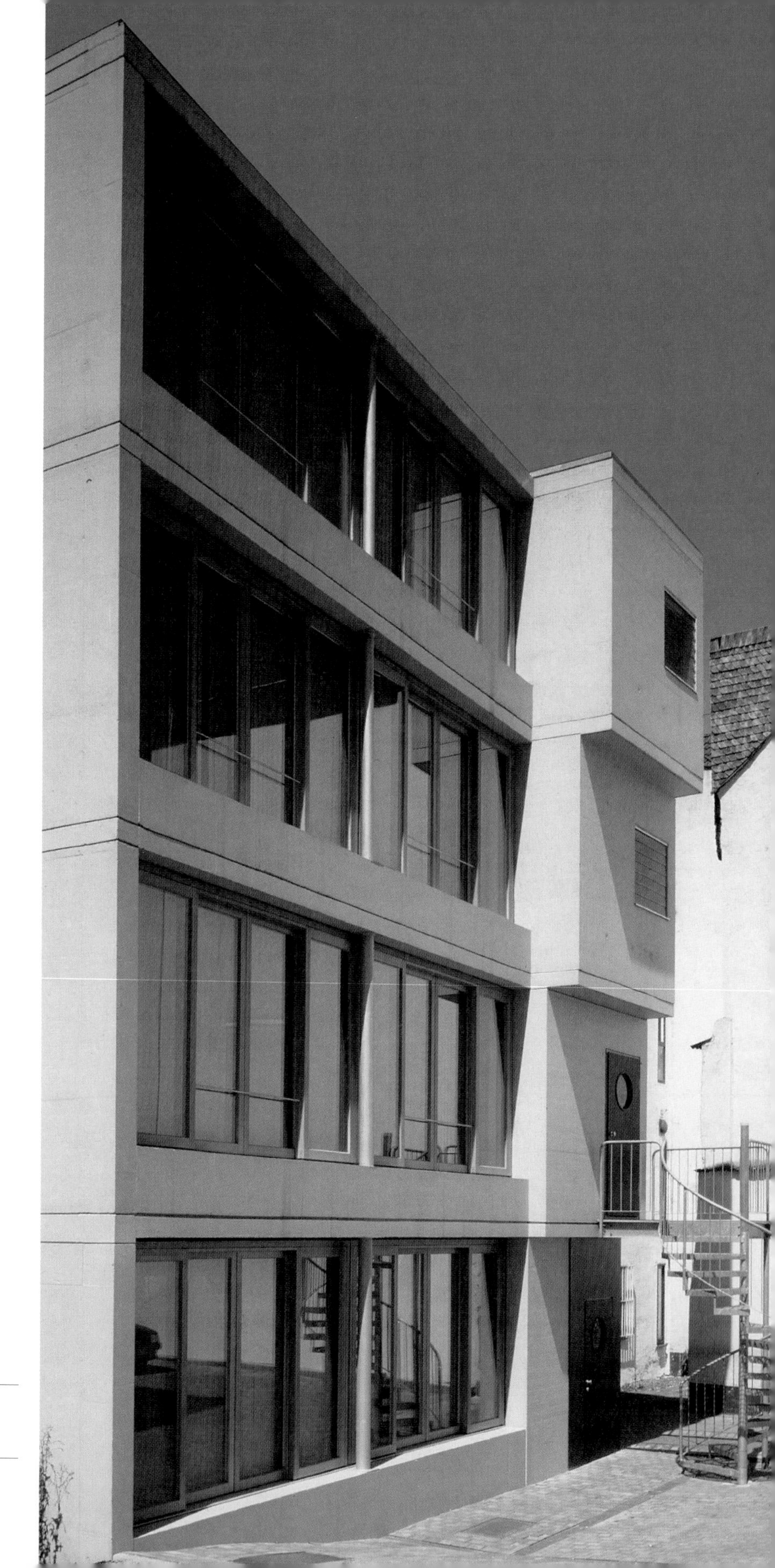

995 **Bingen, Germany**

ffice and apartment house

e 741-m² building echoes itself in a series of steps at emphasise the basic box form. On the street cade, windows across the upper floor cut back into e cube, the corner window leaving a generous space, hich has been defined by the concrete planes of roof d walls. At the rear of the building, the gradation vertical, with successive storeys at one end of the cade pushed further and further out, defining the tside and the staircase inside.

Vor- und Rücksprünge in der Fassade dieses 741 m² großen Büro- und Wohnhauses betonen seine Kastenform. Die Fenster des Obergeschosses auf der Straßenseite springen in der Horizontalen dreifach zurück und schaffen so an der vorderen Ecke eine großzügige Freifläche zwischen Betondach und Wänden. An der Rückseite findet die Staffelung in der Vertikalen statt: Die Geschosse an der Seite der Fassade schieben sich sukzessiv nach außen und betonen so das hinter ihnen liegende Treppenhaus.

Cet immeuble de bureaux et d'appartements de 741 m² se décline en une série de gradins soulignant la forme cubique de base. Sur la façade côté rue, les fenêtres sont en retrait, la fenêtre d'angle définissant un espace généreux délimité par les plans des murs et de la toiture en béton. A l'arrière du bâtiment, la gradation devient verticale ; les étages successifs s'avançant de plus en plus définissent à la fois la façade et la cage d'escalier intérieure.

larmund/Vigsnæs

stian Augusts Gate 11, 0164 Oslo, Norway tel +47 22 994 343 fax +47 22 994 353 e-mail jva@jva.no web www.jva.no

ar Jarmund

'n	1962	Oslo
died	1987	Oslo School of Architecture; 1989 University of Washington, Seattle
ctice	1995	established Jarmund/Vigsnæs

kon Vigsnæs

'n	1962	Oslo
died	1987	Architectural Association, London; 1988 Oslo School of Architecture
vious practice	Sverre Fehn, Oslo	
	1995	established Jarmund/Vigsnæs

lected projects

lier Berge	1997	Bærum, Norway
adquarters for the Governor of Svalbard	1998	Longyearbyen, Norway
astal Traffic Centre	2000	Kvitsøy, Norway
ın Bouvet" summerhouse	2001	Sineu, Majorca, Spain
lo School of Architecture	2001	Oslo, Norway
lde college	2002	Molde, Norway

'mund/Vigsnæs have responded to the dramatic d exposed landscapes of their country with equally amatic buildings. Their best-known work, the head-arters for the Governor of Svalbard in Spitsbergen, s like a fortress in its arctic setting, with sloping lls - a functional response to harsh weather condi-ns as well as an aesthetically exciting solution ere several planes collide. Similarly, Kvitsøy astal Traffic Centre outside Stavanger builds on an sting pilot station to create a monumental edifice t can be seen for miles, elongating the natural cliff. both projects there are also cultural references to area: at Spitsbergen materials such as zinc dding reflect local mining traditions, and at Kvitsøy te-clad sloping walls are an overblown version of pitched roofs of the houses in the village below. ur strategies are generally based on a utilisation aspects of the landscape," says Håkon Vigsnæs.

Jarmund/Vigsnæs haben mit ebenbürtigen Bauten auf die spektakuläre Landschaft Norwegens reagiert. Ihr bekanntestes Werk, das Präsidium des Gouverneurs von Svalbard auf Spitzbergen, sitzt wie eine Festung vor dem arktischen Hintergrund, deren schräge Wände eine funktionelle Antwort auf das rauhe Klima geben und zugleich eine ästhetisch reizvolle Lösung schaffen, wo mehrere Ebenen aufeinandertreffen. Das Coastal Traffic Center in Kvitsøy bei Stavanger bezog die bestehende Lotsenstation ein. So entstand ein imposantes Bauwerk, das Kilometer weit zu sehen ist und die natürliche Felswand optisch verlängert. Beide Bauten stellen außerdem kulturelle Bezüge zu ihrer Umgebung her: In Spitzbergen verweisen Materialien wie Zinkblech auf die örtliche Bergbautradition, und die schräg stehenden, schieferverkleideten Wände in Kvitsøy erscheinen wie eine stark vergrößerte Wiederholung der Dächer des nahen Dorfes.
»Unsere Vorgehensweise basiert in der Regel darauf, dass

Jarmund/Vigsnæs répondent aux paysages rudes et dramatiques de leur pays par des constructions non moins saisissantes. Leur réalisation la plus connue est le bâtiment abritant les services du gouverneur de l'archipel de Svalbard, planté comme une forteresse dans le paysage arctique ; les murs obliques constituent une solution fonctionnelle compte tenu des conditions climatiques rigoureuses, et produisent un effet esthétiquement séduisant grâce au recoupement de plusieurs plans. De même, le Centre de contrôle de la navigation côtière de Kvitsøy, près de Stavanger, crée à partir d'un poste existant un édifice monumental prolongeant la falaise, visible à des kilomètres à la ronde. Les deux projets contiennent également des références culturelles à la région : à Spitzberg, le revêtement en zinc fait écho à la tradition minière locale ; à Kvitsøy, les murs inclinés revêtus d'ardoise constituent une version démesurée des toits en pente du village situé en contrebas.

"However, this attitude might be differently loaded depending on the situation. The architectural relation towards landscape is sometimes integration, sometimes reflection. In other projects this communication is more commenting and challenging."
Also important in their work are spatial dynamics. This might be expressed in the relationship between a new structure and an old at Kvitsøy, in outdoor and indoor space, between transparent and solid as in the Atelier Berge, or between interior spaces and a nearby public park as in the new School of Architecture to be built inside an existing industrial building in Oslo.

wir Aspekte der Landschaft einbeziehen«, sagt Håkon Vigsnæs. »Abhängig von der jeweiligen Situation kann diese Haltung jedoch unterschiedlich betont sein. Das Verhältnis von Architektur und Landschaft hat manchmal mit Integration, manchmal mit Reflexion zu tun. In wieder anderen Projekten kann sich dieser Austausch stärker kommentierend oder provozierend gestalten.«
Räumliche Kräfte spielen in ihrem Œuvre eine wichtige Rolle. Das kann sich, wie in Kvitsøy, in der Beziehung zwischen einem neuen und einem alten Bauwerk niederschlagen, zwischen Außen- und Innenraum, zwischen Transparenz und Massivität wie im Atelier Berge oder zwischen Innenräumen und einem nahen öffentlichen Park, wie bei der neuen Architekturfakultät, die in Oslo in ein vorhandenes Industriegebäude hinein gebaut werden soll.

« Nos stratégies sont généralement fondées sur l'utilisation de certains aspects du paysage, explique Håkon Vigsnæs. Selon la situation, toutefois, cette démarche peut prendre des formes différentes. Parfois l'architect s'intègre au paysage, parfois elle le reflète. Dans d'autr projets, cette relation relève plutôt du commentaire et d défi. »
La dynamique spatiale joue également un rôle importa dans leurs réalisations. Cette dynamique peut s'exprim par la relation entre un bâtiment préexistant et une stru ture nouvelle, comme à Kvitsøy ; entre espaces extérieu et intérieurs dans le cas de la « maison danoise » ; entr transparence et compacité comme dans l'atelier Berge ou encore entre les espaces intérieurs et un parc public situé à proximité comme dans la nouvelle Ecole d'archi tecture, qui sera construite à Oslo à partir d'un bâtimer industriel existant.

Headquarters for the Governor of Svalbard

latitude N78° at Norway's most northern outpost on e island of Spitsbergen it is dark 24 hours during win- r and temperatures can drop to 40°C. So in designing administrative headquarter for the Svalbard island oup, physical and psychological protection from the ements was the dominating challenge.
gled walls and zinc cladding on walls and roofs pro- de protection from snow, rain and gale-force winds. azing is triple-layered, filled with argon gas. Open oden screens shield the office windows, and when ow settles on them, they act as a reflector, throwing tificial light from the offices back through the win- ws as though it is daylight outside.
e 1 900-m² building is based on an existing concrete me left when the previous headquarters burned wn. The angled walls have increased the floor area thout the need for new structural pillars, which would ve been particularly difficult to anchor in this terrain. hile achieving functional requirements such as resi- ntial accommodation, offices, a prison, a library d a garage for snow scooters, the building has not nored aesthetic considerations. Its hunched figure, lf-buried into the landscape, immediately conveys defensive stance, and the materials used suggest e mining traditions of the island, but the generous cades and proud angles have sufficient gravitas for governor's headquarters.

Die Insel Spitzbergen, Norwegens nördlichster Vorposten, liegt auf 78° nördlicher Breite und gehört zur Svalbard- gruppe, wo im Winter 24 Stunden lang Dunkelheit herrscht und die Temperatur bis auf minus 40°C fallen kann. Beim Bau des Präsidiums für den Gouverneur von Svalbard wa- ren daher physischer und psychologischer Schutz vor den Elementen die größte Herausforderung.
Schräge Wände und zinkplattierte Mauern und Dächer bieten Schutz vor Schnee, Regen und Sturmwind. Die dreifache Verglasung ist mit Argongas gefüllt. Offene Holzgitter liegen schützend vor den Fenstern, und wenn Schnee auf ihnen liegt, reflektieren sie das Licht aus den Büros, als sei es Tageslicht.
Das 1 900 m² große Gebäude steht auf einem Betonrah- men, der erhalten blieb, als das alte Präsidium abbrannte. Schräggestellte Wände vergrößern die Fläche, ohne neue tragende Pfeiler erforderlich zu machen.
Der Neubau umfasst Wohnräume, Büros, ein Gefängnis, eine Bibliothek sowie eine Garage für Schneemobile und erfüllt damit alle funktionalen Anforderungen, ohne ästhetische Aspekte zu vernachlässigen. Er fügt sich zurückhaltend in die Landschaft ein und erinnert in der Materialwahl an die Bergbautradition der Insel; die groß- zügigen Fassaden und kühnen Schrägen verleihen ihm jedoch hinreichendes Gewicht für einen Regierungsbau.

Le bâtiment des services du gouverneur est situé à une latitude de 78° N., à l'extrémité nord du Spitzberg, dans l'archipel de Svalbard, où il fait nuit 24 heures sur 24 en hiver et où le thermomètre peut descendre jusqu'à – 40°C. Le problème essentiel était la protection physique et psychologique contre les éléments. Des murs inclinés, revêtus de zinc ainsi que les toits, protègent l'édifice contre la neige, la pluie et les vents violents. Les triples vitrages sont isolés à l'argon. Des écrans à claire-voie en bois protègent les fenêtres des bureaux ; lorsque la neige arrive, ces écrans renvoient la lumière artificielle des bureaux vers l'extérieur, donnant l'impression qu'il fait jour.
Le bâtiment de 1 900 m² est construit sur l'ossature en béton qui subsistait après l'incendie de la résidence pré- cédente. Les murs inclinés ont augmenté la surface au sol sans nécessiter de nouveaux piliers structurels, parti- culièrement difficiles à ancrer dans ce terrain.
Tout en répondant aux exigences fonctionnelles telles que logements, bureaux, prison, bibliothèque et garage pour motoneiges, l'édifice n'ignore pas les considérations esthétiques. La silhouette trapue, à demi enterrée, expri- me d'emblée une attitude défensive, tandis que les maté- riaux évoquant les traditions minières de l'île, les façades généreuses et les angles hardis lui confèrent la dignité convenant à la résidence d'un gouverneur.

By angling the walls, the architects have increased the floor space, left. Far left, Svalbard presents a bleak landscape and harsh climate.

Links: die Architekten vergrößerten die Grundfläche, indem sie die Wände abschrägten. Ganz links: Die Landschaft von Svalbard ist karg und das Klima rau.

A gauche : les murs fortement inclinés augmentent la surface au sol. Page de gauche : le paysage de Svalbard est austère, et son climat est rude.

Generous expanses of triple-layered sandwich glass create a comfortable interior for the public foyer.

Großzügige Flächen gasgefüllter Dreifachverglasung schaffen ein angenehme Atmosphäre im öffentlichen Foyer.

Les triples vitrages isolants créent une ambiance confortable ; ici, le foyer.

, office windows are shielded by wooden screens, ch in the winter double as snow-covered light ectors. Below left, elevations.

.s: Bürofenster werden von Holzlamellen geschützt, im Winter, wenn sie mit Schnee bedeckt sind, auch Lichtreflektoren dienen. Links unten: Aufrisse.

auche: les volets à claire-voie des bureaux protègent soleil, et, l'hiver, diffusent la lumière réfléchie par la e. En bas à gauche, élévations.

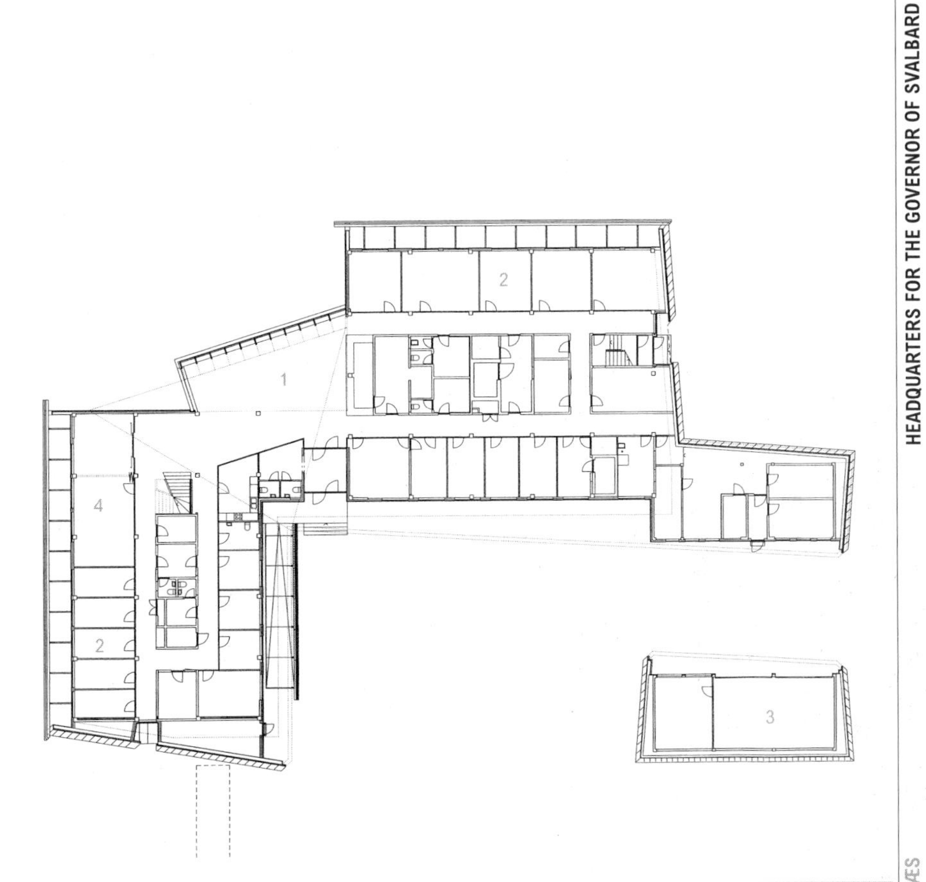

Ground floor plan/ Erdgeschossgrundriss/ Plan du rez-de-chaussée

1 **foyer/** Foyer/ foyer et hall d'accueil
2 **offices/** Büros/ bureaux
3 **garage/** Garage/ garage
4 **conference room/** Konferenzraum/ salle de conférence

2000 **Kvitsøy, Norway**

Coastal Traffic Centre

A competition-winning scheme to design a new pilot station at Kvitsøy on the western coast of Norway. Rather than building next to the old building, the architects decided to build on top of it, minimising construction, but also strengthening the profile of the pilot station as a beacon for sailors. The existing structure forms the core of the new building, with the new construction built around, its surface broken in places to expose the inner structure. Angled walls of the whole building are clad in a unifying coat, a mirror of the pitched roofs of the surrounding village, which picks up the ever-changing conditions of light and moisture of the sea.

Aus dem Wettbewerb für den Bau einer neuen Küstenwachstation in Kvitsøy an der Westküste Norwegens ging dieser Entwurf siegreich hervor. Anstatt den Neubau neben der vorhandenen Station zu errichten, entschieden sich die Architekten dafür, ihn auf das vorhandene Gebäude zu setzen, um den konstruktiven Aufwand zu minimieren und zugleich den Signalcharakter der Küstenwachstation für die Seeleute zu betonen. Das bestehende Gebäude bildet das Herzstück des Neubaus, dessen Außenhaut an einigen Stellen durchbrochen ist, um die Konstruktion freizulegen. Aus Gründen der Einheitlichkeit und als Schutz vor der Feuchtigkeit des Meeres wurden die schrägen Wände des gesamten Baus mit Schiefer verkleidet, der das ständig wechselnde Licht einfängt und die geneigten Dächer der umliegenden Häuser reflektiert.

Ce projet remporta le concours concernant la reconstr tion de la station de pilotage de Kvitsøy, sur la côte ou de Norvège. Au lieu de construire à côté du bâtiment e tant, les architectes ont décidé de construire par-dessu ce dernier, ce qui réduisait l'ampleur des travaux tout e accentuant la forme du repère utilisé par les marins. L' cien bâtiment forme le noyau du nouveau Centre de contrôle de la navigation côtière, dont l'enveloppe s'ou par endroits pour révéler la structure interne. Les murs inclinés revêtus d'ardoise font écho aux toits en pente des maisons à pignon du village, tout en répondant au conditions climatiques sans cesse changeantes dues à proximité de la mer.

The existing coastguard station, the lookout tower, has been enveloped by the new building.

Der Neubau schließt die vorhandene Küstenwachstation mit ihrem Beobachtungsturm ein.

Les nouveaux bâtiments enveloppent la tour de guet de l'ancien poste de gardes-côtes.

Sloping slate-clad walls, right, allude to the pitched roofs of the village below. Below, walls are cut away in places to reveal the inner workings of the building.

Rechts: Schräge, mit Schiefer verkleidete Wände zitieren die Dächer des unten liegenden Dorfes. Unten: An einigen Stellen sind die Wände eingeschnitten, um die Binnenkonstruktion freizulegen.

Les murs obliques revêtus d'ardoise font écho aux toits des maisons du village en contrebas. Ci-dessous : les murs sont percés de vastes baies vitrées.

The nearly totally closed street facade opens occasionally to release the view on to the landscape.

Die fast gänzlich geschlossene Straßenfassade öffnet sich gelegentlich, um den Blick auf die Landschaft freizugeben.

La façade côté rue, presqu'aveugle, s'ouvre soudain pour donner un aperçu du paysage s'étendant au-delà.

997 Bærum, Norway

telier Berge

e architects make the most of the stunning location a hilltop facing the sea outside Oslo. The first-floor ing room is almost entirely glazed, embracing the ew, while the road facade is resolutely closed, allow-g just a glimpse of the distant landscape. The more closed studio space, expressed on the exterior as a be hung off the main house, benefits from generous rth lighting and access to a roof terrace above the ing area. The exterior is panelled with untreated pen, which weathers to a soft silvery grey.

Die Architekten haben sich beim Bau des Ateliers Berge die spektakuläre Lage auf einem Hügel vor Oslo mit Blick aufs Meer zu Nutze gemacht. Der Wohnraum im Erdgeschoss ist nahezu vollständig verglast, um die Aussicht einzufangen, während die bewusst geschlossene Straßenseite nur einen flüchtigen Blick auf die ferne Landschaft zulässt. Der an das Haupthaus angeschlossene Kubus des Ateliers erhält üppiges Nordlicht und hat einen Zugang zur Dachterrasse über dem Wohnbereich. Der Außenbau ist mit unbehandeltem Espenholz verkleidet, das unter dem Einfluss der Witterung eine weiche, silbrig-graue Tönung annimmt.

Pour cette habitation des environs d'Oslo nommée « Atelier Berge », les architectes ont tiré le maximum du site exceptionnel : au sommet d'une colline, face à la mer. Le séjour du rez-de-chaussée est presque entièrement vitré du côté mer, tandis que la façade donnant sur la route, résolument fermée, permet tout juste d'entrevoir l'horizon. L'atelier, exprimé à l'extérieur comme un cube suspendu au corps du bâtiment principal, bénéficie généreusement de la lumière du nord et s'ouvre sur une terrasse constituant le toit des pièces d'habitation. Ses façades sont revêtues de tremble non traité, qui devient d'un gris argenté très doux en vieillissant.

Mathias Klotz

dora Goyenechea 3356 of 60, 6760323 Las Condes, ntiago, Chile

tel +56 2 233 6613 fax +56 2 232 3282 e-mail aymark@entelchile.net

athias Klotz

rn	1965	Santiago, Chile
udied	1990	Pontificia Universidad Católica de Chile
aching	Professor at Taller de Arquitectura, Universidad Federico Santa María de Valparaíso and Universidad Central de Santiago	

lected projects

sa Klotz	1991	Playa Grande de Tongoy, Chile
sa Müller	1994	Isla Grande de Chiloé, Chile
sa Ducaud	1994	La Dehesa, Chile
sa Sadhu	1994	Pirque, Chile
sa Lavados	1995	Volcán Villarrica, Chile
sa Ugarte	1995	Maitencillo Sur, Chile
sa Grudsky	1996	La Dehesa, Chile
sa Úbeda	1996	Chicureo, Chile
sa Reutter	1999	Cachagua, Chile
dega de vinos	2000	Santa Cruz, Chile

ilean architect Mathias Klotz has steadily built up series of weekend houses in dramatic locations re- onding to Chile's diverse topography and climate nge. His simple geometric forms are heavily influ- ced by the Modern Movement, Le Corbusier and e Bauhaus. These houses sit serenely on the land, en presences that could be removed without leaving race: Casa Klotz at Tongoy, a bleached-out box of acting geometry washed up on the barren shore; re white, Casa Ugarte shining from the rich red cliffs Maitencillo Sur; larch-boarded Casa Müller in the rests of Chiloé; light tree-house Casa Reutter on the oded slopes of Cachagua.

he forms these projects follow respond to a sensitive e of the materials creating a type of sanctuary for eir users where they can contemplate nature from a tional and protective space, facing a medium which ey respect without contaminating it. These forms pre-

Der chilenische Architekt Mathias Klotz errichtete eine Reihe von Wochenendhäusern an exponierten Standorten, mit denen er auf die mannigfaltige Topographie und die verschiedenen Klimazonen Chiles eingeht. Seine einfachen geometrischen Formen sind von der Moderne Le Corbusiers und des Bauhauses beeinflusst. Die Häuser wirken heiter und gelassen, wie fremde Geschöpfe, die man entfernen könnte, ohne eine Spur zu hinterlassen. Die streng proportionierte Casa Klotz in Tongoy erinnert an eine ausgebleichte Kiste, die am unwirtlichen Gestade angespült wurde; die rein weiße Casa Ugarte leuchtet von den roten Klippen bei Maitencillo Sur; Casa Müller in den Wäldern von Chiloé ist mit Lärchenholz verschalt; Casa Reutter steht als luftiges Baumhaus an den bewaldeten Hängen von Cachagua.

»Die Bauten zeugen von einer sensiblen Verwendung der Materialien; sie bilden eine Art Refugium für die Bewohner, einen schützenden Raum, von dem aus man die Na-

Au fil des années, l'architecte chilien Mathias Klotz a construit une série de maisons de week-end adaptées à la topographie variée et aux diverses zones climatiques du Chili. Ses formes géométriques simples portent l'empreinte du mouvement moderne, de Le Corbusier et du Bauhaus. Ces maisons sereinement intégrées au paysage sont pareilles à des présences étrangères qui ne laisseraient aucune trace si on les retirait : la Casa Klotz de Tongoy, boîte lavée de blanc d'une géométrie rigoureuse échouée sur la grève ; la Casa Ugarte d'un blanc éclatant, perchée sur les falaises rouges de Maitencillo Sur ; la Casa Müller revêtue de mélèze, dans la forêt de Chiloé ; la légère Casa Reutter, « maison dans les arbres » sur les pentes boisées de Cachagua.

« Les formes de ces projets, correspondant à une utilisation sensible des matériaux, créent pour leurs utilisateurs un espace rationnel et protecteur d'où ils peuvent contempler la nature en la respectant et en évitant de la pol-

tend that they do not belong to the place on which they rest, that they are passing through, like a car that has been parked in the middle of a pasture and could be towed away."

Though his villas best exemplify the architect's lightness of touch, he has also received commissions for more complex commercial projects including an administration building for Pizarras Ibericas in Huechuraba, a hotel on the coast north of Zapallar, a bodega and a suspension bridge in Santiago.

tur erfahren kann, ohne sie zu stören. Dabei erwecken sie den Anschein, als gehörten sie nicht an die Plätze, auf denen sie stehen, als befänden sie sich auf der Durchreise, wie ein Auto, das mitten auf einer Weide geparkt ist und abgeschleppt werden könnte.«

Obwohl Klotz seine Vorstellungen von Architektur in den Landhäusern am deutlichsten zur Geltung bringt, hat er auch komplexere kommerzielle Projekte übernommen, darunter das Verwaltungsgebäude für Pizarras Ibericas in Huechuraba, ein Hotel an der Küste nördlich von Zapallar, eine Bodega und eine Hängebrücke in Santiago.

luer. Ces formes proclament qu'elles ne font pas partie lieu où elles reposent ; elles passent, comme une voitur garée au milieu d'un pâturage, qui pourrait être retirée à tout moment. »

Bien que ses villas constituent le meilleur exemple de la légèreté de son design, l'architecte a également exécuté des commandes commerciales plus complexes, notamment un immeuble administratif pour Pizarras Ibericas à Huechuraba, un hôtel à Zapallar, sur la côte nord, une bodega et un pont suspendu à Santiago.

ain entrance, right, leading through to rear terrace,
ft

chts der Haupteingang; links das Deck auf der Rück-
ite des Hauses

droite : l'entrée principale ; à gauche : la terrasse située
'arrière de la maison

991 **Playa Grande de Tongoy, Chile**

asa Klotz

studiously plain unit 12 x 6 x 6 m, washed in white er every interior and exterior surface, the beach use is closed on three sides opening to the sea on fourth. Inside, a series of symmetrical relation- ips operate around different horizontal and vertical es. Two single-height spaces flank the central uble-height living space. Bedrooms held back from facade are balanced against the enclosed outdoor rraces that are left. The vast window looking out to e sea is dissected by timber mullions into a rectangu- r grid and its outline duplicated in the raised outdoor cking that falls beneath it like a shadow. Throughout, e main ornamentation is provided by the repetitive ometric forms.

Die Casa Klotz, ein Strandhaus von 12 x 6 x 6 m, ist bewusst schlicht gestaltet. Sämtliche Oberflächen wurden weiß gestrichen, drei Seiten sind geschlossen, die vierte öffnet sich zum Meer. Die Räume ordnen sich symmetrisch um verschiedene horizontale und vertikale Achsen an. Zwei eingeschossige Räume flankieren den doppelgeschossigen Wohnraum. Die ins Innere des Kubus verlegten Schlafräume grenzen an die umfriedeten Außenterrassen an. Das riesige Fenster zum Meer wird von hölzernen Sprossen in ein rechtwinkliges Raster zerlegt; sein Umriss wiederholt sich in der aufgeständerten Terrasse, die wie ein Schatten vor ihm liegt. Der gesamte Bau wird von sich wiederholenden geometrischen Formen bestimmt.

Cette maison de plage de 12 x 6 x 6 m, d'une simplicité très étudiée, entièrement peinte en blanc à l'intérieur comme à l'extérieur, est fermée sur trois côtés, le quatrième s'ouvrant sur la mer. A l'intérieur, divers axes horizontaux et verticaux créent une série de relations symétriques. Deux espaces à un seul niveau entourent un séjour double hauteur. Les chambres en retrait sur la façade donnent sur des terrasses fermées occupant l'espace restant. La grande baie vitrée s'ouvrant sur la mer forme une grille de carrés délimités par des meneaux en bois, motif repris dans le plancher extérieur surélevé, semblable à une ombre portée. Ces formes géométriques répétitives constituent la principale ornementation de la villa.

Casa Klotz, a white box in a barren landscape

Casa Klotz: ein weißer Kasten in karger Landschaft

La Casa Klotz : une boîte blanche dans un paysage aride

eft, view from double-height main living space out sea. Above, living and stairs up to mezzanine and edrooms.

inks: Blick aus dem doppelgeschossigen Wohnraum ufs Meer. Oben: Der Wohnraum; rechts im Bild die reppe zum Mezzaningeschoss mit Schlafräumen.

gauche : du living double hauteur, la vue porte jusqu'à mer ; ci-dessus : le séjour et l'escalier montant à la nezzanine et aux chambres (à droite).

rraces and walkways create outdoor platforms from hich to contemplate the ocean view.

rrassen und Stege schaffen Außenräume mit freiem ick aufs Meer.

rrasses et passerelles : autant de plates-formes pour ntempler la mer.

999 **Cachagua, Chile**

Casa Reutter

ocated on a wooded slope in the tropical climes of achagua, 140 km north of Santiago, Casa Reutter is otz's contemporary interpretation of a tree house. It essentially two separate volumes suspended in the r - the larger of wood and glass housing the public eas, the smaller a closed copper box containing the edrooms. A 30-m walkway stretches up from the road the roof terrace with views out to the sea. The sen- ation is one of being lifted up into the trees and living mong them.

Die Casa Reutter, die 140 km nördlich von Santiago im tropischen Klima von Cachagua auf einem bewaldeten Abhang steht, stellt Klotz' zeitgenössische Variante des Baumhauses dar. Zwei separate Baukörper hängen sozusagen in der Luft – der größere aus Holz und Glas enthält die öffentlichen Bereiche, der kleinere, ein geschlossener, mit Kupfer verkleideter Kasten, die Schlafräume. Ein 30 m langer Fußweg führt von der Straße direkt auf die Dachterrasse mit Meerblick. Man hat das Gefühl, hinauf gehoben zu werden und inmitten der Bäume zu leben.

Située sur une pente boisée de la région tropicale de Cachagua, à 140 km au nord de Santiago, la Casa Reutter est une interprétation contemporaine du motif traditionnel de la « maison dans les arbres ». Elle consiste pour l'essentiel en deux volumes distincts suspendus en l'air ; le plus grand, en bois et verre, abrite les espaces communs ; le plus petit est une boîte habillée de cuivre contenant les chambres. Une passerelle de 30 m de long conduit de la route au toit-terrasse avec vue sur la mer. L'ensemble donne l'impression de vivre dans les arbres.

The layered house projects from the wooded hillside, above. Left, secluded entrance to living area.

Oben: Das »geschichtete« Haus ragt aus dem bewaldeten Hang hervor. Links der versteckte Eingang zum Wohnbereich.

La maison semble faire irruption dans la colline boisée (ci-dessus). A gauche, l'entrée discrète du séjour.

Casa Reutter is reached via a treetop walkway.

Ein Steg führt durch die Baumwipfel zur Casa Reutter.

Une passerelle jetée entre les arbres donne accès à la Casa Reutter.

Søren Robert Lund

Kongensgade 110E, 1, 1264 Copenhagen, Denmark tel +45 33 910 100 fax +45 33 914 510 e-mail srl@srlarkitekter.dk web www.srlarkitekter.dk

ren Robert Lund		
rn	1962	Copenhagen, Denmark
udied	1989	Kunstakademiets Arkitektskole, Copenhagen, Denmark
	1991	set up own practice

lected projects		
RKEN Museum of Modern Art	1996	Ishøj, Denmark
la	1997	Allerød, Denmark
tBureau, refurbishment	1999	Copenhagen, Denmark
e Danish House of Contractors, renovation	1999	Copenhagen, Denmark
S Sjællandske Avistryk	1999	Slagelse, Denmark

nd's breakthrough came in 1988 when he won the mpetition to design the ARKEN Museum of Modern t, which allowed him to establish his own studio in 91. The design and construction process was long d drawn out, but it launched Lund onto an internanal stage. Since the museum's opening in March 96, Lund has been invited to participate in numerous estigious international competitions, including the orld Intellectual Property Organisation headquarters Geneva, the Royal Theatre of Copenhagen and a asterplan for the former mining area of Ahlen in ermany.

ather than subscribing to the sort of pared-down late-)th century Modernism that Northern Europe does well, Lund has been influenced by the more flamyant styles of the 90s. Shades of Frank O. Gehry nd Zaha Hadid can be detected in buildings such as e printing plant in Slagelse and the ARKEN Museum Modern Art. Spaces often occur when the various anes of the building collide rather than being designed as rooms in themselves. The exterior form emerges hen a central concept such as a folding newsprint or shipwreck is worked up.

und combines private practice with his role as chief eveloper for the Tivoli Gardens in Copenhagen.

1988 gelang Lund der Durchbruch mit seinem erfolgreichen Wettbewerbsbeitrag für das ARKEN Museum of Modern Art in Ishøj, ein Auftrag, der es ihm erlaubte, 1991 sein eigenes Büro zu gründen. Entwurf und Bau nahmen viel Zeit in Anspruch, ebneten Lund aber den Weg in die internationale Szene. Seit der Eröffnung des Museums im März 1996 wurde er zu zahlreichen internationalen Wettbewerben eingeladen, so zum Beispiel für die Zentrale der World Intellectual Property Organisation in Genf (1999) und den Masterplan für das frühere Bergbaurevier der Stadt Ahlen in Westfalen.

Lund ließ sich mehr von den extravaganten Stilen der 90er-Jahre als von der in Nordeuropa so verbreiteten strengen Moderne des ausgehenden 20. Jahrhunderts anregen. Bauten wie die Druckerei in Slagelse und das ARKEN Museum of Modern Art erinnern an Frank O. Gehry und Zaha Hadid. Hier werden Räume nicht als abgeschlossene Einheiten konzipiert, sondern ergeben sich häufig durch das Aufeinandertreffen verschiedener Ebenen. Der äußeren Form liegt meist ein zentraler Gedanke zugrunde, wie bei der »gefalteten« Zeitungsdruckerei oder dem Museum in Form eines Schiffswracks.

Neben seiner Tätigkeit als selbständiger Architekt ist Lund mit den Planungen für den Tivoli in Kopenhagen betraut.

Lund effectua sa percée décisive lorsqu'il remporta en 1988 le concours pour la construction du musée d'art moderne ARKEN à Ishøj, ce qui lui permit de créer son propre bureau en 1991. Depuis l'inauguration du musée en mars 1996, Lund a été invité à participer à plusieurs concours internationaux, concernant en particulier le siège de l'Organisation mondiale de la propriété intellectuelle à Genève, le Théâtre royal de Copenhague, et le schéma directeur de l'ancienne région minière d'Ahlen en Allemagne.

Plutôt que de souscrire au modernisme atténué tant prisé en Europe du Nord à la fin du XXe siècle, Lund s'inspire de certains des styles les plus vigoureux des années 90. L'influence de Frank O. Gehry et de Zaha Hadid peut être détectée dans des réalisations telles que l'imprimerie de Slagelse et le musée ARKEN. Souvent, les espaces naissent de la collision de plusieurs plans du bâtiment, au lieu d'être dessinés sur le papier. La forme extérieure est issue de la réinterprétation d'un concept de base tel que le pliage des journaux ou l'épave d'un bateau. Lund allie sa pratique privée à ses fonctions de responsable du développement du parc d'attractions de Tivoli à Copenhague.

EGILL JACOBSEN

ARKEN Museum of Modern Art

nd's starting point for the 9 200-m² museum, a com-ssion won in competition in 1988, was a shipwreck, sponding to its site on the Danish coast. The long rizontal building stretches out into the landscape th a variety of sculptural forms and deconstructed ements. Spatially, the museum is organised around 150m-long gently curving "art axis", which broadens 10 m height and 12 m width in the middle and rrows to 3.5 m at either end.

tering the building through the narrow foyer, squeezed tween two convex curving walls, the effect of emerg-g into the art axis is intended to replicate that of tering the nave of a cathedral. Exhibition galleries ad off this long aisle.

e main foyer is dominated by a domed skylight and 36-tonne Norwegian granite block that links the bal-ny of the main axis with the second-floor restaurant. secting the building is the "red axis", a red-tiled rridor leading from the main foyer to the boat-bridge the harbour like a giant artery. Dark and intimate, e contrast with the light white art axis is profound.

In Bezug auf seinen Bauplatz an der dänischen Küste ist die Form des 9 200 m² großen ARKEN Museum of Modern Art einem Schiffswrack nachempfunden. Es erstreckt sich als langer, plastisch ausgeformter Baukörper mit dekonstruierten Elementen in die Landschaft. Räumlich ordnet sich der Bau um eine 150 m lange, leicht geschwungene »Kunstachse«, die in der Mitte 10 m hoch und 12 m breit ist, während sie sich an beiden Enden auf 3,5 m verschmälert.

Man betritt das Gebäude durch ein enges, zwischen zwei konvexe Wände gezwängtes Foyer. Der anschließende Übergang in die »Kunstachse« soll an das Betreten des Mittelschiffs einer Kathedrale erinnern. An diesen langen Trakt schließen sich die Galerieräume an. Das Hauptfoyer wird von einem Oberlicht und einem 36 t schweren Block aus norwegischem Granit beherrscht, der den Balkon der Hauptachse mit dem Restaurant auf der zweiten Ebene verbindet. Einen eindrucksvollen Kontrast zur hellen »Kunstachse« bildet die »Rote Achse«, ein rot gefliester, höhlenartig anmutender Korridor, der, wie eine riesige Arterie vom Hauptfoyer zur Bootsbrücke am Hafen führend, den Bau in zwei Hälften teilt.

Pour ce musée d'art moderne de 9 200 m², l'idée de départ de Lund était une épave de bateau. Faisant écho au site, sur la côte danoise, le long bâtiment horizontal s'étend dans le paysage en présentant divers éléments sculpturaux et formes déconstruites. Spatialement, le musée ARKEN s'articule autour d'un « axe artistique » long de 150 m et légèrement incurvé ; haut de 10 m et large de 12 m au milieu, il ne fait plus que 3,50 m aux deux extrémités.

Après être entré par un étroit foyer comprimé entre deux murs convexes, le visiteur pénètre dans l'axe artistique, expérience comparable à la découverte d'une nef de cathédrale. Les salles d'exposition sont situées de part et d'autre de cette longue galerie.

Le grand foyer est dominé par une coupole vitrée et par un bloc de granit norvégien de 36 tonnes, qui relie le balcon de l'axe principal au restaurant situé à l'étage. L'édifice est traversé latéralement par l'« axe rouge », artère géante revêtue de faïence rouge conduisant du grand foyer à une passerelle de paquebot dominant le port. Sombre et intime, ce couloir présente un contraste saisissant avec l'axe central traité en blanc.

e "red axis", right, and the main circulation route or rt axis" left

echts: Die »rote Achse«; links: Haupterschließungsweg der »Kunstachse«

gauche, l'« axe artistique », principale voie de circulation musée ; à droite, l'axe transversal ou « axe rouge »

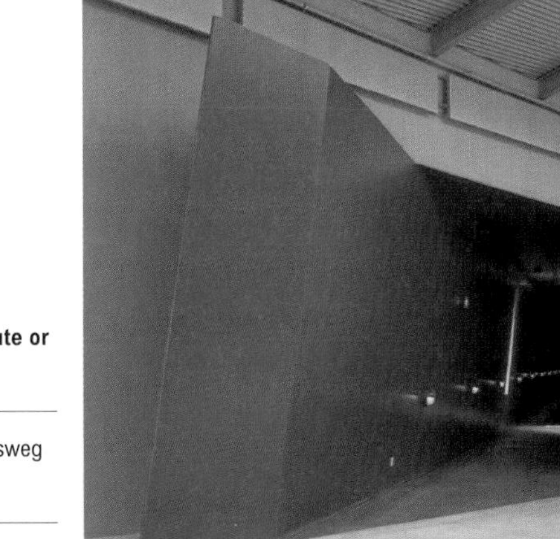

Light plays across the wall of the art axis, left. Above, view of the waterside building at night from Ishøj harbour.

Links: Über die Wände der »Kunstachse« ziehen sich Lichtreflexe; oben: Blick vom Hafen von Ishøj auf die zum Wasser gelegene Gebäudeseite.

A gauche, jeux de lumière sur les murs de l'«axe artistique». Ci-dessus, vue du musée prise du port d'Ishøj.

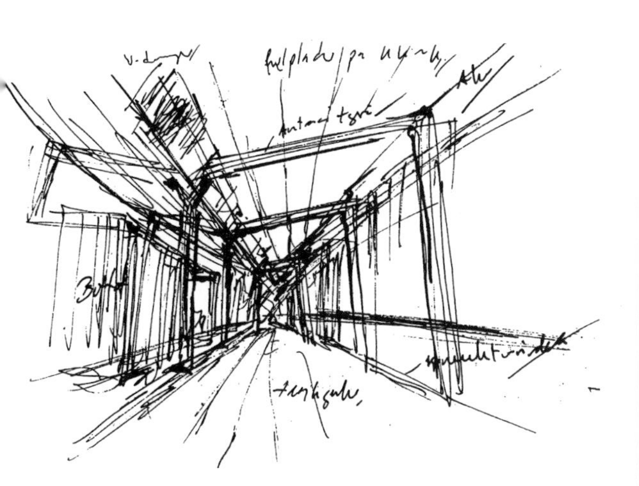

ew from one of the courtyards, left, and sketch for staurant, above

ks: Blick aus einem der Innenhöfe; oben: Skizze für s Restaurant

auche, une cour intérieure. Ci-dessus, ébauche du taurant

Ground floor plan/ Erdgeschossgrundriss/ Plan du rez-de-chaussée

1 **entrance/** Eingang/ entrée
2 **"art axis"/** »Kunstachse«/ « axe artistique »
3 **galleries/** Ausstellungsbereich/ salles d'exposition
4 **main foyer/** Hauptfoyer/ grand foyer
5 **"red axis"/** »rote Achse«/ « axe rouge »

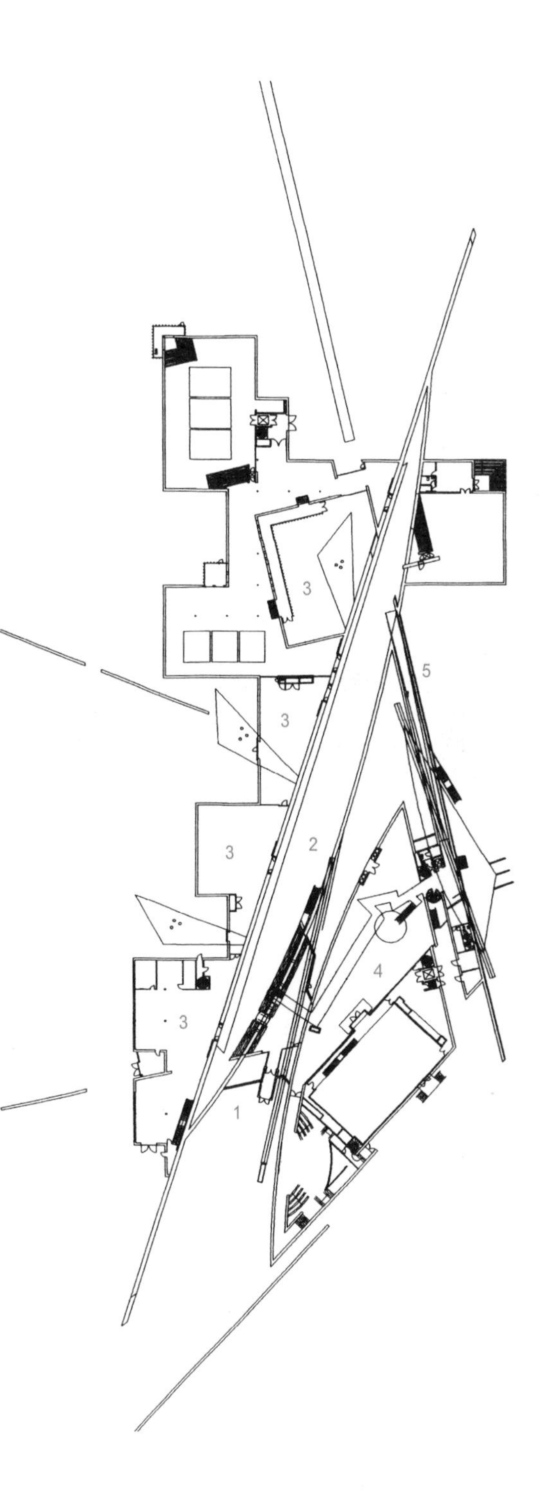

A/S Sjællandske Avistryk

Shades of Frank O. Gehry in the zinc-clad curves that mark the printing and ventilation halls, the folded seams echoing the folding of the newspapers inside. Either side of this central mass, lower rectilinear buildings house administration, storage, packing, and the staff canteen. Here black-stained wood and bare concrete are a deliberate contrast to the shiny facades of the printing and ventilation halls, an oblique reference to their contents - paper rather than metallic machinery. Landscaping using paper birches draws attention to the tree-pulp-paper chain.

Die Druck- und Lüftungshallen der Druckerei Sjællandske Avistryk erinnern mit ihren zinkverkleideten, geschwungenen Wänden an Bauten Frank O. Gehrys und symbolisieren mit ihren gefalteten Kanten das Falten einer Zeitung.
Zu beiden Seiten des zentralen Bauteils sind in flacheren, rechtwinkligen Gebäuden Verwaltung, Materialdepot und Verpackung sowie die Kantine untergebracht. Schwarz gebeiztes Holz und nackter Beton bilden hier einen bewussten Kontrast zu den glänzenden Fassaden der Druck- und Lüftungshallen – ein versteckter Hinweis auf das Papier, das hier gelagert wird. Die Birken der Landschaftsgestaltung assoziieren die Entstehungskette Baum-Papierbrei-Papier.

Les courbes revêtues de zinc des salles d'imprimerie et de ventilation, présentant des pliures qui rappellent le pliage des journaux, ne sont pas sans faire penser à Frank O. Gehry.
De part et d'autre de cette masse centrale, de longs bâtiments rectilignes abritent les services administratifs, les entrepôts, les salles d'emballage, ainsi que la cantine du personnel. Le bois teint en noir et le béton brut forment un contraste délibéré avec les façades luisantes des salles d'impression et de ventilation, allusion à leur contenu – le papier, et non les machines. De même, la plantation de bouleaux sur le terrain attenant attire l'attention sur la chaîne bois-pâte à papier.

The zinc-clad printing and ventilation halls that dominate the building, right, display shades of Frank O. Gehry. Left, the low-key entrance.

Rechts: Die mit Zinkplatten verkleideten Druck- und Lüftungshallen beherrschen das Gebäude und erinnern an Frank O. Gehry. Links der schlichte Eingang.

A droite : les salles revêtues de plaques de zinc de l'imprimerie ne sont pas sans évoquer Frank O. Gehry. A gauche, l'entrée, d'une grande sobriété.

n facade, left, with zinc-clad printing and :ilation halls at its centre

:s die Hauptfassade mit den zinkverkleideten :k- und Lüftungshallen im Zentrum

açade principale, avec les hautes salles de primerie revêtues de plaques de zinc

Level 1 floor plan/ Grundriss Ebene 1/ Plan du niveau 1

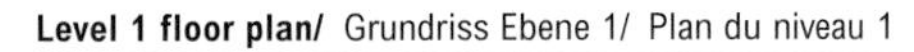

1 **pick up/** Auslieferung/ expéditions
2 **packing/** Verpackung/ emballage
3 **canteen/** Kantine/ cantine
4 **ventilation hall/** Lüftungshalle/ salle de ventilation
5 **printing hall/** Druckhalle/ imprimerie
6 **entrance/** Eingang/ entrée
7 **store/** Lager/ entrepôt

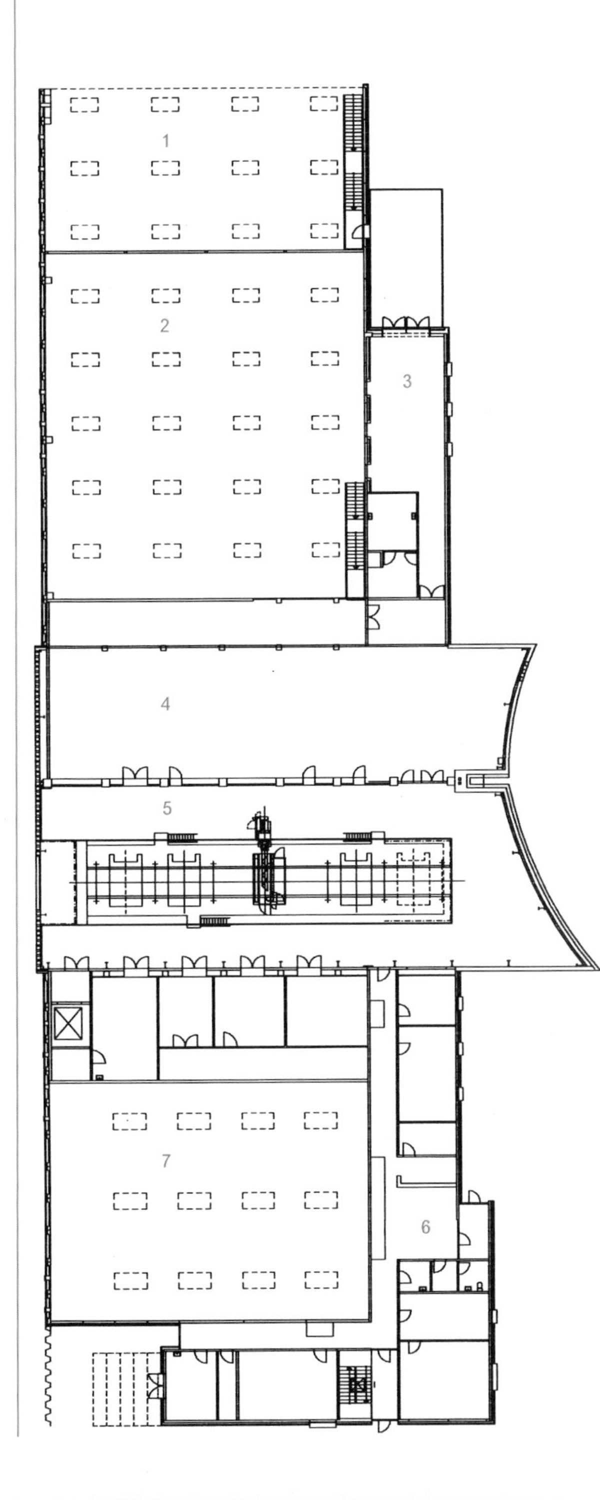

Niall McLaughlin

3 Portobello Road, London W11 2EB, UK tel +44 20 7792 0973 fax +44 20 7243 4081 e-mail nmclaughlin@btconnect.com web www.niallmclaughlin.com

ll McLaughlin

n	1962 Geneva, Switzerland
died	1984 University College Dublin
vious practice	Scott Tallon Walker, Dublin
	1991 set up Niall McLaughlin Architect

lected projects

apel and sacristy, Carmelite monastery	1992 Kensington, London, UK
rden and house remodelling	1995 London, UK
alth spa and pool	1995 Kensington, London, UK
Shack	1996 Northamptonshire, UK
d Stand, De La Warr Pavilion	2000 Bexhill-on-Sea, UK

e use of lighting, both natural and artificial, to cre- texture within an interior is deftly handled within Laughlin's work. Concealed roof lights and glass eens set up layers to diffuse and reflect light, cast- ever changing patterns across walls and floors. roughout his work, a point is made of allowing the cupant to sense the quality of light changing during day as the patterns and colours in the room grad- lly change.

e are less interested in the overall expression of hnology by bolts, junctions and gaskets, more in the erall presence of a space. In particular, the way in ich materials alter space by modulating light, com- ing it, diffusing it, storing it, reflecting it, dulling r changing its speed."

ove of materials - "we work with anything from d to Daz" - and knowledge of the production process ans that all McLaughlin's work is beautifully pro- ced, whether the intricate joinery in the London rmelite monastery or the carefully devised pattern individually cast paving stones in a garden. He rks with the same small group of craftsmen and lders, discussing all his designs with them.

Im Werk McLaughlins fällt der geschickte Einsatz von Tages- und Kunstlicht zur Strukturierung von Innenräumen auf. Versteckte Oberlichter und Glasschirme schaffen Schichten, die das Licht streuen und reflektieren und dabei ständig wechselnde Muster auf Wände und Böden werfen. McLaughlin achtet darauf, dass der Bewohner die im Lauf des Tages wechselnde Lichtqualität spürt, indem Muster und Farben im Raum sich allmählich verändern.

»Wir sind weniger an einem technischen Erscheinungsbild mit Schrauben, Anschlüssen und Dichtungen interessiert als an der Präsenz des Raums; besonders an der Art und Weise, in der Materialien den Raum verändern können, indem sie Licht modulieren, kombinieren, streuen, verstärken, reflektieren, dämpfen oder seine Geschwindigkeit verändern.«

Die Liebe zu den Materialien – »wir arbeiten mit allem von Gold bis Dasch« – und die Kenntnis der Herstellungsprozesse gibt allen Arbeiten McLaughlins ihre hohe handwerkliche Qualität, ob es die kunstvollen Tischlerarbeiten im Londoner Karmel oder das wohlüberlegte Muster der einzeln geformten Pflastersteine in einem Garten sind. Er arbeitet stets mit derselben kleinen Gruppe von Handwerkern und Bauleuten zusammen, mit denen er sämtliche Entwürfe bespricht.

McLaughlin manie avec une grande habileté l'éclairage, tant naturel qu'artificiel, pour donner une texture à des volumes intérieurs. Des ouvertures dissimulées dans la toiture et des écrans de verre diffusent et réfléchissent la lumière, projetant sur les murs et le sol des motifs sans cesse changeants. Dans toutes ses réalisations, il tient à ce que l'occupant sente la différence de qualité de la lumière selon l'heure du jour, grâce à la modification graduelle des motifs et des couleurs.

« Nous nous intéressons moins à l'expression générale de la technologie par les scellements, les boulons ou les joints, qu'à la présence globale d'un espace – et en particulier à la façon dont les matériaux transforment l'espace en modulant la lumière, en la combinant, l'accumulant, la reflétant, en l'atténuant ou en modifiant sa vitesse. »

L'amour des matériaux – « nous travaillons avec n'importe quoi, de l'or au Dash » – allié à une parfaite connaissance des processus de fabrication assure que toutes les constructions de McLaughlin sont superbement exécutées, qu'il s'agisse de la complexe menuiserie d'un monastère de carmélites à Londres ou du motif élaboré des pierres choisies une à une pour le dallage d'un jardin. Il travaille toujours avec le même petit groupe d'artisans et de maçons, et discute avec eux de chaque projet.

1992 **Kensington, London, UK**

Chapel and sacristy, Carmelite monastery

The sacristy is intended as a place of passage, of stillness and meditation for the priest to prepare before going through to the altar. McLaughlin's calm interior reflects this. The flowing planes of the ceiling in the sacristy fold over each other, concealing two roof lights that fill the room with a soft light reflected from the white surfaces. A celestial presence is suggested by the shaft of light cast by the narrower roof-light which the priest must cross on his way to the chapel, a device inspired by Carmelite monk Fra Filippo Lippi's painting of the Annunciation in which a loggia separates the Virgin and the angel. Materials are kept very plain so that the colourful vestments can resonate within the room.

The adjoining chapel is intended to be experienced in the context of the garden. Objects in the chapel are based on pure geometric forms - circle, cube, cone - in contrast to the freer realm of the garden, representing paradise. The twelve chairs around the walls allude to the Last Supper, their backs at shoulder-height to evoke human presence. The tabernacle containing the consecrated host is a solid oak cube that splits in two to reveal a gold-lined cylinder. Joinery and furniture are the work of Westside Workshops in Bath, England.

Die Sakristei des Karmels im Londoner Stadtteil Kensington ist ein Ort des Übergangs, der Stille und Meditation, wo sich der Priester auf den Gang zum Altar vorbereiten kann. McLaughlins ruhiges Interieur antwortet diesem Anliegen. Die fließenden Deckenflächen greifen ineinander und verbergen zwei Oberlichter, die den Raum mit sanftem, von den weißen Wänden reflektierten Licht erfüllen. Ein durch das schmalere Oberlicht fallender Lichtstreifen, den der Priester auf seinem Weg zur Kapelle durchqueren muss, symbolisiert die Präsenz des Himmlischen – angeregt von der Verkündigung des Karmelitermönchs Fra Filippo Lippi, auf dem eine Loggia die Muttergottes vom Engel trennt. Um den farbigen liturgischen Gewändern im Raum den Vortritt zu lassen, wurden äußerst schlichte Materialien verwendet.

Die angrenzende Kapelle soll im Kontext des Gartens erlebt werden. Den Objekten liegen rein geometrische Formen zugrunde – Kreis, Kubus, Kegel –, um den Gegensatz zum freieren Raum des Gartens zu betonen, der für das Paradies steht. Die zwölf Stühle an den Wänden, deren schulterhohe Lehnen menschliche Präsenz andeuten, spielen auf das Letzte Abendmahl an. Der Tabernakel mit der Eucharistie ist ein massiver Eichenholzkubus, der sich teilt und einen innen vergoldeten Zylinder freigibt. Tischlerarbeiten und Möbel wurden in den Westside Workshops in Bath, England, hergestellt.

La sacristie constitue un lieu de passage, de calme et de méditation où le prêtre se prépare à célébrer l'office fonction que reflète l'intérieur paisible dessiné par McLaughlin. Les panneaux du plafond suspendu se ch vauchent, dissimulant une lucarne dont ils diffusent la lumière captée par leur surface blanche. Un rai de lumi projeté par une lucarne plus étroite, que le prêtre doit franchir pour gagner la chapelle, suggère une présence céleste, procédé inspiré de l'Annonciation du carme Fra Filippo Lippi, tableau dans lequel une loggia sépare la Vierge des anges. Les matériaux très discrets mettent e valeur les couleurs vibrantes des vêtements liturgiques La chapelle attenante est destinée à être perçue dans le contexte du jardin. Tous les objets de la chapelle sont basés sur des formes géométriques pures – cercle, cub cône – contrastant avec la plus grande liberté formelle du jardin, symbolisant le paradis. Douze chaises aligné contre les murs font allusion à la Cène ; leurs dossiers très hauts suggèrent une présence humaine. Le tabernacle contenant l'hostie est un massif cube en chêne q s'ouvre pour révéler un cylindre doublé d'or. Les meub et la menuiserie ont été réalisés par les Westside Work-shops de Bath.

Sacristy

Die Sakristei

La sacristie

low, the chapel, opening on to the garden. Left, the elve chairs, evoking the Last Supper, have been ade by Westside Workshops of Bath, England.

ten die Kapelle mit Blick in den Garten. Links: Die an s Letzte Abendmahl erinnernden zwölf Stühle entstan- n in den Westside Workshops in Bath, England.

-dessous : la chapelle s'ouvre sur le jardin. A gauche : douze chaises évoquant la Cène ont été réalisées par Westside Workshops, de Bath.

The photographer's hide. The roof is intended to suggest a feathery wing.

Das Refugium der Fotografin. Das Dach soll eine Vogelschwinge andeuten.

La retraite de la photographe. Notez le toit évoquant un aile brisée.

he Shack

e Shack is a pond-side hide for photographer Gina ver, who specialises in pictures of insects, but ludes a sauna for her partner and a den-cum-bed-m for their daughter to keep the rest of the family ppy.
It in the grounds of a former World War II airbase, hide takes its cues from flying. The plywood and reglass roof canopy of broken wing forms suggests tallic plumage, while scales of polycarbonate and forated metal extend out over the water. A long om with a camera on the end skims over the surface the pond, which McLaughlin likes to think of as reconnaissance flight from base bringing back ages from remote landscapes".
lind wall at the rear of the building captures light ering the shack from the pond, while layers of fins l concealed roof-lights cast ever-changing light terns along its screen-like surface.

The Shack ist das an einem See gelegene Refugium der Fotografin Gina Glover, die sich auf Insektenfotos spezialisiert hat; daneben gibt es eine Sauna für ihren Partner und ein kleines Studio für die Tochter.
Der Bau auf dem Gelände eines Luftwaffenstützpunkts aus dem Zweiten Weltkrieg spielt auf das Fliegen an: Das Schutzdach aus Sperrholz und Fiberglas in gebrochener Flügelform lässt an metallisches Gefieder denken, während Schuppen aus Polycarbonat und perforiertem Metall in den See ragen. Ein langer Ausleger mit einer Kamera am Ende streicht über die Oberfläche des Teiches und unternimmt dabei, so McLaughlin, »vom Stützpunkt aus Erkundungsflüge, um Bilder entlegener Landschaften zurückzubringen«.
Eine Blendmauer auf der Rückseite des Gebäudes fängt das Licht ein, das vom Teich in die Hütte fällt, während gestaffelte Lamellen und verborgene Oberlichter ständig wechselnde Lichtmuster auf die gitterartige Oberfläche werfen.

The Shack (« la hutte »), située au bord d'un étang, est une retraite destinée à la photographe Gina Glover, spécialisée dans les photos d'insectes. Le reste de la famille n'a pas été oublié : il y a un sauna pour son époux et un studio-salle de loisirs pour leur fille.
Construite sur le site d'une ancienne base aérienne de la Deuxième Guerre mondiale, cette tanière s'inspire de l'aviation. La toiture en contre-plaqué et fibre de verre en forme d'ailes brisées s'étendant au-dessus de l'eau est recouverte d'écailles de polycarbonate et de métal perforé évoquant un plumage métallique. Une longue perche portant un appareil photo effleure la surface de l'étang ; cela fait penser McLaughlin à « un vol de reconnaissance ramenant des images de paysages lointains ».
A l'arrière du bâtiment, un mur aveugle capte la lumière réfléchie par l'étang, tandis que des ailerons superposés et des lucarnes dissimulées projettent des motifs lumineux changeants sur sa surface pareille à un écran.

Above, the photographer's lookout tower. Below, northerly light plays across the wall of the main living/working space.

Oben: Der Ausguck der Fotografin. Unten: Auf der Wand des Hauptwohn- und Arbeitsraums spielt das von Norden einfallende Licht.

Ci-dessus : la tour de guet de la photographe. A gauche : jeux de lumière sur les murs exposés au nord.

Floor plan/ Grundriss/ Plan

1 **shower/** Dusche/ douche
2 **work space/** Arbeitsraum/ atelier
3 **sauna/** Sauna/ sauna
4 **pond/** Teich/ étang

The window doubles as bank, left; a silver light box marks the end of the garden, far left.

Links das Fenster, dessen Fensterbank zugleich als Sitzgelegenheit dient. Ganz links der Lichtkasten am Ende des Gartens.

A gauche : la fenêtre en bois dont le rebord sert de banc. Page de gauche : le « caisson lumineux » à l'extrémité du jardin.

995 London, UK

Garden and house remodelling

n earlier project for the same photographer shows cLaughlin's commitment to craftsmanship. A beautilly executed wooden window has back-to-back seats cing both into and away from the house to form the indowsill. Intricate layers of silk blinds, wooden shutrs and sliding folding windows allow a multitude relationships between the room and the garden. A ooden pergola encourages creepers to grow into a nopy above, and paving designed and cast by the aritects, sends a beautiful pattern out across the yard. t the end of the garden, McLaughlin has positioned a lver light box, visible from the front door of the house, linking element through the building. Sandblasted ass is mounted onto the front and laminated with siler-plated strips. Tiny gaps between the ingots glow ith light from behind. As the light changes, so does e silver wall, and throughout the year it builds up a atural layer of patination, changing colour from silver rough yellows to black. The family polishes the wall very Easter.

Das frühere Projekt einer Garten-Umgestaltung für dieselbe Fotografin zeugt von McLaughlins Nähe zur Handwerkskunst. Die Fensterbank eines kunstvoll gearbeiteten Holzfensters fungiert zugleich als Sitz, von dem sich der Blick ins Haus oder hinaus in den Garten öffnet. Komplizierte Schichten von Seidenrouleaus, hölzernen Läden und faltbaren Schiebefenster stellen vielfältige Beziehungen zwischen Raum und Garten her. An einer hölzernen Pergola ranken sich Kletterpflanzen auf das darüber liegende Dach, und der vom Architekten entworfene und gegossene Bodenbelag überzieht den Hof mit einem schönem Muster.
Am Ende des Gartens platzierte McLaughlin einen silberfarbenen Lichtkasten, der von der Eingangstür zu sehen ist und so eine optische Verbindung durch das Haus hindurch schafft. Die Vorderseite des Kastens ist mit sandgestrahltem, versilbertem Glas verkleidet. Eine dahinter liegende Lichtquelle lässt die winzigen Fugen zwischen den Streifen aufleuchten. Mit wechselndem Licht verändert sich auch die Wand, und im Laufe des Jahres entsteht eine natürliche Patina von Silber über Gelbtöne bis hin zu Schwarz. Jedes Jahr zu Ostern wird die Wand von der Familie poliert.

Ce projet antérieur réalisé pour la même photographe témoigne de l'attachement de McLaughlin à l'artisanat. La fenêtre en bois, dont le rebord est formé par des sièges accolés respectivement tournés vers l'intérieur et vers l'extérieur, est d'une exécution superbe. Des couches successives de stores en soie, de volets en bois et des fenêtres coulissantes et pliantes autorisent de multiples relations entre l'intérieur et le jardin. Une pergola en bois se couvre de plantes grimpantes, un dallage entièrement conçu par l'architecte dessine un superbe motif à travers la cour.
A l'extrémité du jardin, McLaughlin a disposé un caisson lumineux argenté ; visible de la porte de la maison, il établit un lien avec celle-ci. Sa face antérieure est en verre dépoli maintenu par des bandes plaquées argent ; à l'arrière, de petits orifices laissent passer la lumière. La paroi argentée change d'aspect selon la lumière du jour ; les ans lui ont donné une patine qui va de l'argent au noir en passant par diverses nuances de jaune. Chaque année, à Pâques, la famille se fait un devoir de la polir.

MVRDV

hiehaven 15, 3024 EC Rotterdam, Netherlands tel +31 10 477 2860 fax +31 10 477 3627 e-mail office@mvrdv.nl www.mvrdv.nl

ny Maas

rn	1959	Schijndel, Netherlands
died	1983	RHSTL Boskoop (Landscape Architecture); 1990 Technical University Delft
actice	1991	co-founded MVRDV

cob van Rijs

rn	1964	Amsterdam, Netherlands
died	1984	The Hague Free Academy; 1990 Technical University Delft
actice	1991	co-founded MVRDV

thalie de Vries

rn	1965	Appingedam, Netherlands
died	1990	Technical University Delft
actice	1991	co-founded MVRDV

lected projects

ban design of Campus Net3, Mediapark	1995	Hilversum, Netherlands
ee porter's lodges	1996	Hoge Veluwe National Park, Netherlands
a VPRO	1997	Hilversum, Netherlands
U Headquarters	1997	Hilversum, Netherlands
ZoCo's apartments	1997	Amsterdam-Osdorp, Netherlands
uble-house	1997	Utrecht, Netherlands (in association with Bjarne Mastenbroek)
ght Forum, masterplan	1999	Eindhoven Airport, Netherlands
uses on Borneo Sporenburg	1999/2000	Amsterdam, Netherlands
rden for Net3 broadcasting companies	2000	Hilversum, Netherlands
tch Pavilion, Expo 2000	2000	Hanover, Germany
veen office building	2000	Amersfoort, Netherlands
odam office/apartment building	2001	Amsterdam, Netherlands

mbining a range of disciplines including urban plan-g, landscape design, furniture design and architec-e, MVRDV have a broad-minded approach to their jects and are not limited by received architectural nking.

he traditional demarcations between the different ciplines are absent. Practical experience of realis- designs has shown that this cross-fertilisation

Ihre große Bandbreite an Disziplinen, darunter Stadtplanung, Landschaftsgestaltung, Architektur und Möbeldesign, ermöglicht es MVRDV, offen an ihre Projekte heranzugehen und sich nicht durch überkommenes architektonisches Denken einengen zu lassen.

»Die traditionellen Grenzen zwischen den verschiedenen Disziplinen sind nicht vorhanden. Die praktische Erfahrung bei der Verwirklichung von Entwürfen hat gezeigt,

Alliant diverses disciplines, de l'architecture et de l'urbanisme à l'architecture de paysage et au design de meubles, MVRDV témoigne d'une grande ouverture d'esprit, et ses projets ne sont pas limités par la pensée architecturale conventionnelle.

« La démarcation traditionnelle entre les différentes disciplines est absente. L'expérience concrète de la réalisation de projets architecturaux a prouvé que cette fertilisation

leads to fruitful solutions. A commission for work on an interior can be approached as if it were a piece of town planning; principles drawn from the field of landscape design can be applied to a piece of architectonic design."

Work to date has been controversial, egotistical, eye-catching, bizarre, but never dull. A combination of lateral thinking and fertile imagination has produced the cantilevered boxes projecting from the facade of WoZoCo's housing, the curled floor slab of the headquarters for broadcaster VPRO, the bulbous concrete shell of the outdoor theatre at Delft, and the jumbled green glass and brown plywood facade of the double-house, Utrecht (executed in association with Bjarne Mastenbroek). Offices and apartment complexes become mini cities, yet remain respectful towards their surroundings.

MVRDV has carried out several urban studies and masterplans. Installations and publications ("FARMAX", "Metacity Datatown", "KM3" and "Costa Iberica", to name but a few) expound one of the practice's core theses: the need to develop high-density building to combat "grey urban sprawl" and preserve what is left of the pastoral landscape.

The cryptic name, MVRDV, is an acronym formed from the surnames of the three founding partners, Winy Maas, Jacob van Rijs and Nathalie de Vries.

dass diese fächerübergreifende Arbeit zu erfolgreichen Lösungen führt. Ein Auftrag für Innenraumgestaltung kann genauso behandelt werden als ginge es um ein Stadtplanungsprojekt; aus der Landschaftsgestaltung abgeleitete Prinzipien lassen sich auf einen Architekturentwurf übertragen.«

Bis jetzt gelten MVRDVs Arbeiten als höchst individuell, auffallend und bizarr; sie sind umstritten, aber niemals langweilig. Unorthodoxe Ideen führen zusammen mit kreativer Phantasie zu ungewöhnlichen Lösungen: vorkragende Kästen, die aus der Fassade des WoZoCo's-Apartmenthauses ragen, die geknickte Bodenplatte der Villa VPRO, die knollenförmige Betonschale des Freilichttheaters in Delft und die Doppelhausfassade aus einer planlosen Mischung von grünem Glas und braunem Sperrholz in Utrecht (entstanden in Zusammenarbeit mit Bjarne Mastenbroek). Büros und Wohnhäuser werden zu Miniaturstädten, die jedoch ihre Umgebung respektieren.

MVRDV hat mehrere stadtplanerische Studien und Masterpläne ausgeführt. In Installationen und Publikationen (»FARMAX«, »Metacity Datatown«, »KM3« und »Costa Iberica«, um nur einige zu nennen) erläutern sie einige ihrer Kernthesen: hoch verdichtete Bebauung, um dem »öden urbanen Wildwuchs« Einhalt zu gebieten, und Erhalt der verbleibenden naturbelassenen Landschaft.

Der rätselhafte Name MVRDV ist ein Akronym aus den Nachnamen der drei Gründungspartner Winy Maas, Jacob van Rijs und Nathalie de Vries.

réciproque génère des solutions efficaces. Une commande d'aménagement intérieur peut être traitée dans l'optique de l'urbanisme. Des principes empruntés à l'architecture de paysage peuvent s'appliquer à un design architectonique. »

Les projets qu'ils ont réalisés à ce jour sont controversés, peut-être bizarres, mais ils accrochent le regard et ne sont jamais ennuyeux. Cette combinaison de pensée non-conformiste et d'imagination fertile a produit les boîtes en porte-à-faux qui percent la façade de l'immeuble WoZoCo's, la dalle de plancher courbe du siège de l'émetteur VPRO, le bulbe en béton qui enveloppe le théâtre de plein air de Delft, et la façade anarchique mêlant verre de couleur verte et contre-plaqué marron de la double maison d'Utrecht (conçue en association avec Bjarne Mastenbroek). Des immeubles de bureaux et des blocs d'appartements deviennent des villes miniatures tout en respectant leur environnement.

MRVDV a réalisé plusieurs études d'urbanisme et schémas directeurs.

Leurs installations artistiques et publications (par exemp « FARMAX », « Metacity Datatown », « KM3 » et « Costa Iberica ») exposent les thèses centrales : la nécessité de développer une architecture à haute densité pour combattre « la grise et tentaculaire extension urbaine » et préserver ce qui subsiste du paysage pastoral.

Le mystérieux acronyme MVRDV est dérivé des noms des trois fondateurs associés de ce bureau d'architectes Winy Maas, Jacob van Rijs et Nathalie de Vries.

Villa VPRO. The floor slab is pulled up at one corner to create a dramatic signpost for the entrance.

Villa VPRO. Die Bodenplatte des Erdgeschosses ist an einer Ecke nach oben gezogen und schafft so einen markanten Eingangsbereich.

La Villa VPRO. La dalle de béton se relève dramatiquement à un des angles de l'édifice, marquant l'entrée principale.

Villa VPRO

he Villa VPRO houses offices, production facilities nd staff restaurant for the successful Dutch media and roadcasting company.
nstantly recognisable for its bent floor slab, expressed n the outside of the building like a giant paper clip, his trademark feature is in fact the main entrance, which is located on the third floor, drawing visitors traight into the heart of the building. Elsewhere, the lock is penetrated by terraces and glazed courtyards hat eat their way into the building and up through the oors in an unpredictable fashion. The idea is to create "continuous interior" that flows from the ground up o the fifth floor, establishing a sense of community within the building.
nlike many modern office buildings, there are no uspended ceilings or prefabricated walls - MVRDV ave gone for a more traditional palette of materials uch as stone, steel, wood, plastic with Persian and isal rugs on the floor, a reference to the company's ormer home in a group of 13 old villas.
adly, an early idea to dispense with glazing and just ave walls of warm air separating "inside" from "outide" had to be discarded on the grounds of safety and nergy consumption. It is, however, typical of the practice to explore such avenues, and has led instead to the se of 35 different sorts of glass of varying colour, reflectivity and transparency across the facade.
ronically, the building has attracted the scorn of Rem Koolhaas, who, as the practice's mentor, could be said o have in some ways inspired it.

Die Villa VPRO beherbergt Büros, Produktionsanlagen und ein Restaurant für die Belegschaft der erfolgreichen niederländischen Medien- und Rundfunkgesellschaft.
Blickfang ist eine geknickte Bodenplatte, die von außen an eine überdimensionale Büroklammer erinnert. Sie bildet als Markenzeichen den Haupteingang auf der dritten Etage und führt Besucher direkt ins Herz des Gebäudes. An anderen Stellen dringen Terrassen und verglaste Innenhöfe in den blockförmigen Bau ein und bahnen sich auf unvorhersehbare Weise ihren Weg durch Räume und Geschosse. Die Idee ist die eines »fortlaufenden Interieurs«, das vom Erdgeschoss in den fünften Stock »fließt« und so ein Zusammengehörigkeitsgefühl entstehen lässt.
Im Gegensatz zu vielen modernen Bürogebäuden gibt es keine abgehängten Decken oder vorgefertigten Wände – MVRDV entschieden sich für traditionelle Materialien wie Stein, Stahl, Holz, Kunststoff; in Erinnerung an die frühere Zentrale, die aus 13 alten Villen bestand, sind die Böden mit Perser- und Sisalteppichen belegt.
Es ist typisch für das Büro, neue Wege zu erkunden. Leider musste jedoch der Plan, Verglasung durch Wände aus warmer Luft zu ersetzen, die Innen- und Außenraum trennen sollten, aus Gründen der Sicherheit und des Energieverbrauchs verworfen werden. Stattdessen kamen an der Fassade 35 verschiedene Glassorten in unterschiedlichen Farben, wechselnder Reflexion und Transparenz zum Einsatz.
Paradoxerweise erregte das Gebäude das Missfallen von Rem Koolhaas, von dem man sagen könnte, er habe den Entwurf als Mentor des Büros in gewissem Sinne inspiriert.

La Villa VPRO réunit des bureaux, des salles de production et un restaurant d'entreprise pour cette société néerlandaise de communication et de radiodiffusion.
Immédiatement reconnaissable à sa dalle de plancher courbe, exprimée à l'extérieur par une forme évoquant un gigantesque trombone de bureau, cet élément typique est en fait l'entrée principale, située au troisième étage, ce qui amène les visiteurs droit au cœur du bâtiment. Ailleurs, le bloc est éventré par des terrasses et des cours vitrées qui envahissent l'espace intérieur, s'étendant d'une manière aléatoire sur plusieurs niveaux. L'idée était de créer un « intérieur continu » unifiant l'édifice entier, du rez-de-chaussée au cinquième étage.
Contrairement à nombre d'immeubles de bureaux modernes, il n'y a ni plafonds suspendus ni cloisons préfabriquées. MVRDV a préféré des matériaux plus traditionnels tels que pierre, acier, bois, plastique ; les sols sont recouverts de tapis persans ou de sisal, référence à l'ancien siège constitué d'un groupe de 13 villas anciennes.
Malheureusement, l'idée primitive – supprimer les vitrages, des « murs » d'air chaud suffisant à séparer l'« intérieur » de l'« extérieur » – dut être abandonnée pour des raisons de sécurité et d'économie d'énergie. L'exploration de telles solutions est cependant typique de la démarche de MVRDV ; elle a conduit à utiliser pour la façade 35 sortes de verres différant par la couleur, le degré de transparence et de réflexivité. Curieusement, cette réalisation a suscité le mépris de Rem Koolhaas qui, en sa qualité de mentor de MVRDV, en est sans doute l'inspirateur, du moins sous certains aspects.

Kitsch meets concrete, far left. Left, outdoor spaces work their way through the building.

Ganz links: Kitsch trifft Beton; links: Innen- und Außenbereiche durchdringen sich.

Page de gauche : le kitsch fait bon ménage avec le béton. A gauche : des espaces à ciel ouvert s'enfoncent profondément dans l'édifice.

Meeting room, far left, and left the entrance

Ganz links der Konferenzraum; links der Eingang

Page de gauche : la salle de réunion ; à gauche, l'entrée

01
Deutsche Post

e surprising Dutch Pavilion is one of the stars of e Hanover Expo 2000.

r ungewöhnliche Pavillon der Niederlande ist eine r Attraktionen der Expo 2000 in Hannover.

étonnant pavillon des Pays-Bas est une des attractions l'Expo 2000 à Hanovre.

000 **Hanover, Germany**

Dutch Pavilion, Expo 2000

n response to their country's most pressing development issues - space, land, ecology, and increasing population - MVRDV proposed a pavilion that would onfront these topics and present "a mix of technology nd nature, emphasising nature's marketability and rtificiality: technology and nature need not be mutually exclusive, they can perfectly well reinforce each ther."

uilt as a tower, the structure, for the Foundation olland World Fairs, is what MVRDV describe as 'a multi-level park" that dissolves boundaries and aves space, energy, time, water and infrastructure, perating its own mini-ecosystem.

Als Antwort auf die dringendsten Entwicklungsfragen ihres Landes – Raum, Land, Ökologie und Bevölkerungszuwachs – schlug MVRDV für die Expo 2000 in Hannover einen Pavillon vor, der diese Fragen in gebauter Form aufnehmen sollte. Er sollte »eine Mischung aus Technik und Natur präsentieren und dabei die Vermarktbarkeit und Künstlichkeit von Natur aufzeigen: Technik und Natur müssen sich nicht ausschließen, sie können sich sehr gut gegenseitig stärken.«

Der als Turm konzipierte Bau für die Foundation Holland World Fairs wird von MVRDV als »Park auf mehreren Ebenen« beschrieben, der Begrenzungen aufhebt und Raum, Energie, Zeit, Wasser und Infrastruktur spart, indem er ein eigenes Mini-Ökosystem schafft.

En réaction aux problèmes de développement les plus pressants auxquels leur pays doit faire face – espace, écologie, accroissement démographique –, les architectes de MVRDV ont proposé un pavillon présentant « un mélange de technologie et de nature, qui souligne le caractère artificiel et plastique de la nature : la technologie et la nature ne sont pas nécessairement incompatibles, mais peuvent fort bien se renforcer mutuellement. »

La structure en forme de tour construite pour la Foundation Holland World Fairs est, selon les architectes eux-mêmes, « un parc sur plusieurs niveaux », écosystème miniature qui efface les limites et économise l'espace, l'énergie, le temps, l'eau et les infrastructures.

EMPTY
FULL

The cave-like interior of the cafeteria (right) and the "flowerpot-level" (left)

Die höhlenartige Cafeteria (rechts) und das »Blumentopf«-Geschoss (links)

La grotte de la cafétéria (à droite) et le niveau « pots de fleurs » (à gauche)

fit the requisite number of apartments onto the site, ditional apartments are cantilevered off the north cade, left. Right, the balconies of the south facade.

n die erforderliche Zahl von Wohnungen auf dem ugrund unterzubringen, kragen einige Apartments s der Nordfassade vor (links). Rechts die Balkone f der Südfassade.

in d'atteindre le nombre requis de logements sur site peu étendu, des appartements supplémentaires t été construits en porte-à-faux sur la façade nord gauche). A droite, les balcons de la façade sud.

997 **Amsterdam-Osdorp, Netherlands**

WoZoCo's apartments

is apartment building set everyone in the Netherlands lking with its bizarre facade of boxes and balconies ooting out in mid-air.
esigned to accommodate elderly people in the Amerdam suburb of Osdorp, the main building is a rrow strip, a ploy by MVRDV to minimise its footprint d maximise the precious green space surrounding it. owever, with a brief to provide 100 apartments, and room for more than 87 in the thin block, MVRDV mply cantilevered the remaining rooms off the north cade. On the timber-clad south facade, windows are aced in different positions and balconies given varyg depths and widths (their colour was the decision each inhabitant, hence the multicoloured result), aking each apartment unique and creating a colour- rhythm across the building.
egularely featured in the international architecture ess, the building was chosen as a finalist for the ies van der Rohe Award for European architecture.

Das Apartmenthaus WoZoCo's erregte mit seiner bizarren Fassade, aus der unvermittelt Kästen und Balkone herausragen, in ganz Holland Aufsehen.
Der Bau im Amsterdamer Vorort Osdorp wurde für Senioren konzipiert. Der Hauptbau ist ein schmaler Riegel, ein Kunstgriff von MVRDV, um die Grundfläche klein und die kostbaren Grünflächen möglichst groß zu halten. Da die Ausschreibung 100 Wohnungen vorsah, in dem schmalen Block aber nur 87 Platz fanden, hängten die Architekten die verbleibenden Räume einfach an der Nordfassade auf. An der holzverschalten Südseite wurden die Fenster unregelmäßig positioniert, und die Balkone variieren in Tiefe und Breite, so dass jede Wohnung einzigartig ist. Da jeder Bewohner zudem die farbliche Gestaltung seines Balkons selbst bestimmen konnte, entsteht auf der Fassade ein farbenfrohes Wechselspiel.
Das in der internationalen Architekturpresse oft besprochene Gebäude gelangte in die Endrunde um den Mies-van-der-Rohe-Preis für Europäische Architektur.

L'immeuble d'appartements WoZoCo's dont la façade bizarre faite de boîtes et de balcons projetés dans le vide fait jaser tous les Pays-Bas.
Destiné à accueillir des personnes agées à Osdorp, localité de la banlieue d'Amsterdam, le bâtiment principal est une bande étroite, stratégie utilisée par MVRDV pour minimiser la surface au sol et préserver les précieux espaces verts qui l'entourent. Le cahier des charges prévoyait toutefois 100 appartements, mais le bloc étroit ne pouvait en contenir que 87 ; pour résoudre le problème, MRVDV a simplement disposé les pièces supplémentaires en porte-à-faux sur la façade nord. Sur la façade sud, revêtue de bois, la disposition des fenêtres est variable, de même que la largeur et la profondeur des balcons. Leurs couleurs étant choisies par les habitants eux-mêmes, chaque appartement est unique ; cela crée également un rythme bariolé qui marque l'immeuble entier. Souvent commenté dans la presse architecturale internationale, l'édifice a été qualifié pour les finales du Mies van der Rohe Award for European Architecture.

MINNAERT

leutelings Riedijk

ıeepmakersstraat 13, 3011 VH Rotterdam, Netherlands tel +31 10 404 6677 fax +31 10 414 2712 e-mail nra.rdam@luna.nl

lem Jan Neutelings

n	1959 Bergen op Zoom, Netherlands
died	1986 Technical University, Delft
vious practice	partnership with Frank Roodbeen, Rotterdam
	1991 co-founded Neutelings Riedijk

:hiel Riedijk

n	1964 Geldrop, Netherlands
died	1989 Technical University, Delft
vious practice	partnership with Juliette Bekkering, Rotterdam
	1991 co-founded Neutelings Riedijk

ected projects

naertgebouw	1997 University of Utrecht, Netherlands
Post	1997 Scherpenheuvel, Belgium
nman Drukkers	1997 Ede, Netherlands
station	1999 Maastricht, Netherlands
station	1999 Breda, Netherlands
ıcert hall (competition entry)	1999 Bruges, Belgium

ɔther Dutch practice derived from the Office for tropolitan Architecture (Neutelings is a contempor- of Winy Maas of MVRDV), Neutelings Riedijk's rk is bursting with humour. It is not a crass, slap- k humour, but the sort that makes you smile when see it.

is essay "On Laziness, Recycling, Sculptural Math- atics and Reason" ("Over de luiheid, recyclage, lpturale wiskunde en vernuftigheid", Fascinaties/4, terdam) Neutelings writes provocatively, "In our jects we try, with tremendous effort and varying grees of success, to apply laziness as a design phil- phy." By this he is advocating a recycling of ideas n history by incorporating existing buildings into v ones. In some cases he may even dissuade a client n building anything at all. He rails against the :herlands' "thundering avalanche of ever more

Wie MVRDV ist auch Neutelings Riedijk eines der holländischen Büros, das aus dem Office for Metropolitan Architecture hervorging (Neutelings ist ein Altersgenosse von Winy Maas von MVRDV). Ihre Arbeiten sind ausgesprochen humorvoll – eine Art von Humor, die einen zum Lächeln bringt.

In seinem Essay »Über Faulheit, Recycling, plastische Mathematik und Vernunft« (»Over de luiheid, recyclage, sculpturale wiskunde en vernuftigheid«, Fascinaties/4, Rotterdam) schreibt Neutelings provozierend: »In unseren Projekten versuchen wir mit enormer Mühe und wechselndem Erfolg, Faulheit zur Entwurfsphilosophie zu machen.« Gemeint ist ein Recycling historischer Ideen, indem vorhandene Bauten in neue inkorporiert werden. Es kommt vor, dass Neutelings einem Bauherrn gänzlich vom Bauen abrät. Er wütet gegen die auf Holland niedergehende »donnernde Lawine von immer mehr launiger

Un autre bureau d'architectes néerlandais issu de l'Office for Metropolitan Architecture (Neutelings appartient à la même génération que Winy Maas de MVRDV). Les constructions de Neutelings Riedijk sont caractérisées par leur humour : pas du genre tarte à la crème, mais de celui qui fait sourire.

Dans son essai « Sur la paresse, le recyclage, les mathématiques sculpturales et la raison » (« Over de luiheid, recyclage, sculpturale wiskunde en vernuftigheid », Fascinaties/4, Rotterdam), texte délibérément provocateur, Neutelings écrit : « Dans nos projets, nous essayons, avec énormément d'efforts et un succès variable, de faire de la paresse une philosophie du design. » Il préconise en fait un recyclage d'idées historiques en intégrant des édifices existants à de nouvelles constructions. Dans certains cas, il va jusqu'à dissuader un client de construire quoi que ce soit. Il fustige « l'avalanche de mobilier urbain toujours

The entrance is spelt out, hiding a bicycle park.

Große Buchstaben am Eingang verdecken die Fahrradständer.

L'entrée, dont les lettres géantes cachent un abri à bicyclettes.

cheerful street furniture, inimitable public works of art, constantly changing traffic situations and a succession of incomprehensible town plans."
Of course, Neutelings Riedijk are not lazy in the literal sense; but the real work behind their buildings is mostly invisible. It would be terribly easy for them to take a copy of the (onerous) Dutch building regulations and build by the book while conforming to a received contemporary style. Far more imagination and lateral thinking has gone into their work.
Their buildings start with a simple mathematical concept - an oval floor plan (Breda Fire Station), a four-bay housing block, an open square (Veenman Drukkers), a wedge-shape (Harlingen Support Building), a slab and tower (Ij Tower Block, Amsterdam) - then carve away at and embellish it. Facades are continuous skins enveloping the building, giving coherence to disparate parts and the external form a monolithic quality. Printed glass, red brickwork, grey concrete bearing a tyre-print pattern (Maastricht Fire Station), corrugated black concrete panels (Harlingen Support Building) become instantly recognisable icons.

Straßenmöblierung, unnachahmlichen öffentlichen Kunstwerke, sich ständig ändernde Verkehrsführungen und eine Reihe unverständlicher Stadtplanungen.«
Freilich sind Neutelings Riedijk nicht wirklich faul, aber die Arbeit hinter ihren Bauten, die sie ihrer Phantasie und unorthodoxem Denken verdanken, bleibt größtenteils unsichtbar. Es wäre sehr einfach, ein Exemplar der (schwerfälligen) niederländischen Bauverordnungen zu nehmen, nach Buch zu bauen und sich an einen anerkannten zeitgenössischen Stil zu halten.
Neutelings Riedijks Bauten gehen von einfachen geometrischen Formen aus: ein ovaler Grundriss (die Feuerwache in Breda), ein vierteiliger Wohnblock, ein offenes Quadrat (Veenman Drukkers), eine Keilform (Harlingen Support Building), eine Scheibe und ein Turm (Ij Tower Block, Amsterdam), die sie dann verändern und gestalten. Fassaden werden als durchgehende Oberflächen aufgefasst, die das Gebäude einhüllen, seinen Teilen Kohärenz und der äußeren Form monolithische Qualität geben. Bedrucktes Glas, roter Backstein, grauer Beton mit Reifenprofil (Feuerwache Maastricht) und gewellte schwarze Betonplatten (Harlingen Support Building) werden zu Markenzeichen mit hohem Wiedererkennungswert.

plus joyeux, d'inimitables œuvres d'art publiques, de situations de circulation sans cesse changeantes, et un succession de plans d'urbanisme incompréhensibles » caractérisant les Pays-Bas.
Il va de soi que Neutelings et Riedijk ne sont pas paresseux dans le sens conventionnel du terme ; pourtant, le travail effectif qui est à la base de leurs constructions e en majeure partie invisible. Il serait terriblement facile pour eux de se procurer un exemplaire des Règlements néerlandais concernant l'architecture et de construire selon les règles, en se conformant à un style contemporain accepté. Leur travail exige bien plus d'imagination de pensée parallèle.
Leurs réalisations commencent par une forme géométrique simple – plan ovale (poste d'incendie de Breda) ; bloc résidentiel présentant quatre renfoncements ; carr ouvert (imprimerie Veenman Drukkers) ; forme de coin (Bâtiment d'assistance de Harlingen) ; bloc bas et tour (Ensemble Ij, Amsterdam) – qui est ensuite entaillée et sculptée. Les façades sont des enveloppes continues q assurent la cohérence d'éléments disparates tout en dc nant une qualité monolithique à l'extérieur. Verre imprimé, brique rouge, béton gris portant des empreintes de pneus (poste d'incendie de Maastricht), panneaux de béton noir ondulé (Bâtiment d'assistance de Harlingen) deviennent des icônes instantanément reconnaissables

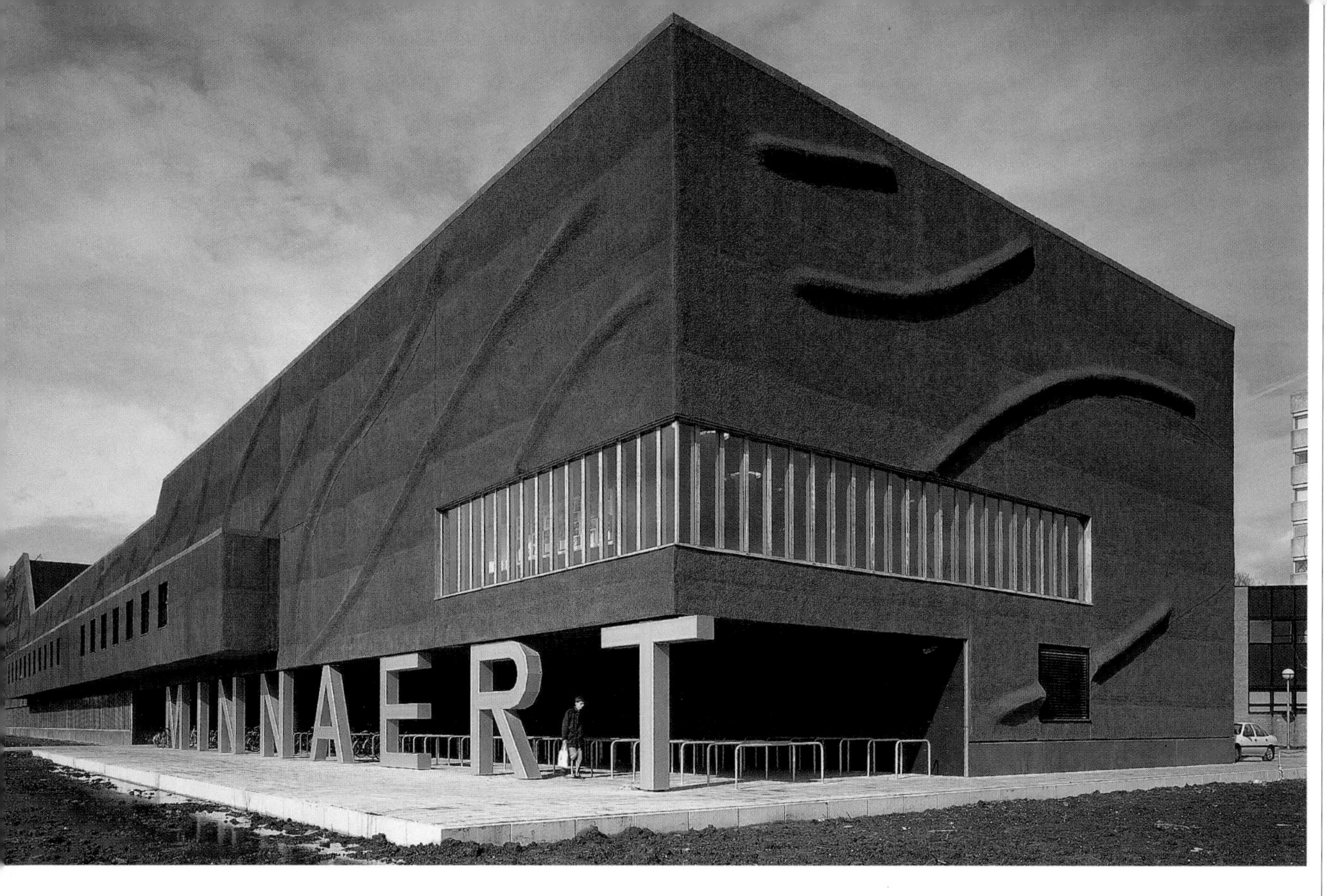

997 University of Utrecht, Netherlands

Minnaertgebouw

ccupying a site in the north-west corner of the Uithof campus of the University of Utrecht, the Minnaertgebouw, named after a famous astrophysicist, houses the mathematics, physics, and geophysics faculties. The much-photographed facade of the building is in sprayed concrete coloured sienna brown. The effect is like elephant hide. The architects had intended to give the building a continuous skin but the fact that only a limited area can be sprayed before the concrete begins to harden means that they have not quite achieved this. Inside, the central hall, the focus for the circulation of the building, is overpowered by an unbounded 10 x 50-m pool, which collects rainwater that comes in through the roof. Water from the pool is pumped around the building as a cooling agent for the air-conditioning system. A dimly lit atmospheric space, the chamber is a peaceful water-garden until it rains; then it reverberates with the sound of falling water. A series of booths containing deep-red velvet banquettes are lined up along one side of the space, cocoons of warmth, light and colour.
The architects comment: "In general, the building is designed around the senses. Sound, smell, humidity, wind, darkness/light and heat/cold area used as architectural instruments."

Das Minnaertgebouw liegt in der nordwestlichen Ecke des Uithof-Campus der Universität Utrecht und ist nach einem berühmten Astrophysiker benannt. Hier sind die Fachbereiche Mathematik, Physik und Geophysik untergebracht. Die oft fotografierte Fassade aus rotbraunem Spritzzement erinnert an Elefantenhaut. Die Architekten hatten ursprünglich vor, dem Bau eine durchgehende Haut zu geben. Diese Idee erwies sich jedoch als nicht durchführbar, da nur eine begrenzte Fläche besprüht werden kann, bevor der Zement zu härten beginnt.
Die zentrale Halle, auf die alle Verbindungswege ausgerichtet sind, wird von einem 10 x 50 m großen Wasserbecken beherrscht, in das das Regenwasser vom Dach fließt, um dann als Kühlungsmittel für die Klimaanlage durch das Gebäude gepumpt zu werden. In dem schwach beleuchteten, stimmungsvollen Raum ist es völlig still, bis es anfängt zu regnen; dann hallt das Geräusch der fallenden Tropfen wider. Eine Reihe von Kabinen mit gepolsterten Bänken in dunkelrotem Samt säumt als von Wärme, Licht und Farbe erfüllte Kokons eine Seite des Raums. Die Architekten bemerken dazu: »Eigentlich wurde das Gebäude um Sinneseindrücke herum entworfen. Geräusch, Geruch, Feuchtigkeit, Wind, Dunkelheit/Licht und Hitze/Kälte werden als architektonische Mittel eingesetzt.«

Construit à l'extrémité nord-ouest du Uithof campus de l'université d'Utrecht, le Minnaertgebouw, du nom d'un célèbre astrophysicien, abrite les facultés de mathématiques, de physique et de géophysique. La façade, souvent photographiée, en béton projeté rouge brun évoque la peau d'un éléphant. Au départ, les architectes se proposaient de revêtir le bâtiment d'une peau continue. Cette idée s'avéra néanmoins irréalisable, vu que l'on ne peut pulvériser qu'une surface limitée avant que le ciment ne commence à durcir.
A l'intérieur, un hall central concentrant la circulation est dominé par une piscine de 10 x 50 m qui recueille l'eau de pluie s'écoulant de la toiture. Cette eau est ensuite pompée dans l'ensemble du bâtiment, où elle sert à la climatisation. Espace atmosphérique faiblement éclairé, cette vaste salle est paisible et silencieuse jusqu'à ce qu'il pleuve ; elle s'emplit alors des multiples échos de l'eau qui tombe. Sur un des côtés, une série d'alcôves meublées de banquettes en velours rouge foncé constituent des cocons de chaleur, de lumière et de couleur. Commentaire des architectes : « Globalement, le bâtiment joue sur les sens. Les sons et les odeurs, l'humidité, le vent, l'obscurité et la lumière, la chaleur et le froid, sont utilisés comme des instruments architecturaux. »

Aerial view of the unconventional building, above; right, study cubicles

Oben: Luftbild des unkonventionellen Gebäudes; rechts Studienkabinen

Vue aérienne de la nouvelle faculté, qui tranche sur son environnement architectural. A droite, les box d'une sal de travail.

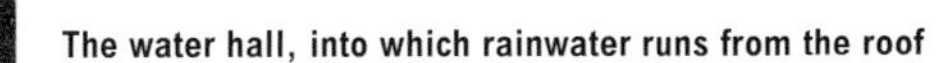

The water hall, into which rainwater runs from the roof

Die Wasserhalle, in die Regenwasser vom Dach fließt

Le grand hall recueillant les eaux pluviales

1999 **Breda, Netherlands**

Fire station

Another textured facade, this time bricks laid like a Hessian weave, wraps around the 6 000-m² complex, making disparate building shapes and outdoor spaces such as a sports field part of the same building mass. Offices are housed in the elongated section that protrudes from the southern edge of the site like a giant eye keeping watch. Bedrooms form two bridges over the garage, minimising the time taken to reach the fire engines, and separated by verdant roof-gardens. Public activities such as the canteen and classrooms are housed in a triangular building next to the offices but with a clear route through to the garage. The oval floor plan helps address Dutch regulations that it should take less than a minute for the fire-fighters to reach their vehicles.

Die Backsteinfassade der 6 000 m² großen Feuerwache von Breda, deren Struktur an Sackleinen erinnert, vereinigt unterschiedliche Gebäudeformen und bezieht auch Außenräume wie die Sportplätze in den Bau ein. Am Südrand des Geländes ragt ein langgestreckter Bürotrakt vor, der einem riesigen wachsamen Auge gleicht. Zwei Brücken mit Schlafräumen überspannen die Garage, was der holländischen Vorschrift Rechnung trägt, nach der die Löschfahrzeuge in weniger als einer Minute zu erreichen sein müssen. Zwischen den Brücken liegen begrünte Dachgärten. Gemeinschaftsräume wie Kantine und Unterrichtssäle sind in einem dreieckigen Bau neben den Büros untergebracht und innerhalb des ovalen Grundrisses durch eine klar erkenntliche Route mit der Garage verbunden.

Une autre façade texturée, cette fois en briques dessinant un motif de tissage, entoure cette Caserne de sapeurs-pompiers de 6 000 m², intégrant des formes architecturales disparates et des espaces extérieurs tels que le terrain de sports dans une même masse architecturale. Les bureaux se trouvent dans la section longue et basse qui s'avance du côté sud du site, tel un œil géant montant la garde. Les chambres forment deux ponts surmontant le garage, dont ils sont séparés par des toits-terrasses verdoyants, ce qui permet de gagner rapidement les véhicules. Les espaces collectifs comme la cantine et les salles de cours, réunis dans un bâtiment triangulaire proche des bureaux, sont reliés au garage par un itinéraire direct. Le plan ovale contribue au respect du règlement, qui prescrit que les pompiers doivent mettre moins d'une minute pour gagner leurs véhicules.

Main facade with offices looking out, far left, side facade, above, and circulation core looking through to fire engines, left

Ganz links: Hauptfassade mit vorkragenden Büros; oben: Seitenansicht; links: zentrales Treppenhaus mit Durchblick auf die Löschfahrzeuge

Page de gauche, la façade principale, dominée par le bloc des bureaux ; ci-dessus, une face latérale ; à gauche, le centre névralgique, donnant accès aux voitures de pompiers

The building is broken down into a series of interlinked blocks and courtyards.

Das Gebäude ist eine Abfolge miteinander verbundener Baublöcke und Innenhöfe.

L'édifice est constitué d'une série de blocs et de cours imbriqués.

Detail of the graphics that characterise the facade

Detail der graphischen Fassadengestaltung

Détail du graphisme caractéristique de la façade

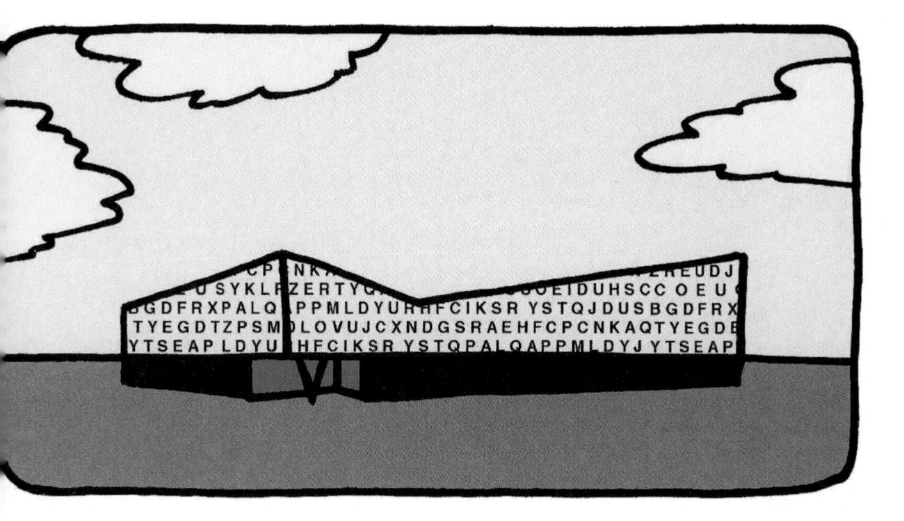

97 Ede, Netherlands

'eenman Drukkers

hough the 4000-m² building houses both offices d printworks for Veenman, it is made to feel like one lding by a continuous elevation that wraps around four sides. In the centre of the plan an open court- d (designed by Dutch landscape architects West 8) rounded by glazed walls provides visual links ween different areas of the building.
facade echoes the function. A text by Dutch poet Schippers is printed in a bold sans-serif typeface on ss panels mounted in a framework similar to that a greenhouse. A bold "Vd" company logo marks the main entrance and is echoed in the shallow V the roof-line. The result is a bold form that acts as D billboard for the company, clearly visible from nearby motorway.

Obgleich der 4000 m² große Bau sowohl die Büros als auch die Druckerei von Veenman Drukkers beherbergt, sind diese unterschiedlichen Bereiche durch die einheitliche Gestaltung aller vier Fassaden außen nicht ablesbar. Ein von den holländischen Landschaftsarchitekten West 8 gestalteter Patio im Zentrum des Grundrisses ist von Glaswänden umgeben und schafft visuelle Verbindungen zwischen den verschiedenen Bauteilen.
Die Fassade spiegelt die Funktion des Bauwerks. Ein Text des holländischen Dichters K. Schippers wurde in einer halbfetten Helvetica auf Glasscheiben gedruckt und in ein Rahmenwerk gefasst, wie man es von Gewächshäusern kennt. Das Firmenlogo »Vd« bezeichnet den Haupteingang und wiederholt sich im flachen V des Dachs. Das Ergebnis ist eine markante Form, die der Firma als dreidimensionale Werbefläche dient und von der nahen Autobahn deutlich zu sehen ist.

Bien que ce complexe de 4000 m² abrite à la fois les bureaux et l'imprimerie de Veenman Drukkers, il doit son unité à une élévation continue entourant ses quatre côtés. Au centre, une cour à ciel ouvert (dessinée par les paysagistes néerlandais West 8) entourée de cloisons vitrées relie visuellement les différentes parties du bâtiment.
La façade reflète la fonction de l'entreprise. Un texte du poète néerlandais K. Schippers est imprimé en caractères gras sans empattement sur des panneaux de verre dont l'encadrement évoque une serre. Le logo de la société, « Vd », marque l'entrée principale, motif repris par la toiture en V ouvert. Cette forme hardie constitue une véritable affiche en relief, nettement visible de l'autoroute qui passe à proximité.

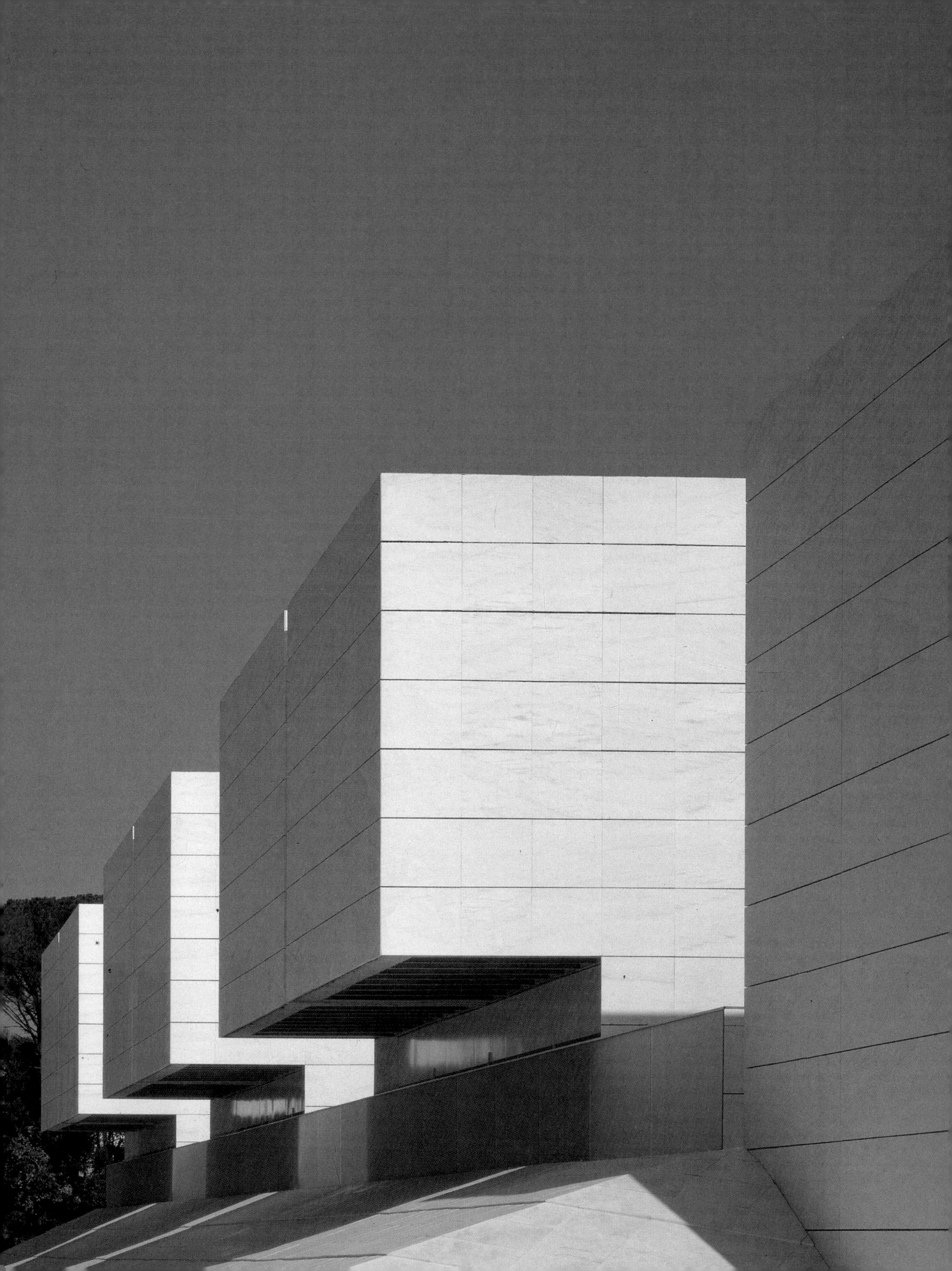

RCR Aranda Pigem Vilalta

sseig de Blay, 34 2on, 17800 Olot (Girona), Spain tel +34 972 269 105 fax +34 972 267 558 e-mail rcr.arquitectes@coac.es

fael Aranda

rn	1961	Olot, Spain
died	1987	Vallés School of Architecture, Barcelona
ctice	1988	co-founded Aranda Pigem Vilalta

rme Pigem

rn	1962	Olot, Spain
died	1987	Vallés School of Architecture, Barcelona
ctice	1988	co-founded Aranda Pigem Vilalta

món Vilalta

n	1960	Vic, Spain
died	1987	Vallés School of Architecture, Barcelona; 1989 Master of Landscape Architecture, Barcelona School of Architecture
vious practice	1987-89	teached at Vallés School of Architecture
	1988	co-founded Aranda Pigem Vilalta

ected projects

nta Aldea Lighthouse	1989	Gran Canaria, Spain
orts stadium	1991	Olot, Spain
sa Margarida	1994	Olot, Spain
trance pavilion to Fageda d'en Jordà	1994	Olot, Spain
hing pavilion	1998	Tussols-Basil, Olot, Spain
v School	1999	University of Girona, Spain
creation and cultural centre	1999	Riudaura, Girona, Spain
sa Mirador	1999	Olot, Spain

e trio live and work in the small town of Olot just tside Girona in Catalonia. Most of their work to date s been in the area. Although Pigem is a professor design and Vilalta is a professor of urbanism and dscape architecture at the Vallés School of Archi-ture in Barcelona, both have distanced themselves m the Barcelona "scene", producing work that is re original.

eir buildings often have a strong horizontal pres-e, like rock strata in the landscape, emphasised

Das Architektentrio lebt und arbeitet in der kleinen katalonischen Stadt Olot nahe bei Girona, wo auch die meisten ihrer bisher realisierten Projekte entstanden. Obwohl Pigem Professor für Entwurfslehre und Vilalta Professor für Stadtplanung und Landschaftsarchitektur an der Vallés-Architekturschule in Barcelona ist, distanzieren sich beide von der dortigen »Szene« und arbeiten ursprünglicher.

Ihre Bauten sind häufig ausgeprägt horizontal ausgerichtet, wie Gesteinsschichten in der Landschaft, ein Eindruck, der von markanten Fassaden aus oxidiertem Stahl,

Le trio vit et travaille dans la petite ville d'Olot, tout près de Gérone, et a surtout construit dans la région. Bien que Pigem enseigne le design, et Vilalta, l'urbanisme et l'architecture de paysage à l'Ecole d'architecture Vallés de Barcelone, tous deux ont pris leurs distances à l'égard de la scène barcelonaise pour réaliser des constructions plus originales.

Leurs bâtiments affirment souvent une puissante horizontalité faisant l'effet de strates rocheuses dans le paysage, soulignée par des façades en acier oxydé, en métal d'un

by facades of oxidised steel, varnished black metal, or white Portland stone. On a small scale, such as the bathing pavilion at Tussols-Basil, their buildings are rich pieces of outdoor sculpture; on a larger scale, such as the Law School of the University of Girona, they have the impact of a lost Inca city.

schwarz lackiertem Metall oder weißem Portlandzement verstärkt wird. Werke in kleinerem Maßstab wie der Badepavillon in Tussols-Basil gleichen differenzierten Freiluftskulpturen; größere Bauten wie die juristische Fakultät der Universität Girona erinnern an verlassene Inkastädte.

noir brillant ou en pierre Portland blanche. A petite éche le, par exemple le pavillon de bains de Tussols-Basil, ce sont des sculptures de plein air ; à une échelle supérieu ils parviennent par exemple à créer l'impression d'une cité inca perdue pour la faculté de droit de l'université d Gérone.

1999 **University of Girona, Spain**

Law School

The steep terrain of the site is evened out by concealed lower floors under ground. The upper floors of the University of Girona Law School leave the impression of a low elegant building defying the true mass of its structure. The interior is organised around three parallel blocks, which are separated by generous courtyards and light wells, pushing out from the side of the building in sober assertive formations. The auditorium facade plays against this, its tall, vertical louvres counterpointing the horizontality of the rest of the building, which is set perfectly perpendicular to the three main blocks. With most of the natural light brought into the core of the building through light wells and courtyards, the exterior facades have been closed, blank expanses of monolithic limestone and white glass that allow the geometric forms of the complex to stand out.

Das steile Baugelände, auf dem sich die juristische Fakultät der Universität von Girona erhebt, wird durch verdeckte unterirdische Geschosse ausgeglichen. Die über Bodenniveau liegenden Etagen verleugnen das tatsächliche Volumen und lassen den Bau flach und elegant wirken. Die Innenräume gruppieren sich um drei durch großzügige Innen- und Lichthöfe getrennte parallele Blöcke, die deutlich aus dem Umriss hervortreten. Die Fassade des Hörsaals bildet mit ihren hohen vertikalen Lamellen ein Gegengewicht zur strengen Horizontalität der Hauptblöcke, die im rechten Winkel zu ihr stehen. Da die Höfe Tageslicht ins Gebäudeinnere lassen, konnten die Außenfassaden als geschlossene glatte Flächen aus Kalkstein und Milchglas gestaltet werden, was die geometrischen Formen des Komplexes unterstreicht.

La forte pente du terrain est compensée en enterrant littéralement les niveaux inférieurs. Les étages supérieurs de la faculté de droit de l'université de Gérone font ainsi l'effet d'un élégant bâtiment bas qui nierait sa propre masse. L'intérieur est structuré autour de trois blocs parallèles séparés par de vastes cours et par des « puits » amenant la lumière, aux formes sobres et puis santes. Les hautes baies à claire-voie de la façade de l'auditorium font contrepoint à l'horizontalité du reste de l'édifice, qui est exactement perpendiculaire aux troi blocs principaux. Comme la lumière du jour entre en majeure partie par les cours intérieures et les puits, les façades extérieures sont aveugles, étendues monolithiques de pierre calcaire et de verre blanc permettant aux formes géométriques du complexe de s'exprimer pleinement.

Classroom blocks project from the main mass, left. Right, internal courtard and light-well.

Links: Die Hörsäle treten als Kuben aus dem Baukörper heraus. Rechts: Der Innenhof lässt Tageslicht eindringe

A gauche : les salles de cours forment des blocs en por à-faux. A droite : une cour intérieure laisse entrer la lumière.

The slope of the site is disguised by partly submerging lower storeys.

Das Gefälle des Geländes wird durch teils unter Bodenniveau liegende Untergeschosse ausgeglichen.

La pente du site est compensée par des niveaux inférieurs en partie enterrés.

Internal circulation space, above, is well lit by natural light. The auditorium projects at right angles to the main horizontal line of the building, left.

Oben: Die Verteilerzonen im Innern erhalten ausreichend Tageslicht. Links: Das Auditorium ragt im rechten Winkel aus dem horizontalen Bau heraus.

Ci-dessus : les espaces de circulation sont généreusement éclairés. A gauche : l'auditorium forme un angle droit avec le corps de bâtiment principal.

Jpper floor plan/ Grundriss Obergeschoss/ Plan du niveau supérieur

1 **courtyard/** Innenhof/ cour
2 **lecture theatre/** Hörsaal/ salle de conférences
3 **teaching block/** Unterrichtsblock/ salles de cours
4 **main stairs/** Haupttreppe/ escalier principal
5 **entrance/** Eingang/ entrée
6 **auditorium/** Auditorium/ auditorium
7 **administration/** Verwaltung/ administration

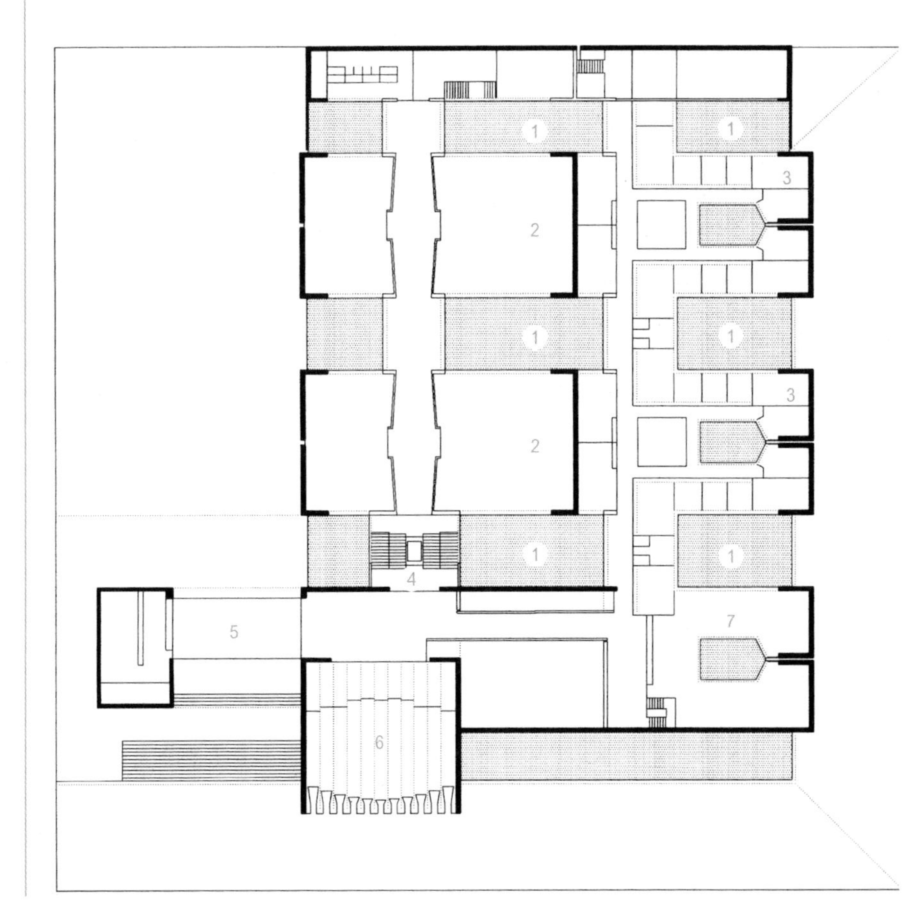

1998 **Tussols-Basil, Olot, Spain**

Bathing pavilion

Perhaps the purest distillation of RCR's architecture, the bathing pavilion is a simple horizontal strip of oxidised steel, the colour of autumn leaves. Blocks of changing modules in stainless steel punctuate the line. Black concrete paving slabs mixed with quartz give a rich texture and moody ambience.

Dieser Badepavillon stellt vielleicht die Essenz von RCRs Architektur dar: ein schlichter horizontaler Streifen oxidierten Stahls in der Farbe von Herbstlaub. Blöcke unterschiedlicher Edelstahlmodule durchbrechen das Band. Bodenplatten aus mit Quarz vermischtem schwarzem Beton schaffen eine vielfältige Textur und stimmungsvolle Atmosphäre.

Représentant peut-être la quintessence de l'architecture de RCR, le pavillon de bains est une simple bande horizontale d'acier oxydé, de la couleur des feuilles d'automne, dont la ligne est ponctuée par des modules d'acier inoxydable de dimensions variables. Le sombre dallage en plaques de béton mêlé de quartz présente une riche texture et génère une ambiance méditative.

The blocks of changing rooms, above, support the roof.

Der Block mit den Umkleideräumen (oben) trägt das Dach.

Les blocs-vestiaires (ci-dessus) soutiennent la toiture.

Oxidised steel roof and black concrete paving slabs blend with their environment.

Das oxidierte Stahldach und der Bodenbelag aus schwarzen Betonplatten passen sich der Umgebung an.

Le dallage en béton noir et la couverture en acier oxydé se fondent dans l'environnement.

Ground plan/ Grundriss/ Plan

1 **changing room/** Umkleideräume/ vestiaires
2 **terrace/** Terrasse/ terrasse

1
1
1
2
0 2.5 5m

Recreation and cultural centre

A new public space for the small town of Riudaura, the horizontality of the recreation centre is a counterpoint to the verticality of another public building, the church. Its main structure is concrete, clad in scales of dark oxidised and varnished steel. Framed by this dark exterior skeleton are white interiors, translucent windows and white stone "lola" benches, designed by the architects, which look like a row of molars. RCR have set the building into its site so that there was space to create a new public square in front.

Das neue Freizeit- und Kulturzentrum der Kleinstadt Riudaura bildet mit seiner Horizontalität ein Gegengewicht zur Vertikalität der benachbarten Kirche. Der Hauptbaukörper aus Beton ist mit Platten aus dunkel oxidiertem, lackiertem Stahl verkleidet. Diese dunkle Außenhaut rahmt die hellen Innenräume und transluzenten Fenster. Die weißen Steinbänke namens »lola«, die an eine Reihe Backenzähne erinnern, sind ebenfalls von RCR entworfen. Das Gebäude wurde auf dem hinteren Teil des Geländes angelegt, um davor einen neuen öffentlichen Platz zu schaffen.

Un nouvel espace culturel conçu pour la petite ville de Riudaura, dont l'horizontalité contraste avec les lignes verticales de l'église. La structure principale est en béton, revêtu d'« écailles » d'acier oxydé et verni, de couleur foncée. Cette peau sombre encadre des intérieurs blancs dotés de fenêtres translucides et meublés de bancs de pierre blanche « lola », conçus par les architectes et évoquant des rangées de molaires. RCR a inséré le bâtiment dans le site de sorte à laisser suffisamment de place pour créer un square à l'avant.

Defiantly monochrome, the recreation centre uses dark oxidised and varnished steel for the exterior cladding, left, contrasted with white interiors featuring "lola" stone benches, above.

Links: Das bewusst monochrom gehaltene Freizeitzentrum ist mit dunkel oxidiertem, lackiertem Stahl verkleidet. Oben: In Kontrast dazu die weißen Innenräume mit den »lola« genannten Steinbänken.

Résolument monochrome, le centre de loisirs est revêtu à l'extérieur d'acier oxydé et peint en noir (à gauche) ; l'intérieur est uniformément blanc, y compris les bancs en pierre « lola » (à droite).

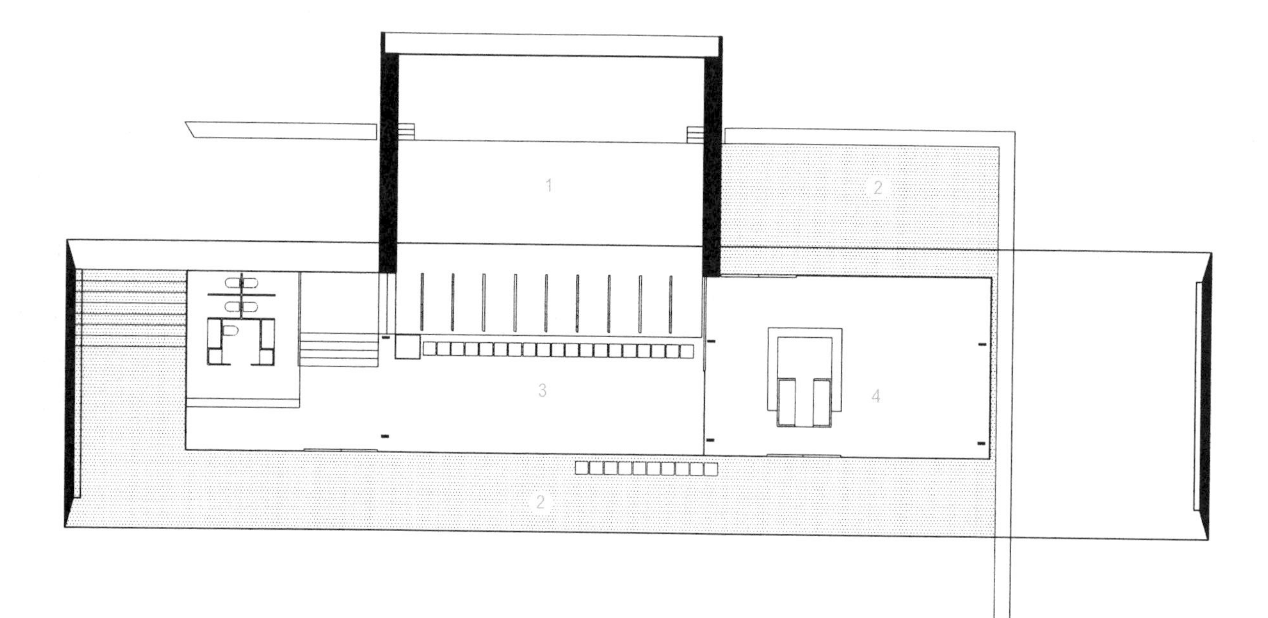

Upper floor plan/ Grundriss Obergeschoss/ Plan du niveau supérieur

1 **hall/** Halle/ hall
2 **terrace/** Terrasse/ terrasse
3 **gallery/** Galerie/ galerie
4 **bar/** Bar/ bar

he low and horizontal building, left; below, ne foyer bar

inks das lang gestreckte, flache Gebäude; unten: ar im Foyer

gauche, le bâtiment bas aux lignes horizontales ; i-dessous, le bar du foyer

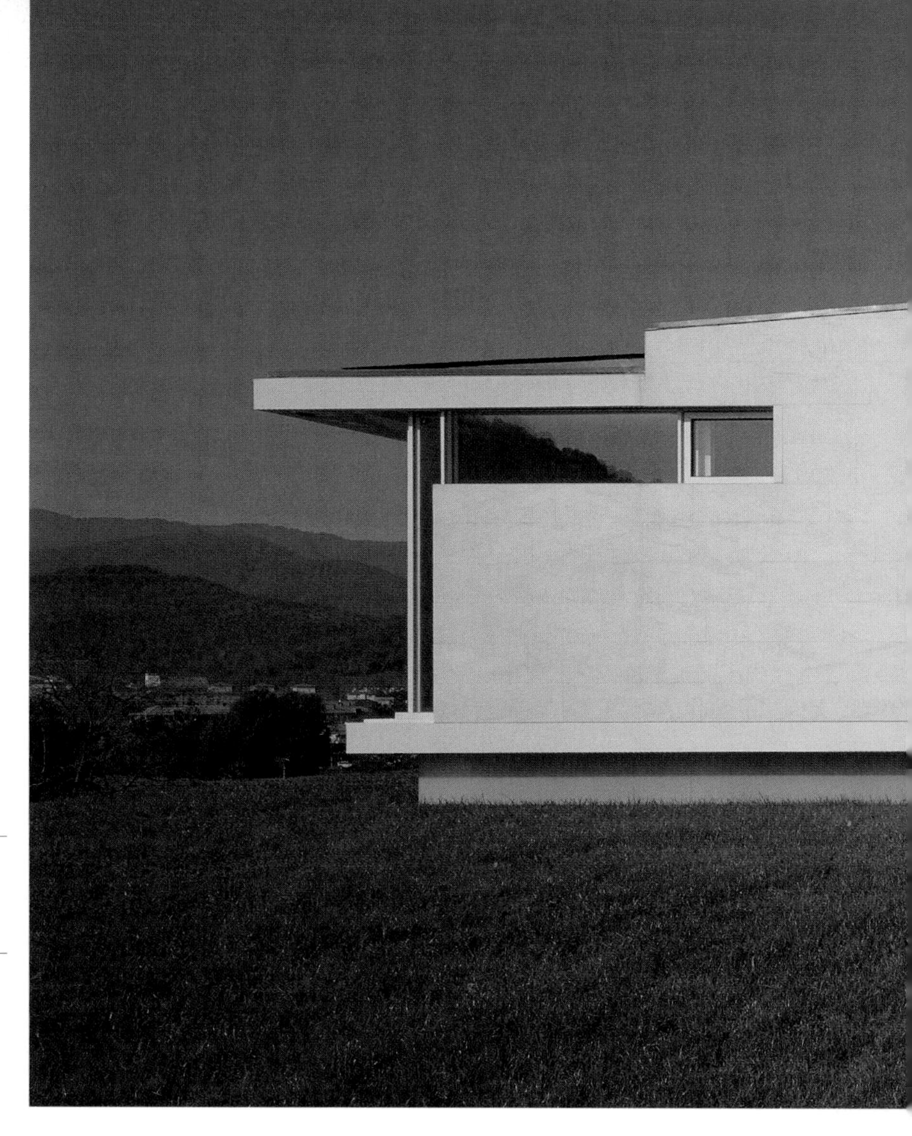

A white stone entrance facade, right. Glazed garden facade, below, with living room on main floor and study half submerged beneath.

Rechts die Eingangsfassade aus weißem Stein; unten die verglaste Gartenfassade mit oben liegendem Wohnraum und halb versenktem Arbeitszimmer.

La façade d'entrée en pierre blanche (à droite). Côté jardin, la maison est entièrement vitrée (ci-dessous). L'espace de vie occupe le niveau principal ; le bureau est en partie caché par la pente du terrain.

999 **Olot, Spain**

Casa Mirador

uilt on a slope, Casa Mirador, or "Viewpoint", makes e most of its elevated location to capitalise on views ıt from the house across the landscape. From the long uthern facade, it is a Miesian pavilion. However, as ıe moves around the building, it becomes more solid ıd complex as planes of white stone frame and close ɔwn views into and through the volume.
ıe building is divided in two along its length by a ɔrridor that runs straight through the plan, separating tchen and gym from living and bedrooms. A glazed wer storey, half dug into the slope of the site, gives e upper storey a certain weightlessness.

An einem Hang errichtet, profitiert die Casa Mirador (»Aussichtspunkt«) von der weiten Aussicht des Bauplatzes. Mit ihrer langen, voll verglasten Südfassade wirkt sie wie ein Mies'scher Pavillon. Bewegt man sich jedoch durch den Bau, so gewinnt er an Masse und Komplexität; weiße Steinflächen rahmen Ausblicke in und durch den Baukörper.
Ein Korridor teilt das Haus der Länge nach und trennt Küche und Sportraum von Wohn- und Schlafzimmern. Das verglaste Tiefgeschoss verschwindet zur Hälfte im Hang und lässt das Obergeschoss fast schwerelos wirken.

Construite sur un versant de colline, la Casa Mirador (« point de vue ») jouit d'un vaste panorama. La longue façade sud, complètement vitrée, lui donne l'aspect d'un pavillon miesien. En parcourant le bâtiment, l'on prend cependant conscience de sa masse et de sa complexité ; les plans de pierre blanche révèlent différentes parties du paysage à l'intérieur et à travers le corps du bâtiment. Celui-ci est divisé dans le sens de la longueur par un couloir séparant la cuisine et la salle de gymnastique du séjour et des chambres. Le niveau inférieur vitré est à demi enterré dans le site abrupt, ce qui donne une grande légèreté au niveau supérieur.

Sancho-Madridejos

os Rosas, 47, Bajo 3 B, 28003 Madrid, Spain tel/fax +34 91 553 6613 e-mail soljc@iberfin.es

l Madridejos Fernández

rn	1958 Madrid
udied	1983 Escuela Técnica Superior de Arquitectura de Madrid (ETSAM)
evious practice	1982-96 worked as Bau Arquitectos
	1997 co-founded Estudio Sancho-Madridejos

an Carlos Sancho Osinaga

rn	1957 San Sebastián, Spain
udied	1982 Escuela Técnica Superior de Arquitectura de Madrid (ETSAM)
evious practice	1982-96 worked as Bau Arquitectos
	1997 co-founded Estudio Sancho-Madridejos

lected projects

llegio Carretas school pavilion	1991 Arganda del Rey, Spain
using Los Rosales	1991 Villaverde, Madrid, Spain (with Javier García García)
n Sebastián de los Reyes sports centre	1996 Madrid, Spain
wn Hall and Civic Centre	1999 San Fernando de Henares, Spain
vic Centre Anabel Segura	1999 Alcobendas, Madrid, Spain
sidence, chapel and hunting pavilion	2000 Valleacerón, Spain

ghly mathematical, the work of Sancho and Madri-jos prides itself on the manipulation of architec-ral components, the interlocking of blocks and voids, d the folding of planes to create three-dimensional apes. Though their buildings appear simple, it is ten impossible to read them correctly from the out-de. Voids and protruding blocks rarely are what ey at first seem. The architects understand the built vironment as a way for mankind to organise its rela-nship to the rest of the world. Architecture is con-dered a means of creating sensitive spaces that bring derstanding and order to society. Their spaces are ulptures that explore the topics of space, density, d tension.

project provides a puzzle of multifaceted fragments d diverse positions which develop into an idea. The ea can be understood in different ways: as a strategy,

Das hoch mathematische Werk von Sancho und Madridejos bedient sich der Manipulation architektonischer Elemente, der Verschränkung von Blöcken und Leerräumen und der Faltung von Flächen, um dreidimensionale Gebilde zu schaffen. Obgleich ihre Bauten einfach erscheinen, ist es häufig unmöglich, sie von außen richtig zu verstehen. Leerräume und vorkragende Blöcke vermitteln auf den ersten Blick meist einen falschen Eindruck von ihrer wirklichen Funktion. Die Architekten verstehen die gebaute Umwelt als Methode, mit deren Hilfe die Menschheit ihr Verhältnis zur Welt ordnen kann. Mit Architektur lassen sich sensitive Räume schaffen, die der Gesellschaft Verständnis und Ordnung geben. Ihre Räume gleichen Skulpturen, die die Themen Raum, Dichte und Spannung ausloten.

»Ein Projekt bringt für uns ein Spiel aus vielfachen Ausschnitten und unterschiedlichen Positionen hervor, die

Hautement mathématique, le travail de Sancho et Madridejos repose sur la manipulation des composants architecturaux, l'emboîtement des pleins et des vides, et le pliage de plans créant des formes tridimensionnelles.

En dépit de l'apparente simplicité de leurs constructions, il est souvent impossible de les lire correctement de l'extérieur. Les vides et les blocs en saillie sont rarement ce qu'ils paraissent. Dans l'optique de Sancho et Madridejos, l'environnement architectural constitue pour les hommes une manière d'organiser leur relation au reste du monde. L'architecture est considérée comme un moyen de créer des espaces « intelligents » apportant ordre et compréhension à la société. Leurs constructions sont des sculptures qui explorent les notions d'espace, de densité et de tension.

« Pour nous, un projet c'est un jeu qui comprend plusieurs facettes et exige diverses attitudes lesquelles engendrent

a design, an approach, a concept ... Essentially, however, it is a concept of space requiring concrete forms, materials and techniques for its realisation. Clarity of conception and the coherence of style are the major interests on which we concentrate our efforts in our projects."

sich zu einer Idee formen. Diese Idee kann man dann unterschiedlich verstehen: als Strategie, Entwurf, Denkweise, Konzept (...). Schließlich jedoch ist es eine Idee vom Raum, die nach Formen, Materialien und einer Technik ruft, um diesen Raum zu konstruieren. Was uns bei unseren Projekten am stärksten interessiert, ist die Klarheit der Konzeption und die Kohärenz der Formensprache – darauf konzentrieren wir unsere Bemühungen.«

une idée. Cette idée peut ensuite se concevoir de diverses manières : comme stratégie, projet, façon de penser, concept (...). Finalement, il s'agit d'une idée de l'espace qui nécessite des formes, des matériaux et une technique pour construire cet espace. Ce qui nous intéresse le plus dans nos projet, c'est la clarté de la conception et la cohérence du langage formel – ceci constitue le but de nos efforts. »

1999 **San Fernando de Henares, Spain**

Town Hall and Civic Centre

The competition-winning design consists of a long white box incorporating the ruin of an 18th-century tapestry factory that stood on the site. Functions are organised into two wings – the council chambers to the north marked by horizontal strips of glazing, the civic centre to the south marked by one glazed storey, joined by the older part of the building as a central uniting force. One very beautiful and unexpected touch is the 8-m^3 void cut out of the main volume. It is lined with thin sheets of onyx, which filter the dappled green light into the corridors of the public areas.

Der siegreiche Wettbewerbsentwurf für das Rathaus und Bürgerzentrum von San Fernando de Henares sah einen lang gestreckten kastenförmigen Baukörper vor, der die Ruine einer ehemaligen Teppichmanufaktur aus dem 18. Jahrhundert einbezieht. Die Funktionsräume sind in zwei Flügeln untergebracht – die Sitzungszimmer des Stadtrats im Norden werden durch horizontale Glasbänder hervorgehoben, das Bürgerzentrum im Süden durch ein rundum verglastes Geschoss, das mit dem älteren Bauteil als zentrales verbindendes Element fungiert. Ein reizvoller und überraschender Aspekt ist der 8 m^3 große Hohlraum, der aus dem Hauptbaukörper geschnitten wurde. Er ist mit dünnen Onyxplatten ausgekleidet, durch die grünlich gesprenkeltes Licht in die Korridore der öffentlichen Bereiche fällt.

Cette mairie et salle municipale, qui avait fait l'objet d'un concours, consiste en une longue boîte blanche intégrant les ruines d'une manufacture de tapis du XVIIIe siècle qui subsistaient sur le site. Les fonctions sont réparties entre deux ailes : au nord, la salle du conseil municipal, caractérisée par des vitrages horizontaux ; au sud, le centre d'activités communales entièrement vitré, qui forme un volume unique avec les bâtiments anciens, force centrale unifiant l'ensemble. Un détail aussi beau qu'inattendu est la découpe de 8 m^3 pratiquée dans le volume principal. Elle est habillée de fines plaques d'onyx qui emplissent les couloirs d'une lumière verdâtre et tachetée.

8 m^3 void cut into the solid side of the building, left; right, the internal corridor

Links der in die geschlossene Seite des Baus eingeschnittene, 8 m^3 große Hohlraum; rechts der innerer Korridor

A gauche, un vide de 8 m^3 entaille le côté du bâtiment ; à droite, le couloir intérieur

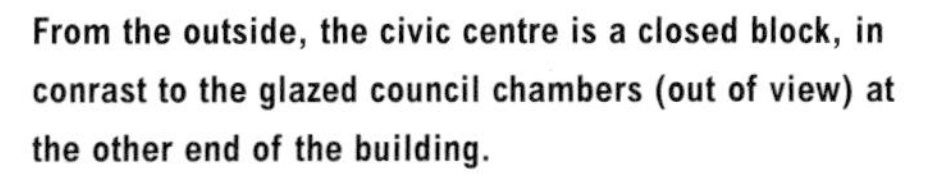

From the outside, the civic centre is a closed block, in conrast to the glazed council chambers (out of view) at the other end of the building.

Von außen erscheint das Bürgerzentrum als geschlossener Block, im Gegensatz zu den hier nicht sichtbaren, verglasten städtischen Büros am anderen Ende des Gebäudes.

De l'extérieur, le centre d'activités communales apparaît comme un bloc aveugle, en contraste avec les bureaux vitrés du conseil municipal (non visible ici) à l'autre extrémité du bâtiment.

Internal circulation behind the onyx screen

Innere Verkehrswege hinter der Onyxwand

Le couloir est recouvert de plaques d'onyx

A glazed box appears to have been dropped into a solid block of stone.

Es scheint, als sei ein gläserner Kasten in den kompakte[n] Steinblock gefallen.

Une boîte en verre qui semble surgie de nulle part est insérée dans le bloc aveugle.

1999 **Alcobendas, Madrid, Spain**

Civic Centre Anabel Segura

Again Sancho and Madridejos begin with a heavy stone box, then cut into it. What appears to be a glass box pushed into the main block is, in fact, the meeting of clerestory windows of the children's library and an outdoor courtyard of the adult library. The visual trickery continues. A glazed lower storey (housing classrooms and a multipurpose hall) makes the stone block appear to be floating rather unnaturally. One end the block is perforated by a grid of small deep-set square windows, making the outer skin of the building seem thick and solid.

Auch beim Bürgerzentrum von Alcobenda bildet eine schwere steinerne Kiste, die eingeschnitten wurde, die Grundlage des Entwurfs. Was aussieht wie ein Glaskasten, der in den Hauptbaublock geschoben wurde, entsteht in Wirklichkeit durch das Aufeinandertreffen der oben liegenden Fenster der Kinderbibliothek und eines Außenhofs der Bibliothek für Erwachsene. Die visuellen Täuschungen setzen sich fort: Ein verglastes Untergeschoss mit Unterrichtsräumen und einer Mehrzweckhalle lässt den Steinblock eher unnatürlich schwebend erscheinen. An einem Ende wird er von einem Raster kleiner, tief liegender Fensterquadrate durchbrochen, die der Außenhaut des Gebäudes eine gewisse Massivität verleihen.

Une fois de plus, Sancho et Madridejos commencent dans ce centre municipal par un massif bloc de pierre, avant de l'entailler. Ce qui ressemble à une boîte en verre enfoncée dans le bloc principal est en fait une forme née de la rencontre des fenêtres à claire-voie de la bibliothèque pour enfants et de la cour extérieure de la bibliothèque des adultes. Le rez-de-chaussée entièrement vitré abritant des salles de classe et une salle polyvalente crée un édifice qui semble flotter de façon irréelle au-dessus du sol. A l'une de ses extrémités, le bloc présente une grille de petites fenêtres carrées profondément enfoncées dans la façade, ce qui donne à celle-ci un aspect solide et compact.

CENTRO CIVICO ANABEL SEGURA

Main entrance, far left, and courtyard, left

Ganz links der Haupteingang; links der Innenhof

Page de gauche, l'entrée principale du centre ; à gauche, le cour

Hunting pavilion, left, and chapel, right

Links der Jagdpavillon, rechts die Kapelle

A gauche, le pavillon de chasse ; à droite, la chapelle

2000 **Valleacerón, Spain**

Residence, chapel and hunting pavilion

The elements of this scheme are scattered across the landscape, different configurations of a folded plane. For the house the plane is bent like a long paper clip, the open end looking out from the slope of the hill. The hunting pavilion is a paper cube with sections of edges pushed back into the volume so that the internal space becomes disjointed. Most spectacular is the chapel, a complex piece of origami developed around a box fold. The irregular interior spaces are dramatic and meditative, with concealed light sources filtering a soft daylight into the enclosed chamber.

Die einzelnen Elemente dieser Anlage, die ein Wohnhaus, einen Jagdpavillon und eine Kapelle umfasst, sind als verschiedenartige Ausformungen einer gefalteten Fläche über die Landschaft verstreut. Das Haus besitzt eine lang gestreckte, an der Kante gefaltete Fläche, deren offenes Ende über den Abhang schaut. Der Jagdpavillon hat die Gestalt eines Papierkubus', bei dem Abschnitte der Ränder zurück in das Innere geschoben wurden und den Innenraum zergliedern. Am imposantesten wirkt die Kapelle, die sich als komplexes Origami aus einer Faltung entwickelt. Die unregelmäßigen Innenräume wirken gleichzeitig spektakulär und meditativ; indirekte Lichtquellen filtern gedämpftes Tageslicht ins Innere.

Les éléments, dispersés dans le paysage, présentent diverses configurations d'un plan replié. Pour la maison, le plan est courbé comme une longue agrafe, dont l'extrémité béante s'ouvre sur la colline. Le pavillon de chasse est un cube en papier dont les bords sont par endroits renfoncés dans le volume, de sorte que la forme extérieure devient discontinue. L'élément le plus spectaculaire est la chapelle, complexe origami tridimensionnel. Les espaces intérieurs irréguliers ont un caractère à la fois dramatique et contemplatif ; des ouvertures cachées baignent l'espace clos d'une douce lumière.

[T]homas Sandell

[sa]ndellsandberg, Riddargatan 17 D 11,
[11]4 57 Stockholm, Sweden

tel +46 8 506 21700 fax +46 8 506 21707 info@sandellsandberg.se www.sandellsandberg.se

[Th]omas Sandell

[Bo]rn	1959 Jakobstad, Finland
[Stu]died	1991 KTH Stockholm
[Pre]vious practices	Jan Henriksson Stockholm
	1989 started up own practice
	1995 set up the multidisciplinary practice sandellsandberg with art director Ulf Sandberg

[Se]lected projects

[Ro]lfs Kök Restaurant	1988 Stockholm, Sweden (with Jonas Bohlin)
[Ev]a Börjesson	1991 Aspö, Sweden
[Ro]dhuset interior design	1991 Stockholm, Sweden (with Love Arbén)
[Ea]st restaurant	1991 Stockholm, Sweden
[Lu]nnberg McCann advertising agency	1992 Stockholm, Sweden
[Lo]we Brindfors advertising agency	1994 Stockholm, Sweden
[Ri]degard restaurant	1994 Stockholm, Sweden
[Ev]a Malm-Hallqvist	1995 Oslo, Norway
[Mo]derna Museet and The Swedish Museum	
[of] Architecture, interior design	1998 Stockholm, Sweden
[Eri]csson St James's Square office	1998 London, UK (through Wingårdhsandellsandberg)
[Wa]llpaper* House	1999 Salone del Mobile, Milan, Italy
[Ha]na Holtblad boutique	1999 Stockholm, Sweden
[Sw]edish Parliament, interior design	2000 Stockholm, Sweden (through Wingårdhsandellsandberg)

[Th]ere is little that is conventional about Sweden's best-[kn]own contemporary designer. Trained as an officer [in] the reserves, Thomas Sandell became an architect [by] accident when he applied to Stockholm's College [of] Architecture on a whim and was accepted. Since [19]95 he has run the multidisciplinary practice sandell-[sa]ndberg with art director Ulf Sandberg (formerly at [Bri]ndfors Advertising and the man behind the Saab [90]0 campaign). The practice is involved in a variety of [cre]ative activities ranging from architecture, interior [an]d furniture design, to advertising, brand develop-[me]nt and exhibitions. The company now employs [ab]out 50 people.

Schwedens bekanntester Designer ist alles andere als konventionell. Der Reserveoffizier kam zufällig zur Baukunst, als er sich aus einer Laune heraus an der Stockholmer Architekturhochschule bewarb und angenommen wurde. Seit 1995 leitet er das multidisziplinäre Büro sandellsandberg zusammen mit Art Director Ulf Sandberg, der früher bei Brindfors Advertising war und maßgeblich an der Anzeigenkampagne für den Saab 900 beteiligt war. Das Büro beschäftigt sich mit einer Vielzahl von Projekten, angefangen mit Architektur, Innenraum- und Möbeldesign bis hin zu Werbung, Markenentwicklung und Ausstellungen. Thomas Sandell hat als führende Persönlichkeit des zeitgenössischen schwedischen Designs großen Einfluss und

Le plus célèbre designer suédois contemporain est certes tout sauf conventionnel. Après une formation d'officier de réserve, Thomas Sandell devint architecte en quelque sorte par hasard, lorsqu'il se présenta par caprice au concours d'entrée de l'Ecole d'architecture de Stockholm et fut accepté. Depuis 1995, il dirige le bureau multidisciplinaire sandellsandberg avec le directeur artistique Ulf Sandberg (ex-collaborateur de l'agence Brindfors Advertising, il réalisa la campagne publicitaire de la Saab 900). Le bureau se consacre à des activités créatrices variées, de l'architecture et du design d'intérieur et de meubles à la publicité et à l'organisation d'expositions.

Thomas Sandell is seen as the leading light in current Swedish design, and is very influential and much copied. Rolfs Kök (designed with Jonas Bohlin in 1988) kick-started Stockholm's designer restaurant boom; he embraces traditional Scandinavian design, in his interiors as well as in his furniture - simple spaces and lots of blond wood, which has helped a younger generation of Swedish designers to rediscover their heritage.
He is also the chairman of SAR, the National Association of Swedish Architects. In the tradition of Alvar Aalto and Gunnar Asplund, he is becoming as well known for his architecture as for his furniture, with commissions from leading international companies such as SCP, Cappellini, Artek, B&B Italia and Ikea.

wird oft kopiert. Rolfs Kök, 1988 mit Jonas Bohlin entworfen, setzte einen Boom von Designer-Restaurants in Stockholm in Gang. Sandells Interieurs und Möbelentwürfe eignen sich mit schlichten Räumen und viel hellem Holz das traditionelle skandinavische Design an – eine Entwicklung, der sich die jüngere Generation schwedischer Designer anschloss.
Sandell ist auch Vorsitzender des Nationalen Schwedischen Architektenbundes SAR. In der Tradition von Alvar Aalto und Gunnar Asplund ist er allmählich für seine Architektur ebenso bekannt wie für seine Möbelentwürfe, die er für internationale Firmen wie SCP, Cappellini, Artek, B&B Italia und Ikea entwickelt.

Sandell est considéré comme le meilleur designer de Suède ; il exerce une grande influence et est abondamment copié. Rolfs Kök (conçu avec Jonas Bohlin en 198 a lancé à Stockholm la vogue des restaurants de décorateurs. Tant pour les intérieurs que pour le mobilier, il reste fidèle au design scandinave traditionnel : des espaces simples et beaucoup de bois clair, qui ont aidé la jeune génération de designers suédois à redécouvrir leur héritage.
Il est également président de la SAR, l'Association nationale des architectes suédois. Dans la tradition d'Alvar Aalto et de Gunnar Asplund, il est aussi célèbre pour ses meubles que pour son architecture, et réalise des commandes pour de grandes entreprises internationales telles que SCP, Cappellini, Artek, B&B Italia et Ikea.

Canteen "Bloni's Bar" for the architecture museum with specially designed lights and furniture

»Bloni's Bar« im Architekturmuseum mit eigens entworfenen Leuchten und Möbeln

Le « Bloni's Bar » du musée d'architecture ; les lampes et le mobilier ont été dessinés par l'architecte.

1998 **Stockholm, Sweden**

Moderna Museet and The Swedish Museum of Architecture, interior design

Sandell received official recognition in 1995 when he was commissioned to design the interiors and furniture for Stockholm's new modern art and architecture museum. The art museum's "Kantyn Moneo" (named after the architect of the new building, Rafael Moneo) is conceived as a "sunny porch" washed in white light. Big round tables of glazed birch make people feel at ease whether they are eating alone or in a crowd, while long banquette tables in the children's area also can be used for guest dinners. Specially designed light fittings include delicate white pendent bells and some framed round refectory trays. Continuing the neutral colour palette, the library is green and the bookshop grey.
In the architecture museum, a converted barrack adjacent to the newly built art museum, spaces have been opened up to make them lighter and more inviting. A small cafe, more intimate than that of the art museum, is lined with specially designed dimpled tiles designed by Pia Törnell that are wonderfully tactile.

Sandell erlangte internationale Anerkennung, nachdem er 1995 mit der Gestaltung der Innenräume und der Möblierung von Stockholms neuen Museen für moderne Kunst und Architektur betraut wurde. Die »Kantyn Moneo« (benannt nach dem Architekten des neu erbauten Kunstmuseums, Rafael Moneo) ist als eine in weißes Licht getauchte »Sonnenveranda« konzipiert. Große runde Tische in polierter Birke schaffen eine behagliche Atmosphäre; durchgehende Tische in einem speziell für Kinder eingerichteten Bereich können auch für Empfänge genutzt werden. Als Beleuchtungskörper dienen eigens entworfene elegante weiße Hängeglocken und runde Tabletts mit einer mittig angebrachten Glühlampe. In Fortsetzung der neutralen Farbwahl ist die Bibliothek in Grün-, die Buchhandlung in Grautönen gehalten.
Das Architekturmuseum ist neben dem neu erbauten Museum in einem ehemaligen Militärgebäude untergebracht, dessen Räume vergrößert wurden, um sie lichter und einladender zu gestalten. Ein kleines Café, intimer als das des Kunstmuseums, ist mit von Pia Törnell eigens entworfenen geriffelten Kacheln ausgekleidet.

Sandell a été reconnu officiellement en 1995, lorsqu'il fut chargé de dessiner l'intérieur et le mobilier des nouveaux musées d'art moderne et d'architecture de Stockholm. Le « Kantyn Moneo » (nommé d'après Rafael Moneo, l'architecte du nouveau musée d'art) est conçu comme un « porche ensoleillé » baigné de lumière blanche. De grandes tables rondes en bouleau verni mettent les gens à l'aise, qu'ils mangent seuls ou en groupe, et les longues tables avec bancs du coin des enfants peuvent également servir pour des réceptions. Les lampes, délicates clochettes blanches, intègrent également quelques plateaux ronds du self-service, spécialement encadrés. Dans la même gamme de couleurs neutres que le reste du musée, la bibliothèque est traitée dans des tons verts et la librairie est en gris.
Au musée d'architecture, caserne réhabilitée adjacente au nouveau musée d'art, les espaces ont été ouverts pour les rendre plus clairs et plus accueillants. Un petit café, plus intime que celui du musée d'art, est habillé d'un carrelage au contact étonnant spécialement dessiné par Pia Törnell.

BRICKOR
BESTICK

Self-service counter in the cafeteria of the architecture museum

Selbstbedienungstheke der Cafeteria im Architekturmuseum

Le comptoir du self-service dans la cafétéria du musée d'architecture

1999 **Salone del Mobile, Milan, Italy**

Wallpaper* House

A prototype mass-produced 117-m² weekend house, which was designed for international lifestyle magazine "Wallpaper*", shown at Milan's Salone del Mobile in 1999 and subsequently sold through the magazine. Sandell calls it his "inside-out house" because of the ambiguous boundaries between indoors and outdoors. Exterior walls continue around the corner at the entrance and into the house; windows wrap around corners; floors become walls; ceilings become windows to another world. At the heart of the floor plan is an open courtyard on to which opens a Zen-style bathroom, with a full view of the courtyard but screened from the entrance and everywhere else inside the house.

The aesthetic is deliberately neutral so that it would be suitable for a variety of locations, though allusions to traditional Scandinavian buildings, Japanese architecture and modernist style are detectable. Black-painted fir panels create a strong facade emphasising the dramatic roof-line, contrasting with a front facade of opalescent plastic, which is neither concealing nor revealing.

White interiors offer a calm serenity. An open-plan living space extends along one side of the house, the roof soaring up over an airy lounge. The master bedroom is no more than a mattress enclosed by four walls with an enlarged photograph of a Swedish birch forest (or any other motif of the client's choosing) on the ceiling.

Das Wallpaper* House ist der Prototyp eines serienmäßig produzierten Wochenendhauses von 117 m², das im Auftrag des internationalen Lifestylemagazins »Wallpaper*« entworfen und auf der Mailänder Möbelmesse 1999 gezeigt wurde. In der Folge wurde das Haus über das Magazin vertrieben.

Wegen seiner Verschränkung von Innen- und Außenraum nennt Sandell es sein »umgekrempeltes Haus«. Wie in einer anderen Welt werden Außenwände im Innern fortgeführt, Fenster umziehen Ecken, Böden werden zu Wänden, Decken zu Fenstern. Ein Zen-Bad ist von den anderen Bereichen des Hauses abgeschirmt und gibt den Blick frei auf den offenen Innenhof im Zentrum des Grundrisses.

Das Haus ist bewusst schlicht gestaltet, damit es sich für eine Vielzahl von Standorten eignet, obwohl Anklänge an traditionelles schwedisches Bauen, japanische Architektur und die Moderne erkennbar sind. Die Fassade mit ihren schwarz gestrichenen Kieferpaneelen unterstreicht die prägnante Dachform und kontrastiert mit der Front aus opakem Kunststoff, die das Innere weder verhüllt noch preisgibt.

Die weiß gehaltenen Innenräume haben eine heitergelassene Atmosphäre. Über dem offenen Wohnbereich schwingt sich das Dach nach oben. Das Hauptschlafzimmer beschränkt sich auf eine von vier Wänden umgebene Matratze, über der eine vom jeweiligen Eigentümer zu wählende Fotografie an der Decke angebracht ist.

Ce prototype d'une maison de week-end de 117 m² destinée à être fabriquée en série, a été conçu pour le magazine international « Wallpaper* ». Après avoir été exposée en 1999 au Salone del Mobile de Milan, la maison est vendue par l'intermédiaire du magazine. Sandell l'appelle sa « maison dehors-dedans » à cause des limites ambiguës entre intérieur et extérieur. Les murs extérieurs dessinent un angle au niveau de l'entrée et se prolongent dans la maison ; les fenêtres épousent les coins du bâtiment ; les planchers deviennent des cloisons et les plafonds deviennent des fenêtres ouverte sur un autre monde. Au cœur de la maison, une cour à ciel ouvert donne sur la salle de bains zen, qui est par ailleurs invisible depuis les autres pièces.

L'esthétique est délibérément neutre afin de pouvoir s'adapter aux sites les plus divers ; elle contient néanmoins de délicieuses allusions à l'habitat scandinave traditionnel, à l'architecture japonaise et au style moderniste. Des panneaux de sapin peints en noir mettent en valeur la forme frappante de la toiture, contrastant avec la façade principale en plastique opalescent qui ne cache ni ne révèle vraiment les intérieurs blancs, lesquels créent une ambiance calme et sereine. Un espace de vie à plan ouvert s'étend sur un des côtés, la toiture se dressant hardiment au-dessus du salon clair et spacieux. La chambre principale n'est en fait qu'un matelas entouré de quatre cloisons, le plafond étant orné d'une grande photo d'une forêt de bouleaux (ou de tout autre motif choisi par le client).

The prototype house at the Milan furniture fair. View of entrance facade.

Prototyp-Haus auf der Mailänder Möbelmesse (Eingangsfassade)

La maison-prototype au Salon de l'ameublement de Milan ; vue de la façade.

THOMAS SANDELL

Living room, above, with chairs designed by Sandell for B&B Italia. Right, rear facade clad in black painted fir to emphasise the inverted roofline.

Oben: Wohnraum mit den von Sandell für B&B Italia entworfenen Stühlen. Rechts: Die mit schwarzer Fichte verschalte Rückseite unterstreicht die markante Dachform.

Ci-dessus : le séjour, avec les sièges dessinés par Sandell pour B&B Italia. A droite, la face postérieure, revêtue de sapin teinté en noir pour souligner la toiture à pente inversée.

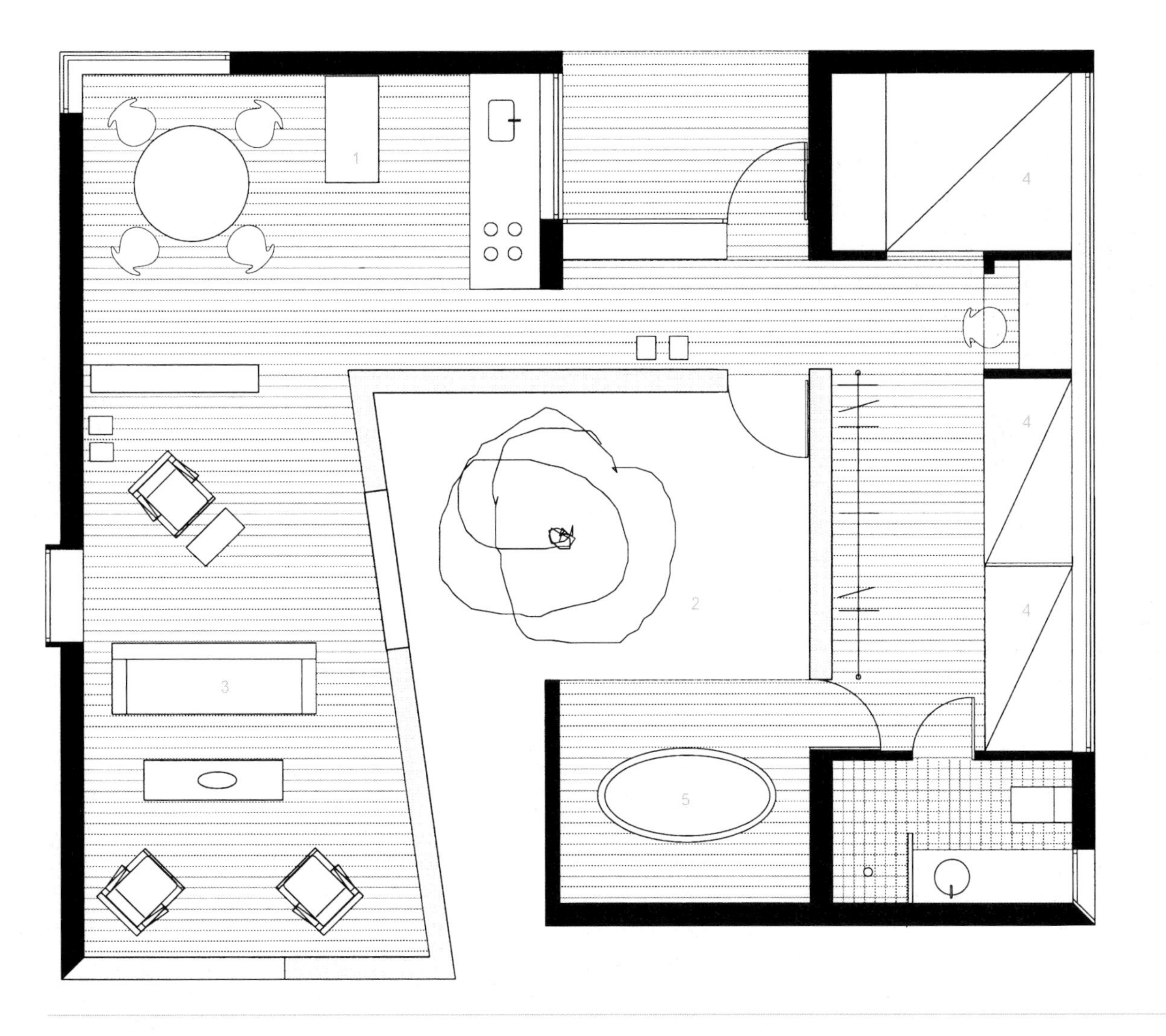

Ground floor plan/ Erdgeschossgrundriss/ Plan du rez-de-chaussée

1 **kitchen/** Küche/ cuisine
2 **courtyard/** Innenhof/ cour
3 **living room/** Wohnraum/ séjour
4 **bed/** Bett/ lit
5 **bathroom/** Bad/ bain

Shop floor with rough oak display table and cash desk

Ladenetage mit Auslagetischen aus unbehandelter Eiche und Kassentisch

Vue partielle du magasin : tables-présentoirs en chêne brut et caisse

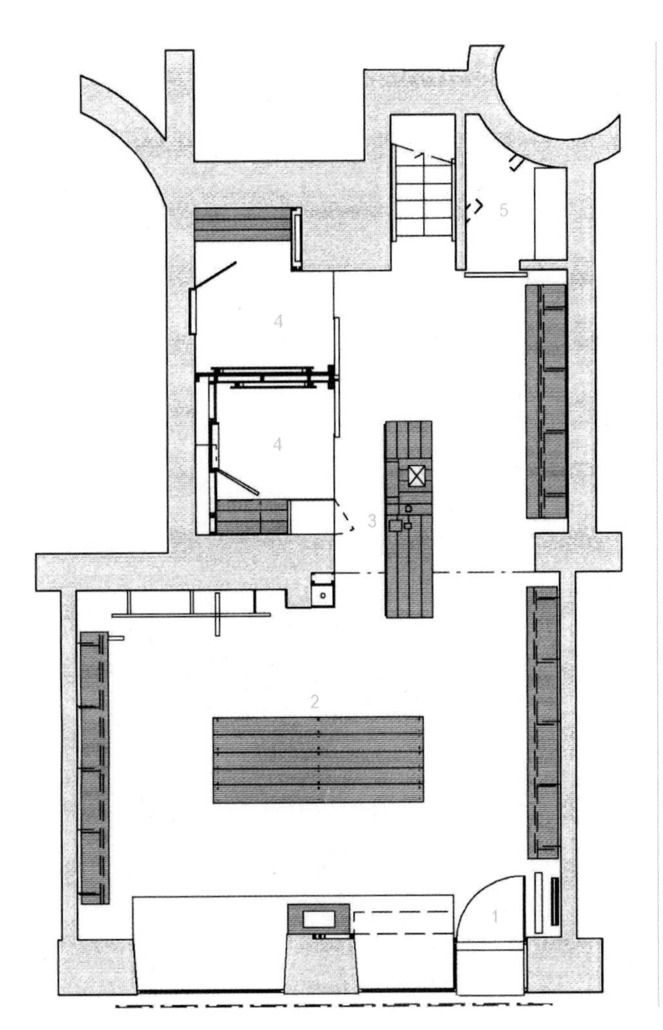

Ground floor plan/ Grundriss/ Plan

1 **entrance/** Eingang/ entrée
2 **display table/** Auslagetisch/ présentoir
3 **cash desk/** Kassentisch/ caisse
4 **changing rooms/** Umkleidekabinen/ cabines d'essayage
5 **store/** Lager/ espace-boutique

1999 **Stockholm, Sweden**

Anna Holtblad boutique

In this store for Sweden's leading young fashion designer Anna Holtblad (also Sandell's partner), the emphasis is on the clothes. In her designs Holtblad works with materials and textures: therefore the interior was to be kept as simple as possible. The walls are painted white, the floor is a terrazzo tile with wide grouting, and the ceiling has smooth oak panelling. Bandsawn oak display cases are deliberately raw to contrast with the luxury of the clothes.

Bei der Boutique für Sandells Partnerin Anna Holtblad, Schwedens führender junger Modedesignerin, dreht sich alles um die Kleider. Da Materialien und Strukturen in Holtblads Entwürfen eine wichtige Rolle spielen, sollte der Raum selbst möglichst schlicht gehalten sein. Die Wände wurden weiß verputzt, der Boden mit breit gefugten Terrazzofliesen belegt, die Decke mit poliertem Eichenholz verschalt. Bandgesägte Eichendisplays sind in bewusstem Kontrast zu den luxuriösen Kleidungsstücken naturbelassen.

Dans cette boutique réalisée pour la jeune dessinatrice de mode Anna Holtblad (qui est également l'associée de Sandell), tout est fait pour mettre les vêtements en valeur. Comme Anna Holtblad accorde une grande importance aux matériaux et aux textures de ses modèles, l'architecture devait être aussi simple que possible. Les murs sont peints en blanc, les sols sont en carrés de terrazzo avec de larges joints, et le plafond est lambrissé de panneaux de chêne poncés. Les présentoirs en chêne scié au ruban sont délibérément bruts afin de contraster avec le luxe des vêtements.

Schneider + Schumacher

hleusenstraße 17, 60327 Frankfurt am Main, Germany tel +49 69 2562 6262 fax +49 69 2562 6299 e-mail schneider+schumacher@schneider-schumacher.com
web www.schneider-schumacher.com

l Schneider

rn	1959 Koblenz, Germany
udied	1986 University of Kaiserslautern; Staatliche Hochschule für Bildende Künste Städelschule, Frankfurt am Main
evious practice	Eisele + Fritz, Darmstadt; Prof. Robert Mürb, Karlsruhe
	1988 set up practice with Michael Schumacher

chael Schumacher

rn	1957 Krefeld, Germany
udied	1985 University of Kaiserslautern; 1986 Staatliche Hochschule für Bildende Künste Städelschule, Frankfurt am Main
evious practice	Foster and Partners, London; Braun & Schlockermann, Frankfurt am Main
	1988 set up practice with Till Schneider
aching	1999 visiting professor Städelschule, Frankfurt am Main

lected projects

Walter Thompson advertising agency	1995	Frankfurt/Main, Germany
fo-Box	1995	Berlin, Germany
MG offices	1998	Leipzig, Germany
aun AG headquarters	2000	Kronberg im Taunus, Germany
bus office and hotel	2001	Düsseldorf, Germany
esthafen Tower	2002	Frankfurt/Main, Germany

e relationship between function and appearance primary in Schneider + Schumacher's work, demon- rating a balance between practicality and aesthetic npact. This quality has attracted creative commercial ients such as J. Walter Thompson and Braun, and eir bright-red Info-Box on Potsdamer Platz injected me fun into Berlin's huge development zone. Big ojects are beginning to come their way, and in 2002 eir Westhafen Tower will add a new landmark to the ankfurt skyline.
-tech glazed facades are a favourite device, perhaps be expected of Schumacher, who has worked in the fices of Foster and Partners, giving their buildings transparency that makes them easy to read from out- de, but can also be used to bring light into deep floor

Die Beziehung zwischen Funktion und Erscheinungsbild, genauer gesagt ein ausgewogenes Verhältnis von Funktionalität und ästhetischer Wirkung, spielt im Werk von Schneider + Schumacher eine herausragende Rolle. Das wirkt anziehend auf kreative Wirtschaftsunternehmen wie J. Walter Thompson und Braun, die zu ihren Auftraggebern zählen. Die knallrote Info-Box auf dem Potsdamer Platz verhalf Berlins bekanntester Großbaustelle zu einem witzigen Farbtupfer. Inzwischen ist das Büro mit größeren Aufgaben betraut, und im Jahr 2002 wird ihr Westhafen Tower als neues Markenzeichen die Frankfurter Skyline ergänzen.
Schumachers Tätigkeit im Büro Foster and Partners mag ihre Vorliebe für Hightech-Glasfassaden erklären. Die Transparenz ihrer Bauten macht diese nicht nur von

La relation entre fonction et apparence joue un rôle essentiel dans le travail de Schneider + Schumacher, l'objectif étant de trouver un équilibre entre utilité pratique et impact esthétique. Cette qualité a attiré des entreprises créatrices telles que J. Walter Thompson et Braun, et leur « Info-Box » rouge vif de la Potsdamer Platz de Berlin a introduit un accent ludique dans cette gigantesque zone de développement. Des commandes importantes commencent à arriver ; en 2002, leur Westhafen Tower ajoutera un nouveau repère au panorama de Francfort.
Les façades vitrées high-tech sont une de leurs solutions favorites, ce qui n'est pas vraiment surprenant de la part d'anciens collaborateurs de Foster and Partners (Michael Schumacher). Cela donne à leurs constructions une transparence qui les rend facilement lisibles de l'extérieur, tout

plans and to promote solar energy, thereby addressing another of the practice's concerns, energy efficiency. Schneider + Schumacher describe their approach to architecture as "poetic pragmatism". "There may be several technical solutions to solve the same problem, but maybe only one that has also got a certain poetic aspect, flair or unexpected point of view. It is this one aspect that we are trying to find."

außen leicht verständlich, sondern dient auch der Belichtung weit innen liegender Bereiche; zudem befürworten sie als Vertreter einer effizienten Nutzung von Ressourcen den Einsatz von Solarenergie. Schneider + Schumacher beschreiben ihre Auffassung von Architektur als »poetischen Pragmatismus«. »Für die Lösung ein und desselben Problems kann es verschiedene technische Möglichkeiten geben, aber vielleicht hat nur eine von diesen eine gewisse Poesie, Flair oder einen überraschenden Blickwinkel. Diesen einen Aspekt versuchen wir zu finden.«

en amenant la lumière du soleil jusqu'au centre d'édific de grande largeur, ce qui correspond à leur souci d'une gestion efficace de l'énergie. Schneider + Schumacher qualifient leur approche de l'architecture de « pragmatisme poétique » : « Il existe sans doute plusieurs solution techniques pour résoudre le même problème, mais peut être une seule qui aura un certain aspect poétique, un style ou point de vue inattendu. C'est cet aspect-là que nous nous efforçons de trouver. »

nfo-Box

rlin's now famous Info-Box began as a competi-n-winning design for a temporary visitors centre Potsdamer Platz to keep people informed of the ogress on what was, at the time, the biggest build-g site in Europe. Schneider + Schumacher's solution s a three-storey red box, which sits 7 m above the ound on concrete-filled steel legs. The box is 23 m gh, 62 m long and 15 m wide, and was built on a dget of 10 million DM. Clad in weatherproof steel nels, it is cut with four large glazed openings that eate unusual views into and through the structure, nphasising the sense of a single floating box rather an a conventional multi-storey building. Inside it uses 2 230 m² of flexible exhibition space and amen-es on three simple levels. A steel staircase zigzags the outside to the popular roof-terrace 22 m above e ground, which provides spectacular views of the ichstag and the new Berlin.

the time of writing, the Info-Box was still scheduled be demolished at the end of 2000, though there are forts to preserve it as a symbol of reunification and e optimism of the time.

Berlins inzwischen berühmte Info-Box nahm ihren Anfang als siegreicher Entwurf in einem Wettbewerb für ein temporäres Besucherzentrum auf dem Potsdamer Platz, um die Öffentlichkeit über die Fortschritte auf der damals größten Baustelle Europas auf dem Laufenden zu halten. Die rote Box ist 23 m hoch, 62 m lang und 15 m breit und wurde für ein Budget von 10 Millionen DM errichtet. Schneider + Schumacher schufen kein herkömmliches mehrgeschossiges Gebäude, sondern eine dreistöckige, mit wetterfestem Stahl verkleidete Box, die auf 7 m hohen betongefüllten Stahlstützen über dem Erdboden zu schweben scheint. Sie öffnet sich mittels vier großer Glasflächen, die ungewöhnliche Ein- und Durchblicke erlauben und den Eindruck des Schwebens verstärken. Im Innern finden auf drei Ebenen 2 230 m² flexibler Ausstellungsfläche und verschiedene ergänzende Einrichtungen Platz. Außen führt eine zickzackförmige Stahltreppe auf die viel besuchte Dachterrasse in 22 m Höhe, von der aus sich spektakuläre Blicke auf den Reichstag und das neue Berlin bieten.

Ob die Info-Box wie ursprünglich geplant Ende 2000 abgerissen wird oder als Symbol der Wiedervereinigung und des Optimismus jener Tage erhalten bleibt, ist zur Zeit noch unklar.

La désormais célèbre Info-Box de Berlin avait fait l'objet d'un concours pour construire sur la Potsdamer Platz un centre d'acccueil provisoire destiné à informer le public des progrès de ce qui était à l'époque le plus important chantier de construction d'Europe. La solution proposée par Schneider + Schumacher était une boîte rouge sur trois niveaux, surélevée de 7 m par des piliers en acier emplis de béton. La « boîte » haute de 23 m, longue de 62 m et large de 15 m a été construite en respectant un budget de 10 millions de marks. Revêtue de panneaux d'acier, elle présente quatre grandes baies vitrées autorisant des vues surprenantes sur l'intérieur de la structure et à travers celle-ci, ce qui renforce l'impression d'un unique volume suspendu et non d'un édifice conventionnel à plusieurs étages. Les trois niveaux totalisent 2 230 m² d'espaces d'expositions modulables et de services. Un escalier extérieur en acier montant en zigzag à l'extérieur permet d'accéder au toit-terrasse, à 22 m au-dessus du sol ; offrant des vues spectaculaires sur le Reichstag et le nouveau Berlin, il est devenu très populaire.

A la date où nous écrivons, il est toujours prévu de démolir l'Info-Box à la fin de l'an 2000, en dépit de tentatives pour préserver ce symbole de la réunification et de l'optimisme de l'époque.

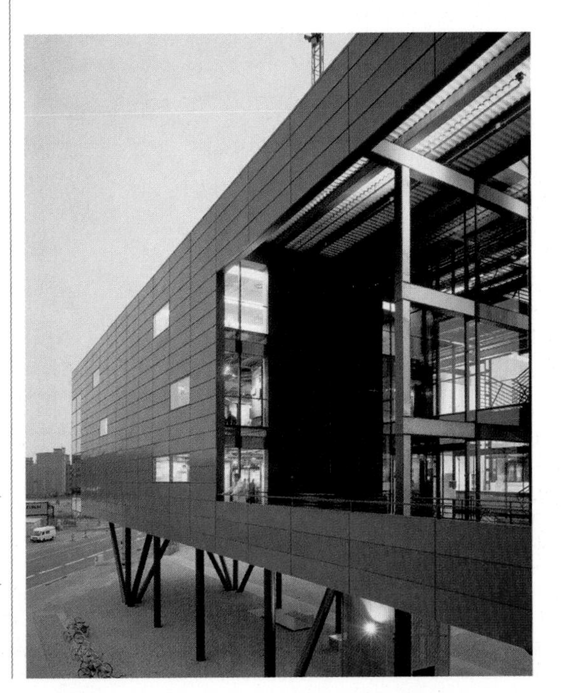

e bright red Info-Box has been focal to Potsdamer atz as the new developments have sprung up around.

e knallrote Infobox war Mittelpunkt des Potsdamer atzes, während um sie herum Großbauten entstanden.

nfo-Box rouge vif de la Potsdamer Platz accrochait les gards à l'époque où n'existait autour d'elle qu'un vaste antier.

ZUBLIN
B GW 338
RZ DR 341

The three-storey box sits on piloti 7 m above the ground.

Die dreigeschossige Box steht auf Stützen 7 m über dem Boden.

La « boîte » à trois niveaux est portés par des pilotis de 7 m de haut.

Left, entrance from ground level. Below, the low-budget exhibition space is used to inform people of the capital's massive regeneration work.

Links: Blick vom Boden auf den Eingang; unten: Im kostengünstig ausgestatteten Innern kann man sich über die umfangreichen Bauvorhaben Berlins informieren.

A gauche : l'accès se fait par des escaliers. Ci-dessous : l'intérieur, aux matériaux « pauvres », sert de centre d'informations sur le plus grand chantier de Berlin.

Left, glazed atrium. Right, at the corner the building appears narrower than it is, adding drama.

Links das verglaste Atrium. Rechts: Die schmal wirkend Ecklösung gibt dem Bau Prägnanz.

A gauche : l'atrium vitré. A droite, le coin du bâtiment semble plus étroit qu'il ne l'est en réalité, ce qui crée un effet surprenant.

1998 **Leipzig, Germany**

Offices for KPMG

Schneider + Schumacher have used a difficult triangular corner site to create drama. The main body of the building has been made narrower than necessary for the confines of the site, bringing it to an acute angle on the corner road junction. The floor plan is then filled out by a transparent box added along one side but held back from the corner, used to house two staircases. Inside, four floors of offices are arranged around a triangular glazed atrium that rises up through the heart of the building, bringing natural light into the core of the deep floor plan.

Schneider + Schumacher gelang es, auf einem schwierig zu bebauenden dreieckigen Eckgrundstück ein höchst markantes Bürogebäude für die Firma KPMG zu schaffen. Der Hauptbau nimmt nicht die gesamte Grundstücksbreite ein, sondern ist so konzipiert, dass sich an der Straßenkreuzung ein spitzer Winkel ergibt. Zurückgesetzt von dieser Ecke wurde dem Gebäude auf einer Seite eine transparente Box mit zwei Treppenhäusern angefügt. Im Innern des Hauptbaus umlagern vier Bürogeschosse ein dreieckiges gläsernes Atrium im Zentrum des Gebäudes, das die weitläufigen Ebenen mit Tageslicht versorgt.

Schneider + Schumacher ont utilisé un difficile site triangulaire pour créer un effet dramatique. Le corps de bâtiment principal, encore plus étroit que le site ne l'exigeait, forme un angle aigu à l'intersection de deux rues. D'un côté, vient s'y ajouter une boîte transparente légèrement en retrait qui abrite deux escaliers. A l'intérieur, quatre étages de bureaux sont disposés autour d'un atrium vitré triangulaire qui s'élève au cœur du bâtiment, amenant la lumière du jour jusqu'aux pièces les plus éloignées de la façade.

eft, detail of glazed circulation wing. Above, the nodern building imposes itself on its low-key eighbours.

inks: Detail des verglasten Treppenhauses. Oben:)er moderne Bau hebt sich von seinem unscheinbaren Jmfeld ab.

gauche : un détail de la cage d'escalier vitrée. ;i-dessus : le bâtiment contraste vivement avec les ieux immeubles qui l'entourent.

A 66 m-long glazed facade acts as animated advertisement for the agency, left. Below left, street facade.

Links: Die 66 m lange Glasfassade fungiert als belebte Werbefläche für die Agentur; links unten die Straßenfassade.

La façade vitrée longue de 66 m (à gauche) constitue une sorte de réclame animée pour l'agence de publicité. En bas à gauche, la façade sur rue.

1995 **Frankfurt/Main, Germany**

J.Walter Thompson advertising agency

The concept behind the offices of advertising agency J. Walter Thompson in Frankfurt am Main is a giant shop window. The 66 m-long glazed hanging facade exposes everything about the building: structure, circulation, occupants. The south-facing facade, which benefits from views of the docks, is protected from excessive sunlight by partial shade from cantilevered balconies. A long steel staircase slashes diagonally across the facade just behind the glass connecting six floors. Outdoor terraces, conference rooms and a cafeteria are located on the roof.

Das Bürogebäude der Werbeagentur J. Walter Thompson in Frankfurt am Main ist als riesiges Schaufenster konzipiert, dessen 66 m lange gläserne Vorhangfassade den Blick auf Konstruktion, Wegeführung und das Geschehen im Innern freigibt. Eine alle sechs Geschosse verbindende lange Stahltreppe verläuft diagonal vor der Fassade unmittelbar hinter dem Glasvorhang. Die Südfassade mit Blick auf die Hafenanlagen wird an einigen Stellen durch vorkragende Balkone vor zu starker Sonneneinstrahlung geschützt. Auf dem Dach befinden sich offene Terrassen, Konferenzräume und eine Cafeteria.

Le concept de base de l'agence de publicité J. Walter Thompson est une gigantesque vitrine. Le mur-rideau vitré long de 66 m révèle tous les aspects du bâtiment : structure, circulation, occupants. La façade sud, qui bénéficie d'une vue sur les docks, est protégée d'un ensoleillement excessif par des balcons cantilever. Un long escalier en acier desservant les six niveaux traverse la façade en diagonale juste derrière la paroi de verre. Sur le toit, des terrasses voisinent avec des salles de conférences et une cafétéria.

Thompson and Rose Architects

1430 Massachusetts Avenue, Cambridge, MA 02138, USA tel +1 617 876 9966 fax +1 617 876 9922 e-mail tranet@ibm.net web www.thompsonandrose.com

Maryann Thompson

born	1960	Cincinnati, Ohio, USA
studied	1983	Princeton University; 1988 Harvard University Graduate School of Design

Charles Rose

born	1960	New York, NY, USA
studied	1983	Princeton University; 1987 Harvard University Graduate School of Design

Selected projects

Atlantic Center for the Arts	1996	New Smyrna Beach, Florida, USA
Bartholomew County Veterans Memorial	1997	Columbus, Indiana, USA
Barn at Staitsview Farm	1997	San Juan Island, Washington, USA
Gulf Coast Museum of Art	1999	Largo, Florida, USA
Amphitheater and Bathhouse	1999	Acton, Massachusetts, USA
Gayhead Residence	2000	Martha's Vineyard, Massachusetts, USA
Paint Rock Camp	2000	Hyattville, Wyoming, USA
Weinstein Residence	2000	New York, NY, USA
Campus Center for Brandeis University	2001	Waltham, Massachusetts, USA

Thompson and Rose relate architecture strongly to its landscape and environmental conditions. Their buildings seem reluctant to impose upon their surroundings yet manage to enrich the experience of them. The Atlantic Center for the Arts buildings slide back into the Florida jungle, leaving space to appreciate the canopy of trees. The Gulf Coast Museum of Art, with its river walks and shaded colonnades, provides vantage points from which to view its botanic garden setting. The Gayhead Residence on Martha's Vineyard is organised around a series of terraces from which to enjoy views of the Vineyard Sound.
"We are interested in creating an architecture that 'sees' its site - an architecture that stands in relationship to its surroundings, heightens the experience and effect on the natural conditions that are at work on the site and focuses, orients or reorients one's perception of the site," say Maryann Thompson and Charles Rose.

Thompson and Rose setzen ihre Architektur konsequent in Bezug zu Landschaft und Umgebung. Die Bauten scheinen sich nur widerstrebend ihrer Umgebung aufzudrängen und bereichern deren Erfahrung. Die Gebäude des Atlantic Center for the Arts gleiten zurück in die subtropischen Wälder Floridas und lassen Raum, das Blätterdach der Bäume zu genießen. Das Gulf Coast Museum of Art bietet mit seinen Wasserläufen und schattigen Kolonnaden Aussichtspunkte in den umgebenden botanischen Garten. Das Haus Gayhead auf Martha's Vineyard ist um eine Folge von Terrassen mit Blick auf den Vineyard Sound organisiert.
Maryann Thompson und Charles Rose: »Wir wollen eine Architektur schaffen, die ihr Gelände ›sieht‹ – eine Architektur, die in Beziehung zu ihrer Umgebung steht, die Erfahrung der natürlichen Gegebenheiten des Geländes verstärkt und unsere Wahrnehmung konzentriert, orientiert und neu ausrichtet.«

L'architecture de Thompson and Rose est fortement reliée au paysage et au contexte. Leurs édifices semblent hésiter à s'imposer à leur environnement, tout en permettant une perception plus riche de celui-ci. L'Atlantic Center for the Arts s'insinue dans la jungle de Floride en laissant suffisamment d'espace pour admirer la voûte des arbres. Le Gulf Coast Museum of Art se déploie tel un balcon sur le jardin botanique, dont il permet d'apprécier la beauté. A Acton, Massachusetts, un amphithéâtre et des bains publics ponctuent le paysage. Une maison privée à Martha's Vineyard est constituée d'une série de terrasses, avec des vues sur le Vineyard Sound.
Pour citer Maryann Thompson et Charles Rose : « Nous cherchons à créer une architecture qui ‹ voit › son site : une architecture en relation avec son environnement, qui nous rend plus sensibles aux forces naturelles à l'œuvre sur le site, et focalise, oriente ou modifie notre perception de ce dernier. »

The museum as seen from the botanic gardens, above. Right, a covered walkway runs along the edge of the site.

Oben: Ansicht des Museums vom botanischen Garten. Rechts: Ein überdachter Fußweg verläuft am Rand des Geländes.

Ci-dessus: le musée vu du jardin botanique. A droite: une allée piétonnière couverte longe le site.

Gulf Coast Museum of Art

A ca. 4600 m² regional museum and arts centre set within an 32-ha botanical garden forming part of the area's plans for an integrated group of cultural institutions. The campus includes exhibition galleries for the museum's permanent collections, and studio classrooms for teaching a variety of arts and crafts. Strongly linear parallel blocks are separated by intimate gardens and sculpture gardens. A sinuous colonnade runs along the edge of the site parallel to the waterway, sheltered by a lightweight steel structure. Walking along this path one enjoys views of the botanical garden, and is aware of the activities in the classrooms that open on to it.
Awnings, tall roof-lights and clerestories provide protection from the strong Florida sun, creating interior spaces filled with a cool, soft light from the north.

Das etwa 4600 m² große Regionalmuseum und Kunstzentrum liegt in einem 32 ha großen botanischen Garten und ist Teil einer geplanten Gruppe von Kulturinstitutionen. Zum Campus gehören Galerieräume für die ständige Sammlung des Zentrums und Lehrateliers für verschiedene künstlerische und kunsthandwerkliche Techniken.
Die Räumlichkeiten sind in deutlich linearen parallelen Blöcken untergebracht, zwischen denen idyllische Gärten und Skulpturengärten liegen. Eine mit einer leichten Stahlkonstruktion überdachte, gewundene Kolonnade begleitet einen Wasserlauf am Rand des Geländes. Von hier aus bietet sich Aussicht auf die Gärten und die Tätigkeit in den Lehrateliers, die sich zur Kolonnade öffnen.
Markisen, hohe Oberlichter und Obergadenfenster bieten Schutz vor der heißen Sonne Floridas und schaffen Innenräume mit kühlem, gedämpftem Nordlicht.

Ce musée communal et centre d'arts d'environ 4600 m², situé dans un jardin botanique de 32 ha, s'intégrera à un groupe d'institutions culturelles projetées par la région. Le campus comporte des salles d'exposition pour les collections permanentes du centre, et des ateliers pour l'enseignement de diverses disciplines artistiques et artisanales.
Il est constitué de deux blocs linéaires parallèles, séparés par un jardin de sculptures intime. Une colonnade sinueuse protégée par une légère structure en acier longe le bord du site et de la rivière. En suivant cette promenade, le visiteur bénéficie de vues du jardin botanique tout en étant conscient des activités des salles de cours situées à proximité.
Des auvents, de hautes lucarnes et claires-voies donnant au nord protègent de l'ardent soleil de Floride et créent des espaces intérieurs baignés par une lumière froide et atténuée.

Light is filtered down into the galleries by tall roof lights.

Durch hoch liegende Oberlichter fällt Tageslicht in die Galerien.

Les bandeaux de verre de la haute toiture éclairent les salles d'expositions

Above, the canopy over the main entrance slices through the covered walkway. Right, gallery space.

Oben: Das Vordach des Haupteingangs unterbricht den überdachten Fußweg. Rechts: Ausstellungsraum.

Ci-dessus : le dais indiquant l'entrée principale surplombe l'allée couverte. A droite, une salle d'exposition.

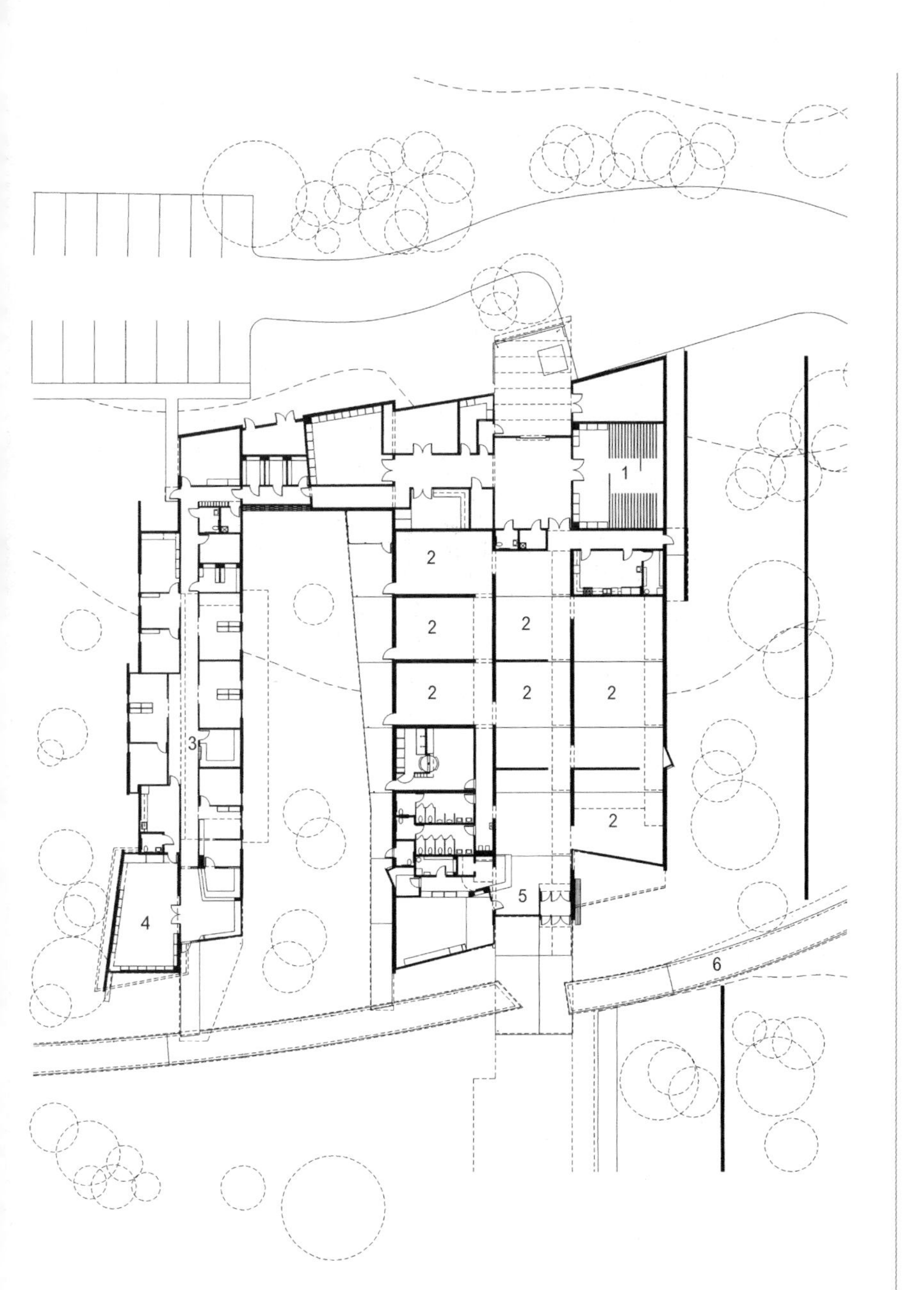

Site plan/ Grundriss der Anlage/ Plan du site

1 **store room/** Lagerraum/ entrepôt
2 **galleries/** Galerien/ salles d'exposition
3 **offices/** Büros/ bureaux
4 **library/** Bibliothek/ bibliothèque
5 **entrance/** Eingang/ entrée
6 **covered walkway/** überdachter Weg/ allée piétonnière couverte

Dance studio; steel awnings will eventually be overgrown by foliage.

Das Tanzstudio; die stählerne Markise wird vermutlich irgendwann überwachsen sein.

La salle de danse ; la pergola en acier sera bientôt recouverte par la végétation.

1996 **New Smyrna Beach, Florida, USA**

Atlantic Center for the Arts

The campus is a labyrinth of seven buildings knitted into the jungle, linked by a boardwalk that threads its way through the landscape. Simple wooden buildings clad in stained cedar are deliberately low key. The architects conceived the project as a series of open spaces between buildings rather than as a series of masses. As intended in much of their work, the architecture is to be experienced by moving through it rather than looking at it.
Each building is designed to house a separate art form and is tailored to its needs - a black-box theatre; painting and sculpture studios with generous north-facing windows under sloping roofs; a light airy dance studio gently lit through a clerestory window of sandblasted glass with a clear glazed strip below the mirrors for views of the tactile vegetation.
The tropical climate has been addressed with louvres subduing direct light, large glass walls maximising northern light, hopper windows, wind scoops and large linear rain scuppers. The surrounding trees are used to create a shady canopy, shedding soft, dappled light over the complex.

Der Campus des Atlantic Center for the Arts gleicht einem in den Dschungel geflochtenen Labyrinth aus sieben Gebäuden, die ein Holzsteg verbindet, der sich durch die Landschaft schlängelt. Die einfache Holzbauten sind mit gebeizter Zeder verkleidet und bewusst schlicht gehalten. Die Architekten verstanden das Projekt nicht als eine Gruppe massiver Volumina, sondern als Folge offener Räume zwischen Gebäuden. Wie vielen ihrer Bauten liegt auch diesem die Idee zugrunde, Architektur weniger durch Betrachten als in der Bewegung durch sie hindurch zu erfahren.
Jedes Gebäude wurde für eine eigene Kunstform entworfen und auf ihre jeweiligen Bedürfnisse zugeschnitten – ein Theater, Maler- und Bildhauerateliers mit großen Nordfenstern unter schrägen Dächern und ein helles, luftiges Tanzstudio, das gedämpftes Licht durch hoch liegende, sandgestrahlte Fenster erhält und unter den Spiegeln einen Klarglasstreifen besitzt, der Blick auf die Vegetation erlaubt.
Dem tropischen Klima entsprechen Jalousien, die den direkten Lichteinfall dämpfen, großflächige Verglasungen an der Nordseite, Kippflügelfenster und große, lineare Regenabzüge. Die umgebenden Bäume bilden ein Schatten spendendes Dach, das die Anlage in gedämpftes Licht taucht.

Le campus de l'Atlantic Center for the Arts est un labyrinthe de sept bâtiments insérés dans la jungle et réunis par une passerelle en bois qui se faufile à travers le paysage.
Les bâtiments en bois habillés de cèdre teinté sont délibérément simples et discrets. Les architectes ont pensé le projet comme une série d'espaces ouverts entre les bâtiments plutôt que comme une succession de masses. Trait commun à nombre de leurs réalisations, il ne suffit pas de regarder l'architecture de l'extérieur; pour la sentir réellement, il faut s'y promener.
Chaque bâtiment est consacré à une forme d'art spécifique, et est conçu en fonction de ses besoins ; une boîte aveugle pour le théâtre ; des ateliers de peinture et de sculpture avec des plafonds rampants et de vastes baies donnant au nord ; un clair et spacieux atelier de danse doucement éclairé par une fenêtre en verre dépoli et, sous le miroir, une bande de verre transparent permettant de voir la végétation.
Le climat tropical a été pris en considération : ouvertures à claire-voie atténuant la lumière directe, pare-soleil, baies vitrées donnant au nord, larges dalots pour l'évacuation des pluies. Les arbres environnants créent un dais diffusant une lumière douce et intermittente sur le complexe.

Above and below right, lead-coated copper roofs tilt towards each other, protruding above the treetops. Above right, the dance studio.

Oben und rechts unten: Mit Blei überzogene Kupferdächer neigen sich gegeneinander und überragen die Baumwipfel. Rechts oben das Tanzstudio.

Ci-dessus et en bas à droite : les toits monopans en cuivre recouvert de plomb, dont les pentes se répondent. En haut à droite, la salle de danse.

Outer pillars are rough-cut, left. Inside, smooth surfaces are inscribed with the writings of the dead soldiers.

Links: Die äußeren Pfeiler sind nur grob behauen. Rechts: In die glatten Flächen im Innern sind Notizen der gefallenen Soldaten eingemeißelt.

A gauche : à l'extérieur, les piliers sont bruts ; sur leur face intérieure polie sont inscrites des réflexions de soldats disparus (à droite).

1997 **Columbus, Indiana, USA**

Bartholomew County Veterans Memorial

A forest of 25 rough-hewn pillars, carved with the names, dates, letters and diary passages of local soldiers who died in 20th-century wars. The outer surface of the rock-cut limestone is intended to be read as a single monumental block, with individual columns disappearing directly into the earth. Inside, surfaces are smooth, and the intimate spaces create an emotionally charged sanctuary for meditation. As one meanders between the columns, the narrowness of the passage forces the eye upward to the sky.

Das Bartholomew County Vetreans Memorial ist ein Wald aus 25 grob behauenen Pfeilern, in die Namen, Daten, Briefe und Tagebuchausschnitte von Soldaten aus der Gegend geritzt sind, die in Kriegen des 20. Jahrhunderts fielen. Die kantigen Kalksteinpfeiler sollen als je ein monumentaler Block verstanden werden, wobei einzelne Pfeiler unmittelbar in die Erde versenkt sind. Im Innern sind die Oberflächen glatt poliert, und die intimen Räume laden mit ihrer emotional dichten Atmosphäre zur Meditation ein. Bewegt man sich zwischen den Pfeilern, so leiten enge Durchgänge den Blick unwillkürlich zum Himmel.

C'est une forêt de 25 poteaux en roche calcaire qui portent les noms et les dates de naissance et de mort de soldats de la région tombés au cours des guerres du XXᵉ siècle, ainsi que des extraits de leurs lettres et journaux intimes. L'extérieur rugueux, grossièrement taillé, est destiné à être lu comme un unique bloc monumental ; quelques colonnes s'enfoncent directement dans le sol. A l'intérieur, les surfaces sont lisses et des espaces intimes créent un sanctuaire à forte charge émotionnelle, invitant à la méditation. Tandis que l'on suit un trajet sinueux entre les colonnes, l'étroitesse du passage contraint à lever les yeux vers le ciel.

Mike Tonkin

1 Goodsway, London NW1 1UR, UK tel +44 20 7837 6255 fax +44 20 7837 6277 e-mail tonkin@zoo.co.uk

Mike Tonkin	
born	1960 Leek, UK
studied	Leeds Polytechnic 1983; Royal College of Art, London 1986
previous practice	Nigel Coates, London; Eva Jiricna, London; Rock Townsend, London
	1994 set up own practice

Selected projects		
Q restaurant	1995	Hong Kong, China
Tong Zhi	1996	Hong Kong, China
Broadway Cinema	1996	Hong Kong, China
Private I hair salon	1997	Hong Kong, China
Lane Crawford store	1997	Hong Kong, China
Hugo House	1997	Hong Kong, China
FLEX	1997	Hong Kong, China
Rhomberg Apartment	1997	Hong Kong, China
Budokan restaurant	1998	Bristol, UK
Camera and Jewel House	2000	London, UK

Mike Tonkin set up his practice almost by accident in 1994 when an around-the-world-trip found him in Hong Kong at the time of the Asian boom and UK bust. Having completed an impressive body of work in the former colony, particularly in the areas of retail, clubs, bars, and housing, Tonkin moved back to the UK in 1998.

The Tonkin design principle is "asking, looking, playing, making". The team begins any commission by playing with the associations coming up from the building's function. "We have a story-telling approach," says Tonkin. "We try to find a new way of approaching every subject by sitting down and asking 'what is it?', 'what was it?', 'what does it want to be?' and playing with these concepts. We see the building as a vehicle for the meaning of something that goes beyond what it is on the surface."

The results are a completely blood-red interior for Broadway Cinema (working on the premise that the

Die Gründung von Mike Tonkins Büro 1994 ist der Tatsache zu verdanken, dass er sich zur Zeit des asiatischen Baubooms und der gleichzeitigen Flaute in England auf einer Weltreise in Hongkong befand. Nachdem er dort eine beachtliche Zahl von Bauten – überwiegend Läden, Clubs, Bars und Wohnhäuser – geschaffen hatte, zog Tonkin 1998 zurück nach England.

Tonkins Entwurfsprinzip lautet: »fragen, schauen, spielen, machen«. Am Anfang eines jeden Auftrags setzt sich das Team spielerisch mit den sich aus der Funktion des Baus ergebenden Assoziationen auseinander. »Wir nähern uns einem Thema auf erzählerische Weise«, sagt Tonkin. »Wir versuchen einen neuen Zugang zu finden, indem wir uns zusammen setzen und fragen ›Was ist das?‹, ›Was war das einmal?‹, ›Was möchte das sein?‹, und dann spielen wir mit diesen Konzepten. Wir verstehen das Gebäude als Träger einer Bedeutung, die unter der Oberfläche liegt.«

Ergebnisse sind das blutrote Interieur des Broadway Cinema in Hongkong (ausgehend von der Annahme, dass das

Mike Tonkin a ouvert son bureau en 1994 presque par hasard, lorsque, au cours d'un voyage autour du monde, il se retrouva à Hong Kong au moment du boom asiatique et de la dépression britannique. Après avoir réalisé un nombre impressionnant de constructions dans l'ancienne colonie, en particulier dans les domaines du commerce de détail, des clubs et bars, et du logement, Tonkin a regagné le Royaume-Uni en 1998.

Le précepte de Tonkin : « poser des questions, regarder, jouer, réaliser ». L'équipe aborde chaque commande en jouant avec les associations suscitées par la fonction du bâtiment. « Nous avons une approche narrative, explique Tonkin. Nous essayons de trouver une nouvelle manière d'aborder un thème en nous demandant, ‹ qu'est-ce que c'est ?›, ‹ qu'est-ce que c'était ?›, ‹ qu'est-ce que ça veut devenir ?› ; et en jouant avec ces concepts. Nous considérons le bâtiment comme le véhicule d'une signification qui va au-delà de la surface. » Les résultats sont un intérieur entièrement rouge sang pour le cinéma Broadway

first theatre was a fight to the blood); the fantasy world of Private I hair salon hung with a forest of paper curls; a studio for the Japanese graphic design company Fontworks that uses a slate floor as a reference to the traditional Chinese ink bowl.
Though strong patterns and wild designs feature strongly in Tonkin's portfolio, his architecture is not just cosmetic, but shows profound spatial awareness, creating spaces that relate to each other and are exciting to move through. The Lane Crawford ladies' fashion boutique uses a circuit board for its plan of counters and display cases, then mirrors it in the ceiling. The Hugo house considers the relationship between rooms and how they penetrate each other. A house under construction near Malaga, Spain, brings a pool into the living room, and another in North London sets up two volumes that face each other across a courtyard.

erste Schauspiel ein blutiger Kampf war); die Phantasiewelt des Friseursalons Private I, der voller Papierlocken hängt; das Atelier der japanischen Grafikagentur Fontworks, das als Bezug auf die traditionelle chinesische Tintenschale mit einem Schieferboden ausgestattet ist.
Obwohl prägnante Muster und verrückte Designs in Tonkins Werk eine große Rolle spielen, ist seine Architektur nicht oberflächlich, sondern zeugt von enormem Raumverständnis, indem sie Räume schafft, die aufeinander bezogen und reizvoll zu erfahren sind. Die Lane Crawford Boutique für Damenmode orientiert sich in der Anordnung der Verkaufstische und Vitrinen an einer Leiterplatte, die sich in der Decke spiegelt. Das Hugo House beschäftigt sich mit der Beziehung zwischen Räumen ihrer gegenseitigen Durchdringung. Ein im Bau befindliches Haus bei Malaga holt den Pool ins Wohnzimmer, ein weiteres in North London stellt zwei Baukörper an einem Innenhof einander gegenüber.

(partant de la prémisse que le premier spectacle était un combat inexorable) ; l'univers fantastique du salon de coiffure Private I, orné d'une forêt de boucles en papier ; un atelier pour la société japonaise de design graphique Fontworks, utilisant un dallage en ardoise se référant à l'encrier chinois traditionnel.
Bien que les motifs vigoureux et les designs déchaînés occupent une place de choix dans les réalisations de Tonkin, son architecture n'est pas uniquement décorative, mais témoigne d'une profonde conscience spatiale ; elle crée des volumes reliés entre eux dont la découverte est fascinante. Le magasin de mode Lane Crawford utilise pour les comptoirs et vitrines une disposition évoquant un circuit imprimé, qui est réfléchie par le plafond. La maison Hugo explore la relation et l'interpénétration des différentes pièces. Une maison en construction aux environs de Malaga fait entrer la piscine dans la salle de séjour ; une autre, édifiée à Londres Nord, se compose de deux volumes situés de part et d'autre d'une cour.

1997 **Hong Kong, China**

FLEX

FLEX bar is conceived as a "cave for men", a series of intimate spaces broken by boxy stalactites that contain video screens, and stalagmites. Cutaways and concealed back lighting give the impression of an abstract interior hewn from a solid block.

Die Bar FLEX ist als »Höhle für Menschen« gedacht, als Abfolge intimer Räume, unterbrochen von kastenförmigen Stalaktiten, in denen Videomonitore untergebracht sind, und Stalagmiten. Einschnitte in den Wänden und indirekte Beleuchtung erwecken den Eindruck eines abstrakten, aus einem massiven Block gehauenen Interieurs.

Le bar FLEX est conçu comme une « caverne pour hommes » : une succession d'espaces intimes coupés par des stalactites et stalagmites trapus abritant des moniteurs vidéo. Des découpes et un éclairage provenant de sources invisibles donnent l'impression d'un intérieur abstrait taillé dans un seul bloc.

Video screens are set into stalactites that hang down from the ceiling, left. Right, the bar.

Links: Von der Decke hängen »Stalaktiten« mit Videomonitoren; rechts die Bar.

A gauche : des moniteurs vidéo sont insérés dans les « stalactites » qui pendent du plafond ; à droite : le bar.

Planes and cutaways along the atmospheric entrance route

Flächen und Einschnitte an der stimmungsvollen Eingangspassage

L'entrée est un jeu « atmosphérique » de plans et de découpes

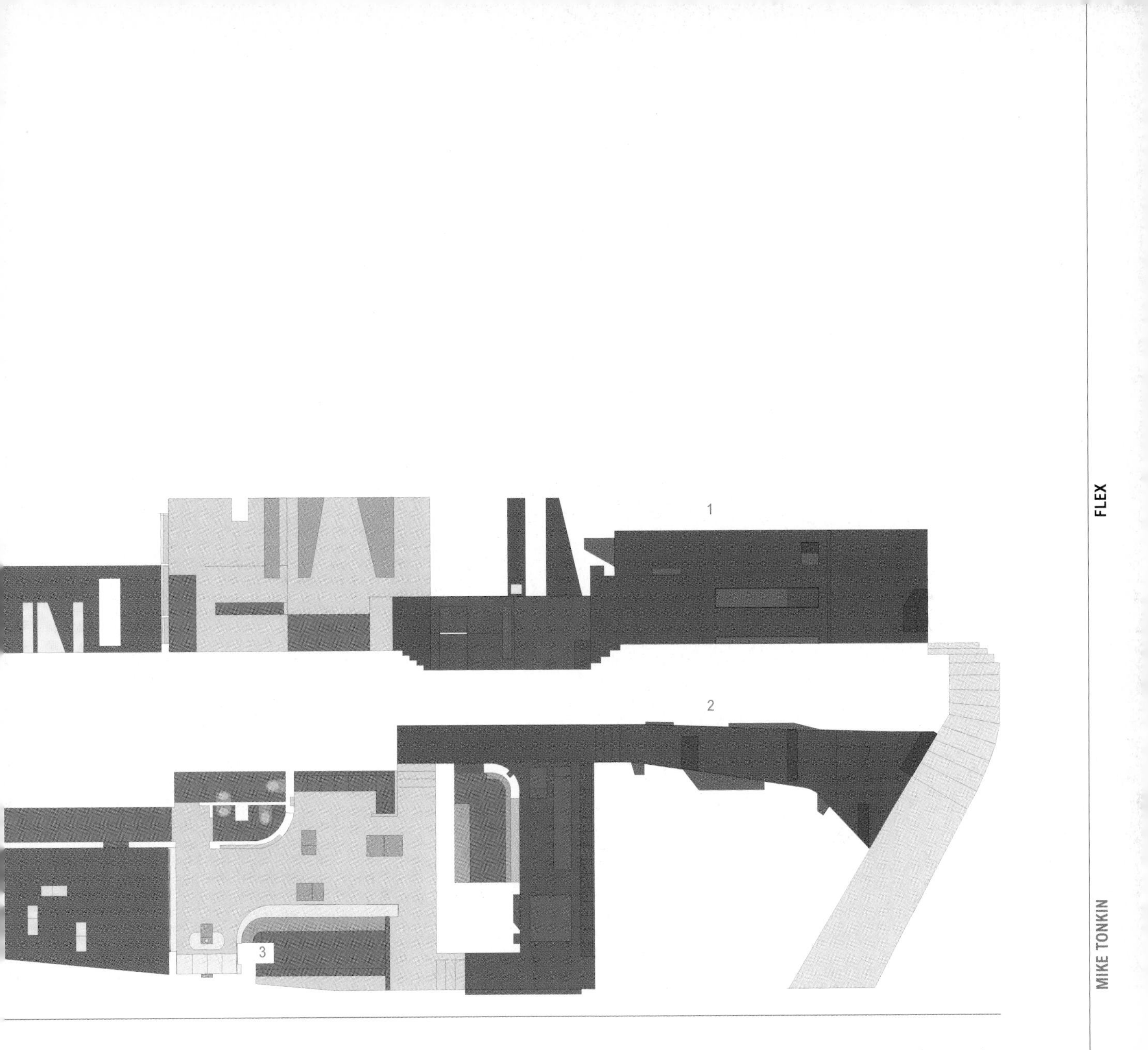

Section and plan/ Schnitt und Grundriss/ Coupe et plan

1 **section/** Schnitt/ élévation

2 **floor plan/** Grundriss/ plan

3 **bar/** Bar/ bar

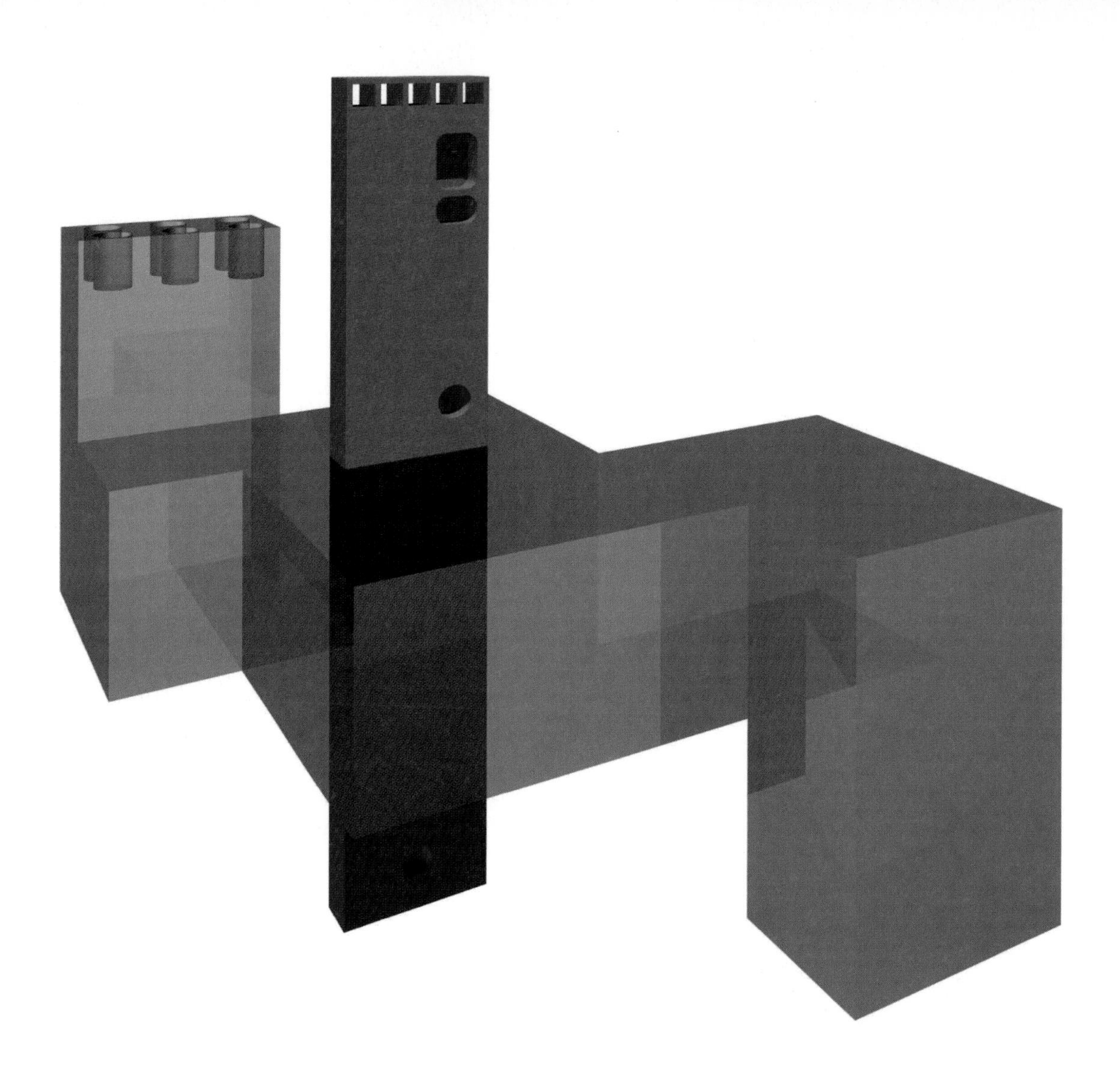

1997 **Hong Kong, China**

Hugo House

The mass of the house is broken down by giving it the appearance of two buildings, one black abutting the road, one white looking out to sea. The internal order is about penetrating space: vertically with a 7 m-high dining space and a red chimney running the full height of the house in the centre of the plan and pushing out through the roof; horizontally as floors cross between the black and white halves of the building; or pushing external windows out to give the illusion that the walls are thicker than they are. Circular holes punched through the flat roof let in light and air.

Das Hugo House wirkt von außen als bestehe es aus zwei separaten Baukörpern: einem schwarzen, der an die Straße grenzt, und einem weißen, der aufs Meer blickt. Im Innern durchdringen sich die Räume: in vertikaler Richtung ein 7 m hoher Essbereich und ein roter Kamin, der das Zentrum des Gebäudes in voller Höhe durchzieht und dann das Dach durchstößt; in horizontaler Richtung überbrücken Böden den Freiraum zwischen der schwarzen und weißen Gebäudehälfte. Fenster treten als Ausbuchtungen aus der Fassade hervor, um die Wände dicker erscheinen zu lassen als sie sind. Kreisrunde Öffnungen im Flachdach lassen Licht und Luft herein.

La masse de la maison Hugo est brisée de sorte à lui donner l'apparence de deux bâtiments distincts ; l'un, noir, tourne le dos à la route ; l'autre, blanc, s'ouvre sur la mer. L'ordonnance interne a pour thème l'interpénétration des volumes : verticalement, un espace-repas de 7 m de haut et une cheminée rouge à position centrale qui perce la toiture ; horizontalement, des planchers s'entrecroisant entre les moitiés noire et blanche de la maison ; ou encore des fenêtres en avancée donnant l'illusion que les murs sont plus épais qu'ils ne le sont en réalité. Des orifices circulaires pratiqués dans le toit en terrasse laissent entrer l'air et la lumière.

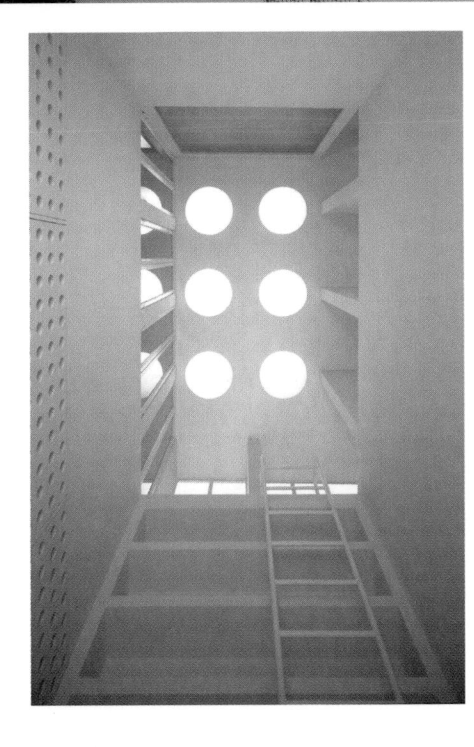

A house of two halves - a white box faces out to sea, a black one on to the road, above, schematically rendered as a solid volume, far left, with the chimney at its heart. Left, the 7 m-high dining space.

Oben: Ein Haus mit zwei Hälften – zum Meer hin ein weißer, zur Straße ein schwarzer Kasten. Ganz links: schematische Darstellung als kompakter Körper mit Kamin im Zentrum. Links der 7 m hohe Essbereich.

Ci-dessus : une maison coupée en deux – une boîte blanche face à la mer, une boîte noire donnant sur la route. Page de gauche : schéma volumétrique de l'édifice avec sa cheminée centrale. A gauche : l'espace-repas, d'une hauteur de plafond de 7 m.

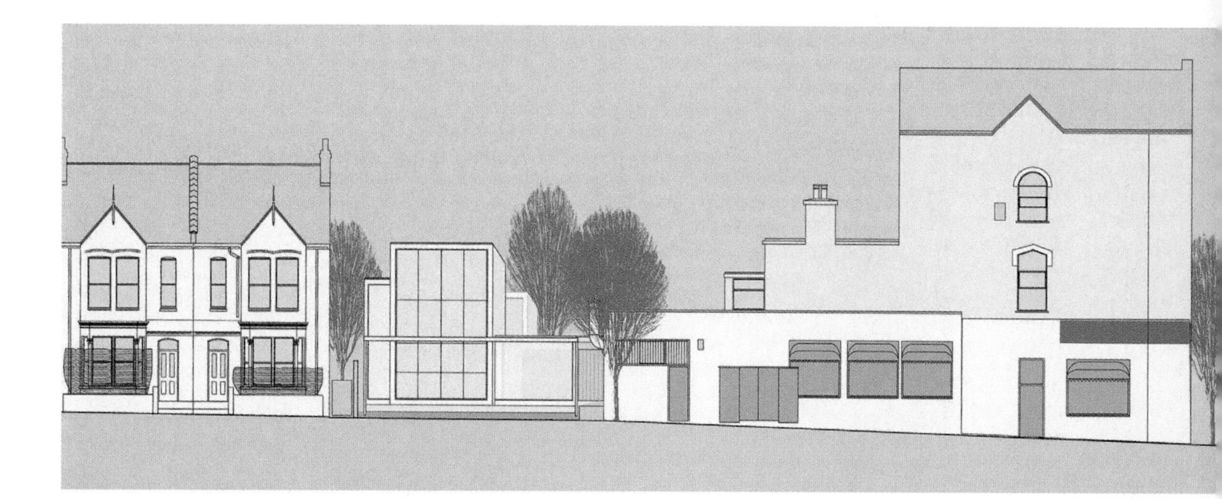

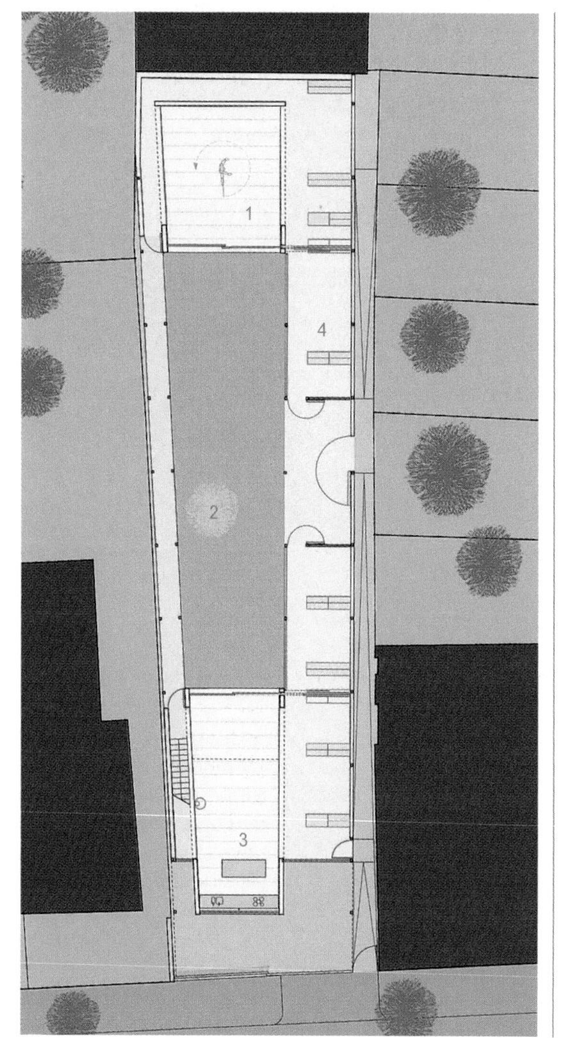

Photomontage of the house in North London, right; elevation, above

Rechts: Fotomontage des Hauses in seiner Umgebung; oben: Aufriss

A droite : photomontage montrant la maison dans son cadre londonien ; ci-dessus : élévation

Ground floor plan/ Erdgeschossgrundriss/ Plan du rez-de-chaussée

1 **photographer's studio/** Photostudio/ atelier photographique
2 **water/** Wasserbecken/ bassin
3 **living area/** Wohnbereich/ séjour
4 **jewellery workshop/** Schmuckwerkstatt/ atelier de bijouterie

2000 London, UK

Camera and Jewel House

A house and studio in North London picks up on the professions of its owners, a jeweller and a photographer, by setting up two units facing each other across a courtyard, one representing a jewel to be looked at, the other a camera from which one can look. The "jewel" will have ground glass mixed in with its render so that it sparkles. The "camera" will have shutters that can be closed to such an exact width that the whole upper-floor studio can be turned into a giant pinhole camera. The shape of the courtyard distorts the perspective so that the apparent distance is shortened from one building and lengthened from the other.

Das Camera and Jewel-Haus mit Atelier in North London nimmt in seiner Gestaltung Bezug auf die Berufe seiner Besitzer – Juwelier und Fotograf – indem sich zwei Elemente an einem Innenhof gegenüberstehen, von denen eines ein Schmuckstück verkörpert, das man anschaut, das andere eine Kamera, durch die man schaut. Damit das »Schmuckstück« glitzert, wird dem Putz gemahlenes Glas beigegeben. Der exakt schließende Verschluss der »Kamera«, die Läden, sollen das gesamte Atelier im Obergeschoss in eine riesige Lochkamera verwandeln. Die Form des Hofs verzerrt die Perspektive, so dass sich der Abstand von einem Bauteil aus gesehen optisch verkürzt, vom anderen aus verlängert.

Cette maison et atelier nommée « appareil photo et bijou » des quartiers nord de Londres s'inspire de la double profession de son propriétaire, à la fois bijoutier et photographe, en plaçant face à face deux unités séparées par une cour, l'une représentant un bijou fait pour être regardé, et l'autre, un appareil photo fait pour regarder. Le « bijou » a un crépi scintillant mêlé de verre broyé. L'« appareil photo » est équipé de volets réglables avec une telle précision que l'atelier du niveau supérieur peut être transformé en une gigantesque chambre noire à sténopé. La forme de la cour déforme la perspective, de sorte que la distance apparente est plus grande vue d'un bâtiment que de l'autre.

The colourful abstract design is based on a leaf pattern.

Das farbenfrohe abstrakte Muster basiert auf einem Blattmotiv.

Le motif abstrait polychrome est basé sur un motif de feuillage.

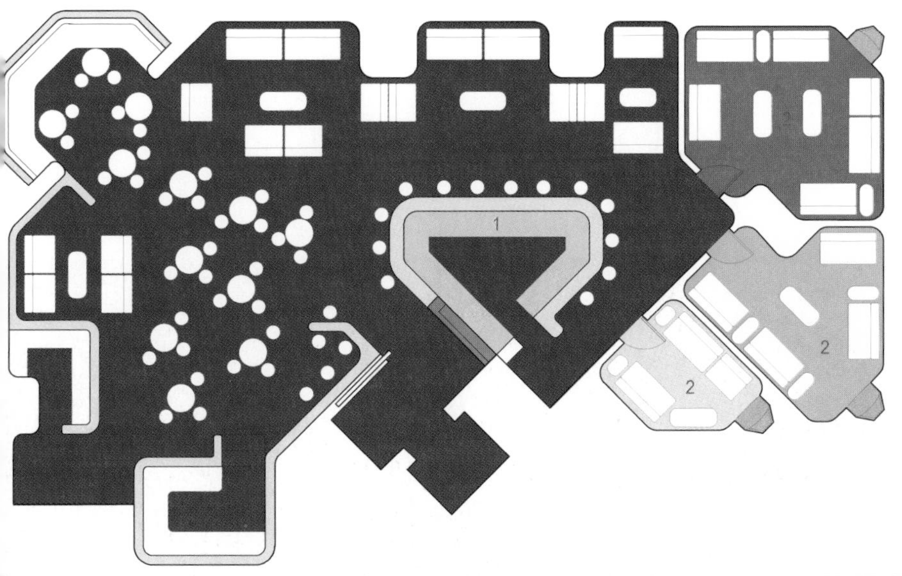

Floor plan/ Grundriss/ Plan

1 **main bar/** Bar/ bar

2 **private rooms/** Privaträume/ pièces privées

996 **Hong Kong, China**

Tong Zhi

Wild decoration derived from a leaf motif takes karaoke "from the living room back to the jungle". The brown walls and funky pattern are carried over almost every wall and partition, enveloping the room. Marshmallow furniture complements the cosy ambience.

Die aus einem Blattmotiv entwickelte wilde Dekoration der Karaokebar Tong Zhi versetzt einen »vom Wohnzimmer zurück in den Urwald«. Die braune Wandfarbe und schrille Musterung überziehen fast jede Wand und jeden Raumteiler. »Marshmallow-Möbel« ergänzen das behagliche Ambiente.

Un décor exubérant inspiré par un motif de feuillage ramène le karaoké « du séjour à la jungle ». La couleur marron et le motif funky sont repris sur la quasi-totalité des murs et cloisons qui délimitent la salle. Un mobilier pastel complète l'ambiance cosy.

Simon Ungers

7 Jay Street #4, New York, NY 10013, USA — tel +1 212 941 7757 fax +1 212 941 1823

imon Ungers		
orn	1957	Cologne, Germany
tudied	1980	B. Arch. Cornell University
revious practice	1982	founded UKZ Inc.; worked on his own as an architect and an artist since 1987

elected projects		
obbs Residence	1980	Lansing, New York, USA
nee Residence	1983	Caldwell, New Jersey, USA
Beam Table, Sophia Ungers Gallery	1989	Cologne, Germany
House (Marcelle Residence)	1992	Wilton, New York, USA
alerie für Junge Kunst, Cantilever	1994	Trier, Germany
ing's Chapel and Gymnasium	1997	Delmar, New York, USA

lonolithic. If there is one word that is inescapable hen describing any project by Simon Ungers it is onolithic. An artist and an architect, his work exemifies the powerful purity characteristic of German esign. Ungers, born in Cologne, but since 1969 a natralised New Yorker, has re-appropriated monolithic rchitecture and rediscovered the beauty of its simicity in the iconic rusted steel T House, the Knee esidence clad in plywood panels like giant bricks, e "I Beam" Table and his "Cantilever" black-slab rt installations.

any of the younger generation of architects work utside the boundaries of what might be termed architecture" and Ungers has established himself as bona fide artist as well as a trained architect. His inallations have an inescapable architectural content, ften one architectural idea distilled down to its esence. A series of installations at the Sophia Ungers allery in Cologne has included rebuilding the ceiling the gallery on the floor to create a mirror effect that onfounds which way is up; a red slab supported on vo of the gallery's structural columns yet seemingly oating in mid-air; three illuminated vertical blocks erfectly positioned to interrelate most harmoniously.

Monolithisch. Wenn sich ein Wort beim Beschreiben eines beliebigen Projekts von Simon Ungers aufdrängt, dann ist es »monolithisch«. Das Werk dieses Künstlers und Architekten verkörpert die kraftvolle Klarheit, die charakteristisch für deutsches Design ist. Ungers, in Köln geboren und seit 1969 in New York lebend, hat sich die monolithische Architektur ganz zu eigen gemacht. In Werken wie dem groben stählernen T House und dem Haus Knee, dessen Sperrholzverkleidung gigantischen Backsteinen ähnelt, dem Tisch »I Beam« und seiner »Cantilever« genannten Installation aus schwarzen Platten hat er die schlichte Schönheit des Monolithischen wiederentdeckt.

Obgleich viele jüngere Architekten die Grenzen dessen, was man gemeinhin als »Architektur« bezeichnet, überschreiten, konnte Ungers sich gleichermaßen als Ernst zu nehmender Künstler und ausgebildeter Architekt etablieren. Seine Installationen sind stets architektonisch, häufig verkörpern sie einen architektonischen Einfall, der auf seine Essenz reduziert ist. So wiederholte er in der Kölner Galerie Sophia Ungers die Decke der Galerie auf dem Fußboden und brachte mit dieser Spiegelung oben und unten durcheinander. Eine rote Platte scheint, von zwei Stützen getragen, frei zu schweben; drei beleuchte-

Monolithique : si un seul terme convient pour décrire les projets de Simon Ungers, c'est celui-là. Tout ce qu'il fait est monolithique. Son œuvre est l'exemple parfait de la puissante pureté qui caractérise le design allemand. Ungers, né à Cologne, New-yorkais d'adoption depuis 1969, s'est approprié l'architecture monolithique et a redécouvert les vertus de sa simplicité, comme en témoignent sa T House en acier, rustique et iconique, et la résidence Knee revêtue de panneaux de contreplaqué pareils à des briques géantes, sans oublier sa table « I Beam » et ses installations « Cantilever » en dalles noires.

Bien que de nombreux architectes de la jeune génération ne se limitent pas à l'architecture proprement dite, Ungers s'est taillé une double réputation d'artiste et d'architecte qualifié. Ses installations « artistiques » ont un évident contenu architectural – souvent une unique idée architecturale dont il a distillé l'essence. Une série d'installations présentée à la galerie Sophia Ungers de Cologne a exigé de reconstituer le plafond de la galerie au sol, effet en miroir qui confond le haut et le bas ; une dalle rouge, en fait soutenue par deux piliers structurels de la galerie, semble suspendue dans le vide ; trois blocs verticaux vivement éclairés sont minutieusement positionnés afin de créer une harmonie parfaite.

To date, Ungers' architectural daring has not been matched by that of those who might commission him. Numerous unbuilt competition entries, including one for the extension of the Prado in Madrid that imposed three glass and steel elements (a tall tower, a stocky slab and an elongated bar) on the city centre, or his concept for a steel and glass sphere on top of the Pan Am Building in New York to house a night-club, give a sense of how exciting it would be to have Ungers work in an urban context rather than in the semi-isolation of a gallery or in a rural setting.

te vertikale Blöcke wurden so positioniert, dass sie in möglichst harmonische Wechselbeziehung treten.
Bis jetzt haben Ungers kühne Entwürfe nur wenige mutige Bauherren gefunden. Zahlreiche Wettbewerbsbeiträge – darunter die Erweiterung des Prado in Madrid, die dem Stadtzentrum drei Elemente aus Stahl und Glas zumutete (ein Hochhaus, eine gedrungene Platte und einen langgestreckten Riegel) oder seine Idee, das Pan Am Building in New York mit einer Kugel aus Stahl und Glas zu krönen, in der ein Nachtclub untergebracht werden sollte – vermitteln einen Eindruck davon, wie spannend es sein könnte, Ungers' Ideen in urbanem Kontext statt in der Abgeschiedenheit einer Galerie oder in ländlicher Umgebung umzusetzen.

A ce jour, l'audace d'Ungers et de son architecture n'a pas été égalée par celle des clients potentiels. De nombreux projets présentés à des concours, notamment pour l'extension du musée du Prado à Madrid, qui prévoyait trois éléments en acier et verre (une haute tour, un bloc compact et une barre allongée), ou son concept pour une sphère en acier et verre abritant une boîte de nuit au sommet du gratte-ciel de la Pan Am à New York, nous donnent une idée de ce que Ungers pourrait accomplir s'il avait la possibilité de travailler dans un contexte urbain et pas seulement dans le cadre relativement discret d'une galerie d'art ou d'un site rural.

1992 **Wilton, New York, USA**

T House (Marcelle Residence)

The Marcelle Residence is a powerful image in the rural landscape, T-shape in section and cruciform in plan. The 230-m² dwelling of a writer houses a double-height 10 000-volume library in the upper section, which is set perpendicular to the linear domestic section half-buried in the ground, the juxtaposition giving the building its dramatic form. For a seamless monolithic finish without differentiation between vertical and horizontal surfaces, the house was constructed in six sections - a double-shell system of weathering steel and wood - then assembled on site.

Das im Schnitt T-förmige, im Grundriss kreuzförmige, 230 m² große Haus Marcelle fällt in der ländlichen Umgebung ins Auge. Für einen Schriftsteller erbaut, beherbergt es eine zweigeschossige Bibliothek mit 10 000 Bänden im oberen Teil, der quer zu dem halb unter Bodenniveau liegenden, langgestreckten Wohnbereich angeordnet ist. Die Kombination dieser beiden Teile macht die spektakuläre Form des Hauses aus. Um eine nahtlose monolithische Oberfläche zu erreichen, die an vertikalen und horizontalen Oberflächen einheitlich ist, wurde das Haus – als doppelschaliges System aus oxidierendem Chromstahl und Holz – in sechs Teilen vorgefertigt und dann in situ zusammengesetzt.

La résidence Marcelle insère une image puissante dans le paysage champêtre : section en T et plan cruciforme. Cette maison de 230 m² destinée à un écrivain comporte une bibliothèque pouvant contenir 10 000 volumes, construite sur deux niveaux dans l'unité supérieure, perpendiculaire à la section domestique qui est, elle, linéaire et à demi enterrée ; cette juxtaposition donne à la maison sa forme caractéristique. En vue d'obtenir un aspect parfaitement homogène, sans la moindre différenciation entre surfaces verticales et horizontales, la maison a été construite en six sections – système à double coque d'acier et bois –, qui ont été assemblées in situ.

The dramatic "T" form in vibrant orange rusted steel dominates the surrounding landscape. The top of the T houses a library for the owner, a writer.

Die markante T-Form in dunkelorangem oxidiertem Chromstahl beherrscht die Umgebung. Im Querbalken des T ist die Bibliothek des Besitzers, eines Schriftstellers, untergebracht.

La dramatique forme en T, en acier oxydé d'un orange vibrant, domine le paysage. La partie supérieure de la maison, construite pour un écrivain, abrite la biblio-thèque.

The house emerges from the sloping site, above. Above right, the library in the upper section.

Oben: Das Haus erhebt sich aus dem abschüssigen Gelände. Rechts oben die Bibliothek im oberen Bauteil.

La maison se dresse sur un site en forte pente. A droite, la bibliothèque dans la partie supérieure du bâtiment.

The prefabricated modules being driven to and assembled on site.

Die Module auf dem Weg zum Bauplatz, wo sie zusammengesetzt wurden.

Les modules préfabriqués sont assemblés sur le site.

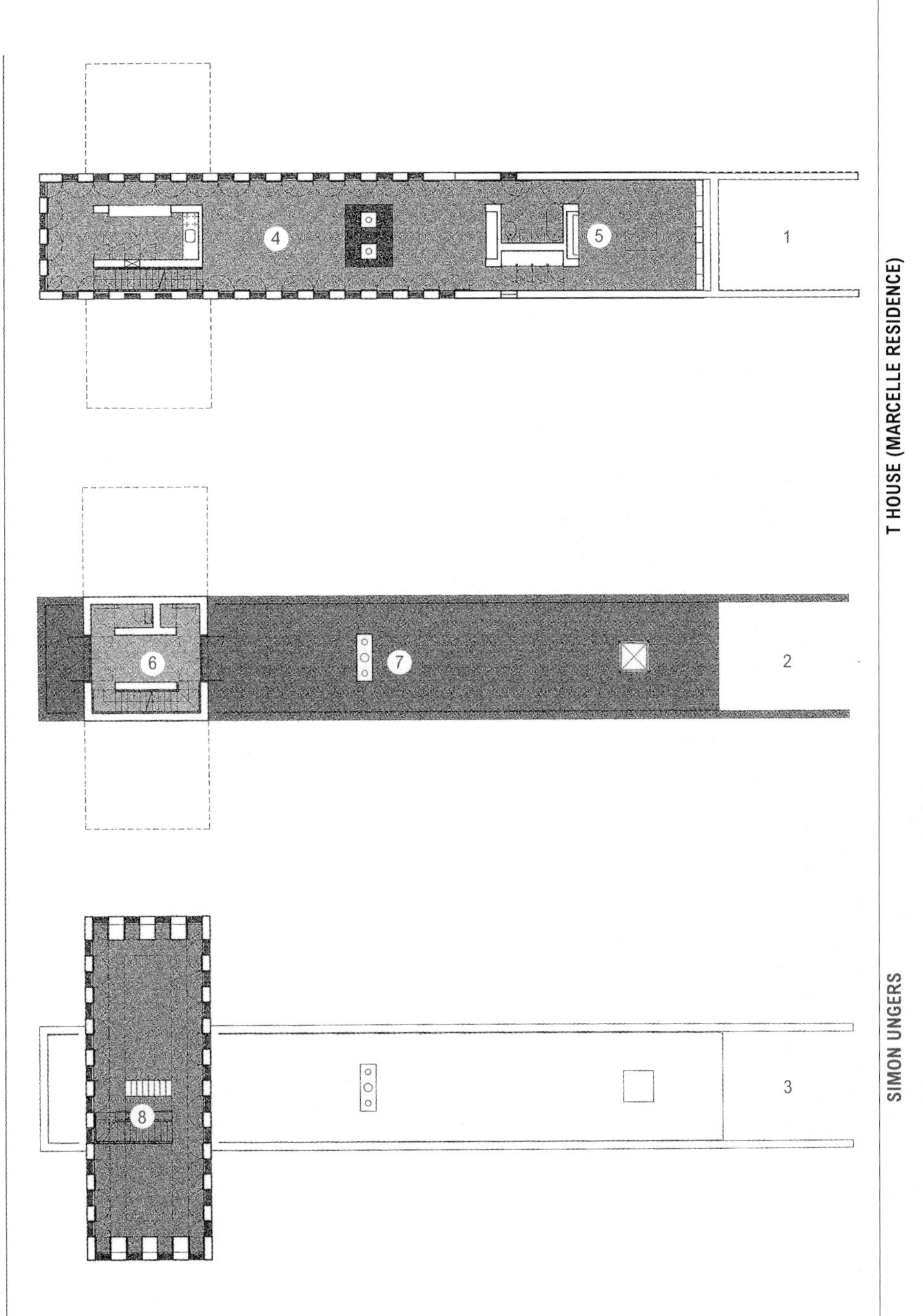

Floor plans/ Grundrisse der Etagen/ Plans des divers niveaux

1 **ground floor/** Erdgeschoss/ rez-de-chaussée
2 **1st floor/** 1. Stock/ premier étage
3 **2nd floor/** 2. Stock/ deuxième étage
4 **living room/** Wohnraum/ séjour
5 **bedroom/** Schlafzimmer/ chambre
6 **entrance/** Eingang/ entrée
7 **roof terrace/** Dachterrasse/ toit-terrasse
8 **library/** Bibliothek/ bibliothèque

An unbuilt scheme for a chapel, gym and classrooms at Delmar, New York

Entwurf für eine Kapelle, Sporthalle und Unterrichtsräume in Delmar, New York

Projet pour une chapelle, un gymnase et des salles de cours à Delmar, Etat de New York

1997 **Delmar, New York, USA**

King's Chapel and Gymnasium

A chapel, gymnasium and classrooms/offices, the project consists of three units, the chapel being the dominant volume. To emphasise the homogeneity of the project, the entire complex, including the steps of the amphitheatre, is constructed of concrete blocks.

Der Komplex setzt sich aus drei Einheiten zusammen: einer Kapelle, einer Sporthalle und einem Gebäude für Klassenzimmer und Büros, wobei die Kapelle den beherrschenden Teil bildet. Um die Homogenität des Projekts zu unterstreichen, soll der gesamte Komplex, einschließlich der Stufen des Amphitheaters, aus Betonblöcken bestehen.

Réunissant une chapelle, un gymnase et des salles de cours plus bureaux, cet ensemble comporte trois unités, dont la chapelle est le volume dominant. Afin d'assurer l'homogénéité du projet, le complexe entier, jusqu'aux marches de l'amphithéâtre, est construit en blocs de béton.

Two competition entries

Even if Ungers' bold competition entries were not chosen by the judges, once such ideas are entered they cannot be ignored.
1) Bucharest 2000 Competition, Romania
Ungers' design for the redevelopment of the area surrounding Ceauşescu's Palace outdoes what he describes as "the bombastic, oppressive architecture of the Ceauşescu regime" with four monumental geometric structures – cube, cylinder, rectangle and sphere – along the central boulevard in Bucharest. The palace itself is caged inside the giant frame, leaving a terrifying impression.
2) German Pavilion, Expo 2000, Hanover, Germany
An orthogonal folded plane, S-shape in section, open to the exhibition at ground level with a parking lot along the upper level. Secondary functions such as offices, meeting rooms and services are housed in a thick wall on the lower level facing the parking lot.

Auch wenn Ungers' kühne Wettbewerbsbeiträge von den Juroren nicht ausgewählt wurden, kann man Ideen dieser Art kaum ignorieren, sind sie einmal eingereicht.
1) Wettbewerb Bukarest 2000, Rumänien
Ungers' Entwurf für die Neugestaltung des Areals um Ceauşescus Palast übertrifft das, was er als »die bombastische, tyrannische Architektur des Ceauşescuregimes« beschreibt. Vier monumentale geometrische Baukörper – Kubus, Zylinder, Rechteck und Kugel – erheben sich entlang des zentralen Boulevards von Bukarest. Der Palast selbst wird in einen riesigen Rahmen gesperrt, was einen beängstigenden Eindruck hinterlässt.
2) Deutscher Pavillon, Expo 2000, Hannover, Deutschland
Eine im Schnitt S-förmige, rechtwinklig gefaltete Fläche ist im unteren Bereich zum Ausstellungsgelände offen und bietet auf der oberen Ebene einen Parkplatz. Sekundärfunktionen wie Büros, Konferenzräume und Serviceeinrichtungen sind in der tiefen Wand unterhalb der Parkebene angesiedelt.

Bien que les projets audacieux d'Ungers n'aient pas été retenus par les juges, ses idées ne peuvent plus être ignorées dès lors qu'elles ont été publiées.
1) Concours pour Bucarest 2000, Roumanie
La proposition d'Ungers pour la réhabilitation du quartier entourant le palais de Ceauşescu dépasse ce qu'il appelle « l'architecture pompeuse et oppressante du régime de Ceauşescu » grâce à quatre structures géométriques monumentales (cube, cylindre, rectangle et sphère) situées le long de l'avenue centrale de Bucarest. Le palais luimême, enfermé dans le cadre géant, paraîtra plus que jamais terrifiant.
2) Pavillon allemand, Expo 2000, Hanovre, Allemagne
Un plan orthogonal à section en S, l'espace d'exposition étant au niveau du sol et un parking tenant une partie du niveau supérieur. Les fonctions secondaires telles que bureaux, salles de réunion et de service sont réunies dans un mur épais placé au niveau inférieur, face au parking.

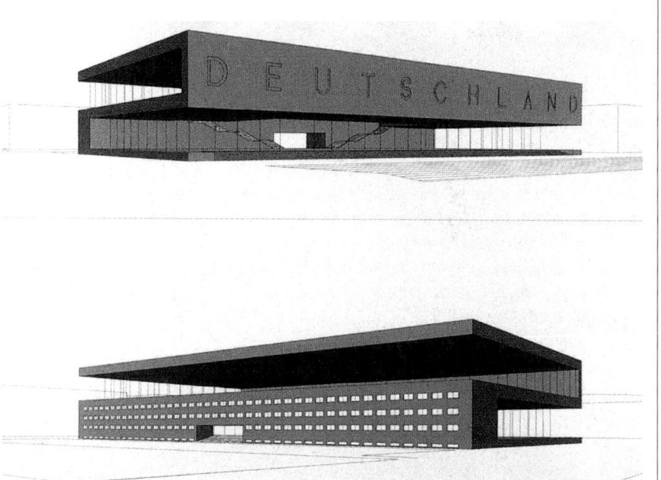

Ungers' unsuccessful proposals for Ceauşescu's palace in Bucharest, above, and the German Pavilion for Expo 2000, above right

Ungers nicht realisierte Entwürfe für Ceauşescus Palast in Bukarest (oben) und den Deutschen Pavillon auf der Expo 2000 (rechts)

Les projets, non réalisés, d'Ungers pour le palais de Ceauşescu à Bucarest (ci-dessus), et pour le pavillon allemand d'Expo 2000 (à droite)

UN Studio

Van Berkel & Bos, Stadhouderskade 113,
1073 AX Amsterdam, Netherlands

tel +31 20 570 2040 fax +31 20 570 2041 e-mail info@unstudio.com web www.unstudio.com

Ben van Berkel

born	1957	Utrecht
studied	1982	Rietveld Academy, Amsterdam; 1987 Architectural Association, London
previous practice	1988	co-founded Van Berkel & Bos Architectuurbureau, Amsterdam
	1998	established UN Studio, Amsterdam

Caroline Bos

born	1959	Rotterdam
studied	1991	History of Art, Birkbeck College, London
previous practice	1988	co-founded Van Berkel & Bos Architectuurbureau, Amsterdam
	1998	established UN Studio, Amsterdam

Selected projects

Villa Wilbrink	1994	Amersfoort, Netherlands
Rijksmuseum Twente conversion and extension	1996	Enschede, Netherlands
Erasmus Bridge	1996	Rotterdam, Netherlands (in collaboration with Gemeentewerken Rotterdam)
Möbius House	1998	't Gooi, Netherlands
Museum Het Valkhof	1999	Nijmegen, Netherlands
City Hall and Theatre	2000	Ijsselstein, Netherlands
NMR laboratory	2000	Utrecht, Netherlands
Electrical substation	2001	Innsbruck, Austria
MuMuTh music theatre	2002	Graz, Austria

"The architect is going to be the fashion designer of the future," say architect Ben van Berkel and art historian Caroline Bos. "Learning from Calvin Klein, the architect will be concerned with dressing the future, speculating on and anticipating coming events and holding a mirror to the world."
Addressing the evolving needs of their architectural projects, the couple expanded their original practice Van Berkel & Bos Architectuurbureau in 1998 with a spin-off firm UN Studio. Standing for United Net Studio, the offshoot is a network of specialists in architecture, urban development and infrastructure. UN Studio responds to their vision of the future of architectural

»Der Architekt ist der Modedesigner der Zukunft«, sagen der Architekt Ben van Berkel und die Kunsthistorikerin Caroline Bos. »Orientiert an Calvin Klein, wird sich der Architekt mit dem Erscheinungsbild der Zukunft befassen, wird Vermutungen über kommende Ereignisse anstellen, sie vorausahnen und dabei der Welt einen Spiegel vorhalten.«
Als Reaktion auf die sich wandelnden Anforderungen an Architektur erweiterte das Paar das Van Berkel & Bos Architectuurbureau 1998 um die Schwesterfirma UN Studio (für United Net Studio), ein Netzwerk von Spezialisten für Architektur, Stadtentwicklung und Infrastruktur. UN Studio antwortet auf ihre Vision von der Zukunft

« L'architecte sera le dessinateur de mode de l'avenir », affirment l'architecte Ben van Berkel et l'historienne de l'art Caroline Bos. « S'inspirant de l'exemple de Calvin Klein, l'architecte se préoccupera d'habiller le futur, spéculant sur les événements à venir et les anticipant, et présentant un miroir au monde. »
Pour répondre aux besoins croissants de leur activité architecturale, ils ont ajouté en 1998 au « Van Berkel & Bos Architectuurbureau » un atelier nommé UN Studio (pour United Net Studio), « réseau » de spécialistes de l'architecture, de l'urbanisme et des infrastructures. UN Studio correspond à leur vision de l'avenir de la pratique architecturale ; cet « hybride de club, d'atelier, de labora-

practice as "a hybrid of club, atelier, laboratory and car plant, encouraging plug-in professionalism", an organisation of trouble-shooters that can move in on projects, drawing on a multitude of professional skills, and devise unique solutions based on accumulated research and experience.

In their manifesto "Move" (Goose Press, Amsterdam, 1999) they expound the virtues of what they call "inclusiveness", - "an integral design process that takes on board all aspects of architecture. The shifting fields of engineering, urbanism and infrastructure form some of the most important parameters of architecture." While the best architects are aware of the importance of collaboration with all members of the construction team, UN Studio has given the complex network of professional relationships formal recognition and equal status.

Their architecture owes much to computer technology, which has allowed them to push form to its mathematical limits, creating complex monolithic structures. The Möbius house, inspired by the mathematical model of the Möbius band, is a twisted contorted form that would have been almost impossible to realise without electronic devices. The 139 m-tall pylon of the Erasmus Bridge now dominating the river Maas at Rotterdam stands proudly astride the roadway, a celebratory feat of engineering.

des Architekturbüros als »Mischform aus Club, Atelier, Labor und Automobilwerk, das auf die Mithilfe anderer Profis angewiesen sein wird«; ein Zusammenschluss von Troubleshootern, die bei Projekten zum Einsatz kommen und dabei auf die unterschiedlichsten professionellen Fähigkeiten zurückgreifen und auf Forschung und Erfahrung basierende, unkonventionelle Lösungen ausarbeiten können.

In ihrem Manifest »Move« (Goose Press, Amsterdam 1999) erläutern van Berkel und Bos die Vorzüge dessen, was sie »Inklusivität« nennen: »ein integraler Entwurfsprozess, der sämtliche Aspekte der Architektur einbezieht. Technik, Stadtplanung und Infrastruktur gehören zu den wichtigsten Parametern.« An ihren Projekten arbeiten alle Mitglieder des Bauteams gleichberechtigt zusammen. Computertechnik ermöglicht ihnen, Formen bis an ihre mathematischen Grenzen weiterzuentwickeln und so komplexe monolithische Bauten zu konzipieren. Das vom mathematischen Modell des Möbius'schen Bandes angeregte Möbius-Haus hat eine gewundene, unregelmäßige Form, die sich ohne elektronische Hilfe kaum hätte verwirklichen lassen. Der 139 m hohe Pylon der Erasmusbrücke, die heute die Maas bei Rotterdam beherrscht, ist ein technisches Meisterstück.

toire et d'usine d'automobiles, favorisant le professionnalisme à la carte », réunit des spécialistes des problèmes difficiles, prêts à intervenir sur des projets exigeant une multitude de connaissances professionnelles en vue de dégager des solutions originales issues de la recherche et de l'expérience.

Dans leur manifeste « Move » (Goose Press, 1999), ils exposent les vertus de ce qu'ils appellent « inclusiveness » : « un processus de design intégré qui embrasse tous les aspects de l'architecture. Les domaines mouvants de l'ingénierie, de l'urbanisme et des infrastructures comptent parmi les paramètres les plus importants de l'architecture. » Les meilleurs architectes sont probablement conscients de l'importance d'une coopération entre tous les membres de l'équipe de constructeurs, mais UN Studio a donné au complexe réseau des relations interprofessionnelles un statut officiel, tout en mettant tous les métiers sur un pied d'égalité.

Leur architecture doit beaucoup à la technologie informatique, qui leur a permis de pousser la forme jusqu'à ses extrêmes limites mathématiques et de créer de complexes structures monolithiques. La maison Möbius, dérivée du modèle mathématique du ruban de Möbius, est une forme contournée qu'il aurait été pratiquement impossible de réaliser sans l'aide de l'informatique. Le pylône haut de 139 m du pont Erasme, qui franchit la Meuse à Rotterdam, est une remarquable prouesse d'ingénierie.

Möbius House

Inspired by the mathematical model of the Möbius band - a twisted loop with a single continuous surface - the Möbius House is based on two intertwining paths that van Berkel describes as "a double-locked torus". Occasionally crossing to form shared spaces, they are an example of how people can live together and yet apart. Areas for work, social life, family life and private space are woven together in a series of irregular yet functional spaces as the two halves of the building wrap around each other.
The concept of two interlocking lines is carried through to the structure of the building, where the architects have established a continually changing relationship between glass and concrete, skin and structure.

Das vom mathematischen Modell des Möbius'schen Bandes – eine gewundene Schleife mit einseitiger Fläche – angeregte Möbius-Haus fußt auf zwei miteinander verwobenen Bahnen, die van Berkel als »doppelt verschlossenen Torus« beschreibt. Bisweilen überschneiden sie sich, um gemeinsame Räume zu bilden und demonstrieren so beispielhaft, wie Menschen zusammen und doch getrennt leben können. Indem sich die beiden Gebäudehälften umeinander legen, bilden die Bereiche für Arbeit, Geselligkeit, Familienleben und Privates ein Geflecht unregelmäßiger, doch funktionaler Räume.
Das Konzept der miteinander verzahnten Linien wurde auch auf die Gestaltung des Gebäudes übertragen, eine sich ständig verändernde Beziehung zwischen Glas und Beton, Flächen und konstruktiven Elementen.

Inspirée par le ruban de Möbius (torsion d'un ruban créant une surface à un seul côté), la maison Möbius est basée sur deux itinéraires entrelacés que Berkel qualifie de « tore à double torsion ». Se croisant parfois pour constituer des espaces communs, ils démontrent comment les gens peuvent vivre ensemble tout en restant indépendants. Les pièces consacrées au travail, aux activités sociales, à la vie de famille et les zones privées s'entre-tissent pour former une série d'espaces irréguliers mais fonctionnels, tandis que les deux moitiés de la maison s'enroulent l'une autour de l'autre.
Le concept de deux lignes entrelacés se poursuit dans la structure du bâtiment, où les architectes ont établi une relation sans cesse changeante entre verre et béton, enveloppe et structure.

The Möbius House is an excercise in how two people can live together yet apart.

Das Möbius-Haus demonstriert, wie zwei Menschen räumlich getrennt und doch zusammen leben können.

La maison Möbius tente de résoudre l'équation : comment vivre ensemble tout en restant indépendants.

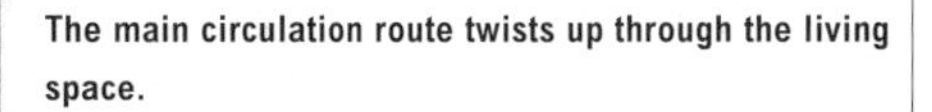

The main circulation route twists up through the living space.

Der Haupterschließungsweg windet sich durch den Wohnbereich.

La principale voie de circulation traverse l'espace de vie en zigzag.

As the floor plan of the house twists round on itself like its mathematical namesake, the Möbius band, it creates dramatic forms and unconventional spaces.

Der Grundriss des Hauses dreht sich wie sein Namensgeber, das Möbius'sche Band, um sich selbst und lässt markante Formen und unkonventionelle Räume entstehen.

La dalle formant le plancher s'enroule sur elle-même comme le ruban de Möbius, créant des formes étonnantes et des espaces hors norme.

Villa Wilbrink

The concept behind Villa Wilbrink is the house as a suburban bunker. Van Berkel and Bos wanted to create an atmosphere of privacy, seclusion and individuality for the inhabitants. Introverted and defensive, Villa Wilbrink hides behind banks of shingles, but once these have been penetrated, the house opens up into a warm, light space. The main domestic space has a glazed facade opening on to a private courtyard behind the shingle banks.

Die Idee hinter der Villa Wilbrink ist die vom Haus als vorstädtischem Bunker. Van Berkel und Bos wollten eine Atmosphäre der Abgeschlossenheit und Individualität schaffen. Introvertiert und abweisend verbirgt sich die Villa Wilbrink hinter Wällen aus Kieseln. Hat man diese überwunden, öffnet sich das Haus in einem warmen, lichten Raum. Durch die Glaswand des Hauptwohnbereichs sieht man in den abgeschlossenen Innenhof, der hinter den Kieselwällen liegt.

Le concept de base de la villa Wilbrink est la maison en tant que forteresse de banlieue. Van Berkel et Bos voulaient faire bénéficier ses habitants d'une ambiance intime et personnelle. Introvertie et sur la défensive, la villa se cache derrière des talus de galets, mais une fois ceux-ci franchis, la maison s'ouvre, volume clair et accueillant. Le principal espace de vie est doté d'une façade vitrée s'ouvrant sur une cour protégée par les talus.

From the street, the house is like a suburban bunker, above, but the living area at the rear, right, opens on to a glazed courtyard.

Von der Straße wirkt das Vorstadthaus wie ein Bunker (oben), der rückwärtige Wohnbereich (rechts) jedoch öffnet sich auf einen verglasten Innenhof.

Vue de la rue, la maison de banlieue est protégée comme un bunker (ci-dessus), mais à l'arrière, le séjour (à droite) s'ouvre sur une cour entièrement vitrée.

Boxed windows project from the rear wall, above. A cutaway window in the bottom corner of the house creates intrigue, below right. Above right, the open-plan living space.

Oben: Fensterkästen treten aus der Rückwand hervor; ein ausgeschnittenes Fenster in der unteren Ecke des Hauses macht neugierig (rechts unten). Rechts oben der offene Wohnbereich.

Sur le mur arrière, des fenêtres en avancée (ci-dessus) ; à l'angle inférieur de la maison, une baie vitrée crée la surprise (en bas à droite). En haut à droite : le vaste living à plan ouvert.

The 139 m-high pylon of the Erasmus Bridge has become a modern landmark for Rotterdam.

Der 139 m hohe Pylon der Erasmusbrücke wurde Rotterdams modernes Wahrzeichen.

La « tour » du pont Erasme, haute de 139 m, est devenue un point de repère de la Rotterdam moderne.

1996 **Rotterdam, Netherlands**

Erasmus Bridge

The new bridge links Rotterdam's new urban quarter of Kop van Zuid to the city for which it has already become a potent symbol. A 139 m-high steel pylon is held at the back by four tension cables. Its dramatic impact matches that of the wide River Maas at this point, but it also works on a smaller scale as the architects' attention to detail goes as far as the handrails and road surface.

Als neues Wahrzeichen von Rotterdam verbindet die Erasmusbrücke das neue Stadtviertel Kop van Zuid mit der Innenstadt. Ein 139 m hoher Stahlpfeiler wird auf der Rückseite von vier Zugseilen gehalten. Die spektakuläre Wirkung betont die gewaltige Breite der Maas an dieser Stelle. Dennoch ließen die Architekten sämtlichen Details, selbst Handläufen und Straßenbelag, große Sorgfalt angedeihen.

Le pont Erasme récemment construit pour relier le nouveau quartier de Kop van Zuid au centre-ville est déjà devenu un puissant symbole. Un pylône en acier de 139 m de haut est maintenu par quatre câbles. Son impact est égal à celui de l'imposante et large Meuse, mais la petite échelle n'est pas oubliée, les architectes ayant minutieusement pensé le moindre détail, jusqu'à la rambarde et au revêtement de la chaussée.

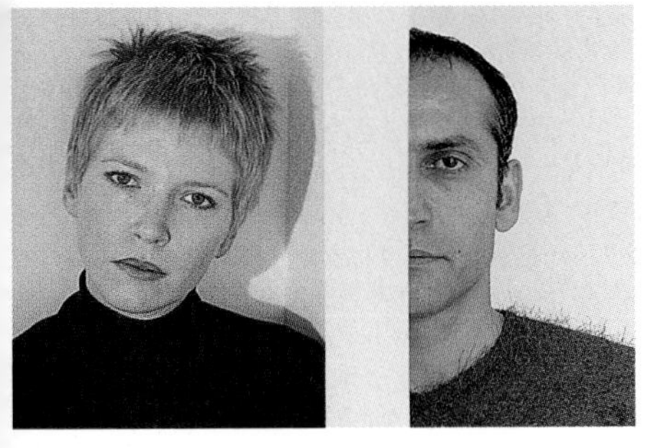

UT

578 Broadway, Suite 506, New York, NY 10012, USA   tel +1 212 966 8815   fax +1 212 966 9148   e-mail ut@utarchitecture.com   web www.utarchitecture.com

Clarissa Richardson

born	1971 Canberra, Australia
studied	1996 Princeton University; 1992 Bartlett School of Architecture, London
previous practice	Alford Hall Monahan Morris, London; Paxton Locher, London
	1998 co-founded UT

Heidar Sadeki

born	1964 Shiraz, Iran
studied	1997 Princeton University; 1994 SUNY at Purchase, NY (BA in Film)
practice	1998 co-founded UT

Selected projects

Peric Residence	1998	New York City, USA
Coty Inc. Gallery	1999	New York City, USA
Bliss Spa	1999	Manhattan, New York, USA
Blissworld Headquarters	1999	Brooklyn, New York, USA
Wink Residence	2000	New York City, USA
Kilgore Boue Residence	2000	Brooklyn, New York, USA

Established in 1998, UT is a very new practice that is already gaining respect and - more importantly - work from influential New York developers. Most of their work to date has been for the health and beauty chain Bliss, part of the LVMH (Louis Vuitton Moët Hennessy) luxury group, and included some re-branding and creating a fresher, chic corporate identity. Projects have also included a headquarters, two spas and an apartment for Bliss's owners. This has brought them to the attention of other companies in LVMH, and should lead to some projects in Los Angeles soon. In addition, UT have been working with New York developer David Walentas on masterplans for the conversion of warehouse buildings to offices in the now fashionable Dumbo ("Down Under Manhattan Bridge") area of Brooklyn.

Though projects have been small-scale and superficially simple, they show a complex analysis of architectural space that adds intricacy to the spatial arrange-

UT, 1998 gegründet, ist ein sehr junges Büro, das schon jetzt Respekt und Aufträge von bedeutenden New Yorker Bauherren erhält. Ein Großteil ihrer Arbeiten entstand für die Wellnessfirma Bliss, die zum Luxuskonzern LVMH (Louis Vuitton Moët Hennessy) gehört. So war UT für die Umgestaltung von Markenartikeln und die Entwicklung einer flotteren Corporate Identity zuständig. Zudem entstanden die Zentrale, zwei Wellnessbereiche und ein Apartment für die Besitzer von Bliss. Diese Projekte machten andere Firmen der LVMH-Gruppe auf UT aufmerksam, was wohl einige Aufträge in Los Angeles nach sich ziehen wird. Daneben war UT unter der Federführung des New Yorker Bauunternehmers David Walentas an Masterplänen für die Umnutzung von Lagerhäusern zu Bürobauten in Brooklyns neuerdings angesagtem »Dumbo«-Distrikt (für »Down under Manhattan Bridge«) beteiligt.

Obgleich es sich eher um klein dimensionierte, auf den ersten Blick einfache Projekte handelt, entwickelte UT

En dépit de sa création récente (en 1998), le bureau UT bénéficie déjà d'une estime certaine, et surtout de commandes d'importants promoteurs new-yorkais. Ils ont principalement travaillé pour la chaîne de magasins « santé et beauté » Bliss, qui fait partie du groupe LVMH (Louis Vuitton Moët Hennessy) ; il fallait en particulier donner à la chaîne une nouvelle image de marque, plus chic. Ils ont notamment dessiné un siège social, deux instituts de beauté et un appartement pour les propriétaires de Bliss. Ces réalisations ont attiré l'attention d'autres membres du groupe LVMH, ce qui devrait leur valoir prochainement des commandes à Los Angeles. UT ont de surcroît travaillé avec le promoteur new-yorkais David Walentas sur la conversion d'entrepôts en immeubles de bureaux dans le nouveau quartier à la mode de « Dumbo » (Down Under Manhattan Bridge) à Brooklyn.

En dépit de la petite échelle et de l'apparente simplicité de ces projets, ils témoignent d'une analyse en profondeur

ment and enhances the experience of moving through the spaces: tapering floor plans, rooms that project slightly into foyers inviting you in, offset angles, ceilings held back from walls, a solid box projecting from and breaking up a glass plane, a sliver of glass inserted to push out a single plane, and their favourite device - which they describe as a "hinge" in the floor plan that twists it around and breaks away from the confines of the four enclosing walls.

On top of this, UT create sensuous interiors by experimenting with materials, objects and texture. Feathers sandwiched between glass walls, a solid concrete bath poured in situ, bubble wrap held between plastic sheets for cheap insulation panels, packing foam infill around frosty acrylic display cases, workstations made from compressed recycled paper, a red make-up booth lined with rubber and ultra-suede, or fluffy Tibetan Mongolian lambskin.

ausgeklügelte, komplexe Konzepte, die neue Möglichkeiten der Bewegung im Raum schaffen: spitzwinklige Grundrisse, Räume, die sich einladend in Foyers schieben, versetzte Ecken, Decken, die nicht in Wände übergehen, ein massiver Kasten, der aus einer Glasfläche ragt, ein Glassplitter, eingefügt, um eine einzelne Fläche hervorzuheben und ihr Lieblingseinfall, den sie als »Scharnier« bezeichnen, um das sich der Grundriss dreht und das ihn von den Beschränkungen der vier Wände befreit.

Darüber hinaus gestaltet UT durch Experimente mit Materialien, Objekten und Strukturen sinnliche Interieurs: Federn zwischen Glasscheiben, ein in situ gegossenes, massives Betonbad, Noppenfolie zwischen Kunststoffplatten als billiges Isoliermaterial, mattierte Acrylvitrinen in Styropor gehüllt, Arbeitsplätze aus Recyclingkarton, eine mit Gummi und Velourleder ausgekleidete, rote Make-up Kabinen, weiches Lammfell aus Tibet und der Mongolei.

du volume architectural qui donne une complexité intéressante à la disposition spatiale : plans de niveau fuselés, pièces empiétant légèrement sur les halls comme pour inviter à y entrer, angles mis en valeur, plafonds en retrait sur les murs, cube solide perçant un pan de verre, lame de verre insérée dans un plan pour le pousser vers l'extérieur, sans oublier leur procédé favori – qu'ils décrivent comme une « charnière » faisant pivoter le plan de façon à le libérer de l'emprise des quatre murs.

Ce n'est pas tout. UT crée également des intérieurs sensuels en expérimentant avec les matériaux, les objets et les textures. Plumes prises en sandwich entre deux cloisons de verre, massive baignoire en béton moulée in situ, emballage à bulles entre deux feuilles de plastique constituant des panneaux isolants bon marché, vitrines en acrylique translucide avec remplissage en mousse de plastique, postes de travail en papier recyclé et compressé, cabine de maquillage rouge habillée de caoutchouc et de suédine, duveteux agneau du Tibet ou de Mongolie.

Reception desk. The double-glazed wall behind has feathers sandwiched within it.

Empfang; zwischen den Scheiben der Doppelglaswand sind Federn eingeschlossen.

La réception ; la double cloison en verre emplie de plumes.

Bliss Spa

The exclusive Bliss Spa is housed on the third floor of Christian de Portzamparc's new LVMH tower. Though its blue-green glazed facade won much applause from the press, the inversion created an awkward floor plan to work with. The pivotal idea for organising the floor plan is a hinge - in this case the main column at the entrance to the staff lockers - from which the rest of the floor plan spirals out. The treatment rooms are pushed to the edge of the floor plan, with the changing rooms and a lounge enclosed in the centre. Changes in flooring signal changes in functions: stone for the reception, tiles for the locker rooms, wood and ultra-suede for the lounge, spongy quiet rubber for the corridors and treatment rooms.

Though the brief was to create a space that was slightly expensive in look, a tight budget provided the catalyst for innovative experimentation with materials: a wall of feathers suspended in sandwiched glass behind the reception desk; Styrofoam packing material around the bespoke shelving grid that has become Bliss's new hallmark; acrylic shelving that seems to disappear when lit from behind; Australian walnut wood (a relatively cheap material most commonly used for hi-fi speakers, which looks expensive); Chinese tiles cut down into tiny tesserae for the showers; thin cream-coloured tiles of different sizes in the changing rooms that, at first glance, could be limestone.

But it was not just a decorating job. Even in seemingly insignificant areas such as the locker rooms, UT have carefully orchestrated the space. Concealed lighting is installed along either side of the ceiling, exaggerating the narrowing soffit, and a vertical panel of translucent glass at the end of the tapering space uses height to overshadow width. All furniture is designed by UT, including the turquoise "O" series coffee table launched in 2000 at the New York ICFF, ultra-suede banquettes and fluffy Mongolian and Tibetan lamb stools.

Das exklusive Bliss Spa ist im dritten Stock des neuen LVMH Tower von Christian de Portzamparc untergebracht. Zwar wurde die blaugrüne Glasfassade von der Presse begeistert aufgenommen, im Innern ist der Grundriss jedoch eine Herausforderung. Die Bliss Spa ist um ein Scharnier herum organisiert – hier ist es der zentrale Pfeiler am Eingang zu den Umkleiden der Angestellten. Die Behandlungszimmer wurden an den Rand der Etage verlegt, Umkleideräume und Lounge ins Zentrum. Wechselnde Bodenbeläge signalisieren verschiedene Funktionen: Stein für den Empfang, Fliesen für die Umkleideräume, Holz und Velourleder für die Lounge, und weicher, dämpfender Gummibelag für Korridore und Behandlungsräume.

Obwohl die Ausschreibung eher kostspielig wirkende Räumlichkeiten verlangte, führte das begrenzte Budget zu innovativ-experimentellem Umgang mit Materialien: hinter der Rezeption hängt eine mit Federn gefüllte Doppelglaswand; Styropor umschließt das maßgefertigte Regalraster, das zum neuen Markenzeichen von Bliss wurde; Ablagen aus Acryl scheinen durch rückwärtige Beleuchtung zu verschwinden; australisches Walnussholz (eigentlich ein relativ billiges Material, das häufig für Hi-Fi-Lautsprecher verwendet wird) wirkt edel; chinesische Fliesen wurden, zu winzigen Mosaiksteinchen zerschnitten, in den Duschräumen verlegt; in den Umkleiden finden sich dünne, cremefarbene Kacheln verschiedener Größe, die man auf den ersten Blick für Kalkstein halten könnte.

Doch die Arbeit von UT beschränkte sich nicht auf Dekoration: Selbst in scheinbar unbedeutenden Bereichen wie den Umkleiden ist der Raum sorgfältig inszeniert. Auf beiden Seiten der Decke wurde indirekte Beleuchtung angebracht, was die Decke optisch erhöht; eine vertikale Opakglasscheibe am Ende des sich verjüngenden Raums spielt Höhe gegen Breite aus. Sämtliches Mobiliar ist von UT entworfen, darunter auch die mit Nubuk/Velourleder überzogenen Polsterbänke und die Hocker mit Auflagen aus weichem tibetischen oder mongolischen Lammfell sowie der türkisfarbene Couchtisch aus der »O«-Reihe, der auf der New Yorker Möbelmesse 2000 vorgestellt wurde.

Cet institut de « remise en forme » très sélect occupe le deuxième étage du nouvel immeuble de bureaux LVMH de Christian de Portzamparc. Bien que sa façade vitrée bleu-vert ait été applaudie par la presse, l'inversion de l'espace a créé un plan dont le traitement s'est avéré difficile. L'idée de base est une « charnière » – en l'occurrence un pilier placé à l'entrée du vestiaire – autour de laquelle le plan pivote et se déroule en spirale. Les cabines de soins sont repoussées à la périphérie, le centre étant occupé par les vestiaires et par un salon. Les revêtements de sol correspondent aux diverses fonctions : pierre pour la réception, carrelage pour les vestiaires, bois et suédine pour le foyer, couche caoutchoutée étouffant les bruits pour les couloirs et les salles de soins.

Le client souhaitait un espace d'aspect cossu et luxueux, mais le budget très serré fut le catalyseur d'un usage novateur des matériaux : derrière le bureau d'accueil, un mur de plumes suspendu entre deux plaques de verre ; du polystyrène expansé entourant la grille de rangement dessinée spécialement pour Bliss ; des rayonnages en acrylique devenant invisibles quand ils sont éclairés par derrière ; noyer d'Australie (matériau relativement bon marché fréquemment utilisé pour des enceintes d'aspect luxueux) ; dans les douches, carreaux de faïence chinois découpés de sorte à constituer une mosaïque ; pour les vestiaires, carreaux crème de dimensions variées ressemblant au premier abord à de la pierre naturelle …

Mais il ne s'agit pas seulement d'un travail de décoration. UT a orchestré l'espace avec soin jusqu'aux endroits les plus insignifiants tels que les vestiaires du personnel. Un éclairage dissimulé aux bords du plafond souligne le soffite de plus en plus étroit, tandis qu'un haut panneau en verre translucide à l'extrémité de l'espace fuselé détourne l'attention de la faible largeur. Tout le mobilier est dessiné par UT, y compris les tables à café turquoise de la série « O », présentée au salon du meuble de New York 2000, les banquettes en suédine et les tabourets recouverts de duveteux agneau tibétain et mongol.

Relaxation lounge featuring furniture designed by UT, such as the "O"-series coffee table

Entspannungslounge mit von UT entworfenem Mobiliar, darunter der Couchtisch aus der »O«-Serie

La salle de relaxation ; le mobilier a été conçu par UT, notamment la table basse de la série « O »

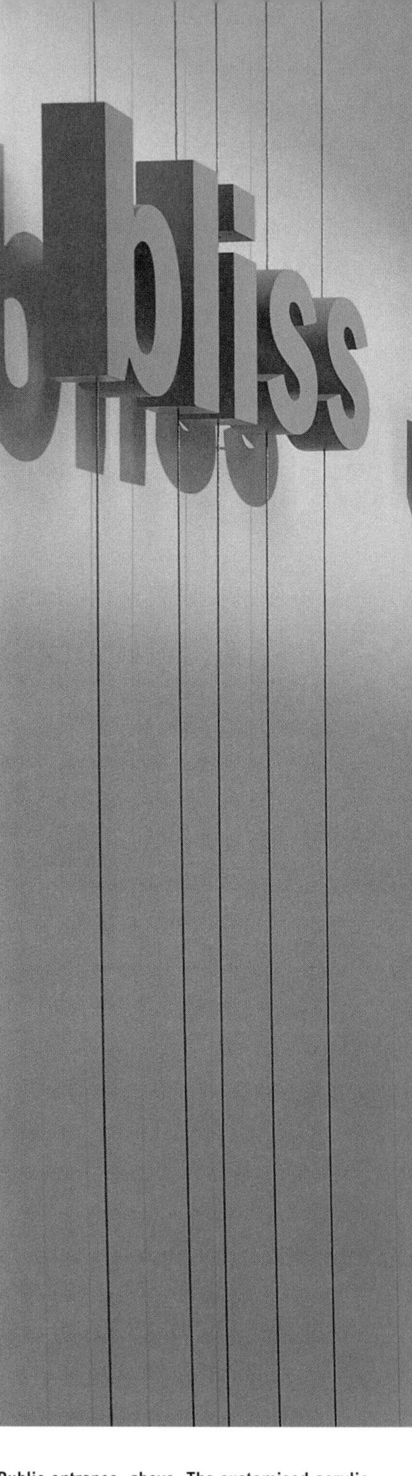

Public entrance, above. The customised acrylic display cases have now become Bliss's trademark. Left, through to the treatment rooms.

Oben der Eingangsbereich. Die eigens angefertigten Acrylvitrinen wurden zum Markenzeichen von Bliss. Links: Durchgang zu den Behandlungsräumen.

Ci-dessus : le hall d'entrée ; les vitrines en acrylique sont devenues un symbole de Bliss. A gauche, le passage menant aux salles de soins.

One arrives in the flat via a narrow passageway, right, which intensifies the shock of the vast living space, below, with views in all directions out over New York.

Man betritt die Wohnung durch einen schmalen Gang (rechts), der die Wirkung des riesigen Wohnraums (unten) mit Panoramablick auf New York noch verstärkt.

A droite : l'étroit couloir donnant accès à l'appartement augmente encore l'effet de surprise créé par l'immense espace (ci-dessous) offrant une vue panoramique sur New York.

2000 Brooklyn, New York, USA

Kilgore Boue Residence

The private residence of the owners of Blissworld, Marcia Kilgore and Thierry Boue lies in the fashionable "Dumbo" area, the former warehouse district between the Brooklyn and Manhattan Bridges. The perfectly square floor plan, which covers the entire 14th floor of a tower block, brings to mind Palladio's Villa Rotonda looking out in all four directions. The Palladian plan has been inverted effectively with only one vertical entrance point in the heart of the plan (by the elevator) rather than having four entrances, one on each facade. An 3.3 m-high narrow hallway compresses the space on arrival, before one emerges at the crossroads of the two main circulation routes, from where one has views out of each facade but also a slight sense of agoraphobia.

As far as possible, domestic spaces such as bedrooms, kitchen and bathrooms have been minimised and held back from the perimeter wall, freeing up maximum space for an open-plan gallery, as well as living and dining areas. The master bathroom is a single block of poured concrete moulded to form a sunken tub. "We wanted to make the apartment into a viewing machine," says Heidar Sadeki. "Our attempt to de-domesticise the apartment met no resistance from our client."

Das Apartment der Blissworld-Eigentümer Marcia Kilgore und Thierry Boue liegt im trendigen »Dumbo«-Distrikt, dem früheren Lagerhausbezirk zwischen Brooklyn- und Manhattan-Bridge. Der quadratische Grundriss erstreckt sich über das komplette 14. Geschoss eines Hochhauses und erinnert an Palladios Villa Rotonda, die Aus-und Durchblicke in alle Himmelsrichtungen bietet. Palladios Grundriss wurde allerdings insofern abgewandelt, als es an Stelle von vier Eingängen (einem auf jeder Seite) nur einen einzigen zentralen per Lift gibt. Man durchschreitet einen 3,30 m hohen, schmalen Flur, ehe man den Schnittpunkt der Hauptachsen erreicht, von wo sich Ausblicke nach allen Seiten öffnen, sich jedoch auch leichte Platzangst einstellt.

Die privaten Bereiche wie Schlafzimmer, Küche und Bäder wurden möglichst klein und auf Distanz zu den Außenwänden gehalten. So stand der Großteil des Raums für eine offene Galerie sowie Wohn- und Essbereiche zur Verfügung. Das Hauptbad ist ein in situ gegossener massiver Betonblock, in den eine Badewanne geformt wurde. »Wir wollten das Apartment zu einem Aussichtspunkt machen«, sagt Heidar Sadeki. »Unser Versuch, die Wohnung zu de-domestizieren stieß bei den Bauherren nicht auf Widerstand.«

La résidence personnelle des propriétaires de Blissworld, Marcia Kilgore et Thierry Boue, dans le quartier chic de « Dumbo », ancienne zone d'entrepôts s'étendant entre les ponts de Brooklyn et de Manhattan. Le plan parfaitement carré tient tout le 14ᵉ étage de la tour : s'ouvrant sur les quatre points cardinaux, il n'est pas sans rappeler la Villa Rotonda de Palladio. En fait, le plan palladien a été modifié : il n'y a pas quatre entrées (une par façade) mais une seule, au centre, desservie par l'ascenseur, d'où un étroit couloir haut de 3,30 m comprime l'espace avant de s'ouvrir sur le croisement des deux principales voies de circulation ; le visiteur découvre alors des vues sur les quatre points de l'horizon, ce qui peut susciter une légère agoraphobie.

Les espaces domestiques (chambres, cuisine, salle de bains) ont été réduits dans toute la mesure du possible et éloignés de la périphérie, libérant un maximum d'espace pour une galerie, les aires de repas et de séjour. La salle de bains principale est un unique bloc de béton moulé de sorte à former une baignoire encastrée.

« Nous voulions faire de cet appartement une machine à voir, explique Heidar Sadeki. Notre tentative de dé-domestiquer l'habitat n'a pas rencontré de résistance de la part du client. »

suds
bath

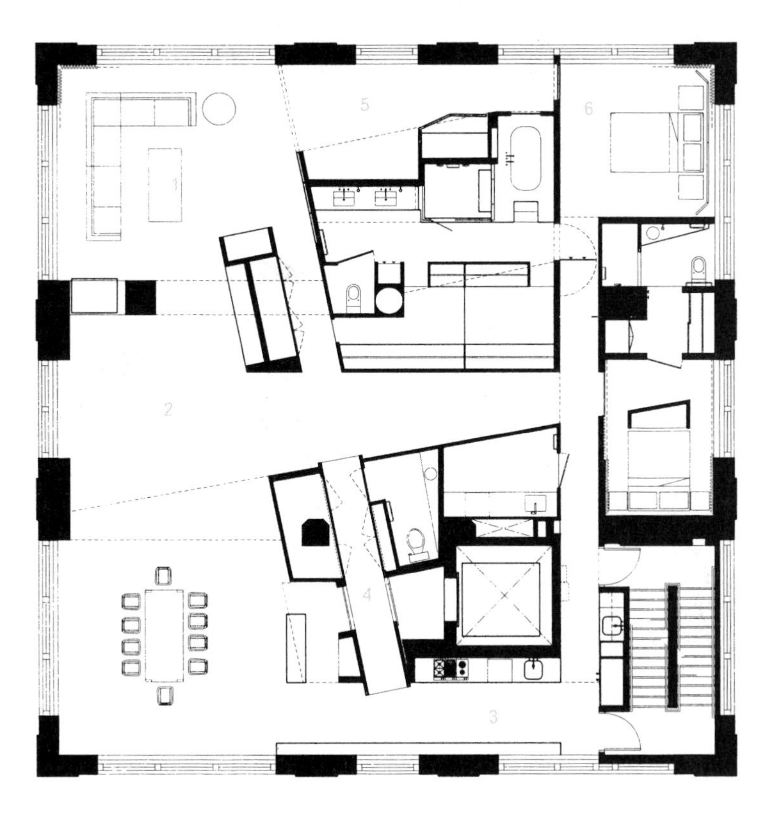

Floor plan/ Grundriss/ Plan d'ensemble

1 **living room/** Wohnraum/ living
2 **gallery/** Galerie/ galerie
3 **kitchen/** Küche/ cuisine
4 **main hall/** Flur/ couloir
5 **study/** Arbeitszimmer/ bureau
6 **master bedroom/** Hauptschlafraum/ chambre principale

The bath is a solid block of concrete cast in situ.

Das Bad besteht aus einem massiven, in situ gegossenen Betonblock.

La salle de bains monobloc en béton.

1999 Brooklyn, New York, USA

Blissworld Headquarters

A wall of 32 numbered pivoting doors lines the main circulation route, separating offices from warehouse and laboratory space - an addressing system by which to locate particular members of the staff. On the opposite wall sandwich panels filled with bubble wrap provide an innovative (and cheap) sound proofing solution. Customised workstations are made from boards of recycled paper sanded to a velvet finish. Most remarkable of all, the fit-out was completed for just $30/m².

Eine Wand aus 32 nummerierten Schwingtüren säumt den Hauptdurchgang, der die Büros von Lagerhaus- und Laborräumen trennt und dem raschen Auffinden der Mitarbeiter dient. An der gegenüber liegenden Wand stellt Noppenfolie zwischen Kunststoffplatten eine innovative und kostengünstige Lärmdämmung dar. Individuell gefertigte Arbeitsplätze aus Recyclingkarton erhielten durch Schmirgeln eine samtige Oberfläche. Am bemerkenswertesten ist die Tatsache, dass sich die Kosten für diese Ausstattung auf lediglich 30 $/m² beliefen.

Un mur percé de 32 portes pivotantes numérotées borde la principale voie de circulation qui sépare les bureaux des entrepôts et des laboratoires et permet de localiser rapidement le personnel. Sur la cloison opposée, une feuille plastifiée à bulles d'air, prise en sandwich entre deux panneaux synthétiques, constitue une méthode inédite (et peu coûteuse) d'isolation phonique. Les postes de travail sur mesure sont faits de papier recyclé et compressé, poncé jusqu'à avoir l'aspect du velours. Performance remarquable, cet équipement fut réalisé pour environ $ 30/m².

The main corridor is lined with pivoting panels: closed, left, and open, right.

Schwingtüren säumen den Hauptflur; links geschlossen, rechts offen.

Le couloir central est entouré de panneaux pivotants, que l'on voit ici fermés (à gauche) et ouverts (à droite).

21
22
23

INDEX OF PLACES

PHOTO CREDITS

Adjaye and Russell

© Ed Reeve 24-26, 28-33, 35-37
© Chris Doyle 27
© David Adjaye 34

Jesús Aparicio Guisado

© Hisao Suzuki 38, 40-47
© Héctor Fernández Elorza 39

Studio Archea

© Pietro Savorelli 48-53, 55-57
© Pietro Savorelli/Alessandro Ciampi 58-59

Architectus

© Duncan Shaw-Brown 60, 62-65
© Mark Henderson 61
© Paul McCreadie and Patrick Reynolds 67-69

Artto Palo Rossi Tikka

© Voitto Niemelä 70, 72-77, 79 t., 80-81
© Sirkku Hölttä 71
© Jari Jetsonen 79 b.

Asymptote

© Asymptote 82-90

Shigeru Ban

© Hiroyuki Hirai 92, 94-103, 105

Marc Barani

© Serge Demailly 106, 108-112, 114-117

Berger + Parkkinen

© Christian Richters 120, 122-125, 128-129, 131
© Ludwig Rusch 121
© Reinhard Görner 126
© Berger + Parkkinen 132-133

Wendell Burnette

© Bill Timmerman 134, 136-141
© Tim Bodell 135
© Timothy Hursley 142-147
© Wendell Burnette 148-149

Camenzind Gräfensteiner

© Patrik Borgeaud 150, 152
© Dominique Meinberg 151
© Serge Kreis 153-154, 156
© Ursula Litschi 155
© Camenzind Gräfensteiner 158-159

Estudio Cano Lasso

© Carlos Roca 160, 163-166
© Hisao Suzuki 168-169
© Leopoldo Lamberti/Jose Criado 170-171

Claesson Koivisto Rune

© Patrik Engquist 174, 177-183, 185-187
© Stefan Borgius 175

Henri Comrie and 'Ora Joubert

© Leon Krige 188, 191 b.
© David Reid 196-197

Crosson Clarke Architects

Patrick Reynolds © Crosson Clarke Architects 204, 207-210
Susanna Burton © Crosson Clarke Architects 205
Donna North © Crosson Clarke Architects 212, 214-215

Vincent Van Duysen

© Alberto Piovano 216, 218-222, 224, 226-229
© Josée Van Riele 217

EDGE (HK) LTD

© Wong Chung Wai 230, 232-235
© Almond Chu 231, 236-239

Shuhei Endo

© Yoshiharu Matsumura 240-242, 244-248, 250-252

© Toshiharu Kitajima 255-256

Engelen Moore

© Ross Honeysett 258-267

Entasis Arkitekter

© Peter Lind Bonderup 268, 270-274

© P. Wessel 269

© Nathalie Kragh 276-279

Manuelle Gautrand

© Philippe Ruault 280, 282-287, 289-293

Gigon/Guyer

© Heinrich Helfenstein 294, 296-305

© Gigon/Guyer 295

© Arazebra, Helbling + Kupferschmid 306-307

Studio Granda

© Dennis Gilbert/View 308, 310-315, 317-319

© Sigurgeir Sigurjonsson 309

Hild & K.

© Michael Heinrich 320, 322-324, 326-333

© Ulrike Mürzik 321

Gerd Jäger

© Gerd Jäger 334-336

© Dirk Altenkirch 337-345

Jarmund/Vigsnæs

© Espen Grønli 346, 348-352, 358

© Jarmund/Vigsnæs Architects 347

© Nils Petter Dale 354-357

Mathias Klotz

© Alberto Piovano 360, 362-368, 370-373

Søren Robert Lund

© Søren Robert Lund 374, 376-380, 382-384

© Jorn Clausen 375

Niall McLaughlin

© Crispin Hughes 386, 389-391

© Nicholas Kane 392, 394

© Niall McLaughlin 393, 396-397

MVRDV

© Christian Richters 398, 401-405, 410-411

© Jeannine Govaers 399

© Rob 't Hart 406, 408-409

Neutelings Riedijk

© Scagliola/Brakkee 412, 415-419, 424

© Leo van Velzen 413

© Christian Richters 420-423

RCR Aranda Pigem Vilalta

© Eugeni Pons/Eidos Photography 426, 428-432, 434-443

© Enric Roca 427

Sancho-Madridejos

© Hisao Suzuki 444, 446-451, 453-457

© Juan Antonio Garrido 445

Thomas Sandell

© Åke E:son Lindman 458, 460-463

© Christian Coinbergh 459

© Tommaso Sartori 465-466

© Stellan Herner 468

Schneider + Schumacher

© Klaus Frahm/artur 470, 472-477
© Christian Matthias Pohlert 471
© Jörg Hempel/artur 478-483

Thompson and Rose Architects

© Chuck Choi 484, 486-490, 492, 494-497
© Jim Harrison 485

Mike Tonkin

© Jonathan Pile 498, 500-502
© Jonathan Rose 499
© Hybrid 503
© Andrew Wood 504-505
© Alex Gino, Julia von Sponeck, Coneyl Jay 506-507
© Freeman Wong 508-509

Simon Ungers

© Eduard Hueber 510, 513-516

UN Studio

© Christian Richters 520, 522-527, 532-533
© Menno Kok 521
© Helene Binet 528-530, 531 t.
© Kim Zwarts 531 b.

UT

© Andrew Bordwin 534, 536, 538-541, 546-547
© Mark Arbeit 535
© Paul Warchol 542, 544

IMPRINT

Dedication

To my father John Cargill Thompson

Project coordination

Caroline Keller

Collaboration

Nicole Bilstein

Karl Georg Cadenbach

Production

Thomas Grell

Design and layout

Stuart Ratcliffe (with thanks to Building magazine)

Design concept

Jonathan Deayton

German translation

Christiane Court

French translation

Frank Straschitz

Cover design

Angelika Taschen

www.taschen.com

Hohenzollernring 53, D–50672 Cologne

Printed in Italy

ISBN 3–8228–6212–6

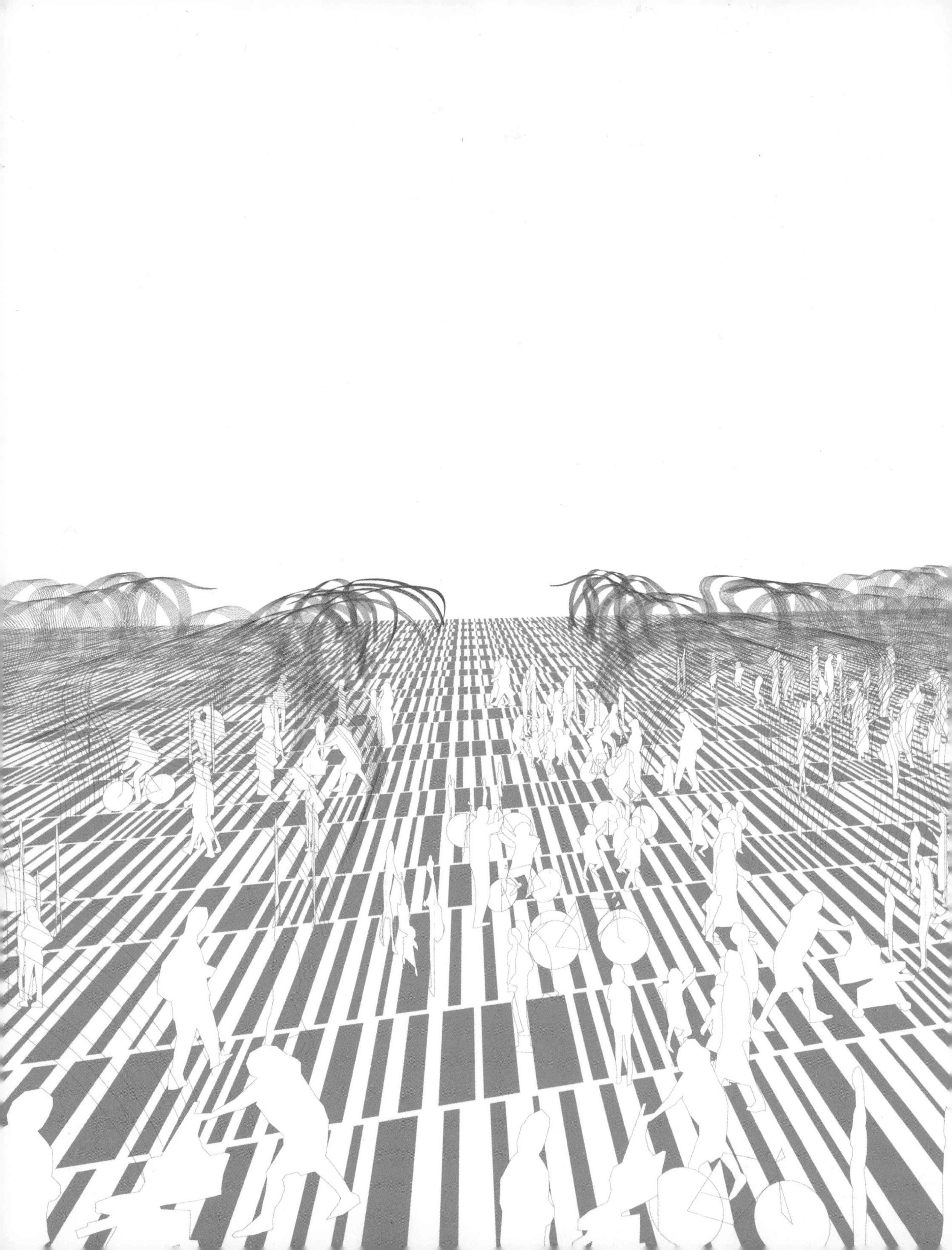